*21st Century*
# AMERICAN ENGLISH
# COMPENDIUM

## *Second Revised Edition*

*21st Century*
# AMERICAN ENGLISH COMPENDIUM

## *Second Revised Edition*

**A Guidebook for Translators, Interpreters, Writers, Editors, and Advanced Language Students**

by **Marv Rubinstein**

*Formerly Adjunct Professor*
**Monterey Institute of
International Studies**

Schreiber Publishing

# 21st Century American English Compendium
## *Second Revised Edition*
### by Marv Rubinstein

Published by:
Schreiber Publishing
Post Office Box 4193
Rockville, MD 20849 USA
spbooks@aol.com    www.schreibernet.com

The article on translating proverbs was reprinted with the kind permission of *Translation Review*.

First Printing

### Library of Congress Cataloging-in-Publication Data

Rubinstein, Marvin.
   21st century American English compendium : a guidebook for translators, interpreters, writers, editors, and advanced language students / by Marv Rubinstein.-- Rev. 2nd ed.
      p. cm.
   Includes bibliographical references and index.
   ISBN: 1-887563-56-3 (pbk. : alk. Paper)
      1. English language--United States--Glossaries, vocabularies, etc. 2. English language--United States--Handbooks, manuals, etc. 3. English language--Translating--Handbooks, manuals, etc. 4. Americanisms--Handbooks, manuals, etc. I. Title: Twenty-first century American English compendium. II. Title.

PE2835 .R83 2000
423'.1--dc21

00-032956

Printed in the United States of America

# TABLE OF CONTENTS

# PREFACE

I certainly wish this book had been available when I first arrived in the United States from Japan. It would have saved me countless hours of browsing through numerous dictionaries and other source material. It would have accelerated my understanding of American culture, as expressed in its language. Most important, it would have helped me achieve fluency and linguistic subtlety sooner and certainly would have added grace and flavor to my early English speech and writing.

At the time of my arrival, I was 17, a freshman in college. Having attended an international school in Japan where all the classes had been conducted in English and French, both my written and spoken English were very good. My grammar was perfect; my vocabulary was quite extensive; I had read Shakespeare as well as many literary classics. And yet, and yet...

That was 22 years ago. Since then I have watched American television, read popular fiction extensively, and conversed with a wide variety of people from all over the United States, as well as the rest of the world. After achieving Bachelor's and Master's Degrees, I worked in a variety of fields, including mental health, advertising, retail, and management consulting. I have been a professional translator of Japanese and teach Japanese to English translation students at the Monterey Institute of International Studies (MIIS).

These experiences have given my English the breadth and depth that it lacked when I arrived in the United States. I now consider English to be my first language, not because it was the language I first spoke in my life, but because it is the language in which I am able to express my thoughts with the highest degree of fluency. Most people who converse with me believe that English is my native language. Achieving this, however, took 22 years of dedicated exposure to the language with all its quirks and flavors.

Even with my language background, a book such as this is very useful. For most translators and students of English, who are not so fortunate in their training and experience, the book can be a timesaver at least and under some circumstances a lifesaver. The majority of my students are native speakers of Japanese, while some are native speakers of English and some of a third language. The challenges that face each of these groups are quite different. For the native speakers of Japanese, comprehension of the source text is usually not a problem, although the nature of the texts faced by professional translators can be quite daunting in its complexity and difficulty, even for native speakers. The problem lies in the smooth, effective communication of the content of the source text in appropriate English.

What exactly is meant by *appropriate* English? First and foremost, the meaning must be accurate, which is achievable through the use of dictionaries and reference material. However, accuracy is not enough. There are other factors such as good grammar, language register, and style.

When I compare the works in English submitted by native speakers of Japanese to those submitted by native speakers of English, there is a often a certain awkwardness, even when the grammar and vocabulary are excellent. I believe this stems from the lack of a cultural context. Their English lacks fluency.

In this book, Marv Rubinstein makes a valiant attempt at defining the less tangible cultural qualities which go into the concept of fluency in a language, and provides a road map of a shortcut to achieving fluency in the American language. Students of the American language, native speakers and non-native speakers alike, can learn a lot from his observations. One of the author's most striking characteristics is his correct, colorful, and creative use of the American language. His students at MIIS have been extremely fortunate to have taken his course, *Quixotic English*, and this book is as close as one can come to capturing the spirit of that course. I have been honored to have made the author's acquaintance and to have been given the opportunity to write this preface, and hope to remain his friend for years to come.

From those of us who work with languages, "Thank you, Marv!"

Tanya Sobieski
Professor GSTI, MIIS
Pacific Grove, CA
June 1997

# ACKNOWLEDGMENTS

*Necessity is the mother of invention.* There was apparently a need for this book so, with the necessary help of both the professors and the students at the Monterey Institute of International Studies, the author was able to invent or write it. For starters, I wish to thank Diane DeTerra, Dean of the Graduate School of Translation and Interpretation, for encouraging me to teach the course on which this book is based, a course with a tongue-in-cheek title—*Quixotic English.*

I also owe a great deal to other professors of the MIIS Graduate School of Translation and Interpretation for helping to head me in the right direction, and particularly to Professor Tanya Fumiko Sobieski for providing the Preface to this book, as well as being of great help in correcting and polishing the sections involving Japanese vocabulary. *Arigato gozaimasu* to Tanya, who is affectionately known by her students as *Sobi-chan.* (*-Chan,* used as a suffix in Japanese, is a diminutive term of affection, much used for children and lovers.)

*Muchas Gracias* also to Professor Lydia Longstreth Hunt who provided yeoman (or should I say yeo-woman) service in correcting my execrable Spanish and bringing up to par any Spanish terminology I have used (or misused) in the chapters on *Proverbs* and *The Birds and the Trees.* Many thanks or *Vielen dank* are also due Professor Manfred J. Heine for similar assistance with and correction of German words and phrases. A good friend, Ling Lau, a former MIIS student and a professional translator and interpreter, has provided assistance with the Chinese terminology.

Perhaps even more so, I owe a debt of gratitude to students in the GSTI Division, and particularly to those in the Japanese/English Section, for making me aware of their needs in the areas covered by this book, for fielding questions from time to time, and for providing additional material when requested.

Even my children have contributed to this book. My daughter Sari and her friend Chris Thomas sent me helpful material on what I choose to call "Youthspeak," the hip language of teenagers and young Americans. My son Jonathan—Executive Vice President of Apple Computers—reviewed the sections on *Computer Acronyms and Abbreviations* to make sure I committed no grievous errors. His

ix

good friend, Tom Berry, of Galileo Systems LLC, was also very helpful in this area. My other son, Doctor Jay, while not a direct contributor, has given me substantial moral support during the ordeal of writing this book.

Many thanks also to my Publisher, Morry Schreiber, for his assistance in preparing this book for publication, for letting me take advantage of his many years of experience in translation and interpretation, and particularly for contributing portions of Chapters One and Five. My thanks also to his able editor, Kimberly Craskey, who spent countless hours bringing this book into its present form.

Most important, if not for my wife, Chie Hamaguchi Rubinstein, I would never have been at the Monterey Institute, would never have taught my course in *Quixotic English*, and never would have even thought of writing this book. I thank her for this experience, for her continuing emotional support, and for her love, which is deeply reciprocated.

## ADDENDUM TO THE REVISED SECOND EDITION

Many who assisted me in the first edition of the *Compendium* contributed additional material for this latest version. I thank them for their continuing help. In addition, I wish to thank Cesar and Sylvia Chelala, Yuko Kashiwagi, Carol Lof, Pedro and Rebecca Mateo-Gelabert, Shoko Matsuzaka-Koestler, Cynthia Raymond and Louise Takata for help with the new sections on Colors and Baby Talk. Yuko made an additional contribution by writing a complimentary review of the first edition for the *ATA Chronicle*.

Finally, thanks to Stephen Want of Schreiber Publishing for his excellent work in assembling and editing the disparate sections of this revised second edition. Stephen is British and consequently was of great additional help in fine tuning the chapter on British vs. American English.

# PROLOGUE TO THE REVISED SECOND EDITION

The first edition of the 21st Century American English Compendium was greeted with approval by translators, interpreters and ESL students throughout the United States, as well as overseas. A number of positive book reviews have appeared in the ATA Chronicle and several other publications. The author and publisher have also received complimentary letters from a number of satisfied readers.

However, even the Garden of Eden had its negatives. As was predicted in the Postscript to the first edition, quite a few readers have phoned or e-mailed or sent us letters pointing out typos, errors and omissions. Such criticisms are welcome, since they enable us to do a better job next time round.

A few readers also suggested additional subjects or areas for future editions—subjects which they felt would be helpful in their work and which are usually neglected in their language education. We particularly thank these contributors, and have tried to incorporate some of their ideas in this volume.

The bottom line is that this revised second edition was prepared in attempt to (1) correct past mistakes, (2) amplify or expand the contents of previous chapters, and (3) add additional sections or chapters which we believe fall into the purview of a compendium of this nature.

# FOREWORD

This 21st Century Compendium should be a valuable addition to the research libraries of those requiring a thorough knowledge of English—and particularly of the American Language—in their daily work. It was originally conceived as an aid to professional translators and interpreters, but should also be of great help to writers, editors, and advanced language students.

Although translators and interpreters of all languages should find this book useful, it will be particularly valuable to those dealing with Far Eastern languages, Middle Eastern Languages, and East European languages such as Russian. The reason is simple: cross-cultural differences which make translation of certain texts troublesome. Much of the contents of this book—proverbs in particular—require of the translator and interpreter not only a wide vocabulary but also some knowledge of the historical, literary, and cultural background of Western civilization. While this 21st Century Compendium cannot totally bridge these differences, it will help narrow the chasm.

One point should be made clear. There is very little in this book that cannot be found elsewhere. But at a price. That price includes not only cash outlays, but also loss of time and efficiency. There are available, for example, several high quality dictionaries of proverbs, slang, and colloquialisms, as well as a few dictionaries covering similes. These can be found in most good libraries. Unfortunately, they are too thick, too heavy to carry, and too time consuming to use on a frequent basis. Many of the proverbs and colloquial expressions given, for example, are archaic and no longer in use. Some proverbs over the years have appeared in different variations, sometimes with only two or three words altered. The researcher has to waste time thumbing through loads of material to reach a nugget of information.

Several small volumes on the difference between American English and British English are available on library shelves. Some of them are good—too good. They contain too many words or expressions which are infrequently used, thus making it harder and more time consuming to find the ones frequently employed. Some have very bad indices or even none at all. The same can be said for books of foreign words and phrases used in English. The author does not know a single book covering expressions from all of the seven foreign languages which most often appear in U.S. books and newspapers. Books providing Latin expressions rarely cover European languages, and vice versa. While Yiddish expressions are widely used in the United States, the researcher must go to a separate reference for these; none of the books covering French and German, for example, include Yiddish.

There are excellent dictionaries covering abbreviations, initialisms, and acronyms, but the best ones run to several volumes. The author knows of only one book covering the vocabulary used for groups of animals. And, to the best of his knowledge, none on baby talk or on the sounds animals make. For translations of the names of birds, fish, plants, and trees, one can only laboriously search through foreign language dictionaries, and may need to consult two or three before finding the translation. Ditto for colors.

A good translator can translate almost anything, given sufficient time. However, to make a living in translation, you must be able to work quickly and efficiently. *Time is money.* This 21st Century Compendium helps you save time by putting in your hands a single portable volume which contains the most important and most frequently used expressions, phrases, words, and abbreviations you need for your work. For interpreters, the Compendium is even more important, since they travel a great deal and cannot carry with them a large research library, even if they have one back at the office. This book is portable, the ideal *vade mecum*.

The 21st Century Compendium will not meet all your needs. You will certainly find some terms missing, even after a diligent search. The book is not a be-all-and-end-all. But you will be surprised at the number of translation and interpretation questions for which you can find a quick answer. In the few cases where you come up empty handed, the huge tomes at the library are still available.

# INTRODUCTION

As previously noted, my wife, Chie, is in a sense responsible for this book. She is Japanese and a professional interpreter and translator of English/Japanese and Japanese/English. While she was working for a master's degree in Conference Interpretation at the T & I program of the Monterey Institute of International Studies in Monterey, California, I had the opportunity to get to know many of her classmates and to converse with them on numerous occasions.

I found their English to be very good indeed; they would never have been admitted to this advanced program had it not been. However, I found that all of them, with virtually no exceptions, were weak in certain areas of English communication, areas normally bypassed when students learn a foreign language. These weaknesses were universal, regardless of the mother tongue of the student, and I am sure this problem exists with Americans learning other languages. The weaknesses occurred mainly in four categories: (a) specialized technical terminology (e.g., medical, commercial, and legal); (b) peripheral areas such as proverbs; similes; acronyms; abbreviations; foreign words and phrases frequently used in English; and the difference between American and British English; (c) slang and colloquial expressions; and (d) names for colors or for birds, fish, plants, and trees.

The first category was recognized at the GSTI division of MIIS. Being aware that most T & I work was not literary in nature, but required skill in handling technical, industrial, legal and commercial terminology, GSTI made it a point to include many translation and interpretation courses covering these particular specialized areas. Even with that, I am reasonably certain that a translator specializing in the medical field, for example, will require several years of experience and the accumulation of a huge specialized vocabulary before being considered a Class A medical translator.

It was the second area which I found intriguing. Several visits to the library convinced me that there was no easily usable text covering these miscellaneous areas. Since nature abhors a vacuum, I volunteered to teach a course covering these subjects, thus effectively filling in the chinks in foreign students' use and comprehension of English. I whimsically dubbed the course *Quixotic English,* because much of the material tended to be benevolently erratic and irregular. With no comprehensive text available to assist my teaching, I had to create a two-inch (now expanded to five-inch) pile of handouts covering the subject. The eventual result: this Compendium.

While this book and my course concentrate on the peripheral areas described above, additional material has since been added to cover some slang and colloquial terminology, as well as an abbreviated dictionary of common birds, fish, plants, and trees, titled *The Birds and the Trees*, plus sections on colors and on baby talk.

As regards slang and colloquial expressions, I found substantial numbers of dictionaries covering this area. However, these dictionaries are just too much of a good thing. Being unwilling to include all the terms available (since we wanted to keep this Compendium portable), we have chosen to concentrate on a number of popular slang or colloquial terms with origins in a variety of fields—from animals to transportation. Terms such as *strikeout* from baseball; *bearish* or *bullish* from business; *beef up* from the food industry; *behind the eight-ball* from the game of pool; *third degree* from the legal field, and *A.W.O.L.* from the military offer us several interesting examples.

With reference to the birds and the trees, the problem is different. Limited knowledge here is less important, unless one plans to specialize in agriculture, forestry, animal husbandry, or ichthyology, in which case an illustrated encyclopedia is recommended. In fact, few native speakers are familiar with more than a handful of plant and fish designations in their own languages. Still, I felt that translators and interpreters were entitled to a quick source for these names, without having to thumb through voluminous dictionaries, most of which provide meager information on the subjects of flora and fauna. One major difficulty here is that there are many varieties of a given species. You have for example rock bass, sea bass, and striped bass. In English, these are all called bass, but in other languages, each may have a different name. The same applies to daisies or jays. Again, I have chosen to economize by translating only the most frequently used family names.

For those who wish to find more information in any of the above areas, an extensive bibliography is provided at the end of this book.

# GUIDE TO THE USE
# OF THIS BOOK

A reference book is only as good as the guidelines enabling you to use it efficiently. Consequently, it is important that you read this brief section before proceeding.

To begin with, an index at the end of this book, covering the key words in the chapters on proverbs, expressions, similes, and slang, allows the reader to find the desired reference where the subject matter is known, but the exact expression vague.

In the chapters on Proverbs and on Popular American Expressions, where identical or similar proverbs or expressions are given to enhance explanations, these are preceded by the equal sign (=) and given in *italics*. (The question as to whether two proverbs are identical or similar is highly subjective, but the author had to make choices.) In a few cases, there are proverbs expressing a sentiment totally contradicting the base proverb. These are preceded by the unequal sign (≠).

A good number of the proverbs have equivalents in a foreign language. These are preceded by the designation "Equiv.," and identified by **Ar, Ch, Fr, Ge, He, It, Ja, Ko, La, No, Ru, Sp,** and **Yi,** which stand for Arabic, Chinese, French, German, Hebrew, Italian, Japanese, Korean, Latin, Norwegian, Russian, Spanish, and Yiddish, respectively. Where the foreign proverb is in a language which uses or is easily transliterated into Roman letters, the proverb is given in *italics* in the original language, followed by a literal translation into American English surrounded by { } (braces).

As indicated above, abbreviations and symbols are used to assist the reader in understanding the way the text is arranged. The following should be helpful:

| | |
|---|---|
| **Ar** | Arabic |
| **Aus** | Australian |
| **Brit** | British English |
| **Ch** | Chinese |
| **En** | English |
| **Fr** | French |
| **Ge** | German |

| | |
|---|---|
| **It** | Italian |
| **Ja** | Japanese |
| **Ko** | Korean |
| **La** | Latin |
| **No** | Norwegian |
| **Ru** | Russian |
| **Sp** | Spanish |
| **Yi** | Yiddish |

| | |
|---|---|
| = | equal or equivalent (synonymous) |
| ≠ | opposite or contradictory (antonymous) |
| ( ) | parentheses, used to show alternate wording and parts of speech |
| [ ] | brackets, used as parentheses within parentheses |
| { } | braces, used to set off foreign language translations |
| **Bold** | bold, used for emphasis, to set off dictionary entries and foreign language abbreviations |
| *Italics* | italics, used to set off English words for distinction and indicate foreign language text and equivalents |

| | |
|---|---|
| adj | adjective |
| adv | adverb |
| Equiv. | equivalent |
| interj | interjection |
| LT | literal translation |
| n | noun |
| phr | phrase |
| pron | pronoun |
| sent. | sentence |
| usu. | usually |
| v | verb |

# Chapter One

# AMERICAN SPOKEN HERE—
# ENGLISH UNDERSTOOD

Dynamic. Versatile. Imaginative. Capable of capturing fine nuances. All these terms can truthfully be used to describe the American Language. "Don't you mean the 'English language'?" some readers may ask. No, I mean the **American Language.** Over many years, American English has vastly expanded and changed, a transmutation which has left it only loosely connected to its mother tongue, British English. (As one chapter in this book will illustrate, the differences are vast. The Reuters News Service in New York has a twelve-page list of British words requiring "translation.")

Someone once jested that the United States and England are two countries separated by a common language. Many a true word is said in jest. Though English is the primary language of many countries—the United States, England, Canada, Australia, New Zealand, South Africa, the Falkland Islands, Belize, Bermuda, and many other countries in the Caribbean—the variations from place to place are humongous. You have to listen only to a street conversation in Singapore—a country in which English and Chinese vie for lingual primacy—to realize the huge number of differences in English usage.

The English spoken in most English-speaking countries has its roots in England; its most polished version, once referred to as "The Queen's English," gave way to another standard, BBC English, which in recent years has somewhat loosened, to say the least. In most of these countries today—and particularly in numerous other places where English is a popular second language—the accents vary widely, and while there are numerous localisms, more and more the terminology, idioms, slang, and colloquialisms smack of American English. Even in England this is slowly but surely happening. The primary reasons are not hard to find—television, movies, and rock music, those pervasive couriers of culture and speaking habits. However, the growth of tourism and the expansion of roads, railroads, and airports into areas previously difficult of access are strong secondary influences.

Canadian English, incidentally, borrows from both American and British usage. Amusing hybrid terms such as "tire centre" are not uncommon. According to humorist Stephen Leacock, Canadians use "[British] English for literature, Scotch for sermons, and American for conversation." Even there, however, particularly in major commercial centers such as Toronto, American English is steadily making inroads.

Things have changed so much, and the use of American English in international communications has grown so much, one can now safely say that most English speakers use (to a greater or lesser degree) Americanized English, i.e. the **American Language.** And rightly so. The American language is so much richer and more adventurous. British English never stood a chance. The bottom line can perhaps be summed up by a sign in the window of a shop in Tel Aviv, which reads:

Ici, on parle français. Se habla español.
English spoken here. American understood.

More than 650 million people in the world speak English, about sixty percent learning it as a first language. As a second language, English is in popular use in Singapore, Hong Kong, Taiwan, the Philippines, India, Pakistan, Burma, Sri Lanka, Israel, the Netherlands, the Scandinavian countries, and half a dozen countries in Africa, among others. In more than fifty countries, English is either a primary language, a frequently used secondary language, or the most popular foreign language chosen by students. More than fifty percent of young people (ages 15 to 25) living in the EEC (European Economic Community) now speak English with at least some competence. The primary language of the airlines and the aircraft industry is English. Every international pilot, every aviation engineer or executive, all control-tower personnel—communicate in English. French was the language of diplomacy. No longer: it is now English. German was the language of scientific writing. No longer: it is now English, as is the primary language of trade, industry, and entertainment. English—and particularly the **American Language**— has become (at least for the immediate future) the *lingua franca*, the Esperanto, the first truly international language of the world.

For a microcosm of what is happening linguistically in the world, one need only look at Morocco, one of several North African countries long dominated culturally and linguistically by France. In the *New York Times*, columnist Thomas Friedman discusses a conversation he recently had with a senior Moroccan government official. This gentleman had been educated in French schools but was now sending his children to an American school in Casablanca. He gave two reasons for this shift. "First," he said, "in the world we are going into, if you don't speak English, you're illiterate." He then opined that, while the French system taught one how to be an administrator, the American schools taught one how to survive on his or her own, providing a better fit with the direction his society is heading. Culture and language are intimately intertwined, and American culture is obviously penetrating many societies where the French and others have long dominated.

There are now four American schools in Casablanca, each with a long waiting list. In addition, English (primarily American English) courses are springing up all over that country. If this is happening in Morocco, a country with long-lasting French connections and traditions, it is undoubtedly happening everywhere. The **American Language** is becoming ubiquitous.

In a similar vein, a pragmatic former president of another Third World country is quoted as saying, "If you want to earn your daily bread, the best thing to do is to learn English. That is the source from which most of the jobs come."

## The Richness of the American Language

While the American language has been adopted worldwide by native speakers of many other languages, the reverse is also true. Much of the richness of the American language lies in the fact that it has absorbed words and expressions from at least fifty other languages. Examples are endless. *Mesa* and *marijuana* from Spanish via Mexico. *Timid* and *morsel* derived from the French *timide* and *morceau*. *Kindergarten* and *FLAK* (*Flieger Abwehr Kanonen*) from German. *Brooklyn, Harlem,* and *poppycock* from Dutch. *Brogue* from Irish Gaelic. *Skedaddle* from Scots Gaelic. *Pal* derived from the Romany Gypsy word for "brother." *Veld* and *wildebeest* from South Africa's

Afrikaans. *Cherub* and *seraphim* from Hebrew. *Camel* and *assassin* from the Arabic *gamal* and *hashish*. *Diva, adagio, fortissimo*, and numerous other musical terms from Italian. *Boogeyman* from the Boogie pirates in Indonesia. *Smorgasbord* from Swedish. *Kosher, shamus*, and *shmear* from Yiddish. *Typhoon* from China. *Kamikaze, bonsai*, and *Geisha* from Japan. Numerous words from the Indian languages (primarily Hindi), e.g. *guru, sahib, brahmin*, and *rajah*. *Cigar* from the Mayan language. *Orangutan* from the Malay language. *Aloha* and *hula* from Hawaiian.

Not to mention a vast international vocabulary of food terms found in many restaurant menus of America's major cities and on television cooking programs: *Biali, enchilada, taco, paella, fritata, farfel, matzo ball, sauerbraten, curry, sushi, tempura, vichyssoise, Vienna schnitzel, strudel, Sachertorte, flan, crème caramel*. The list is indeed endless, and the trend to absorb and adapt foreign words continues apace.

In addition to foreign words absorbed into and becoming part of the American language, there are thousands of foreign words and expressions in their original forms which are frequently used in English sentences for emphasis or to express a thought or feeling more aptly phrased in the language of origin. Such words often appear in *italics* in American texts. Though words or phrases come from many languages, there are seven languages which contribute well over ninety percent of those frequently encountered: French, German, Italian, Japanese, Latin, Spanish, and Yiddish.

Latin is the largest contributor, particularly of legal and academic terminology. *Caveat emptor* (Let the buyer beware.); *stare decisis* (a legal point already binding); *pro bono* (free legal services), and *magna cum laude* (a university degree with highest honors) are typical examples. French is next largest. Though French terms used in English cover many subjects, a large percentage of them deal with culinary arts. *A la carte, à la mode, à votre santé, au jus*, and *au gratin* are typical examples, and that only covers the "A's."

Spanish terms are particularly popular in the Southwest of the United States, due to its proximity to Mexico. *Dinero, fiesta*, and *Gringo* are often used. Many food terms are also popular, e.g. *burrito, tortilla*, and *margarita*. As previously noted, Italian expressions used in English are most commonly known by musicians:

*aria, maestro, glissando,* and many more. Their food names such as *pizza, gelato, cacciatore,* and *al dente* are also used by most Americans. German words and expressions cover a variety of subjects, with emphasis on political and military terms, e.g. *Blitzkrieg, Gestapo, Nazi, and Übermensch.* Though Japanese terms also cover different fields, many such as *bushido, judo, karate,* and *kendo,* deal with martial arts.

Yiddish occupies a special category. Yiddish expressions were brought to the United States by Eastern European Jews. They concentrated in big cities, where some of their ethnic foods became popular. We all know *bagels, lox,* and *blintzes.* Many Jewish writers and stand-up comics became popular, and many others became active in Hollywood and on TV. Consequently, their colorful expressions used in the media were quickly picked up by the American people. Terms such as *chutzpah* (unmitigated gall), *kvetch* (to gripe and complain intensely), *mavin* (a connoisseur), *yenta* (a gossip), *mish-mash* (a hodgepodge), and *tush* or *tushy* (one's behind or buttocks) found an easy place in American English, which always welcomes colorful expressions.

So, in the **American Language**, if you are seeking the *mot juste,* you not only have the choice of hundreds of thousands of English words, you can also include expressions from other languages to provide you with exactly the right nuance you are seeking. (A chapter in this book offers a much larger selection of useful foreign words and phrases commonly found in American English.)

One might well ask, "Don't other languages also derive from and use foreign words and phrases? How does the **American Language** differ?" After all, Spanish and other Romance languages were derived from Latin. Just about every week, Japan borrows American words and changes their spelling and pronunciation, and—*voilà!*—they become Japanese words. When Israel decided to revive Hebrew—a language pretty much dead for nearly 2,000 years—they had almost no words for technical and technological subjects, so considerable borrowing was done from England and the U.S. The author's favorite is *habackax hakidmi* (the back axle in the front) for the front axle of an automobile. Much to the chagrin of the *Académie Française,* young French people still add American expressions to their *franglais* vocabularies, e.g. *les bluejeans* and *le snacquebarre.*

So how does the **American Language** differ from these? The answer lies in two important factors, namely (1) degree and (2) opportunity. As regards the former, there is no question that American English has been like a sponge absorbing and modifying words from many other languages, not just two or three (as is the case with French or Italian). And the opportunity for this variety stems from the fact that English is spoken in many different countries, and that immigration to the United States has brought in not only a variety of different cultures, but their language patterns as well. Not to mention the fact that hundreds of thousands of Americans travel overseas each year, frequently bringing back colorful phrases as well as local bric-a-brac.

**Historical Language Contributions**

The **American Language** has not only imported and adapted foreign words, but also incorporated its own localisms and regional English into itself. Many of these words and expressions have historical underpinnings and relate to significant events or periods in American history, mainly during the nineteenth century, the time of the American frontier experience. One must be careful, however, in attributing a specific word or expression to any specific item or aspect of that period. A good example is the word *highfalutin* (an attitude of self-importance; bombastic language) which has been attributed by some etymologists to the high, flute-shaped smokestacks of the steamboats that sailed the Mississippi River in those days, as popularized by the Broadway musical, *Showboat*. Others consider this word to be de-rived from the term "high flying" or "high floating." Other terms attributed to the riverboat are *letting off steam* (today mainly used figuratively), a process which helped protect the engine from excessive pressure and explosions, and *hogwash* (pretentious talk or nonsense), the run-off from washing the hogs that were transported by those boats.

One of the major events of that era was the Gold Rush, actually a series of events, the best known of which was the California Gold Rush in 1848, when tens of thousands of fortune hunters went out West in search of gold. This experience triggered a large number of neologisms. Stricken by *Gold Fever, prospectors* (a new word based on the term *prospects)* headed West for *El Dorado* (the legendary Kingdom of Gold) in the hopes of *striking it rich*. They *staked their claims*, established their *digs (diggings)*, and in a few cases, achieved a *bonanza*. For most, however, things did not *pan out*, but they remained in the West and built a new state—California. All of these terms are widely used today, but often figuratively and for totally different purposes from the original intent.

The historical trek westward to establish a new frontier was more often based on hunger for land rather than gold. The availability of large tracts of land in the Southwest made cattle raising a prosperous enterprise. The herding of cows required *cowboys*, sociologically a new breed, with their own collection of English words and phrases. *Cowhands*, *cowpokes*, *range-riders*, *bronco-busters*, *mavericks*, *rustlers*, and *hustlers* soon became part of American tradition as well as the American vocabulary. Further, their contact with Mexican horse-handlers and *caballeros* provided additional language enrichment with terms originally of Spanish origin, but important to the cowboy vocabulary and culture. A few of these are *bronco, mustang, pinto, rodeo, lasso, lariat, stampede,* and *ranch*, but there are many more.

Plenty of land was available for cattle grazing, but there was a more serious problem, namely getting the cattle to market. The answer: railroads. And, of course, a side effect of developing a transcontinental rail system was an increase in words based on this new venture. Many railroad-associated terms were simply borrowed from passenger ships, but many new ones also *tracked* their way into the **American Language**. As usual, many terms describing literal activities are now used figuratively. *Railroaded* (coerced), *sidetracked* (diverted), and *backtracking* (retreating) are typical. Additional examples are *gravy train, whistle stop, right of way,* and *end of the line*.

## Localisms as Enrichment

Enrichment of the local varieties of English spoken by settlers on the first boatloads to arrive at our shores started early on. Settlers picked up dozens of words from the first Americans—the native Indians and later the Eskimos. Some obvious ones are *squaw, papoose, teepee, tomahawk, moccasin, wigwam, igloo,* and *kayak*. Others less apparently of Indian origin are *mugwump, powwow,* and *firewater.* Add these words or phrases derived from Indian concepts: *warpaint, Indian Summer, bury the hatchet, peace pipe,* and *playing possum.* Speaking of possums, let us not disregard words for local flora and fauna found in the New World and previously unknown to Europeans, animals such as *skunk, raccoon, chipmunk,* and *moose;* trees such as *pecan* and *hickory.* Not to mention good things to eat: *squash, eggplant, hominy, pemmican,* and *quahog,* among others. Incidentally, finding the proper names for flora and fauna was not only a problem for the early settlers; it is still a bugaboo for translators and, in fact, for anyone learning a second or third language. (The chapter in this book titled *The Birds and the Trees* should be of some help.)

The South contributed mightily to the American language. The best known terms of Southern origin are derived from jazz, probably originating in New Orleans. The musical terms *ragtime, bop, rebop,* and *bebop,* indicating complex jazz forms, also have New Orleans origins. Other words originating in the South include *bellows, bubba, hound dog,* and *hullabaloo.* Colorful expressions such as *Colder than a well-digger's ass in January* and *Stubborn as a mule* also come from the southern regions. Former presidential candidate Ross Perot is fond of a southern expression, *This dog won't hunt,* indicating that an idea or procedure will not succeed. Southern pronunciation was (and is) of course quite different from the Northern varieties, leading to many jokes. For example, one Northerner asks another for the definition of a "poho." When he receives no answer, he provides the definition. "A poho is a destitute prostitute from the deep South." (*Po* would be the way many rural Southerners pronounce *poor,* while *ho* is their rendition of *whore.*)

A particularly rich list of localisms hails from New England. Included are words such as *adrift, astern, avast, blue nose, boodle, cleanser, deacon,* and *flummery.* Interesting expressions such as *cat-and-dog fight, chowder head, come-on, election day,* and *take a gander* are of Boston, Maine, and other New England origin.

California has provided us with *abalone, adobe, Big Foot (Sasquatch), embarcadero,* and many other terms. *Hoosiers* come from Indiana and *Down-Easters* from Maine. Texas and the Southwest also offer abundant terminologies of local origin, e.g. *boll weevil, bracero, buckaroo, chaparral, chaps, corral, ebony,* and _esplanade._ Alaska provides _igloo_ and _eskimo._ And, of course, most of us are familiar with popular Hawaiian expressions—_haole, hula,_ and _wahine._

Then, of course, we have a wide variety of local foods available to Americans: _codfish_ and _geoduck_ from the Pacific Northwest; _Apple Brown Betty, chicken lobster, fiddleheads, finnan haddie, hash,_ and _succotash_ from New England; _crawfish_ and _crawdaddy_ from the Ozarks; _chitlins, corn pone, crackling, grits,_ and _hush puppies_ from the South; _shoofly pie_ and _apple pandowdy_ from the Pennsylvania Dutch; _cioppino, garrupa,_ and _halibut_ from California; _jambalaya_ and _pralines_ from New Orleans; and _ahi, aku,_ and _mahi mahi_ (among others) from Hawaii. All of these foods, once local, are now known in most metropolitan areas of the United States, as are their local names, which now have become part of the **American Language.**

Don't other countries absorb local terms and names into their national languages? They most certainly do. Local French expressions eventually become part of the French language. The same could be said for Germany. However, a major difference is that the United States is much larger than either of these countries. Consequently, there are more local areas. What about China, Russia, and India, which also have vast land masses? Here again, there is a major difference—television and advertising. Even in remote corners of the United States, people soon become familiar with the local terminologies of the rest of the country.

While it is true that the United States in spite of its size does not have as many distinct local dialects and terminologies as Britain, for example, there are still gradations. The author was born in Rochester, New York, where the term _catty-corner_ (diagonally across) was never heard. Instead, we used _kitty-corner._ We also pronounced _Chili_ as "Shylai" and _Charlotte_ as "Shar-lot." In New York City, _Houston_ Street is pronounced "House-ton," and if you order a _soda,_ you get an _ice-cream soda._ In California, you would get carbonated water mixed with syrup, which in New York City would be called an _egg cream._ If you want carbonated water or club soda in New York, ask for a _two-cents plain_ (which will cost you anything from $.50 to $2). In Illinois, the residents of the city of _Cairo_ call it "Kay-row." Order _tea_ in the north, and you get hot tea. Order _tea_ in the South or West, and you get iced tea. Someone once said that language changes every twenty miles. That is a fact, and it is a fact which enriches the **American Language**.

## Youthspeak

Lack of discipline among young people and teenagers in America creates numerous social problems. On the other hand, regarding the **American Language**, it is another source of enrichment. Young people have always tried to develop their own special language so as to communicate with each other while maintaining a degree of privacy from nearby adults. During the last few decades, however, youthspeak vernacular has been drawn out of beatniks, hippies, punk rockers, and other adolescent groups. The problem with writing about these vocabularies is that they provide a moving target. With a few exceptions, the terms change so quickly that, before you get a chance to publish an article or a book on the subject, many terms have become obsolete.

Still, the words with greater longevity do add to the richness and diversity of the **American Language**. Many such terms are commonplace words which have been given a new meaning. *Cool* no longer means low in temperature, but instead implies a degree of sophistication or savvy that enables an individual to handle any situation which may arise, and handle it with confidence and panache. Or if referring to an idea or a situation, cool means OK, free of cant and acceptable to cool people. To *rap* does not mean to knock, but to carry on an informal chat with an exchange of ideas. More recently, it has become a fast-paced type of talking song, often filled with strong comments on our society. *Honcho* (a Japanese word for a group leader) means a big shot or a big chief in "youthspeak."

As noted, most youthspeak terms are evanescent, but some have remained with us as standard American English. In addition to *cool* and *rap* given above, it looks as if *put-down, hassle,* and *uptight* are here to stay. The terms *nerd, geek, bummer,* and *stoned* appear to be holding up as well. There are literally hundreds of ever-changing terms in today's youthspeak, with a large percentage of them occurring regularly in rap and rock songs. A few of the colorful ones are provided below, with the caveat that, by the time you read this, they may be considered obsolete or may have changed their meanings completely:

*Abusak* combines "abuse" and "Musak" to describe what the young call *elevator music*. *Check you later* is a way of saying good-bye. A short word for parents is *rents*, although this might also be an indication of who pays the rent. In the same vein, a *daddylac* is an expensive car paid for by papa. An *organ recital* is a sex education class. *Mickey D's* for McDonalds and *D.Q.* for Dairy Queen. The expressions in this paragraph were current five years ago but may not be active today.

A recent check with the author's daughter brought out the following current "youthspeak," which should be usable for at least another year. *Posse* indicates a group or circle of friends. *Phat* is an updated version of "cool." *Ass* is a suffix added to other words to amplify or intensify their meaning, a stronger version than adding "very." Examples are *bad-ass, smart-ass,* or *dumb-ass.* Typical use would be, "I don't want to hear your *dumb-ass* problems." The term *stupid* now means "exceedingly," as in a *stupid* hot day. A *hottie* is an attractive person, male or female. To *freak* is equivalent to 1960s' *freak out. Ill* used as a verb shows that even the young can convert nouns or, in this case, adverbs to verbs. It means to feel sick or depressed. "I can't go out tonight. I'm *illing*." Strange to say, Shakespeare used similar phraseology.

The author's favorite youthspeak expression is the word *McJob*. Once you think about it, the meaning is dreadfully obvious: a job which brings in some pocket money but has no future. In short, young people are talking about the growing number of low-paid, futureless jobs in the service industries. A *McJob* at McDonalds preparing or serving Big Macs is a prime example. Today's youth might consider these terms *so five-years ago*, indicating that they are old hat.

## Black English

Black English—most recently called Ebonics—has been a highly controversial subject for many years, periodically creating great emotional waves and then dying down as a hot subject. Is it a distinct language, a dialect, or just bad English? Opinions vary. Still, millions of African-Americans speak some form of Black English in their homes, though it varies considerably from one part of the country to another and between country dwellers and city folk.

Whatever your opinion, it cannot be denied that the language of Black America has permeated the **American Language** in a big way. We have already discussed musical terms such as *jazz, bop, bebop, rebop,* and *riff*—all part of today's spoken and written English. *Blues* and *rock 'n' roll* can be added to the list. As previously noted, the popular terms *rap* and *rapper* refer to conversation but also to a type of music. *Jive, jitterbugging,* and *breakdancing* are all dance terms originating with African-Americans. On a non-musical level, *chill,* meaning to relax and take it easy, is now standard American English, as is *crib,* a slang word for "home." Sexually descriptive terms like *jelly roll* or *Having your ashes hauled* add to the many other expressions for describing intercourse.

And these show just the tip of the iceberg. So many words we use regularly are variations of imports from Africa or the Caribbean, and we are not even aware of their source. These include: *banjo, voodoo, banana, jam session, to bad-mouth,* and *nitty gritty.* Furthermore, if you closely examine many of the expressions used by our young people and teenagers, as discussed in the previous sessions, you will find that a good percentage of these terms have Black English origins. As stated, just the tip of the iceberg.

It should be noted, however, that many—probably most—of the differences between Black English and standard American have to do with pronunciation, word clipping, tense, and sentence structure more than with terminology. There is an old joke about a black boy and a white boy arguing about whether God is black or white. They decide to go into a church and ask Him. When they raise their heads and appeal for God to appear, he does so in a blinding flash of light which conceals his visage. The boys ask, "God, are you black or are you white?" God replies in a deep, stentorian voice, "I am what I am!" and disappears. The boys leave the church, and after a few moments of silence, the white boy says, "Well, that didn't settle anything."

"Oh yes, it did," replies the black boy. "God is white. He said, 'I am what I am!' If he were black, he would have said, 'Ah is what Ah is.'"

**Out of the Closet**

Recent sociological events have also expanded the **American Language.** One important change has been the campaign of homosexuals to declare their sexual preferences and to assert their rights. The expression _Coming out of the closet_ is now part of standard English. It has become such a common American term that it is now used, not just in the sense of sexual selection, but to indicate any other previously hidden activity which is now out in the open. Former President Harry Truman was called a _closet intellectual,_ when it was discovered that he read history books and biographies, rather than cowboy soap operas (_a la_ Ronald Reagan). _In drag_ is a term formerly used only by transvestites or cross-dressers to indicate males dressing as females. Today, one hears of _business drag_ (dark blue suits) or _party drag_ (fancy evening gowns).

Open gayness has also popularized words dealing with being gay, e.g. _closet queen_ (one who denies his homosexuality); _drag queen_ (a male transvestite); _fruit_ (a derogatory term for a homosexual); _butch_ (a derogatory term for a lesbian who plays the male role in a relationship); and _homophobe_ and _homophobia_. Gays _turn a trick_ when they pick up a partner for sexual purposes. And _cruising for pick-ups_ is used by both gays and _straights_. The term _gay_ itself, an old word that not so long ago meant happy, now has an entirely different connotation.

## Women's Movement

Chronologically, the gay revolution occurred at about the same time as another cultural change in America: the Women's Movement. Some women's groups insist that language affects action and that terms such as _chairman_ and expressions such as _To each **his** own_, when referring to both men and women, are basically sexist and male chauvinistic. So many common words have undergone changes. Business letters addressed to women are now sent to _Ms._ instead of _Mrs._

_Chairman_ has become _chairperson_ and has been further reduced to _chair_. But many gender-based terms remain unresolved. While, for example, _policeman_ easily becomes _police officer_, other words and phrases resist change. One almost invariably hears expressions such as _Everyone to their own taste_. Grammatically incorrect, but why risk offending potential female customers of advertised products? However, when a woman _mans_ the controls of an aircraft, should the term be changed even though it denotes action, not identity? What should we now call a "*man*hole cover"? The debate over this area of language is clearly unresolved.

## Verbing

Do not try to look in your dictionary for the meaning of the above caption. You will not find it, at least not today. The author made it up by turning the noun *verb* into an operating verb. This was done to emphasize another point in the growth and diversification of the **American Language,** namely turning many nouns (and some adjectives) into verbs. At one time, language specialists, English teachers, and dictionary publishers frowned on this verbal trick, but it has now become commonplace and widely accepted.

As a matter of fact, the practice of "verbing" goes back a long way to Elizabethan England and the time of Shakespeare. Even then, you could *tongue* (talk back to) your husband; *uncle* (act in an avuncular fashion toward) your nieces and nephews; *happy* a friend or *malice* a foe. These were all nouns used as verbs. In present day America, however, the practice has *mushroomed*. Instead of letting them *foot* it, we *bus* children to school where the teachers *school* them. In movies, the cowboys *head* the horses off at the pass. At dinner, we are *wined* and dined in fine restaurants, or we *pig out* at the local beanery. We *horn* our way into difficult situations and then have to *weasel* our way out. In today's American English, hundreds (perhaps thousands) of these noun-to-verb conversions exist. In addition, nouns can also be used as adjectives. Adjectives, in turn, are sometimes used as adverbs.

This new flexibility certainly provides a richer language, but it also provides headaches to translators, interpreters, and those learning English as a second language. Let us look at some examples. When you *chair* a meeting, this is defined as acting as a chairman or chairwoman. However, on first encounter with this usage, one would be equally justified in thinking that the term means *to sit in* at the meeting. To *needle* someone means to tease or taunt that person but could easily be interpreted as jabbing someone with a needle. As described in a subsequent chapter on the differences between the **American Language** and British English, the expression *to table a motion* provides a perfect example of the possible confusion that "verbing" can create. In the United States Congress, *to table a motion* is to lay it aside for possible future consideration, in effect, to kill it. In the British Parliament, *tabling a motion* is putting it on the table for immediate consideration. The bottom line is that for the translator or language student, this practice adds to the complexity of the language, since the meaning of each expression must be learned by rote rather than by a set of rules.

That's the **American Language** for you. All the rules are broken. It ain't elegant, but it *sure* adds versatility, flexibility, and richness. One final example of changing nouns to verbs is the term *stonewall,* which means to erect figuratively a wall or barrier to prevent an opponent from winning or consolidating his gains. U.S. Senators frequently *stonewall* to prevent passage of legislation they dislike. Suspected felons often *stonewall* to prevent prosecutors from obtaining additional evidence against them. The interesting thing about *stonewall* is that it has turned both a noun (wall) and an adjective (stone) into a verb. In addition, it has then compounded these two words to form a single thought, another practice which has expanded and diversified American English.

## Compounding

This practice of adding two or more words together to form a single compound word is known as *compounding* or forming compound words. (*Compounding* itself is a perfect example of "verbing" or converting a noun to a verb.) This practice does not happen all at once. Usually, two words which often appear adjacent to each other are joined by a hyphen and could then be termed hyphenated words. As time goes on, however, when the two words are seen together so frequently that one could consider them as "married," the hyphen is relegated to the trash bin. This frequently happens with adjectives which are normally hyphenated when they both immediately precede a noun. A typical example would be a *week-end* trip, which for years was hyphenated and now usually appears as the single word *weekend.*

Frequently, one of the words used in compounding becomes a common building block for many compound words. The word *wise* provides a good prototype. We now have *streetwise, weatherwise, clockwise, moneywise, timewise,* and *otherwise* (or should we say other *wises*?). The terms *out* and *over* both provide opportunities for numerous compound words, to name a few: *outbid, outcast, outcry, outdistance, outdoors* (formerly *out-of-doors*), *outlive, outlook, output, outmaneuver, outweigh,* as well as *overcome, overcompensate, overdose, overdress, overdue, overhang, overhaul, oversee, overturn,* and *overweight.*

Other compound words include *oddball, goofball, softball; deadhead, butthead, sorehead; deadeye, deadfall, deadbeat, deadlock; downfall, downhill, downtime, downbeat,* and *downpour.* Need I go on?

Compound words exist in almost all languages, but never anywhere near the extent that they do in American English. In French, for example, the word for "to smile" is *sourire*—a compounding of *sous* (under) and *rire* (to laugh). Smiling is, after all, a kind of sub-laughter. In English there have always been some compound words such as *everybody, someone,* and *everyday.* However, during the last few decades, compounding has reached epidemic proportions. The vast majority of compound words are of relatively recent origin *language-wise.*

## Abbreviating and Downsizing

Long "before" American words were starting to get longer by compounding, others were getting shorter by abbreviating or taking only part of the word for the whole. This has been going on for so long that we no longer realize what we are doing. Prime examples are *bus* for autobus, *phone* for telephone, and *taxi* or *cab* for taxicab. *Rep* for reputation, *con* for convict, and *ain't* for "are not" "or" "am not" are more recent contractions.

Since English is a living language, it not only adds words every day, it also sheds them or radically changes their meanings. As noted above, the word "gay" once meant carefree and light-hearted. Today, it is used only for homosexuals. "Nice" once meant precise. It still retains that meaning in terms such as a "nice distinction," but is usually used to mean pleasant, kind, or well-mannered.

Many once-popular words are rarely used any longer, often due to cultural changes. The term "old maid" is a case in point. Being a spinster or old maid once had negative connotations. Today, when women can support themselves and may choose not to marry or can't find a suitable mate, being an unmarried woman on her own no longer has such a social stigma. Since the term "old maid" no longer has a reason to exist, it has disappeared. With a growing, changing language, words come and words go.

## Offshoots of Specialized Activities

Contributing further to the expansion and diversification of the **American Language** are a vast number of recent slang and colloquial terms originating in the professions or in specialized areas of American life. These include words and expressions borrowed from the military, business, sports, games, animals, and food, among others. These days, with a little *strategic planning* (military), it is *as easy as apple pie* (food) to get your *ducks in a row* (animals) and *bank on* (business) *scoring big* (sports) before *cashing in your chips* (games). American English translation: These days, with a precise goal, it is very easy to organize everything in such a way that you can depend on achieving financial success before you die.

That last sentence is highly contrived, but the point is clearly made. If you get the hang of American English slang and colloquial expressions, you can add vitality to your language, give it a little *nouveau* language fillip, and achieve nuances of expression much more difficult to achieve in other languages. Chapter Five is aimed at familiarizing readers with a substantial number of slang and colloquial expressions derived from specialized activities.

It is hoped that this chapter has given the reader a bird's eye view of the American Language, its richness, and its magnificence. It is now time to get into the book itself. Alternatively, the author could say that he has run out of words suitable for this chapter. But that would not be truthful. With the amazing **American Language,** one never runs out of words. Well, hardly ever.

## TOP TEN INTERNATIONAL LANGUAGES

Have you ever wondered what is the most widely-spoken language in the world? Most people would guess English. The correct answer is Chinese. Between 800 million and one billion people speak one or more Chinese dialects as their first (and usually only) language.

If we consider the number of people worldwide who speak English as a first, second, or third language, however, English comes in second, with well over 650 million speakers. English is, in fact, the only truly international language—the primary language in the United States, Canada, Great Britain, South Africa, Australia, New Zealand, the Falkland Islands, Bermuda, and throughout most of the Caribbean — not to mention wide usage as a second language in the Philippines, Singapore, Hong Kong, India, Pakistan, Burma, Sri Lanka, Israel, the Netherlands, and the Scandinavian countries, among others. Perhaps more important, English is the primary language of aviation, diplomacy, religion, industry, and commerce.

Hindi and other Indian dialects are spoken as a first language by about 340 million people and not far behind is Spanish with 335 million. Whether either of these beats out English as a first language is problematic (depending on whose statistics you accept), but neither of these anywhere near approaches the hegemony of English usage on the international scene. Want your children to be linguists? See to it that they learn English, Spanish, and Chinese, and they will feel at home conversing with approximately two billion people almost anywhere in the world.

The following table gives a close approximation of the millions of people who speak the ten most common languages **as a mother tongue**:

| | | |
|---|---|---|
| (1) | Chinese | 800 million to 1 billion |
| (2) | Hindi | 340 million |
| (3) | Spanish | 335 million |
| (4) | English | 300 to 350 million |
| (5) | Bengali | 190 million |
| (6) | Arabic | 185 million |
| (7) | Russian | 170 million |
| (8) | Portuguese | 170 million |
| (9) | Japanese | 125 million |
| (10) | German | 98 million |

# Chapter Two

# PROVERBS, SLOGANS, AND APHORISMS

*Proverbs Are the Wisdom of Nations*
*A Proverb Is a Short Sentence Based on Long Experience*
*Wise Men Make Proverbs and Fools Repeat Them*

A proverb is a popular, pithy saying expressing what is believed to be a well-known truth or fact. A slogan is a catchword or phrase, usually originally associated with advertising or promotion or as a rallying cry for an organization or association, but now in popular use. An aphorism is a terse statement of a truth or opinion. The line between proverbs and aphorisms is blurred and highly subjective but, generally speaking, proverbs tend to have a longer history and more popular usage. Proverbs are also more likely to carry a moral message than are aphorisms. (In order to avoid constant repetition, whenever the term "proverbs" is used below, consider it as including slogans and aphorisms.)

There are literally thousands of proverbs, slogans, and aphorisms, some of American origin and many going back to our English heritage, or even further back, to the Bible. In addition, most have over the years developed variations in which a word or two has changed, but in which the basic thought is still expressed. A number often appear in truncated form, with the first part being explicit and the rest of the proverb implicitly understood due to frequent historical usage. For example, a proverb frequently used by children *Finders keepers, losers weepers* more frequently appears as simply *Finders keepers,* with the second part of the quotation mute but understood. Many proverbs have parallel sayings expressing the same concept but using different words and imagery. Though the topographic areas for *Any port in a storm* and *Any water in the desert* are totally different, the meanings of these two proverbs are identical. As can be seen from the three proverbs quoted at the head of this section, some proverbs directly or indirectly contradict other proverbs, indicating that different people have different concepts of "truth." Finally, many are used so frequently that they have become banal, trite, and hackneyed.

The bottom line is that these sayings are popularly used and, if not overused, add a certain flavor to the English language. All of which provides the professional translator and interpreter with both a challenge and an opportunity. Proverbs can be effective translation tools but unfortunately are rarely taught in language schools. In addition, many defy literal translation and depend on imagery and parallelism. *Never judge a book by its cover,* for example, has nothing to do with books and covers. It deals with the relationship between external appearance and internal realities, particularly with reference to human beings and their personalities. Another translation problem is that most proverbs are short. The proverb *Brevity is the soul of wit* is in no place more true than in the proverbs themselves. The shorter, the better. While this very terseness—*this short sentence based on long experience*—is often the heart of the proverb in all languages, it at the same time provides a difficult hurdle for the translator to clear. A three- or four-word phrase in one language may require an entire sentence, or even a paragraph, in translation, particularly if the translator feels the need to provide a full explanation.

This being said, it is incumbent for the author to state that this chapter will in no way provide a guide as to exactly how proverbs should be translated. That would be an overwhelming task. What the translator will find here is an explanation of the basic meaning in American English of a large group of proverbs. Some of the meanings are self-evident; some are moderately easy to decipher; but a large number of them (probably most) depend on allegories and/or metaphors to get across their ideas. These allegories and metaphors in turn may require an historical or cultural background, a foundation which a translator whose native language is not English may lack. Once the meaning of the proverb is explained, the translator has four choices: (1) he may provide a simple literal translation; (2) he may, where possible, find an identically phrased proverb in his target language; (3) he may try to construct a parallel proverb in his target language, expressing the same thought but using different words or images; and (4) where all else fails, he may need to fall back on using the original English proverb in his translation, highlighted in quotation marks or italics or bold type. Before he can do any of these, however, he needs to feel certain as to the precise meaning of a proverb, and that is what this chapter aims to provide.

For more on these concepts for realizing optimum power in translating proverbs, an article aptly titled "Proverbs" by John Duval is reprinted below with the kind permission of the journal *Translation Review,* in which it first appeared. It provides detailed examples of some of the translation problems described above, and offers examples of constructive approaches. In short, it provides a fitting "appetizer" to the list of proverbs, slogans, and aphorisms which follow. This chapter has attempted to distill about 650 of the most popular expressions, concentrating on those in present-day use and, where variations exist, choosing the ones most frequently encountered.

A few notes are in order. An index at the end of this book, covering the key words of each proverb, allows one to find all the proverbs that contain this noun, verb, or adjective. Many expressions are followed by the designation "LT," which means "Literal Translation" and indicates that the author believes that the thought is so common worldwide that the translator or interpreter is probably safe in translating it literally. This is particularly true for European languages where, in many cases, identical proverbs exist. For Far Eastern languages and for Russian, where cultural and historical differences are great, more care must be exercised by the translator. Consequently, you will frequently find the notation "LT acceptable." While the author believes a literal translation can be used for some languages, extreme care should be exercised with proverbs denoted by this phrase.

It is strongly suggested that translators and interpreters (even when LT is indicated) seek translations from English into another language reflecting, not the literal language of the proverb or aphorism, but the heart of the concept. For example, the American proverb *Every Jack has his Jill* has a Japanese counterpart: *For every cracked pot, there is a cracked lid*. The words are totally different, but the idea is pretty much the same. It must be said that this English version is terser, a characteristic devoutly to be desired when translating proverbs. Furthermore, there is an almost poetic rhythm in the former, which is lacking in the Anglicized version of the Japanese quotation.

Where identical or similar proverbs are given to enhance

explanations, these are marked by an equal sign ( = ), indicating that the alternative proverb given is more or less identical, or not exactly the same but similar. All equivalent proverbs in this chapter are given in *italics*. In a few cases, there are available proverbs with sentiments totally contradicting the base proverb. These are shown as follows with the unequal sign ( ≠ ) preceding the contradictory proverb.

About twenty percent of the proverbs given as **Equivalents** are in a foreign language. These are indicated by **Ar.** (Arabic), **Brit.** (British English), **Fr.** (French), **Ge.** (German), **It.** (Italian), **Ja.** (Japanese), **Ko.** (Korean), **La.** (Latin), **No.** (Norwegian), **Ru.** (Russian), **Sp.** (Spanish), and **Yi.** (Yiddish). Where the foreign proverb is in a language which uses or is easily transliterated into Roman letters, the proverb is given in italics in the original language, followed by a literal translation into American English enclosed within braces.

It should be strongly noted that the limited foreign language translations provided do not constitute an attempt to convert this book to a multilingual dictionary of American proverbs. The purpose of using these is to give the translator and interpreter some feel for the diverse ways that the message or the moral of the proverb can be delivered. Proverbs are based on human experience, and human experience—diverse as it may seem—is basically the same everywhere, regardless of language. These foreign language proverbs more or less provide proof of this statement.

The reader who is interested in the systematic study of proverbs may want to refer to the box at the end of this chapter, which deals with Proverbs on the Internet. These sites on the Web deal with areas of paremiology (the study of proverbs), and paremiography (the writing or collecting of proverbs).

One final point. There are a number of expressions in the American language, which cannot in any way be categorized as Proverbs, Slogans, and Aphorisms. Whatever their category, however, they are commonly used expressions which translators and interpreters should find useful. These will be covered in the next chapter under the title **Additional Popular Expressions.** The notes given above relating to the chapter on proverbs will apply equally to this next chapter.

## Translating Proverbs *(From an article by John Duval)*

Translating proverbs is tricky. Like the best poems, the best proverbs take advantage of the particular features of a particular language and show them off in ways that might be less persuasive in other languages. Also, proverbs are short, leaving little room for the translator to maneuver. The shorter the better.

And yet, proverbs do get translated, usually anonymously, *naturally,* we are tempted to think, effortlessly, almost without thinking. Here is a very short proverb: *Morituri te salutant.* Now I am sure I was familiar with this in English translation before I ever read it in Latin: "Those who are about to die salute you," or perhaps for a little stronger identification with the gladiators in some 1950s toga-and-tunic movie: "We who are about to die salute you." And the saying still can, in English, raise hairs on the back of my neck when I imagine two sharp-sworded Demetriuses standing at attention before Caesar in his front row throne at the arena. So the proverb works in English. But when I compare it to the Latin original, my first impulse is to feel ashamed of the English language. What happened to the brevity, so essential in its implication: *vita brevis,* especially for gladiators? Never mind that the English version is only two syllables longer. The Latin is three words, the all-powerful *te* flanked by death *(morituri)* and ceremony *(salutant),* the flanking words compact, massive and gladiatorial.

A closer look at the English, however, reveals it to be different, but not disappointing. In place of the massive symmetry of the Latin, we have a perfect trochaic pentameter line which builds steadily through a string of function words to the stressed die, then rises surprisingly at the penultimate syllable "salute." As in the Latin, but differently balanced, the ceremony and courage transcend the death. But not even the Latin can compare to the immediacy of the English "about to" tense, a tense that is not discussed in grammar books, precisely because our English descriptive grammar evolved from a Latin that had no analogue for it. At this point, we might feel sorry for the French, whose *future proche* does not come close: *Ceux qui vont mourir te saluent.* They could be *going* to die any time within the next few months, but our gladiators are *about to* die. Nevertheless, as a student of mine, Gabriel Lahood, has pointed out to me, in one way the French is stronger than either the Latin or the English, being more physical. The gladiators *are going* to die. And the rhythm, if I may scan the French sentence accentually instead of syllabically, is in step with their physical determination: *ceux qui vont mourir*.... In this language it is the anapest, *te saluent*, with its sudden departure from the strict duple march to *mourir*, that signals again some transcendence through courage and ceremony. The Latin proverb has evolved easily and successfully into both modern languages.

Let's look at an Italian proverb, shorter in words and perhaps even crueler: *Traduttore traditore*, translated literally as "Translator traitor," which translation looks more like an adjective/noun combination than a statement, or "A translator is a traitor," which is too long, or *translator = traitor*, which also has lost some of the economy of the original as well as its unequivocal oral force. Although "Translation traitor" keeps the alliteration and the assonance, the first word is no longer the same number of syllables as the second, and the English pair of words has lost half of the consonance of the original, orally persuasive equation; so unless we chant it over and over again at all translation conferences to the tune of a child's taunt: "Translation traitor! Nyea, nyea, nyea, nyea, nyea!" this translation is not apt to gain currency as a genuine English language proverb. In the Italian, even the meters are equivalent: each term of the equation is a feminine anapest. Notice even how effective the two differences in the Italian words are. The middle *u* is a slightly heavier vowel than the middle *i*, and the double *t* is more emphatic than the single *t*, both differences making *traduttore* the fuller, more substantial word of the pair and *traditore*, as another of my students, Paula Haydar, puts it, "a diminishing echo of the first word," reminding us that the big *traduttore* is only, merely, simply a little *traditore*.

"Translator traducer" would be more faithful to the sound and have the advantage of an etymological kinship with the original: the Italian *traduttore* and the English "traducer" share the same Latin root. But we are still stuck with the dilemma of whether or not we need or can afford, "A... is a..."; and the somewhat bookish sound of "traducer" makes it uncomfortable in the world of proverbs.

Now it is our turn to envy the French: *Traduire c'est trahir* ("To translate is to betray"). Despite the unobtrusive equal sign, *c'est,* the French is more compact than the Italian, and the "diminishing echo" is perfectly replicated. Only a die-hard translator-hater would object that the phrase loses something by condemning the sin of translation rather than the sinner. By focusing on the sin, the French have played a trick English language translators love to play, activated the nouns by turning them into verbs. But in English "To translate is to betray" loses too much echo. "To translate is to traduce," being unpronounceable, is worse. Maybe, on the other hand, we could claim that any of the English translations is really better than the Italian, because by being worse, it illustrates itself.

However, none of the above-mentioned English translations of the Italian proverb works, because none of them is a proverb. None of them has entered the English language in a way that "Those who are about to die salute you" has entered English or *Traduire c'est trahir* has entered French. Only one translation works, the one that you will hear more often than "Please pass the mustard" at any translation conference in the English-speaking world, spoken vehemently sometimes, sometimes vindictively, most often with chagrin: *Traduttore traditore,* words Italian in origin, of course, but now as English as the Queen, as American as apple pie. Proverbial English language usage has turned *traduttore traditore* into English, and this English translation speaks for the original even better than the original does, because by pretending not to be English in its strict replication of every syllable of the Italian, it hints (falsely) that the Italian original is untranslatable.

However, since the hint is indeed false and since this translation does indeed speak perfectly—better than perfectly!— for the original, it betrays the original in the worst way, because it proves that the original is false even though the original, in all good faith, was meant to be true.

But by betraying the original, the English translation *traduttore traditore* demonstrates the truth of the original Italian *traduttore traditore* and is therefore true and faithful.... We could debate this point until the end of time, but life is short.

**Absence makes the heart grow fonder.** LT acceptable. People tend to miss loved ones who are away. (=) *Absence sharpens love; presence strengthens it.* (≠) *Out of sight, out of mind.* Equiv.: **Fr.** *Loin des yeux, près du coeur.* {Far from one's sight, close to one's heart.}

**Accidents will happen.** LT. An expression frequently used to excuse mishaps or non-fortuitous occurrences. (=) *It can happen in the best of families.*

**Act well your part; there all the honor lies.** LT. Do what is expected of you, and do it well.

**Actions speak louder than words.** LT. One should be judged by one's actions rather than by what one says. (=) *Deeds speak louder than promises. The greatest talkers are the least doers.* Equiv.: **It.** *Tra il dire e il fare c'è di mezzo il mare.* {It is a long haul from words to deeds.} **Sp.** *Gato maullador, nunca buen cazador.* {A mewing cat is never a good mouser.}

**All's fair in love and war.** LT acceptable. No rules apply in emotionally-charged situations. (=) *Necessity knows no law.*

**All that glitters is not gold (All is not gold that glitters).** Appearances can be deceptive; things are seldom what they seem. (=) *Never judge a book by its cover. Appearances can be deceiving.* Equiv.: **Fr.** *L'habite ne fait pas le moine.* {The habit doesn't make the monk.}

**All's well that ends well.** LT acceptable. The final result is what really counts, regardless of how things begin. Equiv.: **Ko.** *Baro gana moro gana Seoul man gamyun guman iji.* {It does not matter what route one takes as long as he can reach Seoul.}

**All the world's a stage (and all the men and women merely players [actors]).** An allegorical statement of the human condition.

**All work and no play makes Jack a dull boy.** Recreation is important. (=) *Variety is the spice of life.*

**Always be nice to people on the way up the ladder because you may meet them again on the way down.** Be kind to people when your career is rising, and they will be more likely to reciprocate if you run into misfortune. (=) *Do not burn your bridges behind you.*

**Always leave them laughing.** LT acceptable. One should end every encounter or presentation with an impressive or amusing statement or action.

**Always tell the truth to your doctor and your lawyer.** Self-explanatory. Lying to them will almost always be detrimental to health and/or may cost more in the long run. Equiv.: **It.** *Al confessor, medico, e avvocato, non si de' tener il vero celato.* {To one's priest, doctor, and lawyer, the truth should always be told.}

**Anything worth doing is worth doing well.** LT. Do not start a job or project unless you are willing to give it your maximum effort.

**Appearances can be deceiving.** LT. (=) *All is not gold that glitters. Never judge a book by its cover.*

**Appetite is the best sauce.** LT acceptable. When you are hungry, everything tastes better. (=) *Hunger is the best seasoning.*

**Apple (acorn) does not fall far from the tree, The.** The characteristics (peculiarities) of parents are passed on to their children. (=) *Like father, like son. A chip off the old block.* Equiv.: **Ja.** *Kaeruno kowa kaeru.* {The child of a frog is a frog.} **Ko.** *Gaiguri seki do gaiguri da.* {The child of a frog is still a frog.}

**Apple a day keeps the doctor away, An.** Living healthy helps one avoid illness.

**April showers bring May flowers.** Do not worry about today's negatives for tomorrow will be better.

**Army travels on its stomach, An.** The most important part of a military maneuver is supplying food and equipment to the troops.

**As the sapling (twig) bends, so grows the tree.** We are all products of our background and environment. Equiv.: **Ko.** *Jal jarul namu ddugnip butu anda.* {A tree that will grow healthy has good buds.}

**As you sow so shall you reap.** Everything we do has future repercussions for which we are responsible. (=) *Sow the wind and reap the whirlwind.*

**Ashes to ashes, dust to dust.** LT acceptable. An expression used in burial services, meaning that the body returns whence it came.

**Ask a silly question (and you get a silly answer).** (=) You get what you pay for.

**Bad money drives out good.** LT. Known as Gresham's Law. If two kinds of money of the same denomination but with different values are in circulation, the more valuable (good) currency will be hoarded, while the cheaper (bad) currency will flood the market.

**Bad news travels fast.** LT. (=) *No news is good news.* Equiv.: **Ja.** *Akuji senriwo hashiru.* {Evil deeds run a thousand leagues.}

**Bad penny always returns, A.** LT. A bad experience tends to come back to haunt us.

**Bad workman always blames his tools, A.** LT. One should not blame his equipment when his own incompetence is at fault. Equiv.: **Ja.** *Kôbô fudewo erabazu.* {Kobo (a master of calligraphy) doesn't choose his brush pen. He can write perfectly with any pen.}

**Barking dogs never bite.** Self-explanatory. LT. (=) *His bark is worse* *than his bite.* Equiv.: **Sp.** *Gato maullador, nunca buen cazador.* {A mewing cat is never a good mouser.}

**Beauty is in the eye of the beholder.** LT. (=) *Beauty may have fair leaves but bitter fruit.* Equiv.: **Ge.** *Was Liebe ist, das ist schön.* {What is love is beautiful.} **Ko.** *Jai nun e angyun.* {Every man sees beauty only through his glasses.}

**Beauty is only skin deep.** LT. The true value of a person is in his kindness, understanding, and intelligence rather than in external appearances. (=) *Handsome is as handsome does.*

**Beauty is truth, truth beauty.** LT. Self-explanatory, but used figuratively.

**Be careful what you wish for because you just might get it (Do not wish too hard; you might just get what you wished for).** Sometimes even the greatest opportunities have their pitfalls, and one might regret ever having wished for them. (=) *Look before you leap. Make haste slowly.*

**Beggars can't be choosers.** LT. When asking for favors or accepting gifts, one should not be entitled to the right to inspect and choose. (=) *Never look a gift horse in the mouth.* Equiv.: **It.** *Chi mendica non può scegliere.* {Beggars cannot be choosers.}

**Behind every great man is a woman.** LT. Historically held back by sexist societal norms, women contribute their talents by helping their husbands or bosses succeed at their goals. (=) *A man without a woman is like a ship without a sail.*

**Believe only half of what you see and nothing you hear.** Be extremely skeptical; carefully consider all evidence.

**Be not the first to quarrel nor the last to make up.** Life is much more pleasant if arguments are avoided or quickly settled.

**Best laid plans of mice and men oft go astray, The.** No matter how carefully we plan, unlooked-for accidents or problems come up which upset our planning. (=) *Nothing is certain but the unforeseen. Nothing in life is certain but death and taxes.*

**Best things come in small packages, The.** Quality has nothing to do with size.

**Best things in life are free, The.** LT. Do not be overly preoccupied with money-making; simple pleasures such as air, sunshine, and laughter are more satisfying.

**Better late than never.** It is better to be tardy than never to arrive at all; it is better to achieve something or complete a job late than never to have attempted it.

**Better safe than sorry.** LT acceptable. Extra caution prevents injury.

(=) *An ounce of prevention is worth a pound of cure.*

**Better that the law be known than that the law be just, It is.** Justice is important, but fairness dictates that people should know in advance if they are breaking a law. (=) *Ignorance of the law is no excuse.*

**Better the devil you know (than the one you don't).** When you have two negative alternatives, choose the familiar one.

**Better to be a has-been than a never-was, It is.** Prior achievements at least give you something to look back on.

**Better to be an old man's darling than a young man's slave, It is.** LT.

**Better to be born lucky than rich, It is.** LT.

**Better to have loved and lost than never to have loved at all, It is.** LT. Self-explanatory. (=) *It is better to be a has-been than a never-was.*

**Better to reign in hell than serve in heaven, It is.** LT. Self-explanatory. (=) *Better to be first in a village than second in Rome. Better to be the head of a lizard than the tail of a dragon.* Equiv.: **Ko.** *So ggori boda dak daiggari go jota.* {Better to be the head of a rooster than the tail of an ox.}

**Better to remain silent and be thought a fool than to speak and remove all doubt, It is.** Do not talk unless you have something intelligent or meaningful to say. (=) *Speech is silver; silence is golden.*

**Beware of Greeks bearing gifts.** Be careful whenever an opponent offers something unexpected.

**Bigger they are, the harder they fall, The.** The more successful a person, the more he has to lose; do not fear a person's size or high position. (=) *He who climbs highest, falls farthest.*

**Bird in the hand is worth two in the bush, A.** Possession is of greater value than promises or possibilities. (=) *Bread today is better than cake tomorrow. Take thou the cash and let the credit go.* Equiv.: **It.** *Meglio un uovo oggi che una gallina domani.* {An egg today is better than getting a hen tomorrow.} **Ja.** *Asuno hyakuyori kyôno gojû.* {Better fifty today than a hundred tomorrow.} **La.** *Ad praesens ova crass pullis sunt meliora.* {An egg today is better than a hen tomorrow.} **Sp.** *Mejor un pájaro en la mano que un buitre volando.* {Better to have a bird in hand than a vulture flying.}

**Birds of a feather flock together.** Like attracts like; people of similar tastes, background, ethnicity, or religion for the most part associate with each other. (=) *A man is known by the company he keeps.* (≠) *Opposites attract.* Equiv.: **Ja.** *Ushiwa ushizure, umawa umazure.* {Oxen with oxen, horses with horses.}

**Blood is thicker than water.** LT acceptable. Family relationships are stronger and more important than friendships, particularly in difficult situations. (≠) *A near friend is better than a distant kinsman.*

**Boy's best friend is his mother, A.** LT. Self-explanatory.

**Boys will be boys.** Males are prone to misbehavior, so why bother trying to change them? Often used lightly to excuse men and boys for behaving crudely or aggressively. (=) *Nits will be lice.*

**Brevity is the soul of wit.** (*Wit* meaning understanding or intelligence.) A brief, pithy comment is more likely to express an idea clearly. Equiv.: **Ja.** *Ja heta no naga-dangi.* {The unskilled talk long.}

**Business before pleasure.** LT. When facing a choice between gainful activities and entertainment, one should do what must be done before doing what he wants to do.

**Calm waters do not a sailor make.** Easy situations teach no lessons; problem-solving leads to expertise. (=) *Experience is the best teacher.* Equiv.: **He.** *Eretz Yisrael niknet b'yisurin.* {The land of Israel is acquired through suffering.}

**Candy is dandy, but liquor is quicker.** One can charm a potential sex partner with simple pleasures, but getting him or her intoxicated is likely to achieve the seduction sooner.

**Cast your bread upon the water.** Be generous, for it pays in the long run.

**Cats are black (gray) in the dark (at night), All.** Without illumination, physical or intellectual, widely different things may seem the same.

**Cat can look at a king, A.** The humble have the right to look at the great. (=) *A dog may look at a bishop.*

**Cat has nine lives, A.** Cats are particularly adapted to survival and seem to escape death more than once in their lifetimes. Sometimes used figuratively about a particular human who lives dangerously.

**Catch more flies with honey than he can with vinegar (flypaper), One can.** Reason, charm, and gentle persuasion are more effective than anger, invective, and vituperation.

**Chain is no stronger than its weakest link, A.** Group activity is limited to the ability of the least able member of the group.

**Change is as good as a rest, A.** LT acceptable. Switching activities is as revitalizing as doing nothing.

**Charity begins at home.** One should give priority to that which touches one most closely. Equiv.: **It.** *La carità comincia in famiglia.* {Charity begins in the family.}

**Child is father of the man, The.** What is learned in childhood, for better or for worse, becomes part of the adult's character. (=) *What youth*

*is used to, age remembers.* Equiv.: **Ja.** *Mitsugono tomasaii hyakumade.*
{The soul of a three-year-old stays until 100.} **Sp.** *Lo que en la leche se
mama, en la mortaja se derrama.* {That which is absorbed with one's
mother's milk remains with one till the grave.}
**Children should be seen and not heard.** LT. Children should be
disciplined and not rowdy.
**Christmas comes but once a year.** Do not expect good fortune to smile
on you perpetually.
**Class will tell.** If you make a good appearance and handle yourself well,
you will make a good impression.
**Cleanliness is next to Godliness.** LT acceptable. Few things in life are
as important as keeping one's self and surroundings clean and healthy.
**Clothes (apparel) make the man.** The impression given by the way
one dresses reflects one's status in an organization or society; likewise, a
destitute person in expensive clothing may be mistaken for a wealthy and
successful one. (=) *The tailor makes the man. Fine feathers make fine
birds.* Equiv.: **Ko.** *Ossi nalgai.* {Clothes are wings.}
**Cold hands, warm heart.** LT. A person with cold extremities is more
likely to be warm on the inside; figuratively, a person with a standoffish
appearance may be quite friendly. (=) *Never judge a book by its cover.
Appearances can be deceiving.* Equiv.: **Sp.** *Las apariencias engañan.*
{Appearances are misleading.}
**Condemn the sin, not the sinner.** People do bad things, but there are
no bad people; there is always room for repentance.
**Consider (go to) the ant, you sluggard; look at her ways and be
wise.** Do not be lazy; be industrious and hard-working.
**Consistency is the hobgoblin of little minds, (A foolish).** It is more
important to find practical solutions than to insist on always doing things
in the same way.
**Constant dripping wears away stone.** LT acceptable. A persistent
effort is highly likely to achieve success. (=) *If at first you do not succeed,
try, try again.*
**Count your blessings.** Be grateful for what you have while you have it;
do not lose sight of the best things in your life. (=) *One never appreciates
what he has until he has lost it.*
**Cowards die many times before their deaths; the valiant only
taste of death but once.** LT acceptable. The ability to conquer fear
makes life far easier. (The first phrase is of course figurative.)
**Crazy man thinks everyone is crazy except himself, A.** Everyone
looks at things from his own viewpoint.
**Curiosity killed the cat.** Do not look for trouble by asking too many

questions. (=) *Search not too curiously, lest you find trouble.* Equiv.: **Fr.** *La curiosité est un vilain défaut.* {Curiosity is a nasty fault.}

**Dead men tell no tales.** The dead cannot testify against you, so leave no witnesses. Equiv.: **Fr.** *Les morts ne parlent pas.* {The dead do not talk.} **Ge.** *Tote Hunde beißen nicht.* {Dead dogs don't bite.} **La.** *Mortui non mordent.* {Dead men don't bite.}

**Death is a great leveler.** No matter one's position in life, we all reach the same end and leave all we have achieved behind. (=) *The paths of glory lead but to the grave.*

**Devil finds work for idle hands to do, The.** People who are not occupied often look for trouble, so keep busy. (=) *Idleness is the mother of evil.*

**Different strokes for different folks.** Everyone to his own taste. (=) *To each his own.* Equiv.: **Fr.** *Chacun a son goût.* {Each to his own taste.} **La.** *De gustibus non disputandum est.* {There can be no disputing about taste.}

**Difficult is done at once; the impossible takes a little longer, The.** LT. A whimsical concept frequently offered as a slogan by optimists or those confident of their abilities.

**Discretion is the better part of valor.** In being brave or heroic, one should be safe and act simply. (=) *He who fights and runs away will live to fight another day. He who fears drowning avoids wells.* (≠) *He who hesitates is lost. Look before you leap.*

**Distance lends enchantment.** Situations which, or people who, seem unfavorable under scrutiny may seem better when viewed from a distance. Equiv.: **La.** *Maior e longinquo reverentia.* {Greater reverence from afar.}

**Do no harm.** A slogan of the medical profession meaning that whether or not medical treatments improve the patient's health, they should not make matters worse.

**Do not (never) bite the hand that feeds you.** Be grateful; do not betray or attack the source of one's income or well-being.

**Do not (never) borrow (go looking for) trouble.** LT. Avoid difficult situations; trouble will find you soon enough without your assistance. (=) *Do not trouble trouble before trouble troubles you.*

**Do not (never) build castles in the air.** Do not live in a dream world; be practical. (=) *Keep your feet squarely on the ground.*

**Do not (never) burn your bridges behind you.** Do not make enemies under the assumption that you will not need those persons' assistance again; always leave yourself the possibility of retreat or backtracking. (=) *Always be nice to people on the way up the ladder, because you might* *meet them again on the way down.*

**Do not (never) carry coals to Newcastle.** An expression indicating redundancy, i.e., do not carry to a place items which already exist there in abundance. Equiv.: **It.** *Vender il miele a chi ha le api.* {To sell honey to a beekeeper.} **Ge.** *Eulen nach Athen tragen.* {To carry owls to Athens.}

**Do not (never) change horses in midstream.** It is not wise to change leadership while in the middle of a major undertaking.

**Do not (never) count your chickens before they hatch.** LT acceptable. Do not anticipate or assume too much; do not reach a conclusion until everything is settled. Equiv.: **Fr.** *Ne vends pas la peau de l'ours avant de l'avoir tué.* {Kill (catch) the bear before you sell its skin.} **Ge.** *Man soll den Tag nicht vor dem Abend loben.* {Do not praise the day before the evening comes.} **Ja.** *Toranu tanukino kawazanyô.* {Do not calculate the value of the fur of a raccoon you have not yet caught.} **Sp.** *No cantes victoria antes de tiempo.* {Do not shout victory too soon.}

**Do not (never) cut off your nose to spite your face.** Be careful not to make a situation worse in order to do harm to or get back at someone else. Equiv.: **Ko.** *Jui jabgi weuhe dog ggeji mara.* {Don't break a jar to catch a mouse.}

**Do not fiddle while Rome burns.** Act quickly; do not waste time in an emergency.

**Do not (never) fish in troubled waters.** LT acceptable. Avoid getting involved in an ongoing fight or any difficult situation. Equiv.: **It.** *Pescare nel torbido.* {To fish in muddy waters.}

**Do not (never) give up the ship.** Never quit.

**Do not (never) have too many irons in the fire.** Do not take on more work or responsibility than you can handle. (=) *Do not bite off more than you can chew.*

**Do not (never) hide your light under a bushel.** Do not be overly modest about your abilities or accomplishments. (=) *Stand up and be counted.*

**Do not (never) judge others by yourself.** LT. Self-explanatory.

**Do not (never) jump out of the frying pan into the fire.** Do not avoid a bad situation by getting into a worse one. (=) *From bad to worse.* Equiv.: **Sp.** *Ir de Guatemala en guate-peor.* {To go from bad to worse.}

**Do not (never) kill the goose that lays the golden eggs.** Do not risk the source of one's wealth out of greed for more.

**Do not (never) kiss and tell.** LT acceptable. Do not boast about private matters, sexual or otherwise.

**Do not (never) let the grass grow under your feet.** Act quickly; do not waste time. (=) *Never put off 'til tomorrow what you can do today.*

**Do not (never) let the tail wag the dog.** Do not let minor or unimportant matters control major, important ones; one should be fully aware of priorities.

**Do not (never) let your heart rule your head.** Do not allow emotions to override rational thinking.

**Do not (never) make a mountain out of a molehill.** Do not over-emphasize; do not make a big deal out of a small matter. Equiv.: **Fr.** *Faire tout un plat de rien du tout.* {To make a whole dish out of nothing.} **Ge.** *Aus einer Mücke einen Elefanten machen.* {To make an elephant out of a mosquito.} **Sp.** *No te ahogues en un vaso de agua.* {Don't drown in a glass of water.}

**Do (not) make a virtue of necessity.** When faced with an unavoidable task, do not claim to be doing it for righteous reasons; however, always try to come out ahead. (=) *If life hands you lemons, make lemonade.*

**Do not (never) put all your eggs in one basket.** Do not commit everything you own at one time, emotionally or financially; distribute your risks. (=) *The mouse with only one hole is quickly captured.* Equiv.: **Sp.** *Poner toda la carne en el asador.* {Don't put all your meat on a single spit.}

**Do not (never) rub salt in a wound.** When someone is hurt, be careful not to make matters worse by what you say or do. (=) *Do not add insult to injury.*

**Do not (never) start anything you cannot finish.** Plan ahead; be sure you know how complicated or substantial a task is before you accept responsibility for completing it. (=) *Never bite off more than you can chew.*

**Do not stir up a hornet's nest.** Do not make trouble. (=) *Do not open up a can of worms.* Equiv.: **Ja.** *Yabuhebi.* {Disturbing a bush you may encounter a snake.} **Sp.** *Meterse en un avispero.* {To put oneself in a wasp's nest.}

**Do not teach your grandmother to suck eggs.** Do not assume that older people are not experienced with life nor would understand how it feels to be young. Equiv.: **Ja.** *Shakani seppô.* {Do not preach Buddhism to Buddha.} **Ko.** *Buchunim ge Bulgyung.* {It is like lecturing the Buddhist scripture to Buddha.}

**Do not (never) tell tales out of school.** Do not snitch or gossip about other people.

**Do not (never) throw out the baby with the bathwater.** When getting rid of something you do not need, take care that you are not simultaneously losing something important or essential.

**Don't tread on me.** A slogan of the American Revolution, meaning that the omnipotent British monarchy should not abuse its power over the American colonies; do not step on the little people, for they will retaliate.

**Do not (never) use a sledgehammer to crack a nut.** Do not use unnecessarily great force; do not overreact or overdo something. (=) *Do not make a mountain out of a molehill.*

**Do not skate (walk; tread) on thin ice.** Be careful; do not expose yourself to precarious situations. Equiv.: **Sp.** *Andar pisando huevos.* {To walk on eggs.}

**Do not (never) wash (air) your dirty linen in public.** Do not tell family secrets or discuss family disputes when strangers are present. Can also refer to insider groups such as clubs, corporations, political parties, etc.

**Do not watch the clock.** LT acceptable. Keep busy. Equiv.: **Ko.** *Mot olragal san un chuda bojido marara.* {Do not even look up the mountain that cannot be climbed.}

**Do not (never) wear out your welcome.** Be a good guest; do not stay too long. (=) *Fish and visitors start to stink after three days.* Equiv.: **Fr.** *Il faut laisser le jeu pendant qu'il est beau.* {Leave the game while it still looks nice.}

**Do not (never) wear your heart on your sleeve.** It is best not to expose one's intense personal emotions to the world.

**Do not wish your life away.** LT. Do not waste real time on fantasies. A quick answer to people who anxiously await some future event and wish that the day of that event were here already.

**Do nothing by halves.** LT. One should give his fullest and best effort to any task. (=) *Anything worth doing is worth doing well.*

**Do or die.** LT acceptable. Give it one's best effort.

**Do right and fear no man.** If one obeys all natural and human-made laws, he should not have to worry about repercussions.

**Do unto others as you would have them do unto you.** Also known as The Golden Rule. LT. Treat other people in the way you would like to be treated.

**Drowning man grasps at straws, A.** When in dire straits, people will reach out for whatever help they can get, even if the attempt seems futile.

**Each man kills the thing he loves.** Almost always used figuratively. When one loves someone, he tends to excesses which are ultimately destructive, e.g., jealousy, possessiveness, emotional smothering, etc.

**Each to his own taste (poison).** LT. Be tolerant of people's different tastes. Equiv.: **La.** *De gustibus non disputandum est.* {There can be no disputing about taste.}

**Early bird catches (gets) the worm, The.** People who are motivated (i.e., who start the day early) are most productive. (=) *Early to bed, early to rise makes a man healthy, wealthy, and wise.* Equiv.: **Fr.** *La vie appartient à ceux qui se lèvent tôt.* {Life belongs to those who get up early.} **Sp.** *A quién madruga, Dios lo ayuda.* {God helps those who rise early.}

**Early to bed and early to rise makes a man healthy, wealthy, and wise.** LT. Self-explanatory. (=) *The early bird catches the worm. He who will thrive must rise at five.* Equiv.: **Ja.** *Hayane hayaoki yamai shirazu.* {Early to bed and early to rise knows no illness.}

**East is East and West is West, and never the twain shall meet.** The mentalities and outlooks of two cultures may be so different that they are bound to be incompatible; cultural differences are often insurmountable.

**Easy come, easy go.** LT acceptable. Something easily gained can be easily lost. (=) *Soon gotten, soon spent.* Equiv.: **Fr.** *Ce qui vient de la flûte s'en va par le tambour.* {What comes through the flute goes through the drums.} **Ge.** *Wie gewonnen, so zerronnen.* {It melted away the same way it came.} **Sp.** *Lo que por agua viene, por agua se va.* {What comes in the stream goes away in the stream.}

**Easy to find a stick (stone) to beat a dog, It is.** If you are determined to do something, you will find the means. (=) *Where there's a will, there's a way.* Equiv.: **Fr.** *Quand on veut, on peut.* {When one wants, one can.}

**Eat, drink, and be merry for tomorrow we die.** Enjoy yourself now, because no one knows what the future holds. Equiv.: **La.** *Carpe diem.* {Seize the day.}

**Empty kettle (pot/drum/barrel) makes the most noise, The.** Rowdy or boisterous people are that way because they usually have nothing substantive to say. (=) *Still waters run deep.* Equiv.: **Ko.** *Bin ggangtong i sori nun du kuda.* {An empty cart can make the most noise.}

**End justifies the means, The.** Good results validate questionable practices. (=) *Two wrongs don't make a right.* Equiv.: **La.** *La exitus acta probat.* {The end justifies the means.}

**Enough is as good as a feast.** LT acceptable. There is no need for excesses. (=) *Show moderation in all things.* Equiv.: **Fr.** *La modération est la santé de l'âme.* {Moderation is the health of the soul.}

**Eternal vigilance is the price of freedom.** For the nation or the individual, maintaining freedom is a constant battle; there are always people who are eager to limit or erase freedom.

**Even a worm will turn.** Eventually, even the quiet and modest will strike back if continually abused. Equiv.: **Ko.** *Sungnan goyangyi bum do munda.* {An angry cat will bite even a tiger.}

**Every cloud has a silver lining.** There is a bright side to even the most gloomy situation. (=) *When things are at their worst, they will mend.* Equiv.: **La.** *Post nubila Phoebus.* {After clouds comes the sun-god.}

**Every dog has his day.** Sooner or later, every individual has a lucky period. Sometimes used negatively for a day of retribution. Equiv.: **Fr.** *La roue tourne.* {The wheel turns.} **Ko.** *Jui gumung edo hedbit dulnal i itda.* {There will be days when sunshine will even reach into a mouse hole.}

**Every family has a skeleton in the closet.** All of us have secrets to hide, truths we are ashamed of.

**Every Jack has his Jill.** For every man, there's a woman. Equiv.: **Fr.** *A chacun sa chacune.* {For everyone (male) there is someone (female).} **Ge.** *Jeder Topf findet seinen Deckel.* {Every pot finds its own lid.} **Ja.** *Warenabeni tojibuta.* {There is no pot so ugly that one cannot find a cover for it.} **Ko.** *Hun sinjjag do jag un itda.* {Even a (poor quality) straw shoe has a mating shoe.}

**Every man has his price.** LT acceptable. Even the most moral or honest person is subject to temptation if the offer is high enough.

**Every man to his trade.** LT acceptable. Everyone should deal with his own area of expertise. (=) *Shoemaker, stick to your last.*

**Every road has its turning.** Nothing remains consistently good or consistently bad; life has its ups and downs.

**Everybody loves a lover.** LT acceptable. People tend to feel warm-hearted when observing people obviously in love.

**Everybody talks about the weather, but nobody does anything about it.** LT. Self-explanatory.

**Everything is either illegal, immoral, or fattening.** The things we enjoy seem to be bad for us.

**Exception that proves the rule, It is the.** LT. When an exception is made, it proves that the rule exists. (=) *Rules are made to be broken.*

**Experience is the best teacher.** LT. Self-explanatory. Equiv.: **Fr.** *C'est en forgeant que l'on devient forgeron.* {It is by working at the forge that one becomes a blacksmith.} **He.** *Eretz Yisrael niknet b'yisurin.* {The land of Israel is acquired through suffering.} **Ja.** *Kamenokôyori, toshinokô.* {The accumulated wisdom of years protects better than hiding in a turtle shell.} **La.** *Experientia docet.* {Experience teaches.}

**Eye for an eye and a tooth for a tooth, An.** Punishment or revenge should be consistent with the crime. (=) *Hand for hand, foot for foot.*

**Eyes are the windows of the soul, The.** LT. A person's eyes can be filled with emotion and expression so revealing that one can get a feeling for the heart and soul of that person.

**Faint heart never won fair lady.** Women appreciate courage in men; courtships should be ardent. (=) *None but the brave deserve the fair.*

**Faith can move mountains.** If you believe long enough and strongly enough, even the impossible is within reach.

**Familiarity breeds contempt.** LT acceptable. Knowing someone well familiarizes you with all his shortcomings. (=) *Distance lends enchantment. No man is a hero to his valet. Good fences make good neighbors.*

**Family that prays (plays) together stays together, The.** LT.

**Fight fire with fire.** If your enemy resorts to dirty tricks and stealth tactics, do the same. (≠) *He who fights and runs away will live to fight another day.* Equiv.: **Ge.** *Mit Dieben fängt man Diebe.* {A thief snares thieves.} **Ja.** *Dokuwo motte, dokuwo seisu.* {Check poison with poison.}

**Finders keepers, losers weepers.** LT acceptable. Self-explanatory. When one happens upon something of value, he can claim that because he found it he can then take possession of it. (=) *Possession is nine points of the law. First come, first served.*

**Fingers were made before forks.** LT. While the rewards of wealth and success are great, be careful not to forget the basics of life.

**First casualty of war is truth, The.** LT. Secrecy and censorship abound during wartime for the sake of national security or military strategy.

**First come, first served.** LT. The quick and motivated individuals are usually the most successful. (=) *The early bird gets the worm. Finders keepers, losers weepers.* Equiv.: **No.** *Den som kommer først til mølla, får først male.* {The first one to the mill is the first one to grind.}

**First impressions are the best impressions.** The initial opinion you form when first meeting a person is probably more accurate than later conclusions. (≠) *Never judge by first impressions.*

**First shall be last, and the last first, The.** Concerning eventual justice meted out by God. (=) *The meek shall inherit the earth.*

**First thrive, then wive.** Be sure you can make a living and support a family before you consider marriage.

**Fool and his money are soon parted, A.** LT. It is easy to swindle money from gullible people. (=) *A fool may make money, but it takes a wise man to spend it.*

**Fools rush in where wise men (angels) fear to tread.** LT. Proceed with caution. Equiv.: **Ge.** *Unwissenheit ist kühn.* {Ignorance is bold.}

**For the want of a nail, the shoe was lost.** Small details often control the results of important undertakings. (≠) *Do not let the tail wag the dog.*

**Forbidden fruit is the sweetest.** LT. Things that, or people, who are forbidden become more intriguing and when indulged more savory; people become more interested when something is forbidden.

**Forewarned is forearmed.** LT. It is much easier to defend oneself when one knows what attacks are coming. Equiv.: **Fr.** *Un homme averti en vaut deux.* {A forewarned man is worth two men.}

**Friend in need is a friend indeed, A.** A true friend is one who helps when you are in trouble. (=) *Prosperity makes friends; adversity tries them.* Equiv.: **It.** *Nel bisogno si riconosce un amico.* {When you are in need, you know who your friends are.}

**Gather ye rosebuds while ye may (Old Time is still a-flying).** Make the most of enjoying life while you are young. (=) *You are only young once. The flower that once has blown (bloomed) forever dies.* Equiv.: **La.** *Carpe diem.* {Seize the day.}

**Give someone an inch (yard) and he will take a mile.** Give some people even a small advantage, and they will use it to get a much greater advantage. (=) *Give him a finger, and he'll take a hand.* Equiv.: **Fr.** *On lui en donne long comme le doigt, il en prend long comme le bras.* {You give someone as much as a finger, he takes a whole arm.} **Ja.** *Kameno toshiwo tsuruga urayamu.* {The crane is jealous of the turtle's age.}

**Give me liberty or give me death.** LT. Equiv.: **Ge.** *Mehr als das Leben lieb' ich meine Freiheit.* {I love freedom more than I love life.}

**Give someone (a thief) enough rope and he will hang himself.** When someone is doing something wrong, give him enough freedom and security and he will become less vigilant and cautious, eventually acting in a way that will ensure his capture.

**Give the devil his due.** Give someone credit for something positive or well done even if he is disliked or untalented. (=) *Give credit where credit is due.* Equiv.: **Sp.** *(Darle) al cesar lo que es del cesar.* {Render unto Caesar what is rightfully his.}

**God gave us our relatives; thank God we can choose our friends.** LT. Self-explanatory. (≠) *Blood is thicker than water.*

**God (Heaven/the Lord) helps those who help themselves.** LT acceptable. Prayer may be good for the soul, but self-reliance is more likely to result in answered prayers. Equiv.: **Ar.** *Siq bellah wa laken ieqel dabatak.* {Trust in Allah but tie your camel.}

**Good fences make good neighbors.** LT. (=) *A hedge between keeps friendships green. Familiarity breeds contempt.* Equiv.: **Fr.** *C'est de la familiarité que naissent les plus tendres amitiés et les plus fortes haines.* {Familiarity creates the most tender friendships as well as the strongest hatreds.}

**Good husband makes a good wife, A.** LT. Treat your wife well, and she will reciprocate.

**Good luck does not always repeat itself.** LT. (=) *One swallow doth not a summer make.* Equiv.: **Ja.** *Yanagino shitano dojô.* {A loach (fish) under the willow.}

**Good reputation is more valuable than money, A.** LT. Self-explanatory. A good name is a valuable asset, harder to achieve than wealth or success.

**Good (all) things come to those who wait.** LT. Self-explanatory. (=) *Patience is a virtue.*

**Government is best which governs least.** LT. Too strong a government results in loss of liberty.

**Grass is always greener on the other side of the fence (hedge), The.** We always think that others are doing better than we are. (=) *The apples on the other side of the wall are the sweetest. Our neighbor's ground yields better corn than our own.* Equiv.: **Ge.** *Die Früchte in Nachbar's Garten sind am süßesten.* {The fruit in the neighbor's garden is the sweetest.} *Fremd' Brot schmeckt wohl.* {Foreign bread seems tasty.} **Ko.** *Nam eu ddug un ku boinda.* {Someone else's rice cake looks bigger than mine.}

**Great minds think alike, All.** LT. Self-explanatory. (=) *All great minds run in the same channels.*

**Great oaks from little acorns grow.** All important things have simple beginnings. Equiv.: **Fr.** *Les petits ruisseaux font les grandes rivières.* {Little streams make up big rivers.} **Ge.** *Große Dinge haben kleine Anfänge.* {Large things have small beginnings.}

**Greater the truth, the greater the libel, The.** When truth is circulated for vicious or irresponsible purposes, the validity or intensity of the truth does not matter; it is the intent which prevails.

**Half a glass (loaf) is better than none.** LT acceptable. Better something than nothing. (=) *Better half an egg than an empty shell. Enough is as good as a feast.* Equiv.: **Fr.** *Faute de grives, on mange des merles.* {When thrushes are not available, one eats blackbirds.}

**Half-truth is worse than a lie, A.** Because the true portion of a statement tends to effectively conceal the falsehood, half-truths are more vicious and more devious than outright lies.

**Hand is quicker than the eye, The.** A person can manipulate things so quickly that others cannot see the change. Can be used figuratively for other manipulative areas.

**Hand that rocks the cradle rules the world, The.** Motherhood is the world's most important and influential occupation.

**Handsome is as handsome does.** One should be judged by one's actions rather than one's appearance. (=) *Beauty is only skin deep.*

**Haste makes waste.** Doing things quickly or hurriedly can result in many mistakes that take time to be corrected. (=) *Make haste slowly.* (≠) *Strike while the iron is hot.* Equiv.: **Ar.** *Al ajalat min al shaitan.* {Haste is the work of the Devil.} **Fr.** *Qui veut voyager loin ménage sa monture.* {He who wishes to travel far spares his mount.} **Ge.** *Blinder Eifer schadet nur.* {Blind zeal only results in harm.} **Sp.** *El que mucho corre pronto para.* {He who runs fast stops soon.}

**He jests at scars who never felt a wound.** Opinions should be based on experience. (=) *Experience is the best teacher. Do unto others as you would have done unto you.*

**He prayeth best who loveth best all things both great and small.** Having a loving nature is the sincerest form of piety.

**He travels fastest who travels alone.** LT. Being unencumbered by the needs of others facilitates rapid movement or activity.

**He who bears children provides hostages for fate.** No parent can overcome the forces of destiny to protect his or her child; bearing children increases parents' chances that bad (or good) luck will affect them.

**He who fights and runs away will live to fight another day.** LT. It pays to be a coward. (=) *Discretion is the better part of valor. A living dog is better than a dead lion.* Equiv.: **Ja.** *Shinitaruhitowa ikerunezuminidani shikazu.* {A live mouse is better than a dead man.}

**He who laughs last laughs best.** Do not conclude that you have won until the contest is totally over. (=) *Don't count your chickens before they hatch. It ain't over 'til it's over. It's not over until the fat lady sings.*

**He who hesitates is lost.** Act quickly before the opportunity disappears. (=) *Strike while the iron is hot. Make hay while the sun shines.* (≠) *Look before you leap. Make haste slowly. Discretion is the better part of valor.*

**He who lives by the sword shall perish (die) by the sword.** LT. One's future is determined by the lifestyle he chooses.

**Health is (better than) wealth.** LT. Equiv.: **Fr.** *Qui a santé, il a tout; qui n'a santé, il n'a rien.* {He who has health has everything; he who doesn't has nothing.}

**Hell knows no fury (wrath) like a woman scorned.** A woman who has been abandoned or cheated may become extremely nasty and vindictive; love often turns to hatred.

**Here today, gone tomorrow.** LT. Nothing is permanent; life is short. (=) *Easy come, easy go. Live today, for tomorrow may not come.*

**Hindsight is always better than foresight.** It is always easier to know what should have been done after an event has happened. (=) *Hindsight has 20/20 vision. The hindsight of a schoolboy is greater than the foresight of the greatest statesman.*

**History will repeat itself.** Events are cyclical, consisting of repeated patterns; people should learn history so as not to repeat it. (=) *Everything's been done before. Forewarned is forearmed.*

**Hitch your wagon to a star.** LT acceptable. Be ambitious; aspire to greater achievements. Equiv.: **La.** *Ad Astra Per Aspira.* {To the stars through bolts and bars (aspirations).}

**Home is where the heart is.** Wherever your family or sentiments lie, that is home. Equiv.: **It.** *Ad ogni uccello suo nido è bello.* {Every bird thinks its nest is beautiful.}

**Home is where you hang your hat.** Anywhere you stay is considered home. (≠) *Home is where the heart is.*

**Home without books is like a house without windows, A.** LT acceptable. Without windows, no light (i.e., the light of knowledge) can enter a home; thus its inhabitants are "unenlightened." (=) *A true university is a collection of books.*

**Honesty is the best policy.** LT. Self-explanatory. (=) *A half-truth is worse than a lie.*

**Honor among thieves, There is (no).** Criminals have their own set of rules and their own "ethical" concepts, or vice versa.

**Hope springs eternal (in the human breast [or heart]).** Human beings are essentially optimistic.

**House divided against itself cannot stand, A.** Internal conflicts bring about destruction. (=) *United we stand, divided we fall. In union there is strength.*

**Hunger is the best seasoning.** When one is really hungry, everything tastes good. (=) *Appetite is the best sauce.* Equiv.: **La.** *Fabas indulcet famas.* {Hunger sweetens beans.}

**If anything can go wrong, it will.** LT. Known as Murphy's Law.

**If at first you don't succeed, try, try again.** LT. Never give up. (=) *Never say die.* Equiv.: **Ge.** *Der Baum fällt nicht vom ersten Streiche.* {The tree will not fall from the first chop.} **It.** *Chi l'ha dura la vince.* {He who has it rough wins.} **Ko.** *Chil jun pal gi.* {Seven falls, eight rises.}

**If it ain't broke, don't fix it.** LT. (=) *Leave well enough alone. Do not tempt fate.*

**If pigs had wings (they might fly).** An expression of extreme doubt about dubious (conditional) statements. Equiv.: **Fr.** *Avec de 'si,' on referait le monde.* {With 'ifs,' one could rebuild the world.} *Avec des 'si's* *et des 'mais,' on mettrait Paris dans une bouteille.* {With 'ifs' and 'buts,' one could put Paris into a bottle.}

**If the mountain won't come to Mohammed, then Mohammed must go to the mountain.** In order to reach agreement, if one side does not yield, then the other must yield. (=) *If you can't beat 'em, join 'em.*

**If the shoe (glove) fits, wear it.** If you fit a certain description, admit it. (=) *If it looks like a duck, walks like a duck, and quacks like a duck, it must be a duck.*

**If wishes were horses, all beggars would ride.** LT acceptable. If we could get everything we wanted, all people would take advantage. (=) *If wishes had wings, all of us would fly.* Equiv.: **Ge.** *Wenn das Wörtchen 'wenn' nicht wär', dann wär' mein Vater Millionär.* {If it were not for the small word 'if,' my father would be a millionaire.}

**If you can build a better mousetrap, the world will beat a path to your door.** LT acceptable. Get an original idea, and others will seek you out.

**If you cannot be good, be careful.** LT. A caveat usually referring to sexual activity, but can be used regarding other situations involving possible peril.

**If you can't beat (lick) 'em, join 'em.** If you cannot get others to change their minds, you may have to change yours. (=) *If the mountain won't come to Mohammed, then Mohammed must go to the mountain.*

**If you cannot say something nice, do not say anything at all.** LT acceptable. Do not go through life criticizing others; do not risk hurting someone's feelings just to voice your opinion.

**If you can't stand the heat, get out of the kitchen.** If you are unable to put up with the rigors or side effects of a job or situation, quit or go elsewhere. Equiv.: **Ko.** *Jul i sirumyun jung i gamyun guman iji.* {If the temple is disagreeable, it is the monk who should leave.}

**If you do not like it, (you can) lump it.** Whether you like it or not, things will be done my way. (=) *Take it or leave it.*

**If you lie down with dogs, you get up with fleas.** People are influenced by their friends and associates. (=) *A man is known by the company he keeps.* Equiv.: **It.** *Chi va a letto con i cani si sveglia con le pulci.* {He who goes to bed with dogs wakes up with fleas.} **Ja.** *Shuni majiwareba akakunaru.* {If you work with red dye, you turn red.}

**If you make your bed, you must lie on it.** People are responsible for the consequences of their actions. Equiv.: **Ge.** *Man muß die Suppe auslöffeln, die man sich eingebrockt hat.* {One must drink as he has brewed.}

**If you play with matches, you will get burned.** Do not tempt fate by exposing yourself to dangerous situations.

**If you want a job right (well done), do it yourself.** Depending on others often leads to disappointment.

**If you want a job well done, give it to a busy man.** LT acceptable. People are usually the most efficient and effective when they have many responsibilities.

**Ignorance is bliss.** LT. Self-explanatory. Sometimes it is better not to know. (=) *Where ignorance is bliss, 'tis folly to be wise.*

**Ignorance of the law is no excuse.** One is not excused from breaking a law just because the perpetrator did not know the law. (=) *It is better that the law be known than that the law be just.* Equiv.: **La.** *Ignorantia legis neminem excusat.*

**Imitation is the highest (sincerest) form of flattery.** LT. When people imitate you, it shows that they respect or admire you.

**In for a penny, in for a pound.** Do not make a small investment or commitment unless you are willing to up the ante, if necessary. Equiv.: **Fr.** *Qui dit A dit B.* {He who says A says B.}

**In the kingdom of the blind, the one-eyed man is king.** A little knowledge or ability is better than none; it is better to know something than nothing. (≠) *A little knowledge is a dangerous thing.* Equiv.: **Ko.** *Bum upnun goljag e toggi ga sunseng norut handa.* {Where there is no tiger, a rabbit will play the king.}

**In the spring, a young man's fancy lightly turns to thoughts of love.** LT. As with all other members of the animal kingdom, spring is the best mating time for humans.

**In union, there is strength.** Combined efforts are more likely to succeed than individual effort. (=) *There is safety in numbers. Two heads are better than one.* Equiv.: **Ko.** *Jongyi hanjang do matdulmyun shibda.* {It is easier to carry something together with someone else rather than by yourself, even if it is very light like a sheet of paper.}

**In wine, there is truth.** People who drink become less inhibited and are more likely to give their honest opinions. Equiv.: **La.** *In vino, veritas.*

**Inch is as good as a mile, An.** Losing by even a small amount is still losing. (=) *A miss is as good as a mile.*

**Into each life, some (a little) rain must fall.** There is no such thing as constant good luck, pleasure, or happiness.

**It is a man's world.** LT. Historically, business, government, and other public endeavors have been controlled by and privy to men only.

**It is a sin to tell a lie.** LT. Lying is a very serious offense. (=) *A half-truth is worse than a lie.*

**It is a woman's privilege to change her mind.** Self-explanatory. (≠)

*Woman is fickle.*

**It is always fair weather when good fellows (friends) get together.** When people are having a good time, camaraderie creates good times; it is the camaraderie and the ambiance that count.

**It is an ill wind that blows nobody any good.** Somebody always profits from the misfortunes of others. Equiv.: **Fr.** *A quelque chose le malheur est bon.* {To something (someone), misfortune is good.} **Sp.** *No hay mal que por bien no venga.* {There is nothing so bad that no good comes of it.}

**It is easier for a camel to go through the eye of a needle than for a rich man to enter the kingdom of heaven.** The means by which people become wealthy involve impious actions that bar them from heavenly salvation.

**It is good to have two strings to one's bow.** Always give yourself a fall-back position in case of failure.

**It is no use locking the stable door after the horse has been stolen (is gone).** Preventive action is more productive than later reaction. (=) *An ounce of prevention is worth a pound of cure. Better safe than sorry.* Equiv.: **Ko.** *Saram juggonasu yiwon burumyum muat hana.* {Don't bother sending for a doctor after the patient dies.}

**It is not what you know but whom you know (that counts).** Success in one's career is often based on the ability to associate with influential people.

**It pays to advertise.** LT. Promotion of oneself or one's products or services has positive results. (=) *There is no such thing as bad publicity. A knock is as good as a boost.*

**It takes a heap of living to make a house a home.** LT acceptable. A house is only a structure of wood or other materials, but a home is established by the memories created in it by the people who live there.

**It takes a thief to catch a thief.** One is judged best by his own kind. (=) *It takes one to know one.*

**It takes all kinds (sorts) of people (to make up the world).** Since the world's population is so diverse, we must learn to tolerate one another. Usually used in a sarcastic sense when one meets an individual of the rarer kinds.

**It takes one to know one.** You are no better than the person you are describing. (=) *It takes a thief to catch a thief.*

**It takes two to tango.** Petty or malicious behavior requires two enemies; cooperation is necessary to get things done. Equiv.: **Ko.** *Du son yi maju chuya sori nanda.* {It takes two hands to make noise.}

**It will all come out in the wash.** It cannot remain a secret; everyone will know eventually. (=) *Time will tell. Murder will out.*

**Jack of all trades is a master of none, A.** A person who dabbles in many areas has a familiarity with each, but is proficient at none. Equiv.: **Sp.** *Aprendiste mucho, maestro de nada.* {You've learned a lot, but you have mastered nothing.}

**Jealousy is a green-eyed monster.** Jealousy is a self-destructive emotion.

**Jealousy is the deadliest of the seven deadly sins.** LT. Jealous thoughts should be avoided.

**Jingle of the Guinea heals the hurt that honor feels, The.** Monetary awards can compensate for damage to one's reputation. A Guinea is an old English coin.

**Job well begun is half done, A.** LT. Preliminary planning makes every task easier.

**Job worth doing is worth doing well, A.** LT. If one starts a task he should put his fullest effort into it. (=) *Do nothing by halves.*

**Join the Navy and see the world.** A slogan of the U.S. Navy designed to attract new recruits.

**Journey of a thousand miles begins with a single step, A.** LT. The most daunting tasks can be broken down into small steps that are more easily surmountable; unless you start something, you will never finish it.

**Joy (pleasure) shared is joy doubled.** Experiences are always more pleasurable when shared with a friend or a loved one.

**Judge not, lest you be judged.** LT. There is always the danger in judging others that the tables may be turned. (=) *Do unto others as you would have done unto you.*

**Justice delayed is justice denied.** If it takes too long a time to right a wrong, the decision may come too late to have a salutary effect.

**Justice is blind.** Judgments should be rendered on the facts of the case and not on the character or background of the individuals involved.

**Keep your ear to the ground.** Pay careful attention to what is going on around you.

**Keep your nose to the grindstone.** Work hard and for long hours; mind your own business.

**Keep your powder dry.** Keep your emotions (temper) under control; be ready to act quickly and rationally. Equiv.: **Fr.** *Garde la tête froide.* {Keep a cool head.}

**Keep your sunny side up.** Be cheerful; keep smiling.

**Kind word goes a long way, A.** LT. Showing a little sympathy and understanding can be helpful to someone in trouble or sorrow.

**King can do no wrong, The.** While kings were once thought to be divine, today this expression is often used sardonically or sarcastically about leaders, implying that the opposite is true.

**Knock is as good as a boost, A.** Any publicity or exposure, good or bad, is useful. (=) *It pays to advertise. There is no such thing as bad publicity.*

**Know thyself.** LT acceptable. It is important to know one's own motivations.

**Know what side your bread is buttered on.** Know where your best interests lie. Equiv.: **Sp.** *Saber uno lo que le conviene.* {To know what suits one's interests.}

**Knowledge is power.** LT. Valid information enables one to prevail over opponents or competitors. (=) *Forewarned is forearmed.*

**Laugh and the world laughs with you; cry and you cry alone.** LT. (≠) *A friend in need is a friend indeed. All the world loves a lover.*

**Laughter is the best medicine.** LT. Humor is good for your health.

**Laws (rules) are made to be broken.** A cynical expression used to excuse those who are planning to break the law, usually in small ways. (=) *It is the exception that proves the rule.*

**Lay your cards on the table.** Be honest and straightforward.

**Lead a horse to water but he cannot make him drink, One can.** You can try to convince people, but you cannot force them to do what you want. (=) *A man convinced against his will is of the same opinion still.*

**Learn from your mistakes.** Gain something even from negative experiences; do not make the same mistake twice. (=) *Those who do not remember the past are condemned to repeat it.*

**Leave no stone unturned.** LT. Explore all possibilities; conduct a meticulous investigation. Equiv.: **It.** *Non lasciare niente di intentato.* {Don't leave anything untried.} **La.** *Omnen movere lapidem.* {To move every stone.}

**Leave well enough alone.** LT. Do not aim for change when things are going well. (=) *If it ain't broke, don't fix it.*

**Left hand does not know what the right hand is doing, The.** Things are disorganized or uncoordinated; part of a team isn't coordinating with the other; part of you does not know what the rest of you is doing.

**Leopard never changes its spots, A.** People do not change their basic natures. Equiv.: **Ge.** *Man kann nicht aus seiner Haut heraus.* {A man can't get outside of his skin.} **It.** *Il lupo cambia il pelo, ma non il vizio.* {A wolf changes its fur, but not its nature.} **Sp.** *Perro que come huevos,* *ni quemandole el hocico.* {A dog that eats eggs won't stop eating eggs, even if you burn his mouth.}

**Let bygones be bygones.** Do not dwell on the past or hold on to grudges.

**Let sleeping dogs lie.** Do not stir up a calm situation that could become tense or explosive. (=) *Leave well enough alone.* Equiv.: **Ko.** *Janun saja ggewuji mara.* {Do not awaken a sleeping lion.}

**Let the buyer beware.** Before purchasing anything (or idea), the sale item must be examined carefully. Equiv.: **La.** *Caveat emptor.*

**Let us hang together or we will hang separately.** Internal disagreements can be dangerous. (=) *In union there is strength.*

**Liar needs a good memory, A.** Unless you remember well the details of your lies, one can easily trip you up.

**Life begins at 40.** LT. Maturity and experience enable one to enjoy life more.

**Life is a comedy to those who think, a tragedy to those who feel.** LT. Emotional people see the world's suffering and injustice; intellectual people see its irony and absurdity.

**Life is but a (an empty) dream.** Life goes by quickly, so try to enjoy it. (=) *Eat, drink, and be merry for tomorrow we die.*

**Life is not a bowl of cherries.** Living can be difficult.

**Life is short, art is long, decision difficult, and experiment perilous.** LT. Self-explanatory. Equiv.: **La.** *Ars longa, vita brevis.* {Art is long, life is short.}

**Lightning never strikes twice in the same place.** Past events do not guarantee similar future events. (≠) *History repeats itself.*

**Like father, like son.** Children often resemble their parents in habits, personality, and appearance. (=) *The apple doesn't fall far from the tree.* Equiv.: **Ja.** *Kaerunokowa kaeru.* {The child of a frog is a frog.}

**Little knowledge (learning) is a dangerous thing, A.** It is easy to make mistakes or assumptions when one knows only a little about a subject. (≠) *In the kingdom of the blind, the one-eyed man is king.* Equiv.: **Ko.** *Suturun jumjengyi saram juginda.* {An unfamiliar shaman leads a man to death.}

**Little pitchers have big ears.** Be careful what you say; children are listening. (=) *The walls have ears.*

**Live and learn.** LT. Experience is valuable. (=) *Experience is the best teacher.* Equiv.: **La.** *Experientia docet.*

**Live and let live.** Do things your way, but do not insist on others following. (=) *Different strokes for different folks. Each to his own taste.*

**Live today, for tomorrow may not come.** LT. Self-explanatory. (=)

*Here today, gone tomorrow. Eat, drink, and be merry, for tomorrow we may die.*

**Long road that has no turning, It is a.** Change is almost always inevitable. (=) *Every road has its turning.*

**Look for the silver lining.** Try to find the good in any situation. (=) *Every cloud has a silver lining.*

**Look (think) before you leap.** LT. Think and observe carefully before acting. (=) *Make haste slowly.* (≠) *He who hesitates is lost.* Equiv.: **Ja.** *Ishibashiwo tataite wataru.* {Rap on the stone bridge before you cross it.}

**Lord giveth and the Lord taketh away, The.** Used to indicate the uncertainty of possession, material or otherwise. (=) *Easy come, easy go.*

**Love is blind.** LT. Emotion and passion prevent clear thinking. Equiv: **La.** *Suum cuique pulchrum.* {To everyone, his own is beautiful.}

**Love me, love my dog.** If one wants to have a relationship with someone, he or she must accept everything about him or her. Equiv.: **Ko.** *Manura ga guiyuumyun chuga jib malddug edo julhanda.* {If one loves his wife, he will bow even to the cornerstone of his wife's (in-laws') house.}

**Love of money is the root of all evil, The.** LT. Equiv.: **La.** *Radix omnium malorum est cupiditad.* {Cupidity is the root of all evil.}

**Love will find a way.** LT. People in love will always be inspired to overcome difficulties.

**Love (work) conquers all.** LT. (=) *Love will find a way.* Equiv.: **La.** *Amor omnia vincit.*

**Love your neighbor as yourself.** LT. Self-explanatory. (=) *Do unto others as you would have done to you.*

**Lucky at cards, unlucky in love.** LT. Material success is not necessarily condusive to romantic success.

**Maids say "no" and mean "yes."** Women are alleged to have equivocal feelings about men's sexual advances.

**Majority is always right (wrong), The.** LT. Exactly as stated, depending on your point of view. Used either positively or cynically. Equiv.: **Ko.** *Du babo saram dungshin mandunda.* {Two fools make one genius appear a fool.}

**Make haste slowly.** One should take his time in doing things to ensure that he is doing them well. (=) *Look before you leap.* Equiv.: **It.** *Chi va piano, va sano e va lontano.* {He who travels softly stays healthy and goes far.}

**Make hay while the sun shines.** Take advantage of favorable conditions. (=) *Strike while the iron is hot. He who hesitates is lost.* Equiv.: **La.** *Carpe diem.* {Seize the day.}

**Man convinced against his will is of the same opinion still, A.** LT. You may try to persuade, but you cannot force people to believe as you do. (=) *You can lead a horse to water, but you cannot make him drink.*

**Man does not live by bread alone.** Food is essential, but a good life must include recreation and spiritual values.

**Man is known (judged) by the company he keeps, A.** Knowing a person's friends provides a fair idea of that person's character because people generally associate with others with similar interests and character. (=) *Birds of a feather flock together. Show me your friends, and I will tell you who you are. It takes one to know one.* Equiv.: **It.** *Chi dorme con i cani si sveglia con le pulci.* {Those who sleep with dogs wake up with fleas.}

**Man proposes; God disposes.** The most carefully thought out plans can go wrong because of unanticipated or uncontrolled circumstances. (=) *The best laid plans of mice and men go oft astray.* Equiv.: **Ge.** *Der Mensch denkt; Gott lenkt.* {Man thinks (plans); God directs.}

**Man who is his own lawyer has a fool for a client (and an incompetent for an attorney), A.** LT. Never try to represent yourself in a court trial.

**Man who makes no mistakes never accomplishes anything, A.** LT. Only from errors does a person learn how to do better; if one is involved in any activity, he is certain to make some mistakes.

**Man who pays the piper (fiddler) calls the tune, The.** LT. Whoever pays for an activity has the right to direct or control it.

**Man with a fair (beautiful) wife needs more than two eyes, A.** The husband of a beautiful woman needs to watch her as carefully as her admirers to make sure she remains faithful to him.

**Man without a woman is like a ship without a sail, A.** Men benefit from a woman's guidance. (=) *Behind every great man is a woman.*

**Man's home is his castle, A.** One should be entitled to privacy and security in one's own home. Equiv.: **Fr.** *Charbonnier est maître chez lui.* {Even a coalman is master at his home.}

**Man's reach should exceed his grasp (or what's a heaven for?).** We should all strive for more than we can possibly obtain.

**Man's work is till set of sun, (but a) woman's work is never done.** LT. Being a housewife and mother is a 24-hour-a-day job.

**Manners make the man.** LT acceptable. People are judged by their manners and social graces.

**Many a man digs his grave with his teeth.** LT acceptable. Overeating is unhealthy.

**Many a slip 'twixt cup and lip, There is.** One's plans do not always give the hoped-for results; plans miscarry and go awry between start and conclusion. (=) *The best laid plans of mice and men go oft astray. Nothing in life is certain but death and taxes.* Equiv.: **Ge.** *Der Mensch denkt; Gott lenkt.* {Man thinks (plans) and God directs.} **It.** *Dalla mano alla boca si perde la zuppa.* {Between the hand and the mouth, much soup is lost.} **Sp.** *Del dicho al hecho hay mucho trecho.* {There is plenty of space between what is said and what is done.}

**Many a true word is said (spoken) in jest.** LT. Serious meaning is often concealed behind levity.

**Many hands make light work.** LT. A cooperative effort makes a job easier. (=) *Two heads are better than one.*

**March comes in like a lion and goes out like a lamb.** LT. In temperate climates, early March often has wintry weather which usually turns mild by month's end.

**Marriage is made in heaven.** LT. (≠) *The path of true love never runs smooth. A woman is the woe of man. Can't live with them, can't live without them.*

**Marry in haste, repent at leisure.** Give serious thought before undertaking any irreversible or difficult to reverse step. Refers to marriage, but is occasionally used with reference to other important steps. (=) *Measure twice, cut once.*

**Meal without wine is like a day without sunshine, A.** LT.

**Measure twice, cut once.** Take great care before making an irreversible step. (=) *Marry in haste; repent at leisure.*

**Meek shall inherit the earth, The.** LT. When Judgement Day comes, the quiet God-fearing people shall reign.

**Might makes right.** LT. Power enables one to enforce one's beliefs. (=) *Money talks.*

**Millions for defense; not one cent for tribute.** A jingoistic cry stating that one's country should not give in to the demands of another country and be willing to risk military activity to enforce the principle.

**Mills (wheels) of the gods grind slowly, but they grind exceedingly small, The.** Retribution for bad deeds eventually catches up with one. (=) *Murder will out.*

**Mind your p's and q's.** Pay attention to details; be extremely careful. (=) *Dot your i's and cross your t's.*

**Misery loves company.** Sharing your hardships with another person can halve unhappiness. (=) *Joy (pleasure) shared is joy (pleasure) doubled.*

**Miss is as good as a mile, A.** A near success, or losing by a little, is no better than losing by a large margin or failing completely; i.e., not winning is equivalent to losing. (=) *An inch is as good as a mile.*

**Money burns a hole in the pocket.** Having money easily accessible is much easier to spend.

**Money doesn't grow on trees.** LT. Money must be earned; it is not easy to come by. Equiv.: **Fr.** _L'argent ne tombe pas du ciel._ {Money doesn't fall from the sky.} **Ko.** _Ddang ul pado naoji annunda._ {You cannot find money by digging in the ground.}

**Money makes the world go round.** Money has a vast influence. (=) _Money talks._ Equiv.: **La.** _Pecunia obediunt omnia._ {All things yield to money.}

**Money talks.** Money is a powerful tool to get what one wants. (=) _Money makes the world go round._ Equiv.: **Ge.** _Geld behält das Feld._ {Money controls the field.} **It.** _Chiave d'oro apre ogni porta._ {A gold key opens all doors.} **La.** _Aurio hamo piscari._ {To fish with a golden hook.}

**More the merrier, The.** The more people there are, the happier the occasion and the better the results.

**More you have (eat), the more you want, The.** People are often gluttonous or greedy.

**Mountain labored and brought forth a mouse, The.** Little has been achieved despite a major effort. Equiv.: **Ge.** _Viel Lärm um nichts._ {A lot of noise over nothing.}

**Murder will out.** Those who act badly will eventually be apprehended (discovered); guilt will always betray. (=) _Give someone enough rope and eventually he will hang himself. It will all come out in the wash. The mills of the gods grind slowly, but they grind exceedingly small._

**Music hath charms to soothe the savage breast.** LT acceptable. Music helps calm down angry or tense people.

**Nature abhors a vacuum.** Literal or figurative. In physics, an unoccupied space sooner or later gets filled; likewise, an empty heart or an open job will eventually find tenants. (=) _Every Jack has his Jill. Necessity is the mother of invention._

**Necessity is the mother of invention.** LT acceptable when _mother_ also means _creator_. Things happen when there is a need for them. (=) _Nature abhors a vacuum._ Equiv.: **It.** _La necessità fa virtù._ {Virtue is born of necessity.} **La.** _Magister artis ingeniique largitor venter._ {The belly is the teacher of art and the bestower of genius.}

**Never (do not) bark up the wrong tree.** Be careful not to pursue erroneous ideas or detrimental people.

**Never (do not) be the first by whom the new is tried, nor the last to lay the old aside.** Do not be an innovator, but do not resist change either.

**Never (do not) bite off more than you can chew.** LT. Never undertake more work or accept more responsibility than you can handle. (=) *Do not have too many irons in the fire. Do not start anything you cannot finish.* Equiv.: **Sp.** *El que mucho abarca, poco aprieta.* {He who tries to cover too much squeezes too little.}

**Never (do not) buy a pig in a poke.** Always examine a potential purchase carefully and ascertain its value before you buy. (=) *A fool and his money are soon parted. Look before you leap.* (≠) *Beggars cannot be choosers.* Equiv.: **Ge.** *Die Katze im Sack kaufen.* {To buy a cat in a bag.} **No.** *Å kjøpe katta I sekken.* {Never buy a cat in the bag.}

**Never (do not) despair.** Do not ever give up; be positive and optimistic. (=) *If at first you do not succeed, try, try again. Keep your sunny side up.* Equiv.: **La.** *Nil desperandum.*

**Never give a sucker an even break.** When you have someone at a disadvantage, finish him off. (≠) *Never kick a man when he is down.*

**Never (do not) judge a book by its cover.** Surface characteristics are insufficient for judging character and other attributes. (=) *All that glitters is not gold. Appearances are deceiving.* (≠) *Cold hands, warm heart.* Equiv.: **La.** *Fronti nulla fides.* {No reliance can be placed on appearance.}

**Never (do not) judge by (rely on) first impressions.** LT. Take a closer look. (=) *Never judge a book by its cover. Appearances are deceiving.* (≠) *First impressions are the best impressions.* Equiv.: **La.** *Fronti nulla fides.* {No reliance can be placed on appearance.}

**Never (do not) kick a man when he is down.** Do not take advantage of people in trouble; try to be just and compassionate. (≠) *Never give a sucker an even break.*

**Never (do not) let the left hand know what the right hand is doing.** Operate with a degree of secrecy; compartmentalize your actions.

**Never (do not) look a gift horse in the mouth.** When one is given a gift, it is ungrateful and insulting to the donor to check for possible defects. (=) *Beggars can't be choosers.* (≠) *Never buy a pig in a poke.* Equiv.: **Sp.** *A lo dado no se busca lado.* {When receiving a gift, don't look for the angle (reasons).}

**Never (do not) put off for tomorrow what you can do today.** LT. Do not delay; do it now. (=) *No time like the present. The early bird catches the worm.*

**Never say die.** Never quit. (=) *If at first you don't succeed, try, try again.* Equiv.: **Ko.** *Chil jun pal gi.* {Seven falls, eight rises.} **La.** *Nil desperandum.* {Never despair.}

**Never too late (old) to change (learn), It is.** LT. Self-explanatory. (=) *You can't teach an old dog new tricks.* Equiv.: **Ja.** *Rokujûno tenarai.*

{One can learn calligraphy at 60.}

**New broom sweeps clean, A.** New managers or supervisors make many changes.

**No accounting for taste, There is.** LT. People enjoy different things or experiences. (=) *Each to his own taste. One man's meat is another man's poison.* Equiv.: **Fr.** *Chacun a son goût.* {Everyone to his own taste.} **La.** *De gustibus non est disputandum.*

**No business like show business, There is.** No other industry is as fun or bizarre as the entertainment business.

**No fool like an old fool, There is.** LT acceptable. Age may bring wisdom, but the foolish mistakes of the elderly can be particularly foolish.

**No harm in asking (trying), There is.** Take a chance, for you have nothing to lose; the worst you can get is a negative answer.

**No man is a hero to his valet.** No one remains a hero to an intimate. (=) *Familiarity breeds contempt.* Equiv.: **La.** *Maior e longinquo reverentia.* {Greater reverence from afar.}

**No man is above the law.** LT. Self-explanatory.

**No news is good news.** If the news were bad, you would have heard it already. (=) *Bad news travels fast.*

**No one has ever been killed with kindness.** There is no such thing as being too kind. (≠) *Each man kills the thing he loves.*

**No pain, no gain.** Without effort or risk, no positive results occur. (=) *Nothing ventured, nothing gained. There is no free lunch.*

**No rest for the wicked (weary), There is.** LT. Those who do evil shall never have peace because of their own consciences or of their fear of the repercussions of their actions.

**No time like the present, There is.** LT. Do not procrastinate; do it now. (=) *Seize the day. Do not let the grass grow under your feet. Do not put off until tomorrow anything you can do today. He who hesitates is lost.*

**No use crying over spilled milk.** What is done is done; regrets over what might have been are a waste of time if nothing can be changed. (=) *Measure twice, cut once.* Equiv.: **Ar.** *El-ifat matt.* {What is dead is dead.} **Ja.** *Fukusui bon-ni kaerazu.* {Spilt water never returns to the bowl.}

**Nobody is perfect.** LT. Self-explanatory. (=) *To err is human; to forgive is divine.*

**None are so blind as those who will not see.** It is difficult or impossible to convince people who stubbornly refuse to listen to reason; be open-minded.

**None but the brave deserve the fair.** Courtships should be ardent and persistent. (=) *Faint heart never won fair lady.*

**Nothing in life is certain but death and taxes.** LT. Self-explanatory.

( = ) *The best laid plans of mice and men go oft astray.*

**Nothing new under the sun, There is.** LT. Fundamentally, every idea or thing we create has existed at some prior time; anything new is essentially a variation on a previous theme. ( = ) *Everything has been done before.*

**Nothing succeeds like success.** Success often follows itself; winning streaks seem to continue for a period of time.

**Nothing ventured, nothing gained.** LT. There is never profit without risk. ( = ) *No pain, no gain.* Equiv.: **Ja.** *Koketsuni irazunba, kojiwo ezu.* {If you don't enter the tiger den, you will never get tiger cubs.} **La.** *Audaces fortuna iuvat.* {Fortune favors the brave.} **Sp.** *Quien no se arriesga, no cruza el mar.* {He who doesn't take risks will never cross the ocean.}

**Of all sad words of tongue or pen the saddest are these, "It might have been."** Lost opportunities always lead to lasting regrets. ( ≠ ) *Far sadder still we daily see: it was but it hadn't ought to be.*

**Oh tempore, oh mores!** My, how customs (times) have changed!

**Oh, what a tangled web we weave when first we practice to deceive.** Lies and deception tend to get complicated, and sometimes become impossible to walk away from unscathed.

**Oil and water do not mix.** Some people (depending on their personality traits, race, sex, religion, generation, etc.) will never get along with each other.

**Old soldiers never die; they just fade away.** Soldiers survive in tales of their bravery and sacrifice; soldiers who survive a long time never quite disappear but seem to lose the attention they previously attracted.

**Once bitten (burnt), twice shy.** People who have had a bad experience are more careful in the future. Equiv.: **Ge.** *Ein gebranntes Kind scheut das Feuer.* {A burnt child fears the fire.} **It.** *A cane scottato l'acqua fredda pare calda.* {To a scalded dog even cold water seems hot.} **Ja.** *Atsumononi korite, namasuwo fuku.* {Having been taught a lesson from hot soup, he now even blows on fish salad.} **No.** *Brent barn skyr ilden.* {A burnt child avoids the fire.}

**One cannot breathe life into a corpse.** Once a person, idea, or activity is dead, it is foolish to try resurrecting it. Equiv.: **Ar.** *El-ifat matt.* {What is dead is dead.}

**One cannot make bricks without straw.** Nothing can be built or assembled without the proper materials.

**One cannot drive a square peg into a round hole.** LT. Some things are simply impossible to accomplish, particularly trying to change people.

**One cannot get blood out of a stone (turnip).** One cannot do the impossible; usually applied to getting money from a miser. Equiv.: **La.** *Ab asino lanam.* {You can't get wool from a donkey.}

**One cannot live on love alone.** LT. A relationship requires other principles such as trust, honesty, and selflessness besides love. (=) *When poverty comes in the door, love flies out the window.*

**One cannot make a silk purse out of a sow's ear.** One cannot do the impossible; usually applies to changing a person from an uncouth, ill-mannered person to a civil one. (=) *One cannot drive a square peg into a round hole.* Equiv.: **Sp.** *La mona, aunque de seda se vista, mona se queda.* {Even when a monkey is dressed in silk, it is still a monkey.}

**One cannot make an omelet without breaking eggs.** Every constructive operation requires some preliminary destruction or demolition that will trouble or offend some people. (=) *One cannot please everyone.*

**One never gets a second chance to make a first impression.** LT.

**One good turn deserves another.** LT. Favors should be returned; reciprocation is in order. Sometimes used sardonically. (=) *One hand washes the other. Scratch my back and I will scratch yours.*

**One hand washes the other.** Cooperation provides benefits to all parties. (=) *One good turn deserves another.*

**One man's meat is another man's poison.** What is good for one person may be bad for another; people have different tastes. (=) *Each to his own taste. Different strokes for different folks.* Equiv.: **Fr.** *Chacun a son goût.* {Everyone to his own taste.} **La.** *De gustibus non disputandum est.* {There can be no disputing about taste.}

**One may as well be hung for a sheep as a lamb.** If you are going to be punished for a small indiscretion, you might as well do it wholeheartedly and enjoy it. (=) *In for a penny, in for a pound.*

**One may smile and smile and be a villain still.** You cannot tell a person's character by his demeanor or facial expression only. (=) *Appearances can be deceiving. Never judge by first impressions.* (≠) *Cold hands, warm heart.*

**One must learn how to walk before he can run.** One should practice simple preliminary steps to develop experience before trying difficult activities (physical or mental).

**One never appreciates what he has until he has lost it.** LT. Be grateful for what you have while you have it. (=) *Count your blessings.*

**One swallow does not a summer make.** A single indicator of things to come does not necessarily indicate a trend.

**Only the good die young.** LT acceptable. People who die young are often immortalized and remembered as being greater than they actually were.

**Opportunity knocks but once.** Good opportunities do not frequently present themselves, so you had better seize on one when it does appear. (=) *He who hesitates is lost. Make hay while the sun shines.* (≠) *Look before you leap.* Equiv.: **La.** *Carpe diem.* {Seize the day.}

**Ounce of prevention is worth a pound of cure, An.** LT. A bit of planning will save you from hardship later. (=) *Do not lock the stable door after the horse has been stolen. A stitch in time saves nine.* Equiv.: **He.** *L'hakdim refuah lamakah.* {Use medicine before the affliction.} **Sp.** *Hombre prevenido vale por dos.* {A man who anticipates or prevents is worth two men.}

**Ours not to reason why; ours but to do and die.** Soldiers have no right to question, only to obey authority.

**Out of sight, out of mind.** LT. We tend to forget people who are away for very long; also, simple-minded creatures like babies or dogs quickly forget about a toy when it is removed from their line of sight. (≠) *Absence makes the heart grow fonder.*

**Paddle your own canoe.** Make your own way at your own pace; do not judge your success by others' progress. (=) *March to the beat of one's own drummer.*

**Parting is such sweet sorrow.** Leaving someone you love is sad, but the memories of your encounter can be comforting. (=) *To say good-bye is to die a little.*

**Path of true love never runs smooth, The.** LT. Self-explanatory. (≠) *Marriage is made in heaven.*

**Paths of glory lead but to the grave, The.** No matter how rich or how high and mighty you become, you will die like everybody else. (=) *Death is a great leveler.*

**Patience is a virtue.** LT. Self-explanatory. (=) *Good things come to those who wait.* Equiv.: **La.** *Vincit qui patitur.* {Patience wins out.}

**Patriotism is the last refuge of scoundrels.** Many people, particularly politicians, use a false patriotism to attack their opponents or to cover up their own misdeeds.

**Pen is mightier than the sword, The.** Being able to distribute written or printed material to the public is an extremely mighty weapon, often more effective than military action. (≠) *Actions speak louder than words.*

**Penny saved is a penny earned, A.** LT.

**Penny wise, pound foolish.** One who is stingy about spending small amounts, but is profligate with large expenditures. Can also be used figuratively in areas other than financial ones.

**People who live in glass houses should not throw stones.** Do not be hypocritical; be sure you have no skeletons in your closet before you criticize others. (=) *Let he who is without sin cast the first stone.*

**Pick on someone your own size.** LT. Do not be a bully.

**Picture is worth a thousand words, A.** LT. Self-explanatory. Equiv.: **Ja.** *Hyakubunwa ikken-ni shikazu.* {One picture is worth hearing about the subject one hundred times.}

**Pitcher may go to the well too often, The.** Abusing privileges may result in losing them.

**Place for everything, and everything in its place, There is a.** LT. A proper formula for neatness and organization. (=) *Cleanliness is next to Godliness.* Equiv.: **Fr.** *Mise en place.* {Put in place.}

**Possession is nine points (nine-tenths) of the law.** Legally speaking, if you exercise control over something, you have an overwhelming chance of retaining ownership. (=) *Finders keepers, losers weepers.* Equiv.: **La.** *Beati possidentes.* {Blessed are those who possess.}

**Pot calling the kettle black, That is the.** Being hypocritical; accusing others of your own faults.

**Practice makes perfect.** LT. Self-explanatory. (=) *If at first you do not succeed, try, try again. Constant dripping wears away stone.* Equiv.: **La.** *Usus promptos facit.* {Use makes men ready.}

**Practice what you preach.** LT. Do what you tell others to do. (≠) *Do as I say, not as I do.*

**Pride goeth before a fall.** LT. Being overly proud courts disaster.

**Procrastination is the thief of time.** Putting off important acts wastes time. (=) *Never put off for tomorrow what you can do today. No time like the present. Do not let the grass grow under your feet.*

**Proof of the pudding is in the eating, The.** Speculation is fine, but only the end results are important.

**Prophet is without honor in his own country, A.** People tend not to respect local folks with vision or experience as much as they do outside experts or consultants. (=) *An expert is someone from out of town.*

**Public office is a public trust.** Public servants and officials should be mindful of the nature of their duty; citizens expect honesty and integrity from the officials they elect.

**Put that in your pipe and smoke it.** This is the situation whether you like it or not. (=) *Like it or lump it. Take it or leave it.* Equiv.: **Ge.** *Schreib' dir das hinter die Ohren.* {Write it behind your ears.}

**Putting the cart before the horse, That is.** You are doing things in reverse order, misplacing your priorities.

**Put up or shut up!** Do not just talk, but act; are you willing to bet money or put some effort into proving your point? (=) *Put your money* *where your mouth is.*

**Put your money where your mouth is.** Be willing to back up your claims or stop talking. (=) *Put up or shut up.*

**Put your shoulder to the wheel.** Start working hard.

**Race is not always to the swift nor the battle to the strong, The.** LT. Intellectual endeavors such as foresight and planning can be more valuable than physical strength and agility in producing results.

**Rain falls on the just and unjust alike.** Everyone experiences hardships in life; there are more similarities than differences between human beings, particularly on basic matters.

**Rainbow (red sky) in the morning, sailor take warning; rainbow (red sky) at night, sailor's delight.** A morning rainbow precedes an evening storm, while an evening rainbow foretells fair weather the following day. Equiv.: **Fr.** *Araignée du matin chagrin, araignée du soir, espoir.* {Spider in the morrow, sorrow; spider in the evening, hope.}

**Rats desert a sinking ship.** Deserting a friend in trouble marks one as an unprincipled, nasty, mean person.

**Rich get richer and the poor get poorer, The.** LT. The wealthy have advantages that are unavailable to the poor.

**Rising Tide Lifts All Boats, A.** Prosperity benefits everyone.

**Road (way) to hell is paved with good intentions, The.** Good intentions are not enough; concrete actions to bring about intended results are more important. Equiv.: **Sp.** *El inferno está lleno de buenos propósitos, y el cielo de buenas obras.* {Hell is full of good intentions, but heaven is full of good works.}

**Rolling stone gathers no moss, A.** Wanderers and vagabonds are non-productive and rarely achieve anything; for success, one must establish a base and work hard toward an aim.

**Rome was not built in a day.** It takes time to accomplish something substantial. (=) *A thousand mile journey begins with a single step.*

**Rose becomes more beautiful between two thorns, A.** Contrast intensifies the perception of beauty.

**Rose by any other name would smell as sweet, A.** Names are really of no great significance; it is character or personality that counts.

**Rotten apple spoils the barrel, One.** In a group or organization, it takes only one bad individual to corrupt the others. Equiv.: **Ko.** *Nagji hanmari hemuljumbang mangchinda.* {A small octopus can spoil the reputation of a seafood store.}

**Sauce for the goose is sauce for the gander.** Men and women should have the same rights and/or obligations.

**Save your money for a rainy day.** It is important to save some money for emergencies. (=) *A penny saved is a penny earned.*

**Scratch my back, and I'll scratch yours.** You do something for me, and I will return the favor. (=) *One hand washes the other. One good turn deserves another.* Equiv.: **La.** *Quid pro quo.* {Something for something.}

**Secret shared is not a secret, A.** LT. Once somebody knows something, the word tends to spread. (=) *Even the walls have ears. A slip of the lip might sink a ship.*

**Seeing is believing.** LT. Just hearing or reading about something is often not enough; actually seeing something provides a better source of judgment. (≠) *Believe only half of what you see and nothing you hear.*

**Seek and ye shall find.** LT. Diligent searching usually gives results. Equiv.: **He.** *Yagatah u'matzatah ta'amin.* {If you look hard, you will find.}

**Self-praise is no praise.** LT. (=) *A legend in one's own mind.*

**Separate the men from the boys.** Separate the strong from the weak, the mature from the immature, the bright from the dull, the capable from the incapable. (=) *Separate the sheep from the goats.* Equiv.: **Fr.** *Il ne faut pas mélanger les torchons et les serviettes.* {Do not mix dish towels and hand towels.}

**Shared joys (pleasures) are doubled; shared sorrows are halved.** LT. (=) *Joy shared is joy doubled. Misery loves company.*

**Sharper than a serpent's tooth it is to have a thankless child.** One of the most terrible things in life is to have an ungrateful, spoiled child.

**Shoemaker (cobbler) should stick to his last, The.** People should stick to the things they know. (=) *Every man to his trade.*

**Shortest distance between two points is a straight line, The.** LT. The simplest way is the best way; keep to the topic when speaking. (=) *Keep it simple, stupid.*

**Show me your friends, and I will tell you who you are.** Friends usually have much in common. (=) *A man is known by the company he keeps. Birds of a feather flock together.*

**Shroud has no pockets, A.** Wealth will not follow you into the grave. (=) *You can't take it with you. The paths of glory lead but to the grave.*

**Sin in haste, repent at leisure.** The guilt and regrets of having done something wrong quickly without thinking may take a long time to get over.

**Sing for your supper.** Perform a task in return for something desired. (=) *There is no free lunch.*

**Six of one, half a dozen of the other.** Known as Hobson's choice; an innocuous choice, in which nothing is lost or gained either way. Equiv.: **Fr.** *Blanc bonnet ou bonnet blanc.* {White hat or hat that's white.}

**Slip of the lip can sink a ship, A.** Do not discuss even small military matters during wartime for security reasons. (=) *Small leaks sink big ships.* Equiv.: **He.** *Mavet v'hayim b'yad halashon.* {The tongue has power over life and death.}

**Slow and steady (easy) wins the race.** LT. (=) *Haste makes waste.*

**Small leaks sink big ships.** A wartime warning that people should not discuss even trivial military activities in fear of treasonous spies. (=) *A slip of the lip might sink a ship.*

**Small world, It's a.** Expression used when an unlikely meeting or coincidence occurs.

**So (as) Maine goes, so goes the nation.** An American political slogan; the State of Maine almost always voted the same way as the nation as a whole in national elections.

**Soft answer turns away wrath, A.** To avoid arguments or fights speak quietly without any apparent anger showing.

**Something is rotten in (the state of) Denmark.** Something peculiar or fishy is going on. Equiv.: **No.** *Det er ugler i mosen.* {There are owls in the moss.}

**Something there is that does not love a wall.** Barriers between people tend to come down; nature hates separation.

**Sometimes one can't see the forest for the trees.** The obvious or simple is often obscured by the complex.

**Sometimes the remedy (cure) is worse than the disease.** LT. The steps needed to fix something may be more onerous or dangerous than the problem itself. (≠) *The end justifies the means.*

**Son is a son until he gets him a wife, but a daughter's a daughter the rest of her life, A.** It is easier for a man than it is for a woman to be considered an independent person; after marriage, daughters tend to stay closer to their original families than do sons.

**Sound mind in a sound body, A.** Physical exercise and thoughtful education are both needed to form a substantial and meaningful human being. Equiv.: **La.** *Mens sana in corpore sano.* {A sound mind in a sound body.}

**Sow the wind and reap the whirlwind.** Everything we do has future repercussions, sometimes disproportionate to the original deed. (=) *As you sow, so shall you reap. Bread cast upon the waters will return as cake.*

**Spare the rod and spoil the child.** A lack of childhood discipline leads to a uncontrollable and ungrateful adult. (=) *Sharper than a serpent's tooth it is to have a thankless child.*

**Speak of the devil (and he is sure to appear).** An expression used when one is talking about someone, and that person unexpectedly arrives. Equiv.: **Ko.** *Bum do jemal hamyun natananda.* {Even a tiger will appear when people speak of him.} **No.** *Snakk om sola så skinner den.* {Speak of the sun and it shines.}

**Speak only when you are spoken to.** LT. Be silent unless answering a question or address. (=) *Children should be seen and not heard. Speech is silver, but silence is golden.*

**Speak softly, but carry a big stick.** Try to be accommodating, but be sure to show that you have the substantial evidence or power to enforce your point of view. (=) *The greatest talkers are the least doers. The iron fist in the velvet glove.*

**Speak the truth and shame the devil.** The Devil likes to hear lies, so be honest in what you say.

**Speech is silver, but silence is golden.** LT. It is frequently more valuable to hold your tongue than to speak out. (=) *It is better to remain silent and be thought a fool than to speak and remove all doubt.* Equiv.: **He.** *Yafah shtikah l'chachamim.* {Silence becomes the wise.}

**Spirit is willing but the flesh is weak, The.** LT acceptable. One does not always have the physical strength or capacity to carry out one's wishes or desires. (≠) *It is easy to find a stick to beat a dog.*

**Squeaky wheel (hinge) gets the grease (oil), The.** People pay attention to active, outspoken human beings. (≠) *Speech is silver, but silence is golden.*

**Stand on your own two feet.** LT. Do not depend on others for help; be independent.

**Stand up and be counted.** Let everyone know your views. (=) *Do not hide your light under a bushel.*

**Sticks and stones may break my bones, but names will never hurt me.** Name-calling is less harmful than physical abuse.

**Stiff prick knows no conscience, A.** A determined man does not consider the niceties of right or wrong when sexually aroused and trying to seduce a woman.

**Still waters run deep.** Benign outward appearances often conceal depth, intelligence, and character. (=) *Speech is silver, but silence is golden. It is better to remain silent and be thought a fool than to speak and remove all doubt.* Equiv.: **He.** *Yafah shtikah l'chachachim.* {Silence becomes the wise.} **La.** *Altissima quaeque flumina minimo sono labi.* {Deepest rivers flow with the least sound.}

**Stitch in time saves nine, A.** Taking care of small problems now will prevent them from becoming larger problems later. (=) *An ounce of* *prevention is worth a pound of cure.*

**Stolen kisses are the best.** LT. (=) *Forbidden fruit is the sweetest.*

**Stone walls do not a prison make (nor iron bars a cage).** The only true prison a human being can experience is in his own mind; a free spirit will survive anywhere.

**Strike while the iron is hot.** Act quickly while the opportunity is still there. (=) *Make hay while the sun shines. He who hesitates is lost.*

**Strong back and a weak mind, A.** LT. People who are physically powerful are often perceived to be stupid. (=) *All brawn and no brains.* (≠) *A sound mind in a sound body.*

**Success (achievement) is one percent inspiration and ninety-nine percent perspiration.** LT. Ideas begin a project, but hard work and diligence finish it.

**Sucker (one) is born every minute, A.** The world is full of gullible people; there is a constant supply of people who are easily cheated or fooled. Equiv.: **La.** *Mundus vult decipi.* {The world wants to be deceived.}

**Sweet are the uses of adversity.** LT. One can always find something advantageous in a bad situation. (=) *If they sell you a lemon, make lemonade. Every cloud has a silver lining.*

**Take care of your pennies, and the dollars will take care of themselves.** LT. Look after the small details and the bigger things will come out well. (=) *Save your money for a rainy day. A penny saved is a penny earned.*

**Take it or leave it.** This is the only choice whether you like it or not. (=) *Like it or lump it.*

**Take the rough with the smooth.** LT. Accept disadvantages as well as advantages. (=) *Take the bitter with the sweet.*

**Talk is cheap.** Ideas are cost-free, but implementing them requires an investment of time, labor, and often money. (=) *Put your money where your mouth is. Put up or shut up.*

**Taxation without representation is tyranny.** LT. People should not have to subsidize a government that excludes them.

**Them as has gets.** The rich get richer.

**There are many ways to skin (kill) a cat (to cook a goose).** There are a variety of ways to solve the same problem.

**There are more horses' asses than horses.** The world is full of stupid people. (=) *There is a sucker born every minute.*

**There are no atheists in foxholes.** LT acceptable. Religious belief returns when one thinks he is about to die.

**There are (many) plenty of fish in the sea.** Do not worry too much about lost chances or broken romances, because life provides many new opportunities.

**There are two sides to every story.** LT. Do not accept one person's version of an incident unless you have heard another's. Equiv.: **La.** *Audi alteram partem.* {Hear the other side.}

**There is a black sheep in every flock.** In every group, there is at least one misfit or undesirable person.

**There is a tide in the affairs of men which when taken at the flood leads on to fortune.** LT. (=) *Opportunity knocks but once.* Equiv.: **La.** *Carpe diem.* {Seize the day.}

**There is always room at the top.** LT acceptable. People determined to succeed will always find a way.

**There is no free lunch.** LT. There is always a price to a person's generosity. Be wary of too-good-to-be-true deals and offers; do not expect life to be easy.

**There is no place like home.** LT. Self-explanatory. Equiv.: **It.** *Ad ogni uccello, suo nido è bello.* {Every bird thinks its nest is beautiful.}

**There is no royal road to learning.** LT acceptable. Learning requires hard work and discipline.

**There is one law for the rich and another for the poor.** LT. The wealthy are privileged to a different lifestyle and stereotype than that of the poor or working class. (=) *The rich get richer and the poor get poorer.*

**There is safety (strength) in numbers.** LT acceptable. Being surrounded by many people makes you more secure. (=) *We must all hang together or we will hang separately. In union there is strength.*

**There never was a good war or a bad peace.** LT. Self-explanatory.

**These are the times that try men's souls.** LT acceptable. Today's situation is bad, possibly worse than ever before.

**They also serve who only stand and wait.** Movers and shakers are important, but ordinary people who perform smaller services are important as well.

**Thing of beauty is a joy forever, A.** LT. Self-explanatory.

**Things are never as bad as they seem.** LT. Self-explanatory.
(=) *Every cloud has a silver lining.*

**Things are not always what they seem.** LT. Self-explanatory.
(=) *Appearances are deceiving. Never judge a book by its cover.*

**(This above all) to thine own self be true.** It is important to be honest with others but absolutely necessary to be honest with yourself. (=) *Be yourself.*

**This too will pass (away).** Be patient; in time things will get back to normal. (=) *Time heals all wounds.*

**Those who can, do; those who can't, teach.** LT. A mildly derogatory saying implying that teachers do not choose their profession, but have settled for it because they failed in the "real world."

**Those who do not remember the past are condemned to repeat it.** (=) *History repeats itself.*

**Thousand-mile trip begins with a single step, A.** Unless you start something you will never finish it; break a giant task into small steps that seem less daunting. (=) *Rome wasn't built in a day. One must learn to walk before he can run.* Equiv.: **Ko.** *Manun gusul do itji anumyun moggori nun andenda.* {A myriad of beads will not make a necklace until they are strung together.}

**Thrift is a fine virtue in ancestors.** LT. It is great to have a rich parents or relatives.

**Throw out a sprat to catch a mackerel.** One should risk a small item or bet in the hopes of netting a substantial windfall. Equiv.: **Ja.** *Ebide taiwo tsuru.* {Catch a sea bream with a shrimp.}

**Time and tide wait for no man.** LT. Life continues whether one's ready or not. (=) *Eat, drink, and be merry for tomorrow we may die. Life is but a dream.*

**Time flies.** LT. Life passes quickly. Equiv.: **Ge.** *Nutze die Zeit!* {Make good use of your time!}

**Time heals all wounds.** Both body and mind eventually forget all previous grievances and damages. (=) *This too will pass.* Equiv.: **He.** *Hazman oseh et shelo.* {Time does its own work.}

**Time is money.** LT acceptable. Since time is required to earn money, wasting time is like wasting money. Equiv.: **Ja.** *Tokiwa kanenari.* {Time is money.}

**Time will tell.** Eventually we will know the truth. (=) *It will all come out in the wash.*

**To each his own.** Let individuals have their individual oddities and desires. Equiv.: **Fr.** *Chacun a son goût.* {Everyone to his own taste.} **Ja.** *Tadekuu mushimo sukizuki.* {Even the insect that eats smartweed has its taste preference.} **La.** *De gustibus non disputandum est.* {There can be no disputing about taste.}

**To err is human; to forgive divine.** LT. Humans regularly make mistakes, so do not hold grudges against anyone. Equiv.: **La.** *Errare humanum est. Hominus est errarum* {It is human to err.}

**Tomorrow never comes.** LT.

**Too many chiefs and not enough Indians, There are.** A situation where too many people are trying to lead with a few followers. (=) *Too many cooks spoil the broth.*

**Too many cooks (chefs) spoil the broth.** A successful enterprise requires a single capable leader. Equiv.: **Ja.** *Sendô ôkushite fune yamani noboru.* {Too many helmsmen (captains) let the ship sail up a mountain (on the rocks).} **Ru.** *U syemi nyanyek ditya byez glaza.* {A child with seven nursemaids has no eyes watching him.}

**Too much of a good thing, There can be.** There is such a thing as excess—even with things we like. Equiv.: **Yi.** *Der Kallah is tzu shein.* {The bride is too beautiful.}

**Tree is known by its fruit, A.** LT acceptable. One is judged by one's accomplishments.

**True university is a collection of books, A.** LT acceptable. All the knowledge one needs can be found in books. (=) *A home without books is like a house without windows.*

**Truth always pays.** LT. Truth is the best option in many cases.

**Truth is stranger than fiction.** LT acceptable. Things happen in real life that a novelist would never imagine.

**Turnabout is fair play.** If you do it to me, it is fair that I do it to you. (=) *Fight fire with fire. All's fair in love and war. What's sauce for the goose is sauce for the gander.*

**Two can live as cheaply as one.** Sharing expenses cuts costs.

**Two can play at the same game.** LT acceptable. Anything you can do, I can do better; I can be just as sneaky and unfair as you. (=) *What's good for the goose is good for the gander. Turnabout is fair play. Fight fire with fire.*

**Two heads are better than one.** A discussion between two (or more) people is more likely to result in the right decision than a conclusion by one person only. (=) *Many hands make work light.*

**Two is company; three is a crowd.** Friends or lovers often resent others joining them.

**Two wrongs do not make a right.** LT. Self-explanatory. Even in retribution, a second wrong does not rectify (or justify) the first one.

**United we stand, divided we fall.** LT. A group of people is more powerful and effective than a single individual. (=) *We must hang together or we shall hang separately. In union there is strength.*

**Vanity of vanities, all is vanity.** All conscious action is essentially based on selfishness. Equiv.: **La.** *Vanitas vanitatum, omnia vanitas.*

**Variety is the spice of life.** LT. Having many interests and/or changing

your activities, work, friends, etc. makes life more interesting.
**Virtue is its own reward.** LT. Self-explanatory.

**Want makes strife between husband and wife.** Married or co-habitating couples fight most about finances, sometimes ruining the marriage. (=) *When poverty comes in the door, love leaps out the window. First thrive, then wive.*

**War is hell!** LT. Equiv.: **It.** *Guerra cominciata, inferno scatenato.* {When a war begins, all hell breaks loose.}

**Waste not, want not.** If you are not wasteful or overly extravagant, you will always have enough to live on.

**Watched pot (kettle) never boils, A.** When you are waiting impatiently for something, it never seems to happen fast enough.

**Water over a dam never returns.** Some things cannot be undone. (=) *Do not cry over spilled milk.* Equiv.: **Ar.** *El-ifat matt.* {That which is dead is dead.}

**Water seeks its own level.** People tend to associate with their own kind. (=) *Birds of a feather flock together.*

**Way of the transgressor is hard, The.** Those who violate the law or go against accepted social norms will find life difficult. (=) *There is no rest for the wicked.*

**Way to a man's heart is through his stomach, The.** If you want something from a man, cook him his favorite meal; good cooks keep their husbands happy and stay married.

**We can resist anything except temptation.** LT.

**We grow too soon old and too late smart.** LT.

**We have nothing to fear but fear itself.** Fear and worry about a possible forthcoming event is often more injurious than the event itself.

**We must all eat a peck of dirt before we die.** LT. Everyone, regardless of how successful he is born or becomes, must experience some hardship or humiliation in life. (=) *Rain falls on the just and the unjust alike.*

**We must stoop to conquer.** Sometimes one must appear to grovel or be subservient in order eventually to get one's way.

**We will cross that bridge when we come to it.** LT acceptable. There is no need to decide an issue prematurely; wait until all the facts are in. (=) *Do not cry before you are hurt. Do not trouble trouble before trouble troubles you.* Equiv.: **No.** *Ikke ta sorgene på forskudd.* {Don't worry about your troubles beforehand.}

**What cannot be cured must be endured.** One must put up with things which one does not have the power to change. (=) *If you can't lick 'em,* *join 'em. Like it or lump it.*

**What goes around comes around.** Your deeds (good or bad) will eventually catch up with you. (=) *What you lose on the roundabouts, you gain on the swings.*

**What goes up must come down.** One who becomes successful must also be disgraced or ruined; anything good must turn bad eventually. (=) *Always be nice to people on the way up the ladder, because you might meet them again on the way down.*

**What is good for the goose is good for the gander.** If one spouse is unfaithful, the other has the right to retaliate in kind. (=) *Sauce for the goose is sauce for the gander.*

**What is learned in the cradle is carried to the grave.** Early association and learning of the child strongly influence the personality of the adult. (=) *The child is father of the man. As the sapling bends, so grows the tree.* Equiv.: **Ja.** *Mitsugono tamashii hyakumade.* {What's learned at the age of three stays until the age of 100.} **Ko.** *Sesal ddai burud yudunsal ggaji ganda.* {A bad habit established at the age of three will last until eighty years of age.}

**What you don't know won't hurt you.** Sometimes being unaware of a problem may be less troublesome than knowing about it. (=) *Ignorance is bliss.*

**Whatever will be will be.** LT. Equiv.: **Sp.** *Que será será.*

**What you lose on roundabouts, you gain on the swings.** Disadvantages in one area can be compensated by advantages in another. (=) *What goes around comes around.*

**When in Rome, do as the Romans do.** One should fall in line with local customs; one should follow the example of one's friends or companions.

**When it rains, it pours.** Misfortunes tend to pile up one after another; bad things always come in bunches. Equiv.: **Fr.** *Un malheur ne vient jamais seul.* {Misfortune never comes alone.}

**When poverty (the wolf) comes in the door, love leaps out the window.** LT. Financial need puts great strain on a relationship. (=) *When money flies out the window, love flies out the door. Want makes strife between man and wife. First thrive, then wive.*

**When the cat is away, the mice will play.** When there is lack of authority, people try to get away with things. Equiv.: **It.** *Quando il gatto manca i topi ballano.* {When the cat is away, the mice dance.} **Ja.** *Onino inumani sentaku.* {Do laundry while the demon is away.} **Sp.** *Cuando el gato duerme, bailan los ratones.* {While the cat sleeps, the mice dance.}

**When the going gets tough, the tough get going.** When a situation becomes difficult, the stronger, more determined individuals do not hesitate to act.

**Where ignorance is bliss, 'tis folly to be wise.** LT acceptable. Sometimes in life it is better not to know certain things. (=) *Ignorance is bliss.*

**Where law ends, tyranny begins.** LT acceptable. Leaders' power must be kept in check by the rules of the citizens; laws limiting the government's actions are *sine qua non* in a democracy.

**Where there is a will, there is a way.** If you really want to do something, you will find the method for doing it. (=) *It is easy to find a stick to beat a dog.* Equiv.: **Ge.** *Wenn man erst will, dann kann man auch.* {If once we have the will to do something, then we can do it.} **Yi.** *Az du vilst shlugen a hund, du kenst gefinen a stekn.* {If you want to beat a dog, you will always find a stick.}

**Where there is smoke, there is fire.** If there is an indication that something is happening, there is a strong likelihood that that event is happening. (=) *If it looks like a duck, waddles like a duck, and quacks like a duck, it must be a duck.* (≠) *Appearances can be deceiving.* Equiv.: **Ja.** *Hinonai tokoroni kemuriwa tatazu.* {There can't be smoke without fire.}

**While there is life, there is hope.** As long as one is still alive, there is the possibility of things getting better. (=) *Hope springs eternal.* Equiv.: Fr. *Tant qu'il y a de la vie il y a de l'espoir.*

**Wish is father to the thought, The.** Before developing an idea or inventing an object, there must first be a need or desire for it. (=) *Necessity is the mother of invention.*

**Woman is fickle (changeable).** Women are inconsistent; they have a fickle and inconstant temperament. (=) *It's a woman's privilege to change her mind.* Equiv.: **Fr.** *Souvent la femme varie, bien fol est qui s'y fie.* {A woman changes so often, only a fool would trust her.} *Comme la plume au vent, femme est volage.* {Like a feather in the wind, a woman is flighty.} **It.** *La donna è mobile.* {The lady is inconstant.}

**Woman is only a woman, but a good cigar is a smoke, A.** LT acceptable. A vintage macho expression; the whimsical cry of the misogynist.

**Woman is the woe of man, A.** LT. Self-explanatory. (≠) *Behind every great man is a woman.*

**Woman's hair is her crowning glory, A.** Self-explanatory. A bad pun, indicating that a woman's hair (crown) is her most attractive feature.

**Woman's place is in the home, A.** LT. Women were once relegated to the home to perform housekeeping and child-rearing duties while men pursued occupations in the public sphere. Today's woman would say: *A* *woman's place is in the House—and the Senate.* (=) *It is a man's world.*

**Woman's tears are her strongest weapons, A.** LT. Women play on the sympathies of men by crying.

**Woman's work is never done, A.** LT. Responsible for housekeeping, child-rearing, and their own careers, women find themselves busy or preoccupied 24 hours a day. (=) *Man's work is till set of sun; woman's work is never done.*

**Wonder lasts but nine days, A.** Awesome or unique events and people enjoy a brief period of fame before being forgotten. (=) *Everybody is famous for fifteen minutes. Easy come, easy go.*

**Wonders will never cease!** LT. Self-explanatory.

**Word to the wise is sufficient, A.** A few words or a brief explanation are enough for a learned person to understand a larger concept. Equiv.: **La.** *Dictum sapienti sat est.* {A word to the wise is sufficient.}

**Work makes life sweet.** LT. Self-explanatory. Equiv.: **Ge.** *Arbeit macht das Leben süß.* {Work makes life sweet.} **La.** *Omnia Vincit Labor.* {Work conquers all.}

**World is one's oyster, The.** Life has all kinds of good possibilities and luxuries to take advantage of.

**World is too much with us (late and soon), The.** The wearisome aspects of life can be a heavy burden. (=) *Life is not a bowl of cherries.*

**Worst is yet to come, The.** LT acceptable. A proclamation of doom.

**You always hurt the one you love.** LT. Self-explanatory. (=) *Each man kills the thing he loves.*

**You are only as old as you feel.** LT. One should not let age interfere with the activities one loves or the dreams one has.

**You are what you eat.** LT acceptable. One's choice of food affects one's physical and psychological development. (=) *Many a man digs his grave with his teeth.*

**You are only young once.** Take advantage of the joys of youth, for they will not last long. (=) *Gather ye rosebuds while ye may.* Equiv.: **La.** *Carpe diem.* {Seize the day.}

**You'd better get what you want in life, or you will end up wanting what you get.** People eventually settle for what life gives them and then rationalize that all is well.

**You can fool some of the people all of the time, all of the people some of the time, but not all of the people all of the time.** LT.

**You cannot beat somebody with nobody.** Even a mediocre candidate will beat an unknown or unpresentable candidate.

**You cannot have your cake and eat it, too.** You cannot have it both ways; choices have to be made.

**You cannot keep a good man down.** LT. A determined individual will usually win.

**You cannot please everyone.** LT. Self-explanatory. (=) *You cannot make an omelet without breaking eggs.*

**You cannot take it with you.** Wealth will not follow you into the grave. (=) *A shroud has no pockets.*

**You cannot teach an old dog new tricks.** It is difficult to change old habits, particularly with people well on in years and set in their ways. (≠) *It is never too late to learn.* Equiv.: **Fr.** *Ce n'est pas à un vieux singe qu'on apprend à faire des grimaces.* {You can't teach an old monkey how to make funny faces.}

**You get what you pay for.** LT. Price depends on quality. (=) *There is no free lunch.*

**You must take the bad with the good (the bitter with the better; the sour with the sweet).** LT. Life offers both wonderful and horrible moments; savor the wonderful and learn from the horrible. (=) *Take the rough with the smooth.*

**You pays your money, and you takes your chances.** Several equally risky choices are available. While the expression appears ungrammatical, it is colloquial and accepted.

**You shall not bear false witness against your neighbor.** LT. Testifying falsely is a cardinal sin.

**You will be a long time dead.** LT acceptable. Enjoy life today, for it passes by quickly. (=) *Live today for tomorrow may never come. Enjoy yourself. It's later than you think.*

**You never know (what you can do) until you try.** LT. Self-explanatory.

**Youth is a wonderful thing; it is a shame it is wasted on the young (a bunch of kids).** LT acceptable. Self-explanatory.

# WHY ENGLISH DRIVES INTERPRETERS AND TRANSLATORS CRAZY

Inconsistencies and contradictions—the American English language is full of them. So, if you expect logic in a language, you are doomed to disappointment. Contrary to expectations, there are no eggs in eggplants, nor ham in hamburgers. Pineapples are even less logical. They contain neither pine nor apples. Sweetbreads are neither sweet nor bread. They are an internal meat, namely the pancreas. Sweetmeats are sweet, but are not meat. They are a type of candy.

Nor can you count on words to advise you of their country or city of origin. Canadian bacon is not from Canada. In Canada, it is known as *back bacon*. Neither French toast nor French fries are natives of France. English muffins did not originate in England. In France, our French fries are known as *frites*, and in England as *chips*. The scone is about as close as the English get to an English muffin. That cuddly little pet called the Guinea pig is not from Guinea. Nor is it a pig; it is actually a rodent.

Speaking of inconsistencies, in English, you park on a driveway, and drive on a parkway. Actors recite in a play, while musicians play at a recital. We make shipments by truck, but send cargo by ship. A slim chance and a fat chance are the same. Ditto for flammable and inflammable. But a wise guy and a wise man are probably opposites. At gambling if you have few chances to win, you should be pessimistic, but if you have a few chances, there is room for optimism. Finally, when I wind up my watch, it starts, but when I wind up this paragraph, it is finished.

The problems facing translators continue: is hell cold or hot? Sometimes we say "hot as hell!" but on other occasions, "cold as hell!" My house burns up while it is burning down. And, when I fill out an insurance form, I am filling it in. In the morning my alarm clock goes off, but is really going on. Logic deserts you when you expect a boxing ring to be round; it is square. And, incidentally, if you are sinking into quicksand, it is a very slow process.

Let's not forget crazy English plurals: for example, the plural of goose is geese, so the plural of moose should be *meese*, right? Wrong! Similarly, the plural of booth is booths, but the plural of tooth is teeth. House—houses, but mouse, certainly not *mouses*. Try mice. Sometimes, however, inconsistency can be creative. The plural of spouse is spouses, but, in some cases, *spice* would be more realistic.

# Chapter Three

# POPULAR
# AMERICAN EXPRESSIONS

The popular sayings in this chapter were originally included in the previous chapter. However, it was pointed out to the author that these particular expressions definitely did not fit the description of proverbs. That is true. Whether they could be classified as slogans or aphorisms is debatable. Since *discretion is the better part of valor,* it was decided to place them in this separate chapter.

With the decision as to which expressions belong in which chapter being to some extent subjective, the author has no quarrel with any reader who would have classified them differently. From a practical point of view, however, it makes little difference. If a translator is uncertain as to where to find an expression he has in mind, the index at the back of the book will enable him to locate the proverb or slogan or aphorism or popular expression.

From the author's point of view, the chief criteria used in selecting expressions for this chapter was that they be "popular." All chosen find extensive use with one or more groups of Americans. Like proverbs, they do provide a type of shorthand for expressing complex ideas or feelings in a few words.

Be advised that the notes, guides, abbreviations, and symbols discussed in the introduction to the previous chapter and in the **Guide to the Use of this Book** also apply here. Similarly, any caveats or suggestions given for translating proverbs should also be followed in translating expressions in this chapter. Perhaps a little more leeway on freedom of choice of words applies here, since most of these expressions are not laden with history and tradition in the way that proverbs are.

**Add insult to injury.** To not only hurt someone, but also insult that person as well; to make matters worse. Equiv.: **Ko.** *Tanun bul e girum budgi.* {To add oil to the fire.}

**Age before beauty.** Older people should have priority over younger people; often used facetiously when permitting someone else to enter or exit a door before you.

**Always a bridesmaid, never the bride.** Some people never quite succeed.

**Ants in one's pants, To have.** To fidget; to be nervous or anxious.

**Any (old) port in a storm.** Try to do something constructive, even if it is minimal and not really what you would like to achieve; use any imperfect solution that at least partially works. (=) *Any water in the desert.*

**Any Tom, Dick, or Harry.** Anyone will do.

**Ask me no questions and I'll tell you no lies.** I do not want to answer you.

**Bark is worse than his bite, His.** This person threatens a lot, but he does not follow through with actions. (=) *Barking dogs never bite.* Equiv.: **It.** *Abbaia ma con morde.* {He barks better than he bites.} **Sp.** *Gato maullador, nunca buen cazador.* {A mewing cat is never a good mouser.}

**Batten down the hatches.** Prepare yourself for trouble; get ready for a storm.

**Beat around the bush.** Go around in circles without getting to the point.

**Before you can say Jack Robinson.** Immediately; instantaneously. (=) *In the blink of an eye.* Equiv.: **Brit.** *Before you can say knife.* **Fr.** *Avant d'avoir le temps de dire 'ouf.'* {Before you can say 'Phew.'} **It.** *In un batter d'occhio.* {In the blink of an eye.} **Sp.** *(Tan rápido) como un dos por tres.* {As quickly as saying 'one, two, three.'}

**Between a rock and a hard place.** In a very difficult (almost impossible) situation. (=) *Between the devil and the deep blue sea.* Equiv.: **Fr.** *Tomber de Charybde en Scylla.* {Between scylla and charybdis} {Between a sharp jutting rock and a whirlpool.} **La.** *A fronte praecipitium, a tergo lupi.* {A precipice in front, a wolf behind.} **Sp.** *Entre la espada y la pared.* {Between the sword and the wall.}

**Between the devil and the deep blue sea.** Between two dangerous or unpleasant alternatives. (=) *Between a rock and a hard place.* Equiv.: **Ge.** *Zwischen Scylla und Charybdis.* {Between a sharp jutting rock and a whirlpool.}

**Big fish in a small pond, A.** LT acceptable. An important person within a small, limited place where it is easy to be important. (=) *A big frog in a small puddle.* Equiv.: **Ko.** *Ummul ane gaigori.* {A frog in a well.}

**Buck stops here, The.** Final responsibility lies with me. (=) *Passing the buck.*

**Burn the candle at both ends, To.** To be working or active both night and day; to live life too fully. Equiv.: **It.** *Non mettere troppa carne al fuoco.* {Don't put too much meat on the fire.}

**Bring home the bacon, To.** To support one's family; to earn a living. Equiv.: **Fr.** *Gagner son pain.* {To earn one's (daily) bread.} **Ko.** *Jib uro ssal gajigo onda.* {To bring home the rice.}

**By the skin of one's teeth.** By the tiniest margin; barely. Equiv.: **It.** *Per il rotto della cuffia.* {Through the chink in one's cap.} **No.** *På hengende håret.* {On the hanging hair.}

**By hook or by crook.** Any method that works, legal or illegal. Equiv.: **It.** *Di riffa o di raffa.* {By hook or by violence.} *Con le buone o le cattive.* {With goodness or wickedness.}

**Call a spade a spade, To.** To be very honest or outspoken. (=) *To tell it like it is.* Equiv.: **Fr.** *Appeler un chat un chat.* {To call a cat a cat.} **La.** *Ligonem ligonem vocat.* {To call a hoe a hoe.}

**Calm after the storm, The.** LT acceptable. Self-explanatory; usually used figuratively, e.g. lovers reconciling after an argument or stocks leveling off after a crash. (=) *After rain comes fair weather.*

**Carrot and the stick, The.** LT acceptable. A combination of an inducement (reward) and a threat; a means of convincing misfits.

**Cast pearls before swine, To.** To waste time, money, humor, logical argument, or sentiment on people incapable of appreciating or understanding.

**Come out in the wash.** To be revealed; to get the final result when things calm down.

**Cross someone's palm with silver, To.** To bribe someone. Equiv.: **Fr.** *Graisser la patte à quelqu'un.* {To grease someone's palm.}

**Damned if you do, damned if you don't.** A paradoxical situation in which whatever you do is wrong.

**Dig one's own grave, To.** LT acceptable. To do things which are detrimental to one's health and/or success.

**Dog eat dog world.** Every person is concerned with his own goals and desires.

**Draw the short straw, To.** To be selected for an undesirable job.

**Drink someone under the table, To.** To keep drinking alcoholic beverages with a partner, until the other party quits or passes out.

**Drive (send) somebody up a wall, To.** To tax someone's patience; to drive someone crazy.

**Easier said than done.** LT. It is easier to have an idea to do something that it is to follow through and complete it.

**Eggs teaching the chickens, The.** Self-explanatory. (=) *Goslings lead the geese to water. The scholar may educate the master.*

**Every man for himself.** An expression used either literally or jokingly in emergency situations.

**Fall between two stools, To.** LT acceptable. To take on too many projects so that one cannot stay focused and avoid failure. Equiv.: **Ja.** *Nitowo oumonowa, ittowomo ezu.* {If you run after two hares, you will catch neither.}

**Fasten your seat belts.** Be prepared for a surprise, pleasant or unpleasant; take precautionary measures.

**Fine kettle of fish, A.** A quixotic or difficult situation; a sad mess. Equiv.: **It.** *Un bel pasticcio.* {A fine mess.}

**Finger in the pie, Have a.** To have some control or financial interest in an undertaking. Equiv.: **It.** *Avere le mani in pasta.* {To have one's hand in the dough.}

**For the love of Pete (Mike)!** An exclamation of frustration.

**Fox in the henhouse.** Figurative. Anybody with a selfish interest in a business, government, or organization who is put in charge of regulating the very group from which he hopes to profit.

**From the frying pan into the fire.** From a bad situation to a worse one. (=) *From bad to worse.* Equiv.: **Fr.** *Ne te jette pas à l'eau de peur de la pluie.* {Do not jump into the water for fear of the rain.} **Ge.** *Vom Regen in die Traufe.* {From the rain into the gutter.} **Sp.** *Salir de Guatemala para caer en Guatepeor.* {From bad to worse.}

**Full of piss and vinegar.** Describes a vigorous individual, full of energy and ambition.

**Game is not worth the candle, The.** The effort required is greater than the likely rewards.

**Go back to square one.** Start all over. Equiv.: **Fr.** *Reprendre tout à zéro.* {To go back to zero.}

**Go in one ear and out the other, To.** To ignore what someone is saying. Equiv.: **Ge.** *Das geht bei ihm zum einen Ohr 'rein, zum andern wieder 'raus.* {Goes in one ear and out the other.}

**Go to the dogs, To.** To have one's life or undertaking go downhill. Equiv.: **It.** *Andare in malora.* {To go to ruin or perdition.}

**Good riddance to bad rubbish.** Glad to get rid of someone or something. Equiv.: **It.** *Un buon repulisti.* {A clean sweep.}

**Grin and bear it.** LT acceptable. Make the best of, or at least endure, a bad situation. Equiv.: **Fr.** *Faire contre mauvaise fortune bon coeur.* {To prevail against bad luck, have a good heart.}

**Grow old gracefully, To.** LT. To age gradually and discreetly; to age naturally without using artificial means to retain youth.

**Hair of the dog that bit you, A.** To partake of the same thing, person, or place that caused you previous trouble or distress; e.g., to have another drink of the liquor that caused your hangover. (=) *Like cures like.* Equiv.: **Fr.** *Soigner le mal par le mal.* {Cure the bad using the bad.}

**Have a whale of a time.** Thoroughly enjoy yourself; have a grand time.

**Have a yellow streak down one's back, To.** To act cowardly.

**Have an ace up one's sleeve, To.** To have a hidden advantage to be used when needed.

**Have someone in the palm of your hand, To.** To be in total control. Equiv.: **No.** *Å snurre noen rundt lillefingeren.* {To twist someone around one's little finger.}

**Heads I win, tails you lose.** LT acceptable. No matter what happens, I will always win. (=) *Damned if you do, damned if you don't.*

**Heads or tails?** Make a choice.

**Here's mud in your eye!** A drinking toast; to your health. (=) *Bottoms up! Cheers!* Equiv.: **Ja.** *Kampai!* **Ge.** *Prosit!* **He.** *L'chaim!* **Fr.** *Santé!* **Sp.** *Salud!*

**His eyes are bigger than his stomach.** Refers to someone who is greedy or overconfident, who orders more food than he can finish, or who takes on a task too large for his strength or talents.

**Hit the road, Jack.** Get lost; get out of here. (Within a group of people it means, "Let's take off; let's leave.")

**Hold your horses.** Do not get excited; be patient.

**Hook, line, and sinker.** Totally and completely.

**Horse of a different color, A.** A totally different person or situation. (=) *A whole new ball game.* Equiv.: **Brit.** *Another pair of shoes.* **Sp.** *Esa es harina de otro costal.* {That is flour from a different bag.}

**Hunt with the hounds and run with the hare, To.** To be on both sides of an issue or action.

**I'll be a monkey's uncle!** I am astonished; I am amazed.

**Iron fist in a velvet glove, An.** Toughness behind a gentle exterior.

**It is no skin off your (my) nose.** It does not harm you (me).

**It is papa who pays.** In general, the father of the family is ultimately the one who covers the family's expenditures; sometimes also used by men with reference to the expenditures of their girlfriends.

**Jack of all trades.** Someone who is knowledgeable in many areas but not proficient at one. Equiv.: **Sp.** *Aprendiste mucho, maestro de nada.* {You have learned a lot, but you have mastered nothing.}

**Keep it under your hat.** Keep something secret.

**Keep a stiff upper lip.** Maintain a calm or stoic appearance in a trying or emotional situation.

**Keep the wolf from the door, To.** To earn enough to keep oneself and one's family from starving or being evicted. (=) *To bring home the bacon.* Equiv.: **Fr.** *Gagner son pain.* {To earn one's (daily) bread.} **Sp.** *Cerrar la puerta al hambre.* {To close the door to hunger.}

**Keep your cool.** Do not get excited, angry, or upset.

**Keep your shirt on.** Do not get angry, excited, or upset.

**Keeping up with the Joneses.** Maintaining a lifestyle (or an economic class) at least as good as your friends or neighbors.

**Kill two birds with one stone, To.** LT acceptable. To accomplish two aims with a single act. Equiv.: **It.** *Prendere due piccioni con una fava.* {Catch two pigeons with one bean.} **No.** *Å slå to fluer I ett smekk.* {To kill two flies with one blow.}

**Kiss and makeup.** Settle your dispute and show forgiveness. Equiv.: **Ko.** *Sarang ssaum un kal ro mul binum gud gatda.* {A quarrel between lovers is like cutting water with a knife.} **La.** *Amantium irae amoris.* {Lovers' quarrels are the renewal of love.}

**Knock the stuffing out of someone.** To beat up someone; to badly defeat someone.

**Knocked over with a feather.** To be surprised. Equiv.: **Sp.** *Mátame de un Pestañeo!* {Kill me with the blink of an eye.}

**Know when one is well off, To.** To realize how fortunate one is. (=) *To know which side one's bread is buttered on.*

**Lead someone up the garden path, To.** To lead someone on; to deceive someone.

**Least said, the better, The.** LT. There are situations in which it is better not to talk. Equiv.: **La.** *Vir sapit qui pauca loquitor.* {The man is wise who talks little.}

**Let it all hang out.** Relax; take it easy; do what pleases you.

**Like a bull in a china shop.** Clumsy, awkward, uncoordinated aggressive—either physically or socially.

**Like a fish out of water.** Being away from one's natural surroundings; clumsy, inept, and unable to cope. Equiv.: **It.** *Essere come un pesce fuor d'acqua.* {To be like a fish out of water.} **Sp.** *Una gallina en corral ajeno.* {A hen in a foreign coop.}

**Like (as if) there is no tomorrow.** Doing something hurriedly as if today were the last opportunity. Equiv.: **Sp.** *Como si fuera el fin del mundo.* {As if the world were ending.}

**Like shooting fish in a barrel.** Extremely easy.

**Like the black hole of Calcutta.** Very hot and extremely crowded; a cell that leaves no escape but death.

**Like taking candy from a baby.** LT acceptable. Extremely easy.

**Like two peas in a pod.** LT acceptable. Identical; cozy.

**Like a needle in a haystack.** LT acceptable. Something small or camouflaged by its surroundings, thus extremely difficult to find; to attempt the unlikely or impossible.

**Lock, stock, and barrel.** Totally; completely. (=) *Hook, line and sinker.*

**Loose lips sink ships.** Careless sharing of information has damaging effects. (=) *Careless talk costs lives.*

**Many happy returns.** May life continue with good fortune.

**May the best man win.** LT acceptable. The strongest or most capable person should be the winner.

**Meet one's Waterloo, To.** To be utterly defeated.

**Monkey see, monkey do.** What one sees or hears, one will mimic or repeat.

**More than flesh and blood can stand.** LT acceptable. Beyond endurance.

**More trouble (fun) than a barrel of monkeys.** Full of mischief and problems.

**My mama didn't raise no dummy (any foolish children).** I am not stupid or naive.

**Need something (someone) like a hole in the head, To.** To be in excess to the point of being annoying or burdensome. (=) *Who needs it?*

**Neither fish nor fowl (nor good red herring).** Not easily categorized. (=) *Falling between two stools.*

**Night has a thousand eyes, The.** LT acceptable. The stars are out.

**No flies on him (me), There are.** He is (I am) not stupid; you should not expect to get away with anything with him (me).

**No matter how you slice it.** It does not matter how you look at or manipulate something, it is still no good; the truth is the truth. Equiv.: **Ge.** *Ein kleine Wurst ist auch eine Wurst.* {A little sausage is still a sausage.}

**Not for all the tea in China.** Never; not at any price. Equiv.: **Sp.** *Ni por todo el oro del mundo.* {Not for all the gold in the world.}

**Not to be sneezed at.** Not to be disregarded; not to be made light of. Equiv.: **Sp.** *No ser de despreciar.* {Not to be rejected or scorned.}

**Not to know one's ass from one's elbow.** To be dumb-witted or ignorant. (=) *Not to know one's ass from a hole in the ground.*

**Not worth a tinker's dam(n).** Of little value; worthless.

**One foot in the grave.** LT acceptable. Close to death; extremely old. Equiv.: **Sp.** *Tiene un pie aqui y el otra allá.* {He has one foot here and the other there.}

**Patience of Job, The.** Infinite patience.

**Penny for your thoughts, A.** You look so pensive that I am curious as to what you are thinking; What's on your mind?

**Pie in the sky.** Hope or desire for something impossible or highly unlikely. Equiv.: **Ko.** *Gurim ane ddug.* {A piece of rice cake in a picture.}

**Plain as the nose on one's face, As.** LT acceptable. Obvious. (=) *As clear as day.*

**Pouring oil on troubled waters.** Trying to make peace; smoothing things over. (=) *Do not fish in troubled waters.*

**Pull a rabbit out of the hat, To.** To solve a problem in an immediate, unusual, or surprising manner; to produce a minor miracle.

**Punch your way out of a paper bag, To.** To be able to do easy things; used in the negative to indicate lack of ability.

**Put one's head in the lion's mouth, To.** LT acceptable. To take risks; to put oneself in grave danger.

**Put one's house in order, To.** To arrange one's affairs, often prior to death or a long trip.

**Rob Peter to pay Paul.** To take something (usually money) from one source and use it for an unintended beneficiary. Equiv.: **Sp.** *Descubrir un santo para cubrir otro.* {To uncover a saint in order to cover another.}

**Rough (dirty) end of the stick, The.** Unfair treatment.

**Save one's bacon, To.** To preserve one's life or to recover one's position and/or reputation. Equiv.: **Sp.** *Salvar el pellejo.* {To save one's hide.}

**See Naples and die.** A person should never depart this world without having seen extremely beautiful places.

**See the forest for the trees, Not able to.** To pay too much attention to details and not enough to the overall picture. (=) *You cannot see the city for the houses.*

**See which way the wind blows, To.** LT acceptable. To try to gather more information before taking any action.

**Sell like hot-cakes, To.** To have a rapid turnover; to sell in large quantities very quickly. Equiv.: **Ge.** *Weggehen wir warme Semmeln.* {To sell like warm rolls.} **Ja.** *Hanega haetayoni ureru.* {To sell as if wings had grown.}

**Ships that pass in the night.** LT acceptable. People who experience a brief chance meeting, usually never to see each other again.

**Sky is the limit, The.** The possibilities are limitless; you can have anything you want.

**Sleep like a log (baby).** To sleep soundly. Equiv.: **No.** *Å sove som en stein.* {To sleep like a rock.}

**Snake in the grass, A.** A sneaky or deceitful individual.

**Soft soap someone, To.** To sell someone on an idea or purchase by means of flattery. (=) *To sweet talk someone.* Equiv.: **Fr.** *Lécher les bottes de quelqu'un.* {To lick someone's boots.} **Ge.** *Jemandem Honig ums Maul schmieren.* {To smear honey on someone's mouth.} **Ja.** *Higeno chiriwo harau.* {To brush the dust off someone's beard.}

**Speak with a forked tongue, To.** To lie; to be deliberately deceitful.

**Stew in one's own juice, To.** To pay for one's mistakes; to suffer the results of one's own efforts. (=) *You have made your bed, now lie on it.*

**Stick out like a sore thumb, To.** To be conspicuous; to appear out of place or obvious. (=) *Plain as the nose on your face.*

**Storm in a teacup, A.** Making a big deal out of something trivial. (=) *Much ado about nothing.* Equiv.: **It.** *Perdersi in un bicchiere d'acqua.* {To get lost in a cup of water.} **Sp.** *Mucho ruido y pocos nueces.* {A lot of noise and no nuts.}

**Straight from the horse's mouth.** Directly from a reliable source.

**Straw that broke the camel's back, The.** When doing things to excess, there is always a final point where even a small amount of additional activity results in total destruction; usually shortened as *The last straw.* Equiv.: **Sp.** *La gota que colmó el vaso.* {The drop that overflowed the glass of water.}

**Strictly for the birds.** Of very limited value; almost useless.

**Sword of Damocles, A.** Impending disaster (hanging over one's head).

**Take a load off your feet.** Sit down and relax.

**Take something with a grain (pinch) of salt, To.** To be skeptical or dubious. Equiv.: **La.** *Cum grano salis.* {With a grain of salt.}

**Taste of one's own medicine, A.** One's bad behavior or bad attitude being used against him; paying someone back in kind for nasty or unpleasant things he has done.

**Tempest in a teapot, A.** A brouhaha over a small matter. (=) *Storm in a teacup. Much ado about nothing.*

**Thank your lucky stars.** To be aware of how fortunate one is.

**This is the last straw.** This is the last time I am agreeing to this; I cannot take any more. Equiv.: **It.** *Questo è colmo.* {It is full to the brim.}

**Tilt at windmills, To.** To battle imaginary enemies; to fight ridiculously unwinnable battles. Equiv.: **Ja.** *Hitori-zumôwo toru.* {To sumo-wrestle alone.}

**Turn up one's nose at, To.** To reject or look down on people, things, or ideas; to treat with contempt or disdain. Equiv.: **Sp.** *Mirar con desprecio.* {To look at scornfully.}

**Too many irons in the fire.** More activities than one is capable of doing well. Equiv.: **Sp.** *Tener demasiado asuntos entre las manos.* {To have too many businesses in one's hands.}

**Try to put a quart into a pint.** To attempt the impossible.

**Until (when) hell freezes over.** LT acceptable. Forever; never. Equiv.: **La.** *Ad calendas graecas.*

**Voice crying in the wilderness, A.** An ignored point of view. Equiv.: **La.** *Vox climantis in deserto.* {A voice in the desert.}

**Walls have ears, The.** There is always someone listening, so be careful when telling secrets. Equiv.: **Sp.** *Las paredes oyen.* {The walls hear.}

**What's yours is mine, and what's mine is yours.** LT. We share everything.

**When you have seen one you have seen them all.** People or events which are not different from others seen before.

**Whistle while you work.** LT. Enjoy your work; keep a cheerful attitude.

**With his tail between his legs.** To retreat in a dejected fashion after having lost badly. Equiv.: **It.** *Con la coda fra le gambe.* {With his tail between his legs.}

**Wild horses couldn't make me do it.** Nothing can force (convince) me to do it.

**Wise after the event (fact).** LT. To have the benefit of hindsight.

**Wrong end of the stick.** Making a misjudgment; reaching the wrong conclusion. Equiv.: **It.** *Prendere lucciole per lanterne.* {Mistaking a firefly for a lantern.}

**Wolf in sheep's clothing, A.** An aggressive person posing as a mild-mannered individual. Equiv.: **Fr.** *Un loup déguisé en agneau.* {A wolf desguised as a lamb.} **Ja.** *Gemenji bosatsu, naishin nyoyasha.* {Kind face, false heart.}

**Your guess is as good as mine.** LT. I know as little about it as you do.

## SIGNS AND NOTICES:
## AMUSING MISTRANSLATIONS

As a well traveled international salesman for many years, the author has had ample opportunities to observe frequent examples of translation confusion, particularly on public signs and notices. (Apparently, many other travelers have observed the same signs, for a number of the examples given below have been getting wide exposure on the Internet.) Some errors are annoying, but many are very amusing, resulting from the fact that American English abounds in words having double meanings.

Unintentionally amusing signs can be found almost anywhere in the world, but are particularly common in countries where English is a frequently used second language, and the locals believe that they speak it well. Following are some rib-tickling examples:

*In an Athens tailor shop*: Order your Suit Now, because is Big Rush. We Will Execute Customers in Strict Rotation.
*On an Israeli butcher shop door*: Sol Ben Ami, Butcher— Slaughters Himself Daily at 4:00 P.M.
*In a Japanese hotel*: Please take advantage of the chambermaids.
*In a Mexican hotel*: The manager has personally passed all water served here.
*In a Moscow hotel room*: If This is your First Visit to the USSR, You Are Welcome to It.
*In a Paris hotel elevator*: Please Leave your Values at the Front Desk.
*In a Paris rooming house*: Please Clean Tub after Washing Land-lady.
*In a Rome laundry*: Ladies, Leave your Clothes here. Spend the Afternoon Having a Good Time.
*In a Spanish hotel*: We highly recommend the hotel tart.
*In a Swiss restaurant*: Our wines leave nothing to hope for.

# Chapter Four

# SIMILES AND METAPHORS INDICATING EXTREMES

Similes are comparisons of two essentially different things which share one identical or similar characteristic. The two items are connected by explicit words such as "as" or "like." *Heavy as lead* or *black as coal* would be typical examples. Metaphors, on the other hand, compare similar items or objects in an implicit way, that is, one item is substituted for the other and their similarity is understood. *Twilight of life* or *pitch black* are typical metaphors.

The expressions in the following list use similes or metaphors to indicate the extremes of the condition being described. Translations are for the most part direct and literal. For example, *Happy as a lark* means very happy or extremely happy. Whether larks are actually happy is debatable, but the origin of the expression is lost in antiquity, while the present day meaning remains clear. *Tired as a dog* means very tired. The others can be translated in a similar fashion. In a few cases, more economical alternative designations are given. For example, *Tired as a dog* can be translated as "exhausted" and *Crazy as a loon* as "loony." Similarly, "crafty" provides more linguistic punch than "extremely clever."

Though literal translations of similes are very common, some can be tricky. *Black as the ace of spades* would probably be understood everywhere. One could assume that *White as a sheet* would similarly be understood but, since most sheets in the United States are no longer white, it may lead to confusion. What is meant is *White as sheets used to be*. Other translation difficulties are cultural. *Stubborn as a mule*, for example, is easy to understand if you come from a country where mules exist in large numbers or are part of the country's history. For countries where mules are rare, *Stubborn as an ox* (or some other animal) may be substituted. *Bare as a Scotchman's knee* is similar. If you or your reader know nothing about mules or the wearing of kilts in Scotland, a literal translation is worthless. In such cases, "exceedingly stubborn" or "very bare" will have to suffice.

Thousands of similes and metaphors exist. Only the more popular ones (and, in a few cases, the more intriguing ones) are given below, together with a few samples of foreign equivalents. Abbreviations for foreign equivalents are identical to those used in the previous chapters. (Depending on sentence structure, the terms "as" or "like" can precede many of the following.)

**Agile as a monkey.**

**Amorous as a pair of love-birds.**

**Bald as a billiard ball.** (=) *Bald as an egg.* Equiv.: **Fr.** *Chauve comme un oeuf.* {Bald as an egg.} *Son crâne ressemble a un patinoire a mouches.* {His head resembles a skating rink for flies.}

**Bare as a Scotsman's knee.**

**Bashful as a schoolgirl.**

**Big as an elephant.** (=) *Big as a house. Big as life. Big as all outdoors.* Equiv.: **Sp.** *Más grande que la madre.* {Bigger than the mother.} *Más largo que el pedo de una víbora.* {Longer than a python's fart.}

**Bitter as gall.** (=) *Bitter as hemlock.*

**Black as the ace of spades.** (=) *Black as the night.* Equiv.: **Fr.** *Noir comme dans un four.* {Black as the inside of an oven.} *Noir comme de l'encre.* {Black as ink.}

**Black hole of Calcutta, Like the.** Very hot and extremely crowded; a cell that leaves no escape but death.

**Blind as a bat.** Equiv.: **Ge.** *Blind wie ein Maulwurf.* {Blind as a mole.}

**Bold as brass.**

**Blunt as a meat-ax.**

**Brave as a (mad) bull.** Equiv.: **Fr.** *Courage de lion.* {Brave as a lion.}

**Bright as a (new) penny.** Equiv.: **Ko.** *Dainnad gatchi babuda.* {Bright as daytime.}

**Brown as a nut.**

**Buck naked.**

**Bull in a china shop, Like a.** Clumsy, awkward, uncoordinated—physically or socially.

**Busy as a bee.** (=) *Busy as a one-armed paperhanger (with the hives). Busy as a beaver.* Equiv.: **Ja.** *Komanezuminoyoni hataraku.* {Working like a Japanese dancing mouse.} *Mega mawaru-hodo isogashii.* {So busy the eyes start to swim.} *Nekono temo karitaihodo isogashii.* {So busy that even help from cats is appreciated.} **Ko.** *Gaimi gatchi barga.* {Busy as an ant.}

**Chaste as ice.** (=) *Chaste as marble. Chaste as a lily.*

**Clammy as death.**

**Clean as a whistle.**

**Cheap as dirt.** (=) *Cheap as borscht.* Equiv.: **Fr.** *Ça ne vaut pas un clou.* {Not worth a single nail.}

**Clear as a bell.** (=) *Crystal clear.* **No.** *Klart som dagen.* {Clear as the day.} **Ko.** *Sujung churum marga.* {As clear as crystal.} **Sp.** *Claro como el agua.* {Clear as water.}

**Clever as a wagonload of monkeys.**

**Cold as ice.** (=) *Cold as the grave.*

**Cold as a banker's heart.**
**Colder than a well-digger's ass in January.** (=) *Colder than a witch's teat.*
**Common as dirt.** Equiv.: **Ge.** *Wie Sand am Meer.* {Common as sand by the sea.}
**Comfortable as an old shoe.**
**Cool as a cucumber.**
**Crazy as a loon.** (=) *Crazy as a fox; loony.* Equiv.: **Sp.** *Más loco que una cabra.* {Crazier than a goat.}
**Crooked as a ram's horn.**
**Cross as a (an old) bear.**
**Cunning as a fox.** Equiv.: **Ge.** *Schlau wie ein Fuchs.* {Clever as a fox.}
**Curious as a magpie.**
**Cute as a button.** Equiv.: **Fr.** *Mignon comme un coeur.* {Endearing as a heart.}

**Dark as a dungeon.** (=) *Dark as midnight. Dark as the bottom of a well.* Equiv.: **Fr.** *Noir comme un four.* {Dark as inside an oven.} **No.** *Bekmørkt.* {Pitch dark.} *Mørk som graven.* {Dark as the grave}
**Dead as a doornail (mackerel).**
**Deaf as a post.** Equiv.: **Fr.** *Sourd comme une pioche.* {Deaf as a pickaxe.} *Sourd comme un pot.* {Deaf as a pot.}
**Deep as a well.** (=) *Deep as the grave.*
**Docile as a lamb.**
**Dumb as a dodo.** Equiv.: **Fr.**

*Bête comme un âne.* {Dumb as a donkey.} *Bête à pleurer.* {So dumb you want to cry.}**Ge.** *Dumm wie Stroh.* {Dumb as hay.} **Ko.** *Gom churum miryun hada.* {Stupid as a bear.} **No.** *Dum som en geit.* {Dumb as a goat.}

**Easy as falling off a log.** Equiv.: **Ko.** *Nuesu ddug muggi gatda.* {As easy as eating rice cake while lying on one's back.} *Siggun jug muggi gatchi shibda.* {As easy as eating cooled-down soup.}
**Easy as (apple) pie.** Equiv.: **Ko.** *Nuesu ddug muggi gatda.* {Easy as eating rice cakes while lying on one's back.}
**Effective as cupping the dead.** Useless. ("Cupping" is an archaic medical practice.) (=) *One cannot breathe life into a corpse.* Equiv.: **Ar.** *El-ifat matt.* {What is dead is dead.}

**Fair as fair can be.**
**Faithful as a dog.**
**Familiar as a popular song.**
**Far as the eye can see.**
**Fast as lightning.** Equiv.: **Ge.** *Schnell wie ein geölter Blitz.* {Fast as greased lightning.} *Schnell wie der Wind.* {Fast as the wind.}
**Fat as a pig.** Equiv.: **Fr.** *Gras comme une caille.* {Fat as a quail.} *Gras comme un chanoine.* {Fat as a cannon.}
**Fickle as the weather.** Equiv.:

**Ja.** *Onnagokoroto akinosora.* {Changeable as a woman's heart and the sky of autumn.} **Ko.** *Ggulnun jug churum byundug i shimhada.* {Fickle as boiling porridge.}

**Firm like a rock.**

**Fish out of water, Like a.** Being away from one's natural surroundings; clumsy, inept and unable to cope. Equiv.: **It.** *Essere come un pesce fuor d'acqua.* {To be like a fish out of water.} **Sp.** *Una gallina en corral ajeno.* {A hen in a foreign coop.}

**Flat as a pancake.** (=) *Flat as a flounder.*

**Flimsy as gossamer.**

**Free as a bird.** (=) *Free as an eagle. Free as the breeze.*

**Fresh as a daisy.** (=) *Fresh as a flower.* Equiv.: **Fr.** *Frais comme une rose.* {Fresh as a rose.} *Frais comme la rosée.* {Fresh as the dew.} **Sp.** *Fresco como una lechuga.* {Fresh as a lettuce.}

**Fit as a fiddle.** In good health and spirits.

**Gentle as a turtle dove.**

**Gloomy as night.**

**Good as gold.** Equiv.: **Fr.** *Bon comme le pain.* {Good as bread.}

**Good as new.**

**Graceful as a fawn.**

**Green as grass.** Equiv.: **Ge.** *Grün wie Gras.*

**Grim as death.**

**Growing like a weed.**

**Happy as a lark.** (=) *Happy as the day is long. Happy as a pig in shit (muck).* Equiv.: **Fr.** *Heureux comme un roi.* {Happy as a king.} *Heureux comme un pape.* {Happy as a Pope.} **Ko.** *Bai burun dwaiji churum pun hada.* {Happy as a pig with a full stomach.}

**Hard as flint.** (=) *Hard as a rock (granite; nails).* Equiv.: **Fr.** *Dur comme pierre.* {Hard as a stone.} **Ge.** *Hart wie Kruppstahl.* {Hard as Krupp steel.} **Ko.** *Shae churum yumulda.* {Hard as iron.} **Sp.** *Duro como piedra.* {Hard as a rock.}

**Hard to find as a needle in a haystack.**

**Heavy as lead.** Equiv.: **Ko.** *Taisan churum yumulda.* {Heavy as a Thai mountain in China.}

**Helpless as a baby.**

**High as a kite.** (=) *High as an elephant's eye.* Equiv.: **Sp.** *Alto como las nubes.* {High as the clouds.}

**Head over heels in love.**

**Honest as the day is long.**

**Hot as hell (Hades).**

**Hungry as a horse.** (=) *Hungry as a wolf.* Equiv.: **Ge.** *Hungrig wie ein Bär.* {Hungry as a bear.}

**Impatient as a lover.** Equiv.: **Ko.** *Dduguun nambi wui e itnun*

*gaimi churum sunggub hada.*
{Impatient as an ant on a hot
pan.}
**Innocent as a lamb.**

**Kind as Santa Claus.** Equiv.:
**No.** *Snill som et lam.* {Kind as
a lamb.}

**Light as a feather.** (=) *Light
as air.* Equiv.: **Ko.** *Som gatchi-
gaigubda.* {Light as cotton.}
**Like two peas in a pod.**
Equiv.: **Fr.** *Comme deux
gouttes d'eau.* {Like two drops
of water.}
**Limp as a rag.** Equiv.: **Ja.**
*Kurageno youni kunya-kunya.*
{Limp as a jellyfish.}
**Loathsome as a toad.**
**Lonely as a cloud.**
**Loud as thunder.** Equiv.: **Ko.**
*Gijug ul muggun nom churum
ddudulsug hada.* {Loud as a
man who ate a train horn.}
**Low as a snake's belly.**

**Mad as a hatter.**
**Meek as a lamb.**
**More trouble than a barrel
of monkeys.**
**Musical as rain on the roof.**
**Mysterious as the (a) sphinx.**

**Naked as a babe.** Equiv.: **Fr.**
*Nu comme un ver.* {Naked as a
worm.}
**Narrow as an arrow.**
**Neat as a pin.**
**Nervous as a kitten (cat).**

**Numberless as the dead.**

**Old as Methuselah.** (=) *Old
as the hills.* Equiv.: **Fr.** *Vieux
comme le monde.* {Old as the
world.} **Sp.** *Mas viejo que Ma-
tusalén.* {Older than Methuselah.}
**Opposite as night and day.**

**Pale as parchment.**
**Pitch black.** Equiv.: **No.** *Bekk
moerkt.* {Dark as a brook.}
**Placid as a mill (duck) pond.**
**Plain as the nose on one's
face.** (=) *Clear as glass.*
Equiv.: **No.** *Klart som dagen.*
{Clear as the day.}
**Plump as a pudding.**
**Poor as a church mouse.**
Equiv.: **Ge.** *Arm wie eine Kir-
chenmaus.*
**Pretty as a picture.**
**Proud as a peacock.** Equiv.:
**Fr.** *Fier comme un âne qui a un
bât neuf.* {Proud as a donkey
with a new packsaddle.} *Fier
comme un pet.* {Proud as a
fart.}
**Pure as the driven snow.** (=)
*Pure as mountain dew.* Equiv.:
**Ko.** *Sujung churum margda.*
{Pure as a crystal.}
**Queer as a three-dollar bill.**
(=) **Brit.** *Queer as a three-
pound note.*
**Quick as you can say "Jack
Robinson."** (=) **Brit.** *Quick
as you can say knife. Quick as a
bunny. Quick as a wink.*
Equiv.: **Fr.** *Pressé comme un*

*lavament.* {As quickly as an enema.} **Ko.** *Bungaibul churum bbaruda.* {Quick as lightning.} *Bungaibul e kong gguemugdushi bbaruda.* {Quick as frying beans using a thunderbolt.}

**Quiet as the grave.** (=) *Quiet as a mouse.* Equiv.: **Ko.** *Juggun jui churum joyong hada.* {Quiet as a dead mouse.}

**Rare as a day in June.** Equiv.: **Ko.** *Gamulum e kong churum dumuda.* {Rare as a bean in a drought.}

**Red as a rose.** (=) *Red as a cherry. Red as a ruby.*

**Rich as Croesus.** Equiv.: **Ge.** *Reich wie ein König.* {Rich as a king.}

**Right as rain.**

**Scarce as hens' teeth.**

**Sharp (keen) as a razor.**

**Shooting fish in a barrel, Like.** Extremely easy.

**Sick as a dog.**

**Silent as a tomb.** (=) *Silent as the sphinx.* Equiv.: **No.** *Stum som en østers.* {Silent as a clam.}

**Simple as ABC.** (=) *Easy as pie.* Equiv.: **Ko.** *Sonbadag jechida sipi shibda.* {Easy as turning your palm.}

**Sky high.**

**Sleep like a log.** (=) *Sleep like a baby. Sleep like a top.* Equiv.: **Fr.** *Dormir comme un sabot.* {Sleep like a clog (wooden shoe)} *Dormir du*

*sommeil du juste.* {Sleep the sleep of the Just.} **Ko.** *Dweiji churum janda.* {Sleep like a pig.}

**Slender as a reed.** (=) *Thin as a skeleton. Thin as a bean-pole.* **Ko.** *Gaimi huri churum malshin hada.* {Slender as an ant's waist.}

**Slick as a whistle.** (=) *Slick as greased lightning.*

**Slower than molasses.** Equiv.: **Fr.** *Lent comme un escargot.* {Slow as a snail.} **Ko.** *Gum-baingyi churum nurida.* {Slow as a worm.}

**Sly as a fox.** Equiv.: **No.** *Slu som en rev.* {Sly as a fox.}

**Smart as a whip.**

**Smooth as a baby's bottom.** (=) *Smooth as glass. Smooth as silk. Smooth as a billiard ball.* Equiv.: **Ko.** *Huin jinju churum banjil hada.* {Smooth as a white pearl.}

**Snug as a bug in a rug.**

**Sober (solemn) as a judge.**

**Soft as putty.** (=) *Soft as mush. Soft as velvet. Soft as a pillow. Soft like a summer night.* Equiv.: **Ja.** *Tofuno youni yawa- rakai.* {Soft as tofu.) **Ko.** *Tul churum bodurabda.* {Soft as a feather.}

**Solid as the rock of Gibraltar.**

**Sound as a dollar.**

**Spineless as a jellyfish.** Equiv.: **Ko.** *Nagji churum jutdai ga upda.* {Spineless as an octopus.}

**Stark naked.**
**Stately as an oak (pine).**
**Steady as a rock.**
**Stealthy as a cat.**
**Stiff as a board.** (=) *Stiff as a ramrod.* Equiv.: **Sp.** *Tieso como un muerto.* {Stiff as a corpse.}
**Straight as an arrow.**
**Strong as Hercules.** (=) *Strong as Samson. Strong as an ox.* Equiv.: **Ge.** *Stark wie ein Bär.* {Strong as a bear.}
**Stubborn (obstinate) as a mule.** Equiv.: **Ko.** *Hwangso churum gojibjengyi da.* {Stubborn as an ox.}
**Sure as death (and taxes).** (=) *Sure as God's in heaven. Sure as the night succeeds the day. Sure as shootin'.* Equiv.: **Ko.** *Bul bodusi tulim upda.* {As certain as fire.} **Sp.** *Tan seguro como que me llamo...* {Sure as my name is...}
**Sweet as honey.** (=) *Sweet as sugar. Sweet as honeysuckle.*
**Swift as the wind.** (=) *Swift as light. Swift as lightning.*

**Taking candy from a baby, Like.** Effortless; easy.
**Tall as a Maypole.**
**Taut as a fiddle string.**
**There is no tomorrow, Like (as if).** Doing something hurriedly as if today were the last opportunity. Equiv.: **Sp.** *Como si fuera el fin del mondo.* {As if the world were ending.}

**Thick as thieves.** (=) *Thick as pea soup.* Equiv.: **No.** *Å henge sammen som erteris.* {Sticking together like pea sticks.}
**Thick as a plank.**
**Thin as a rail.** (=) *Thin as a toothpick. Thin as a reed. Thin as a skeleton.* Equiv.: **Fr.** *Maigre comme un clou.* {Thin as a nail.} **Ko.** *Judgarag churum yabda.* {Thin as a chopstick.} *Sotul gatchi yabda.* {Thin as cow fur.}
**Thirsty as a sponge.** (=) *Thirsty as a fish.*
**Tight as a drum (drumhead).**
**Timid as a mouse.**
**Tired as a dog.** (=) *Tired as the Dickens.* Equiv.: **Ko.** *Sugurujin kimchi churum pigon hada.* {Tired as drooping kimchi.}
**Tough as leather (shoe leather).** (=) *Tough as nails.* **Ko.** *So himjul gatchi jjilgida.* {Tough as a cow's muscle.}
**Trackless as the desert.**
**Transparent (clear) as glass.**
**Trapped like a rat.**
**True as holy writ.** (=) *True as the Gospel.*
**True blue.**
**Two peas in a pod, Like.** Identical; cozy.

**Ugly as sin.** (=) *Ugly as a scare-crow.* Equiv.: **Fr.** *Laid comme un pou.* {Ugly as a louse.} **Ko.** *Hobag gatchi motnatda.* {Ugly as a squash.}
**Unattractive as a gargoyle.**

Uncertain as the weather.
Unexpected as chastity in a pick-up bar. (=) *Unexpected as a fifth ace in a deck of cards.*
Unfeeling as cold marble.
Unhappy as King Lear.
Unkind as fate.
Unreal as a dream.
Unwelcome as snow in summer.
Unyielding as a rock.
Useless as a gun without a trigger. Equiv.: **Ja.** *Nekoni koban.* {Useless as money to a cat.} *Butani shinju.* {Useless as pearls to a swine.} *Umani nen-butsu.* {Useless as a Bhuddist invocation for a horse.}

Vague as a shadow.

Vain as a peacock.
Vast as a cathedral.

Warm as toast.
Wary as a fox.
Weak as a kitten.
Welcome as the flowers that bloom in the spring.
Wet as a drowned rat. Equiv.: **No.** *Våt som en drukna katt.* {Wet as a drowned cat.}
White as a sheet. Equiv.: **Ge.** *Weiß wie ein Leintuch.* {White as a sheet.} **Ko.** *Nari churum huida.* {White as a lily.} **Sp.** *Blanco como la nieve.* {White as snow.}
Wise as (King) Solomon.
Work like a horse. (=) *Work like a dog. Work like a Turk.*

**Note:** Some similes are only used in a negative sense, i.e., sardonically or sarcastically. They consequently mean the opposite of the condition being described. There are only a few of these. *As clear as mud*, for example, means the opposite of clear, namely murky or opaque. *As funny as a crutch (as a wooden leg)* clearly indicates that something is not funny at all, since crutches are used by the disabled and unfortunate. The meanings of *As useful as a screen door in a submarine* or *As welcome as water in a leaking ship* are obvious. Similarly contrary expressions of course exist in other languages. A Japanese example is *Natsuno Kosode*, which literally translates as "long sleeves in summer." A better translation in simile form would be *As seasonable as snow in summer.*

### LETTER WORDS AND NUMBER WORDS

"Letter Words" are words made up of the pronunciation of individual letters. Typical examples are SA for **essay** and NME for **enemy.** Letter words may consist of one to five letters. The most frequently found letter words contain two letters, with the existing number of words decreasing as the number of letters expands. We have found 14 single letter words, 29 double letter words, 11 consisting of three letters, 6 with four and only one with five letters. The longest letter word we have found is XPDNC for **expediency.**

Number words contain numbers as well as letters, with the pronunciation of the numbers used instead of their numerical value. Thus the number 1 can be read as **won;** 2 can be used for **to** or **too;** the number 4 as **for;** and 8 read as **ate.** Or, the sound of any number can be used as a word building block when combined with letter sounds. In word games, numbers are always mixed with letters, resulting in such letter-number words as K9 for **canine** and 10NC for **tenancy.**

The longest number word we have found is **(NOT)2B4GO10** (not) to be forgotten.

The tables below combine letter words and letter-number words, thus increasing the total in each category.

### LETTER/NUMBER WORD GLOSSARY

**B** be or bee; **B4** before; **BB** bees; **C** see; **CC** sees; **CD** seedy; **CDR** seedier; **CU** see you; **D** Dee; **DV8** deviate; **EZ** easy; **G** gee!; **GG** Gigi; **IC** icy or I see; **ICY** I see why; **II** aye, aye; **IV** Ivy; **J** Jay or jay; **JJ** jays; **K** Kaye; **LEV8** alleviate; **LC** Elsie; **NTT** entity; **NV** envy; **NRG** energy; **R** are; **RT** Arty; **U** you; **Y** why; **10NC** tenancy; **4C** foresee

# Chapter Five

# AMERICAN SLANG AND COLLOQUIALISMS

There are just too many *cotton pickin'* slang and colloquial expressions in the **American Language**. Several thick tomes covering these expressions exist. One recent set is planned for three volumes of over 1,000 pages each. The first two (A - G and H - O) are already in print, with the third volume about to be published. None of these slang "dictionaries" is complete, and all are to some degree out-of-date as soon as they are published.

We felt, however, that this compendium would be incomplete without some coverage of slang. A compromise was reached. While this chapter makes no attempt to cover all slang and colloquial expressions—not even all of the most important or frequently used ones—we chose to cover what we consider the most representative areas of the mainstream of American culture and activities: The Animal Kingdom, Arts and Entertainment, Business and Industry, Food and Drink, Games and Sports, the Human Body, Law, Medicine, the Military, Senses and Feelings, and Transportation. A few examples are found in more than one category. While most of these expressions are still used in the area of their origin, this chapter will concentrate only on how they are used in other fields. Some have a standard English meaning as well as a slang meaning; only the slang definitions will be given here.

Slang is a difficult term to define. It is definitely nonstandard vocabulary. It is often ephemeral, its popularity vanishing after a few years of use. Some slang terms, however, are perennial. Their use diminishes over a period of time and then blooms again. Slang is inclined to be salty or pungent, characterized by spontaneity and raciness. In short, its meaning, like love, is difficult to pin down, but you know it when you see it.

Colloquialism or colloquial expressions also fail to fit into a narrow definition. They are always informal. They are more likely to be found (at least originally) in conversation rather than in writing. Their written usage is limited to newspapers and certain types of fiction, rather than scholarly or technical writing. Unfortunately, this description *skirts* the definition rather than defining it precisely.

There is often a fine line between slang and colloquialisms. In fact, many words or expressions start as slang, then become colloquial, and finally (sometimes) become part of standard English. In any case, as you will see in this chapter, both slang expressions and colloquialisms share one characteristic: They are fun. For example, the terms "A.W.O.L." and "flak" originated in the military but are more frequently used today for non-military areas. A student may be A.W.O.L. (Absent Without Official Leave) from his class. When he finally does show up, his teacher may give him plenty of flak (criticism, trouble, or problems). A doctor applies a Band-Aid to a patient. The same doctor may be seriously in debt, and to take the pressure off, he borrows $1,000 as a Band-Aid (a temporary remedy) to cover his interest payment. The same is true for many (but not all) other expressions in this chapter. They originated in specific activities or with certain organizations, but their uses today are frequently of a general nature or have at least partially shifted to a different activity.

The abbreviations used in this chapter are identical to those used in earlier chapters on proverbs and similes. Where a slang term originated from games or sports, even if now used for other purposes or even for another sport, the specific originating game or sporting event is given in parentheses, e.g. (Poker) and (Baseball).

By its very nature, slang can be pungent and earthy. Many words originally referring to food or animals have slang parallels in sexual activities of various kinds. There are numerous slang names for prostitutes, and a variety of expressions for narcotics and drug users. Expressions of military origin are full of four-letter words. Many terms used to describe people have derogatory connotations. These are marked (derog) to indicate that care should be exercised in using these terms. For recognition purposes, however, they must become part of your passive vocabulary. If some readers find any terms offensive, the author apologizes, but still insists that a list of expurgated slang terms defeats the purpose of a chapter such as this.

## ANIMAL KINGDOM

**alligator** (n) An assertive person; flashy dresser.

**ants in the pants** (n phr) Restless; anxious.

**antsy** (adj) Restless; jittery.

**ape** (v) To imitate someone's behavior, often making fun of it.

**apeshit** (adj) Obsessed; crazy.

**beach bunny** (n) An attractive girl who hangs out with surfers.

**bear** (n) A pessimist; someone with a difficult or aggressive personality; a pessimistic stock investor; a capsule for narcotics.

**bearish** (adj) Pessimistic about the outcome of any enterprise.

**beat a dead horse** (v phr) To continue arguing or discussing after a matter has been settled.

**beaver** (n) The female genital area.

**bee** (n) A small narcotics measurement.

**bee in one's bonnet** (n phr) Bizarre notion; obsession.

**beeswax** (n) Business; concern.

**bird** (n) An airplane; a girl (in UK); derogatory gesture or sound.

**birdbrain** (n) Idiot.

**bird circuit** (n) Tour of gay bars.

**bird dog** (n) Someone who looks for something to blame someone else for; anyone who follows the lead of another.

**bird dog** (v) To follow closely on someone else's heels.

**bird farm** (n) An aircraft carrier.

**birds, (strictly) for the** (adj phr) Unacceptable; unbelievable; improbable.

**bitch** (n) An unpleasant or remarkable event; an ill-tempered woman.

**bitch** (v) To complain incessantly.

**booby hatch** (n) Mental hospital.

**buck** (n) One dollar.

**buck for** (v phr) To work hard (for a promotion, etc.).

**buck up** (v phr) To cheer up.

**buck naked** (adj) Stark naked.

**buffalo** (v) To intimidate; bamboozle.

**bug** (n) A small defect, often difficult to find; a small vehicle; a joker; an enthusiast.

**bug** (v) To bother or pester someone; to eavesdrop using hidden microphones.

**bughouse** (n) Mental hospital.

**Bug off!** (v phr) Go away; get out of here.

**bull** (n) Nonsense; lies.

**bulldoze** (v) To force through an opinion or policy.

**bulldyke** (n) A lesbian taking the male role.

**bullfeathers** (phr) An expression of disbelief.

**bullhorn** (n) Hand-held loudspeaker.

**bullish** (adj) Optimistic about the stock market or about any other enterprise.

**bullpen** (n) An area where baseball pitchers warm up; any reserve of workers.

**bullshit** (n) Nonsense; rubbish. (Also **B.S.**)

**bunny-fuck** (n) Quick sex.

**calf love** (n)  Preadolescent or adolescent love.

**canary** (n)  A singer; an informer; a young girl.

**can of worms** (n)  Potential trouble.

**capon** (n)  An inept person; a bungler.

**cash cow** (n)  A source of seemingly endless funds.

**cat (cool cat)** (n)  A "cool" individual; one who stays calm under all circumstances.

**catbird seat, the** (n)  A favorable position; success; wealth.

**cat fight** (n)  An out-of-control brawl among women.

**cathouse** (n)  A house of prostitution.

**cat out of the bag, to let the** (v phr)  To reveal a secret; to betray a confidence.

**catspaw** (n)  A dupe.

**catch flies, to** (v phr)  To yawn.

**catty** (adj)  Spiteful.

**Charlie horse** (n)  Calf-muscle cramp.

**chauvinist pig, male** (n phr)  A male who treats women as, or considers them to be, inferior.

**chick** (n)  Any young, attractive girl.

**chicken** (n, adj)  Coward(ly); a young boy partner for an adult homosexual.

**chicken feed** (n)  Small change; of low importance.

**chickenhearted** (adj)  Cowardly; soft and sentimental.

**chicken livered** (adj)  Cowardly.

**chicken out** (v phr)  To become scared and decide not to go through with something.

**chickenshit** (adj)  Dictatorial adherence to details, rules, discipline.

**chicken switch (button)** (n phr)  Abort button for in-flight missile.

**chicken tracks** (n)  Illegible handwriting.

**chow hound** (n)  A hearty eater; a glutton.

**clam up** (v phr)  To withdraw into oneself; to stop speaking suddenly. **clothes horse** (n phr)  Someone overly dedicated to dress and style.

**cock-and-bull story** (n phr)  A lie; a fable; an unbelievable story.

**cockeyed** (adj)  Drunk; crazy; confused; chaotic.

**cocksucker** (n)  A despicable, low person.

**cocksman** (n)  A man who sleeps with many women and boasts about it.

**cold fish** (n)  An unemotional person.

**cold turkey** (adv phr)  To try to break a habit or addiction in one motion rather than gradually.

**cook one's goose** (v phr)  To cause someone's downfall.

**coop** (v)  To take a nap in a police car while on duty.

**copycat** (n)  Someone who imitates or mimics another's actions.

**cowhide** (n)  A baseball.

**cow juice** (n)  Milk.

**crab** (n)  A consistent complainer.

**crab** (v)  To complain repeatedly; to be cross.

**crabs** (n)  Pubic lice.

**crow, to eat** (v phr)  To display humility; to be humiliated.

**cry wolf** (v phr)  To give a false alarm.

**cub** (n) An inexperienced person; a beginner.

**cuckoo** (adj) Crazy; eccentric.

**culture vulture** (n phr) Someone to whom cultural activities become a fetish; overactive culture seeker.

**dark horse** (n phr) An unlikely winner; a long shot.

**day the eagle (screams) shits, the** (n phr) Pay day.

**dead duck** (n phr) A hopeless loser or situation; a lost cause.

**dead horse** (n phr) An issue or situation which cannot be rectified or changed.

**desert rat** (n phr) An old, grizzled prospector or hermit.

**dinosaur** (n) An obsolete object, person or activity.

**dodo** (n) A stupid person.

**dog** (n) An unattractive woman; a prospective loser.

**dog-and-pony show (act)** (n phr) An elaborate, showy presentation or display.

**dog collar** (n) A collar closing in the back, worn by the clergy.

**dog days** (n phr) Hot, humid, enervating days.

**dogeared** (adj) Folded down at the corner; worn or damaged.

**dog(gy) fashion (style)** (n phr) Sexual intercourse entering the vagina from behind.

**dogfight** (n) An aerial battle between fighter planes.

**doggone** (adj) Darned; damned; a mild expression of irritation.

**doghouse, in the** (phr) In disfavor or disgrace.

**dog, to put on the** (v phr) To flaunt one's wealth or position; to dress or act in an excessive manner.

**dog tags** (n) Identification tags worn by soldiers in battle.

**dogs, to go to the** (v phr) To become a failure; to decline.

**doggy bag** (n) A bag for taking leftovers home from a restaurant.

**donkey** (n) A stupid person.

**donkey roast** (n) A large, noisy party.

**dove** (n) A non-belligerent person; one dedicated to peace.

**duck** (n) A peculiar or eccentric person.

**duck soup** (n) A very easy task.

**dumb bunny** (n phr) Someone who is mildly stupid.

**dumb cluck** (n phr) A stupid person.

**eager beaver** (n phr) One overly anxious to perform a task.

**eagle** (n) A topnotch pilot.

**eagle eyed** (adj) Being very observant; not missing anything.

**early bird** (n phr) One who always arrives or starts the day early.

**fast buck** (n phr) Money made quickly, perhaps unscrupulously.

**fat cat** (n) Someone who is rich, famous, living in luxury.

**feather one's nest** (v phr) To increase one's financial base; to take an unfair share, often illegally.

**filly** (n) A young woman.

**fish** (n) An easily victimized person; a heterosexual woman.

**fish eye** (n) An expressionless glance; a questioning stare.

**fishbowl** (n)  Exposed surroundings where everyone can watch; no privacy.

**fishtail** (v)  To drive a vehicle in a way that makes the rear end waver back and forth.

**fish (story) tale** (n)  A story of dubious validity.

**fishwife** (n)  A gossipy, difficult woman.

**flea** (n)  Something small but annoying; an insignificant person.

**flea bag (trap)** (n)  A shabby and run-down room (usually a hotel room).

**flea in one's ear, to have a** (v phr)  To be so disturbed that some thought or action is required.

**fleece** (v)  To swindle; to deprive someone of money or assets.

**flock** (n)  A large number.

**fly** (n)  A baseball hit which rises high in the air.

**fly** (adj)  Stylish and attractive.

**fly** (v)  To be high on drugs or alcohol.

**fly chaser** (n phr)  A baseball outfielder.

**fly, on the** (adv phr)  Doing something while on the way to somewhere.

**fly the coop** (v phr)  To escape.

**fly trap** (n)  One's mouth.

**fox** (n)  Someone very sly or clever; an attractive, desirable girl.

**fox (outfox)** (v)  To outwit.

**foxhole** (n)  A trench where soldiers stay concealed during a battle; any hiding place.

**foxy** (adj)  Stylish, attractive, sexy; clever or sly.

**'fraidy cat** (n)  A shy or timid person, often a child.

**Frog** (n)  A Frenchman. (derog.)

**frogman** (n)  A scuba diver; an underwater specialist (particularly in the military).

**frogskin** (n)  A one-dollar bill.

**frog-sticker** (n)  A pocket knife.

**full of bull** (phr)  Grossly misinformed.

**get one's goat** (v phr)  To get a rise out of someone; to make a person lose control.

**gills, green around the** (adj phr)  Showing outward signs of nausea or gastric upset.

**give (flip) someone the bird** (v phr)  To raise the middle finger in a gesture of defiance; to make a farting noise with lips and tongue.

**go ape** (v phr)  To become frenzied; uncontrolled.

**goldfish bowl, in a** (phr)  Living with no privacy.

**goose** (n)  A silly person.

**goose** (v)  To poke someone between the buttocks to make them jump.

**goose bumps** (n phr)  Momentary roughness of the skin caused by fear or cold.

**goose egg** (n)  A zero.

**goose pimples** (n phr)  See goose bumps

**goose step** (n phr)  A military parade step carried out without bending the knee.

**gopher (gofer)** (n)  An errand boy or girl.

**gorilla** (n)  A muscular hoodlum; a strongman.

**grasshopper** (n)  A crop duster.

**graze** (v)  To eat a meal.

**greasemonkey** (n) Auto mechanic; garage attendant.

**groundhog** (n) An unwilling pilot.

**grouse** (v) To complain; to whine.

**gull** (v) To deceive, cheat, or dupe.

**guttersnipe** (n) A bum; shoplifter; thief.

**hair of the dog that bit you** (n phr) A drink of what gave you a hangover; a cure with more of that which caused the problem.

**hawk** (n) A militant, feisty, belligerent individual.

**hawk** (v) To sell something.

**have a cow** (v phr) To get upset.

**have kittens** (v phr) To be openly nervous.

**hellcat** (n) A spirited, reckless uncontrollable woman.

**hen** (n) A woman.

**hen coop** (n) Women's dorm in a co-educational school.

**hen party** (n) A party or gathering of women only; a gossip session.

**henpecked** (adj) Man dominated by a woman.

**high horse, get on one's** (v phr) To assume an air of superiority.

**high on the hog** (adv phr) Living with the best of everything.

**hip chick** (n) A young woman who is up-to-date with current trends.

**hippo (hippopotamus)** (n) A fat person. (derog.)

**hog** (n) A selfish, greedy person; a Harley-Davidson motorcycle.

**hog** (v) To try to have everything for oneself.

**hogwash** (n) Nonsense.

**hog-wild** (adj) Excited; temporarily irrational; uncontrollable.

**Holy cow!** (phr) An expression of astonishment.

**horse** (n) Heroin; a prison guard who is paid to smuggle items in or out for prisoners.

**horse and buggy, that went out with the** (phr) Old-fashioned; obsolete.

**horse around** (v phr) To play around; to act foolishly.

**horsehide** (n) A baseball.

**horseshit** (n) Nonsense; lies.

**horse's ass** (n) A fool; idiot; know-nothing.

**horse's mouth** (n) Direct source of information.

**Horsefeathers!** (phr) An expression of disbelief.

**hound** (v) To pester; to pursue relentlessly.

**hound** (n) Enthusiast; overeager (as in "publicity-hound.")

**hung like a horse** (adj phr) Having extra large male genitals.

**iron horse** (n) A military tank; a railway locomotive; a tractor.

**jackass (ass)** (n) An ignorant person; a real fool.

**Jane Crow** (adj) Laws discriminating against women.

**Jim Crow** (adj) Laws discriminating against African-Americans.

**kangaroo court** (n) A trial deliberately designed to convict, regardless of the evidence.

**kid** (n) A child.

**kid** (v) To make a joke of; to tease.

**lamb** (n) An easy-going type; an

innocent; one easily deceived.

**lame duck** (n) A politician who has lost an election, but is still hanging on until the end of his term; a politician who cannot run again.

**leech** (n) A parasite; a hanger-on.

**legal beagle** (n) An astute and successful lawyer.

**legal eagle** (n) A cunning attorney.

**litterbug** (n) Someone who throws trash on the street.

**loaded for bear** (adj phr) Ready for a fight.

**loan shark** (n) One who lends money at exorbitant interest rates with extreme penalties for nonpayment, usually criminal.

**lock horns** (v) To engage in a struggle.

**lone wolf** (n) Antisocial; someone who keeps to himself.

**Longhorn** (n) A Texan.

**loon** (n) A crazy person.

**loose as a goose** (adj phr) Relaxed; without a care.

**lounge lizard** (n) A gigolo, usually found stalking hotel lobbies.

**louse** (n) A disliked individual; one with no ethics.

**louse up** (v phr) To spoil; ruin; botch.

**lousy** (adj) Very bad.

**lousy with** (adv) Full of; infested with.

**lovebird** (n) A lover.

**lovey-dovey** (adj) Amorous; affectionate.

**mad as a wet hen** (adj phr) Extremely angry.

**Mickey Mouse** (adj) Unprofes-sional; phony; cheap; inferior; shoddy; an easy task.

**Mickey Mouse** (v) To fool around; to waste time.

**mole** (n) An infiltrator.

**monkey act** (n) A sensational show biz performance.

**monkey around** (v phr) To fool around.

**monkey business** (n) Unethical acts; extramarital sexual activity.

**monkey on one's back** (n phr) Drug addiction.

**monkey suit** (n) A formal suit with tailcoat.

**monkeyshines** (n) Trifling, foolish conduct; endearing pranks.

**mountain canary** (n) Burro.

**mountain oysters** (n) Sheep's testicles.

**mouse** (n) A black eye.

**mule** (n) A stubborn person; a narcotics smuggler.

**nag** (n) A beat-up old horse; a contentious woman.

**nitpicker** (n) One overly concerned with minute details; a pedant.

**no flies on, have** (v phr) To have no impediments.

**old goat** (n) An elderly person, usually disliked; an elderly lecher.

**one-horse town** (n phr) A small, rural, unexciting village.

**ostrich** (n) One who denies reality.

**owl** (n) A night person.

**ox** (n) A dumb, usually physically powerful, person.

**packrat** (n) One who never discards anything.

**panther** (n) Cheap liquor (see *panther sweat* below).

**panther sweat (piss)** (n) Raw whiskey.

**paper tiger** (n) Someone or something that appears threatening but lacks substance.

**parlor snake** (n) A would-be seducer.

**paw** (v) To manhandle.

**pecking order** (n) Order of rank or importance.

**pelican** (n) A prostitute.

**penguin** (n) A nun; someone who works for or serves in the Air Force but doesn't fly.

**pet peeve** (n) Major or primary dislike.

**pig** (n) A police officer; a sloppy person; an ugly woman; a promiscuous woman; a selfish or greedy person.

**pig boat** (n) Submarine.

**pig-headed** (adj) Stubborn.

**pig in a poke** (n phr) An unknown product; something accepted sight unseen.

**pig meat** (n) A promiscuous woman.

**pig out** (v) To overindulge in food or anything else.

**piggyback** (v) To attach something to something else, so that the first item may support the second.

**pigpen** (n) A dirty, untidy, disorderly person or room.

**pigskin** (n) A football.

**pigsticker** (n) Bayonet.

**pig sweat** (n) Beer; raw whiskey.

**pig's eye, in a** (phr) An expression of extreme doubt.

**pigeon** (n) An easy mark; an apparent loser.

**pony** (n) A translation book used to cheat in a language class; any unethical aid.

**pony up** (v) To make a payment; to pay up.

**poor fish** (n) Human being with problems.

**porcupine** (n) Frayed wire rope or cable.

**prairie oysters** (n) Bull's testicles.

**pup** (n) Someone young and inexperienced.

**pup tent** (n) A small tent large enough for one or two persons.

**pups, to have** (v phr) To have conniptions; to have kittens; to be extremely nervous.

**puppy-dog feet** (n) The club suit in cards.

**puppy love** (n) Pre-adolescent love.

**puss** (n) Face.

**pussy** (n) Female genitalia; a cowardly man.

**pussycat** (n) A sweet, agreeable, easy-going person.

**pussy whipped** (adj) Man dominated by a woman.

**pussyfoot** (v) To hesitate; to treat gingerly.

**quail** (n) Sexually attractive girl.

**quail roost** (n) Women's dormitory.

**rabbit** (n) A shy, timid, or cowardly person; someone very active sexually.

**rabbit food** (n) Salad; raw vegetables.

**railbird** (n) Horse-racing enthusiast.

**raining cats and dogs** (phr) Raining heavily.

**rat** (n) A despised, totally untrustworthy person; an informer or tattletale.

**rat** (n) (*Preceded by a location*) A frequenter of; e.g. mall rat, alley rat.

**rat (on)** (v) To tell on, betray.

**rat-faced** (adj) Sneaky; underhand.

**rat fink** (n) Treacherous, despicable, unpleasant person.

**rat-fuck** (n) Socially and morally unstable person.

**rat race** (n) Life dedicated to action without any real goals.

**Rats!** (phr) An expression of disgust or disappointment.

**rat's ass, don't give a** (v phr) To have no interest in.

**roach** (n) A marijuana cigarette butt; an unattractive, unescorted girl.

**road hog** (n) Driver who occupies more than his fair share of the road.

**road monkey** (n) Member of a road repair crew.

**round robin** (n) A match where several teams play one another consecutively.

**ruptured duck** (n) An honorable military discharge; the pin indicating such a discharge.

**sea dog** (n) An experienced sailor; a merchant seaman.

**see a man about a dog** (v phr) To go to the bathroom.

**see snakes** (v) To be drunk.

**shark** (n) Expert who hides his talents so he can make money from dupes; anyone who operates in a predatory manner.

**sheep dip** (n) Cheap, inferior liquor.

**sheepskin** (n) A diploma.

**shit for the birds** (n phr) Nonsense; lies; exaggerations.

**shoot the bull** (v phr) To chatter; gossip.

**shorthorn** (n) A novice; a tenderfoot.

**shrew** (n) An argumentative, vicious woman.

**sidewinder** (n) A hard swinging blow from a fist; a feisty tough man.

**sitting duck** (n) An easy target.

**skunk** (n) An unpleasant or nasty person; unidentified object on a radar screen.

**skunk** (v) To win a game before the opponent has even scored.

**slick chick** (n) A lively or sophisticated girl; well-dressed, hip, sexy woman.

**slippery as an eel** (adj phr) Elusive; hard to pin down.

**slug** (n) A low-down person; a disliked person; a bullet; a feature-less, counterfeit coin.

**Smokey Bear** (n) A highway patrolman.

**sowbelly** (n) Bacon; salt pork.

**snake** (n) Unpleasant, cheap, despicable person; male deceiver or seducer.

**snake-eyes** (n) The number "2" in a dice game; a total loss.

**snipe hunting** (n) A fool's errand.

**snowbird** (n) A Florida migratory worker; a Northerner who winters in Florida.

**S.O.B. (son of a bitch)** (n)   A really lousy, bad, unethical person.

**social butterfly** (n phr) Someone who is very active socially.

**Sonofabitch!** (phr) An expression of frustration.

**songbird** (n) A singer.

**sourpuss** (n) A sour-faced, angry-looking person.

**southpaw** (n)   A left-handed person; someone whose actions are difficult to predict.

**sparrow grass** (n) Asparagus.

**split beaver** (n) Woman's exposed genitalia when she sits with her legs apart.

**sponge** (n) A parasite; freeloader; moocher.

**sponge** (v)  To live off others; to scrounge.

**squirrel** (n)   A crazy person; a hoarder.

**squirrel** (v)  To hoard; store up.

**stag** (n)  One who attends a social event without a partner.

**stag party** (n) A males-only gathering. (see *hen party)*

**stallion** (n) Stud; sexually powerful man.

**stool pigeon** (n)  An informer.

**Suffering catfish!** (interj) Expression of surprise and annoyance.

**swan song** (n) A farewell effort.

**take a gander** (v phr)  To take a look.

**talk turkey** (v)  To talk openly and frankly.

**throw the bull** (v phr) To shoot the bull; chat; gossip.

**tiger** (n)  A strong, dangerous person.

**tiger by the tail, have** (v phr) To be in a dangerous situation, from which it is difficult to extricate oneself.

**tight as a tick (newt, owl, goat, mink)** (adv phr)  Very drunk.

**trout** (n)   An old cantankerous woman.

**turkey** (n)  Worthless or unsuitable thing or person.

**turkey shoot** (n)  An easy task.

**turtle** (n)  An armored car.

**turtle** (v) To move very slowly.

**two shakes of a lamb's tail** (n phr) A very short time.

**viper** (n)   A vicious person; a traitor.

**walrus** (n)  A short, fat person.

**WASP** (n)   Acronym for White Anglo-Saxon Protestant.

**weasel** (n)  An informer; a snitch.

**weasel out** (v phr)  To renege on a promise or obligation.

**whale** (n) Anything large or gross.

**whale of a, a** (n phr) An excellent example or sample of something.

**whirlybird** (n)  A helicopter.

**white mule** (n)   Illegal whiskey; moonshine.

**whole hog** (adv)  Completely; all the way.

**wildcat** (n)   Spirited, active energetic person.

**wildcat** (v) To work secretly, particularly in prospecting.

**worm** (n)  Cad; bounder.

**worm** (v)   To elicit information by devious means.

**yardbird** (n) Convict; prisoner; rookie; raw recruit.

**yellow dog** (n) Worthless; inferior.

**yellow dog contract** (n phr) Contract between company and employees forbidding labor unions. Now an illegal practice.

**zebra** (n) A referee.

# ARTS AND ENTERTAINMENT (Theater, Dance, Music, Cinema, Visual Arts)

**all that jazz** (n phr) Other such things.

**artsy-fartsy (adj)** Pompously esthetical; pseudo-artistic.

**Aztec two-step** (n) Diarrhea.

**back to the drawing board** (phr) Start over again from the beginning.

**bandwagon, on the** (adv phr) Joining a cause or movement.

**Barnum and Bailey world** (n) Make-believe surroundings; a fantasy existence. (Circus)

**beat the band, to** (adv phr) In generous quantities.

**bellringer** (n) Something that jogs the memory.

**bells and whistles** (n phr) Frills; unessential embellishments.

**big picture, the** (n) The overall view.

**big time, the** (n) Top success. (Show business)

**blow (toot) one's own horn** (v phr) To promote oneself.

**blow the whistle** (v phr) To inform.

**bogart** (v) To take more than one's share. (Cinema)

**bombed in New Haven** (v phr) A failed production (mainly stage).

**boogie** (v) To get down to business; go into action. (Music)

**bring down the house** (v phr) To score a resounding success.

**call the tune** (v phr) To be in control.

**catch-22** (n) A directive that cannot be obeyed without violating another. (Literature)

**change one's tune** (v phr) To change one's attitude.

**chime in** (v phr) To offer one's opinion or information in a discussion.

**chin music** (n) Idle chatter.

**class act, a** (n phr) A person of admirable style. (Show business)

**clown** (n) An incompetent, unreliable person; someone not to be taken seriously.

**curtains** (n) Death or disaster. (Theater)

**dance around** (v phr) To avoid a confrontation or commitment.

**different drummer, march to a** (v phr) To have priorities or to follow rules different from established standards.

**draw a picture** (v phr) To explain in simple terms.

**drum-beater** (n) An enthusiastic promoter.

**drum up** (v) To stimulate; to promote.

**elevator music** (n) Dull, uninteresting, soporific music.

**end on a high note** (v phr) To finish something in a friendly or positive way.

**etched (carved) in stone (granite)** (adj phr) Unchangeable; irreversible. (Printmaking, sculpture)

**face the music** (v phr) To accept the situation.

**fiddle around** (v phr) To tinker or tamper with; to idle about.

**fiddle-faddle** (n) Nonsense.

**Fiddlesticks!** (phr) Expression of disbelief or disappointment.

**fit as a fiddle** (adj phr) In good health.

**from the top** (adv phr) From the beginning. (Music)

**gag** (n) Joke.

**geek** (n) Awkward in appearance; one who does not fit in. (Carnival)

**get the picture** (v phr) To understand a situation.

**get the show on the road** (v phr) To get something started.

**golden oldie** (n phr) An old record, song, etc., that is still popular.

**groove, in the** (adj phr) On target; on the right path; working smoothly. (Jazz)

**ham** (n) One who likes to act.

**ham up** (v phr) To exaggerate.

**hard rock** (adj) Severe, tough.

**hit** (n) A success. (Theater)

**horse opera** A Western movie.

**in like Flynn** (adj phr) Done easily, effortlessly. (Cinema)

**in the picture** (phr) Under consideration; in the plans.

**jazz** (n) Ornamentation; nonsense.

**jazz** (v) To copulate; increase the level of excitement.

**jazz, on the** (adv phr) Excited; energized.

**jazzed** (adj) Alert, energetic.

**jazz up** (v) To ornament; embellish; make more exciting.

**jazzy** (adj) Exciting, stimulating.

**lip music** (n) An obscene or derisive sound made by vibrating the lips together.

**Mae West** (n) A life vest. (Cinema)

**make a big production** (v phr) To overstress the importance of; blow out of proportion.

**make a scene** (v phr) To have an emotional outburst.

**melodrama** (n) An overly emotional situation.

**Mickey Mouse** (adj phr) Silly; of little consequence.

**oldie but goodie** See *golden oldie*.

**on a high note** (adv phr) With a positive attitude; energetically.

**on that note** (phr) At this point.

**one-liner** (n) A witty remark. (Stand-up comedy)

**one night stand** (n phr) Casual sex.

**opera is never over till the fat lady sings, The** (sent.) One should not assume anything until the final results are determined.

**paint the town (red)** (v phr) To go

on a spree; carouse.

**pay the piper** (v phr) To reap the consequences of one's actions.

**play in Peoria** (v phr) To succeed outside of the main centers of power. (Theater)

**play it by ear** (v phr) To improvise; act spontaneously.

**play second fiddle** (v phr) To always be in an inferior position.

**pooh-bah** (n) A person of inflated importance; one who holds several high offices. (Operetta)

**preaching to the choir** (v phr) Persuading those who already agree with you.

**prima donna** (n phr) A person with a big ego who must have it all his or her way.

**pull strings** (v phr) To manipulate. (Puppetry)

**ring a bell** (v phr) To seem familiar; to provoke a memory.

**ring true** (v phr) To have an air of authenticity.

**rock** (v) To perform really well; to be really great.

**rock and roll** (v phr) To get down to business; go into action.

**scam** (n) A swindle. (Carnival)

**shill** (n) One who tries to induce customers to buy. (Carnival)

**Simon Legree** (n) A brutal taskmaster; a sadist. (Literature)

**sing** (v) To inform on someone.

**sing a different tune** (v phr) To change one's attitude.

**sing out** (v phr) To speak up; make oneself heard.

**snapshot** (n) A short description.

**soap opera** (n) Any situation involving exaggerated sentimentality or emotional crises.

**song-and-dance** (n phr) A pat routine; nonsense.

**stand-in** (n) A substitute. (Show business)

**swan song** (n) A farewell effort.

**swing** (v) To be up-to-date; to have a good time; to perform well.

**swing both ways** (v phr) To be bisexual.

**take** (n) Opinion; view. (Photography)

**tango, it takes two to** (sent.) It cannot be done by one person alone.

**to the tune of** (phr) Costing a certain amount.

**touch dancing** (n) Ballroom dancing.

**trump up** (v phr) To build up; exaggerate; invent. (Music)

**tune in** (v phr) To become aware; pay attention.

**tune out** (v phr) To stop paying attention; stop listening.

**turn a trick** (v phr) To perform sex for money. (Magic)

**waltz** (n) Non-aggressive sparring between two antagonists; an easy task.

**waltz through** (v phr) To get through something easily.

**war paint** (n) Cosmetics; makeup.

**whistle Dixie** (v phr) To engage in wishful thinking. (Song)

**X-rated** (adj) Obscene; pornographic. (Cinema)

# BUSINESS & INDUSTRY

**AC/DC** (adj) Bisexual. (Electronics)

**ball the jack** (v phr) To work rapidly. (Logging)

**bank on** (v) To rely on.

**bankable** (adj) Worth money; reliable; dependable.

**bankroll** (v) To finance; provide funds for.

**battery acid** (n) Coffee.

**bay window** (n) A protruding stomach. (Architecture)

**bearish** (adj) Pessimistic. (Stock market)

**bellringer** (n) Something that refreshes the memory.

**big bucks** (n phr) A large sum of money.

**big deal** (n phr) Very important. (Often used sarcastically.)

**big production, make a** (v phr) Make more of something than it really is.

**big wheel** (n) High level business operator.

**big nickel** (n ) A $5,000 wager or bet.

**big one** (n) A $1,000 wager or bet.

**black money** (n phr) Illegally-earned money which needs to be "laundered."

**blow a fuse** (v phr) To lose one's temper. (Electronics)

**blow a gasket** (v phr) To lose one's temper. (Mechanical)

**boilermaker** (n) Mixture of beer and whiskey. (Plumbing)

**boilerplate** (n) Standard, frequently repeated sections of legal or journalistic document.

**boss** (n) Person in charge; chief.

**boss (around)** (v) To order someone (around).

**bossy** (adj) Domineering.

**bottom line** (n) A final decision or judgment; a fundamental or crucial point or fact.

**bulldoze** (v) To force through an opinion or policy. (Construction)

**bullish** (adj) Optimistic. (Stock market)

**business as usual** (n phr) To go about one's affairs as normal, regardless of circumstances.

**business, give someone the** (n) To treat roughly; punish, rebuke.

**business end** (n) The operating end; the important part.

**buy and sell** (v phr) To go back and forth on something; be unable to make a decision.

**buy into** (v phr) To accept; to acquiesce.

**buy someone off** (v phr) To bribe.

**buy time** (v phr) To gain time; gain a postponement of an unpleasant situation.

**cash cow** (n) A source of seemingly endless funds.

**century, a** (n) A $100 bill.

**chamber of commerce** (n phr) A toilet.

**chump change** (n) A small amount of money.

**clip joint** (n phr) A business establishment that overcharges.

**copper (cop)** (n) A police officer.

**cobbler** (n) A passport forger. (Shoemaking)

**crank out** (v phr) To produce automatically and incessantly.

**deuce** (n) A two-dollar bill.

**dime** (n) A ten-year prison sentence; a $1,000 wager.

**dime a dozen** (adj phr) Cheap and plentiful.

**dime bag** (n) Ten dollars' worth of drugs.

**dime store** (adj) Inexpensive; of little value.

**double nickel** (n) 55 mile-per-hour speed limit.

**double sawbuck** (n) A twenty-dollar bill. (Carpentry)

**down the drain (tubes)** (phr) Lost; wasted. (Plumbing)

**fast buck** (n) Money made unscrupulously.

**filthy lucre** (n) Money.

**fin (finif)** (n) A five-dollar bill.

**five-and-dime** (adj) Cheap.

**four bits** (n) Fifty cents.

**frogskin** (n) A one-dollar bill.

**funny money** (n) Counterfeit currency; play money.

**gave at the office** (v phr) An excuse for not giving a donation or charity.

**gelt** (n) Money.

**get down to brass tacks** (v phr) To deal with the essentials. (Carpet laying)

**get down to business** (v phr) To start working; commit oneself.

**get off the dime** (v phr) To get moving; stop stalling.

**give someone the business** (v phr) To give someone a hard time.

**give someone the walking papers** (v phr) To dismiss from a job.

**go public** (v phr) To reveal one's secrets publicly.

**golden parachute** (n phr) High severance pay or compensation.

**green (greenback)** (n) Dollar bill.

**hard sell** (n phr) An aggressive deal.

**have a short fuse** (v phr) To have a quick temper.

**haywire, go** (v phr) To lose control; go crazy. (Agriculture)

**hit the nail on the head** (v phr) To be exact; to say the precise thing. (Carpentry)

**in business** (phr) In operation; in a working condition.

**in the toilet** (phr) Ruined; wasted. (Plumbing)

**jack up (the price)** (v phr) To increase a price unfairly. (Automotive)

**look like a million dollars** (v phr) To look terrific.

**mad money** (n) Money saved personally to be used for emergencies or small pleasures.

**make a killing** (v phr) To make a large profit.

**mechanic** (n) A card shark; a slick cheater; a hired gun.

**mind the store** (v phr) To attend to routine business.

**mom and pop** (adj phr) A small business run by a family.

**money in the bank** (n phr) Something safe and assured.

**money talks** (phr) Wealth is power.

**moneybags** (n) A very rich individual.

**moola** (n) Money.

**nickel** (n) Five-year prison sentence.

**nickel and dime** (v phr) To eat away at; quibble. (also *Nickel and dime someone to death*)

**nickel bag** (n) Five-dollar bag of drugs.

**nickel nurser** (n) A stingy person.

**nine to five** (adj phr) A regular job; a dull job.

**nuts and bolts** (n phr) The basics.

**off the top** (n phr) Without any deductions.

**on the money** (adj phr) Accurate; perfect.

**O.P.M.** (n phr) Other people's money.

**other side of the coin** (n phr) The opposite opinion or point of view.

**out to lunch** (adv phr) Not with it; not in full possession of one's faculties; not concentrating on what one is doing.

**penny-pincher** (n) A stingy person.

**perk** (n) Benefit; advantage.

**phony as a three-dollar bill** (adj phr) Totally false.

**pink slip** (n) A discharge notice.

**powerhouse** (n) A formidable organization; an energetic person. (Electrical Engineering)

**pull the plug** (v phr) To abort the operation. (Plumbing, Electrical)

**push someone's buttons** (v phr) To set off an emotional reaction in someone; to manipulate their feelings.

**put one's money where one's mouth is** (v phr) To support one's statement; back up one's claim.

**queer as a three-dollar bill** (adj phr) Phony; eccentric; homosexual. (derog.)

**right on the money** (adj phr) Accurate; on target.

**roll out the red carpet** (v phr) To welcome enthusiastically.

**run-of-the-mill** (adj) Ordinary; common. (Textiles)

**sawbuck** (n) A ten-dollar bill. (Carpentry)

**sell someone down the river** (v phr) To betray someone.

**sell-out** (n) A betrayal.

**sell out** (v) To betray.

**shekels** (n) Money.

**shoot one's wad** (v phr) To spend everything; to be wiped out.

**simoleon** (n) A dollar.

**six bits** (n) Seventy-five cents.

**small change** (n) Unimportant; trivial; small potatoes.

**small nickel** (n) A $500 wager.

**soft money** (n) Bills; political donations made to a party rather than to an individual.

**sold on, to be** (v phr) To be convinced of the value of something.

**stop on a dime** (v phr) To brake quickly without skidding.

**TCB (Take [Taking] Care of Business)** (v phr) Doing what

needs to be done.

**ten-spot** (n) A ten-dollar bill.

**thou** (n) A thousand dollars.

**throw good money after bad** (v phr) To continue on an unprofitable course.

**tightwad** (n) A stingy person.

**turn on a dime** (v phr) To make a sharp or very tight turn.

**two bits** (n) Twenty-five cents.

**two-bit** (adj) Trivial; unimportant; of little value.

**two cents (worth), put in one's** (v phr) To express an (often unsolicited) opinion.

**wheeler-dealer** (n) A person who engages in all sorts of business deals, often questionable ones.

**working girl** (n) A prostitute.

## FOOD, DRINK, COOKING & CULINARY ARTS

**apple pie** (adj) Easy; simple.

**apple-pie order** (adj phr) Neat; organized.

**apple-polisher** (n) A sycophant or flatterer.

**applesauce** (n) Nonsense.

**Apple, the (The Big Apple)** New York City.

**bad apple** (n) An evil person; a bad influence.

**bad egg** (n) An undesirable or evil person.

**baker's dozen** (n) Thirteen.

**baloney** (n) Utter nonsense.

**bananas** (adj) Crazy; insane.

**bean** (n) One's head.

**bean** (v) To hit someone on the head.

**bean counter** (n) An auditor or accountant; one who monitors every expenditure.

**bean eater** (n) A Bostonian.

**beans, doesn't know** (v phr) Does not know anything.

**beef** (n) A complaint or gripe.

**beefcake** (n) A nude or near-nude muscular male on display; muscular male legs.

**beef up** (v phr) To reinforce.

**big butter-and-egg man** (n phr) An important person in business.

**big cheese** (n) An important person. (Often used sarcastically.)

**big enchilada** (n) Chief; boss; head man; Mexico City.

**boiled (stewed, fried)** (adj) Drunk.

**breadbasket** (n) Stomach; agricultural sector.

**bring home the bacon** (v phr) To earn a living for one's family; to deliver on a promise.

**buns** (n) Buttocks.

**butter-and-egg money** (n phr) Funds for household expenses.

**cabbage (kale; lettuce)** (n) Money.

**cabbagehead** (n) A stupid person.

**can opener** (n) Tool for breaking into a safe; any tool used to open a metal container.

**candy-assed** (adj) Irresolute; cowardly.

**candy man** (n) A drug pusher.

**carrot top** (n) A red-headed person.

**champagne trick** (n phr) A prostitute's rich customer.

**cheesecake** (n) A nude or near-nude woman on display. (see *beefcake*)

**cheesed off** (v phr) Annoyed; angry.

**cheesy** (adj) Cheap; flimsy; inferior.

**cherry** (n) A virgin; one's virginity; the hymen.

**cherry** (adj) New; virginal; inexperienced; untouched.

**cherry-top fuzzmobile** (n) A police car.

**chestnut** (n) An old joke or story.

**chew out** (v phr) To take someone to task, loudly and abusively.

**chew someone's ear off** (v phr) To talk incessantly.

**chew the fat** (v phr) To chat or gossip.

**chicken** (adj) Cowardly.

**chicken feed** (n) Small change; something of little importance.

**chickenhearted** (adj) Faint hearted; cowardly.

**chicken livered** (adj) Cowardly.

**chickenshit** (adj) Dictatorially adhering to rules and discipline.

**chowder head** (n) A stupid person.

**clam** (n) A silent, secretive, uncommunicative person.

**clambake** (n) A party; a picnic; an entertainment.

**clam up** (v phr) To shut up suddenly; remain silent; withdraw into oneself.

**coffee grinder** (n) A striptease or its performer.

**cook** (v) To die in the electric chair; to excel; to tamper with.

**cooking (cooking with gas; now you're cooking)** (v) Doing something right or well.

**corn** (n) Trite comments; bad or old jokes.

**corn rows** (n) Multiple-braided hair.

**cornball** (adj) Trite; simpleminded.

**cornhole** (v) To have anal sex.

**corny** (adj) Trite; overused; overly sentimental.

**couch potato** (n) Someone who spends an inordinate amount of time in front of the television.

**cow juice** (n) Milk.

**crabby** (adj) In a bad mood; irritated.

**cracker barrel** (adj) Rustic; unsophisticated.

**creampuff** (n) A weakling; a pushover; a sissy; a used car in mint condition.

**cream** (v) To beat up physically; to defeat totally; to completely destroy.

**crock (of shit)** (n) Lies; exaggerations; total misinformation.

**crumb** (n) An untrustworthy person.

**crumb-bum** (n) An untrustworthy, totally worthless person.

**cup of tea** (n) What one likes; to one's taste.

**cut a melon** (v phr) To divide profits.

**cut and dried** (adj) Obvious; leaving no room for disagreement.

**cut the mustard** (v phr) To be equal to the task.

**cuts no ice** (v phr) To be unconvincing; prove nothing; make no difference.

**dark meat** (n) A black person desired by a white person.

**deadpan** (adj) Emotionless; expressionless.

**dish** (n) A beautiful girl.

**dish** (v) To gossip about.

**dish it out** (v phr) To punish or abuse.

**dish the dirt** (v phr) To gossip.

**dishwater** (n) Thin soup; weak tea; something undesirable.

**dishwater (ditchwater), dull as** (adj phr) Lifeless; lacking sparkle.

**dishy** (adj) Attractive and desirable.

**dough** (n) Money.

**doughnut** (n) A spare (usually not full-size) automobile tire; a round cushion with a hole in the middle.

**drink, the** (n) Any large body of water.

**duck soup** (adj phr) Very simple; easy.

**easy as pie** (adj phr) Extremely easy.

**eat shit** (v phr) To be repulsive or contemptible.

**egg** (n) A person (e.g. good egg, swell egg; tough egg).

**eggbeater** (n) A helicopter; a propellor; an outboard motor.

**egghead** (n) An intellectual.

**egg on** (v phr) To goad; to encourage.

**egg-sucker** (n) Flatterer.

**fat farm** (n) Resort promoted as a place to lose weight; health farm.

**fat city** (adj) Excellent condition or mood; prosperous.

**fat of the land, living off the** (v phr) Enjoying the best available.

**feedbag, put (tie, strap) on the** (v phr) To eat a meal.

**fish** (n) One easily duped; an inexperienced individual; a torpedo.

**fish bowl, living in a** (v phr) Exposed; lacking privacy.

**fish eye** (n) A sinister or expressionless stare.

**fishtail** (v) To swing side-to-side.

**fishy** (adj) Dishonest; deceptive; suspect.

**fizzle out** (v phr) To fade and disappear gradually.

**fork over (out)** (v phr) To hand over (usually money).

**Fork you!** (phr) Euphemism for *Fuck you!*

**free lunch** (n) Advantage or pleasure received without obligation. (Common expression: *There is no such thing as a free lunch.*)

**from hell to breakfast** (adv phr) Thoroughly and violently.

**from hunger** (adj phr) (see *strictly from hunger*)

**fruit** (n) A homosexual.

**fruit salad** (n) Campaign ribbons or military decorations displayed together.

**fruitcake** (n) Crazy person.

**Fudge!** (phr) Mild epithet indicating frustration, annoyance, or disappointment.

**fudge** (v) To cheat; to hedge; to fake.

**full of beans** (adj phr) High-spirited.

**full of piss and vinegar** (adj phr) Lively; energetic.

**gel** (v)  To come together (as plans); to solidify.

**George Washington pie** (n) Cherry pie.

**get one's nuts off** (v phr)  To ejaculate; to have an orgasm.

**gin mill** (n)  A bar or saloon.

**ginger** (n)  Spirit.

**ginger-peachy** (adj)  Great; fine and admirable.

**goober** (n)  A peanut; a stupid person; a pimple.

**goose egg** (n)  A zero.

**grape, the** (n)  Wine; any other alcoholic beverage.

**gravy** (n)  Extra money; any unanticipated benefit.

**gravy train** (n phr)  Easy money for little work.

**grease the palm** (v phr)  To bribe.

**greasy spoon** (n)  An inexpensive restaurant, not known for its cleanliness.

**gridiron** (n)  American football field.

**grill** (v)  To question intensely.

**grub** (n)  Food.

**grubstake** (n)  Money for food or necessities; startup funds for a new enterprise.

**gum up the works** (v phr)  To spoil; to stop an operation, usually through stupidity or incompetence.

**hair pie** (n)  The pudendum.

**ham** (n)  An actor or performer who overacts, exaggerates, or makes himself ridiculous; an amateur radio operator.

**ham** (v)  To overact.

**happy juice** (n)  Liquor.

**hardboiled** (adj) Unemotional; devoid of pity and understanding.

**hard boiled egg** (n phr) Severe and pugnacious person.

**hard cheese** (n phr) An unfortunate outcome of a situation.

**hash** (n) Hashish.

**hash out** (v phr)  To work out details.

**hash over** (v phr)  To discuss at length, particularly with regard to pros and cons.

**hayseed** (n) A hick; a rural person.

**herb** (n)  Marijuana.

**hold water** (v phr)  To have validity.

**honey** (n)  A term of endearment.

**hot dog** (n phr)  Skilled surfer; a show-off.

**Hot dog!** (interj) Oh boy!; Great!

**hot potato** (n) An embarrassment; something difficult to handle.

**hot potato, drop something like a** (v phr) Get rid of something very quickly.

**hot water** (n)  Trouble.

**icing on the cake** (n phr)  An embellishment; an added reward.

**I'll drink to that!** (phr)  I strongly agree.

**jam, a** (n)  Trouble.

**jarhead** (n)  A Marine.

**jug** (n)  Prison.

**jugs** (n)  A woman's breasts.

**jughead** (n)  A stupid person.

**juice** (n)  Energy; liquor; fuel; clout; electrical current.

**juice** (v)  To get all one can get.

**juniper juice** (n)  Gin.

**junk food** (n)  Anything of dubious

physical or mental benefit.

**know one's onions** (v phr) To be well informed; to be up on the subject.

**lay an egg** (v phr) To fail abysmally.

**lemon** (n) An unsatisfactory, inferior, troublesome product.

**lick one's chops** (v phr) To anticipate with pleasure; to gloat.

**licorice stick** (n) A clarinet.

**limey** (n) An Englishman.

**loaf** (v) To be idle.

**long drink of water** (n phr) A tall, very thin individual.

**love apple** (n) A tomato.

**make (a) hash of** (v phr) To defeat totally; destroy; cause to fail.

**marshmallow** (n) A white man (derog.); a weakling.

**meal ticket** (n) A person, talent, skill, or other asset that provides a source of sustenance.

**meat** (n) A sex object; a penis.

**meat-and-potatoes** (adj) Basic; primary.

**meatball** (n) An obnoxious, stupid individual.

**meathead** (n) A stupid individual.

**meathooks** (n) Hands; fists.

**meat rack (market)** (n) Pick-up bar.

**meat wagon** (n) An ambulance.

**melon** (n) Gross; total gain; spoils; female breast.

**melon-belly** (n) A protuberant abdomen.

**milk** (v) To exploit to the utmost.

**milk run** (n) An easy job or mis-

sion.

**Molotov cocktail** (n) A bomb made by igniting gasoline-soaked rags in a bottle.

**moo juice** (n) Milk.

**munchies** (n) Snacks or the craving for them.

**muttonhead** (n) A stupid person.

**needle candy** (n) Narcotics injected with a syringe.

**nest-egg** (n) Savings.

**noodle** (n) Head; brain.

**noodle around** (v phr) To fool around; wander aimlessly.

**noodlehead** (adj) Stupid.

**nose candy** (n) Cocaine.

**nut house** (n) Mental hospital.

**nuts** (adj) Crazy; mad; out of one's mind.

**nuts** (n) Testicles.

**Nuts!** (interj) Damn!; (an expression of irritation, contempt or disgust.)

**nuts about** (adj phr) Madly in love with.

**nutty as a fruitcake** (adj phr) Really crazy.

**oat burner** (n) A horse.

**oater** (n) A Western movie or television show.

**off one's nut** (adj phr) Crazy.

**onion** (n) The head.

**orange** (n) A baseball.

**Oreo** (n) African-American who acts Caucasian (i.e., black on the outside, white on the inside).

**out to lunch** (adj phr) Removed from reality.

**oyster berry** (n) A pearl.

**palm oil** (n) Bribe money.

**pancake landing** (n) Landing on a plane's belly because the landing gear failed to come down.

**panhandle** (v) To beg on the streets.

**peabrain** (n) A stupid person.

**pea shooter** (n) A rifle.

**pea souper** (n) A very heavy fog, difficult to see through.

**peach** (n) An attractive girl or woman; a great idea.

**peachy** (adj) Splendid; going very well indeed.

**peanut(s)** (n) Insignificant; unimportant; a very short person.

**peanut gallery** (n) Cheap seats far from the action; top gallery.

**peel** (v) To perform a striptease.

**pepper (pep)** (n) Vitality; enthusiasm.

**pepper-upper** (n) Refresher.

**percolate** (v) To run smoothly.

**pickle, be in a** (v phr) To be in trouble.

**pickle puss** (n) A sour faced, unhappy looking individual.

**pie-eyed** (adj) Drunk.

**pie-face** (n) Someone with a round face.

**pie-in-the-sky** (n phr) Unrealistic goals or hopes.

**pie wagon** (n) Police arrest van.

**piece of cake** (n) An easy task.

**piece of cheese** (n) Undesirable person of questionable ethics; woman's breast

**pineapple** (n) Hand grenade.

**plum** (n) Desirable job given for service and loyalty, rather than ability or experience.

**pork** (n) Unnecessary political expenditures.

**pork** (v) To engage in sexual intercourse.

**pork barrel** (adj) Politics involving padded expenditures.

**pot** (n) Marijuana.

**potato head** (n) A stupid person.

**potboiler** (n) A book of little literary substance, written solely for the income.

**pot luck** (n) Whatever is immediately available; odds and ends.

**prune, prune-face** (n) An old, dried-out individual.

**pudding head** (n) A stupid person.

**pumpkin [punkin]** (n) A term of affection.

**radish** (n) A baseball.

**raspberry** (n) A vulgar derisive noise.

**rehash** (v) To discuss a subject over and over again.

**rhubarb** (n) Noisy argument or fight.

**rib** (v) To tease.

**rib joint** (n) A brothel; whorehouse.

**road apples** (n) Horse droppings.

**roast** (v) To make light of; (n) a party or celebration where someone is roasted by friends.

**rock candy** (n) A diamond.

**rummy** (n) A drunkard; an alcoholic.

**rutabaga** (n) A dollar.

**sad apple** (n) A gloomy person.

**salad days** (n) Times of youthful exuberance; one's young years.

**salt, old** (n) An experienced, often retired, sailor.

**salt mines, back to the** (phr) To return to work.

**sardine can** (n) Crowded subway or train; a submarine.

**sauce** (n) Whiskey; gasoline.

**sauce, on the** (adj phr) Drinking or drunk.

**sauce for the goose** (n phr) What works for one person.

**schmaltz** (n) Excessive sentimentality; bathos.

**scrambled eggs** (n) Gold braid, embroidery, or other gold embellishments on a military uniform.

**sling hash** (v) To wait tables.

**Sloppy Joe's** (n) Any cheap restaurant.

**small beer** (n) A person or matter of little significance.

**small fry** (n) A child; an unimportant person.

**small potatoes** (n) Of little consequence or value.

**smart cookie** (n) Clever, self-confident person.

**smooth apple** (n) One using charm to get his way; suave; slick; seductive.

**soul food** (n) Anything profoundly satisfying.

**soup** (n) Nitroglycerine; foam or froth formed by waves or surf.

**soup, in the** (phr) In trouble.

**souped up** (adj) Designed or retrofitted for increased power.

**spaghetti Western** (n) A Western movie directed and filmed in Italy.

**spam** (v) To deluge an e-mail address with commercial messages.

**Spam cluster** (n) *S*houlder *P*atch for *A*r*M*ed service force.

**spill the beans** (v phr) To betray a secret.

**spinach** (n) A beard; nonsense.

**spoon** (n) Nose-to-tail bow or curve on a surfboard.

**spoon** (v) To sleep nestled front to back with another person; kiss; fondle; neck; pet.

**spring chicken, no** (n phr) Past one's prime.

**sprout** (n) Young son or daughter.

**spud** (n) A potato.

**squab** (n) Girl or young woman; chick; quail.

**square the beef** (v phr) To take care of complaints.

**steam** (v) To make angry.

**stew** (n) Chaos; confusion; flight attendant.

**stew** (v) To nurse one's anger.

**stir** (n) Prison.

**stir-crazy** (adj) Having one's wits dulled by long imprisonment.

**strictly from hunger** (adj phr) Inferior; cheap; undesirable.

**sucker** (n) A potential dupe; an easy person to cheat.

**sucker for, a** (n phr) A fan of.

**sugar** (n) A term of endearment; money; LSD.

**sugar-coat** (v) To make something appear or sound more agreeable.

**sugar daddy** (n) A wealthy older man supporting a young woman so she can live in style.

**swamp water** (n) Coffee.

**sweet** (adj) Lucrative; easy; advantageous.

**sweet pea** (n) A term of affection; easy person to take advantage of.

**sweetie pie** (n) A term of affection.

**sweet potato** (n) An ocarina.

**taffy** (n) Flattery.

**take the cake** (v phr) To win; to be improbable or incredible.

**tart** (n) A promiscuous woman; a prostitute.

**'tater trap** (n) Mouth.

**t-bone** (n) A trombone.

**tea** (n) Marijuana.

**teakettle** (n) Old steam locomotive.

**tea party** (n) An uneventful gathering.

**tenderloin** (n) Night life area of a major city, particularly one with gambling, prostitution, and vice.

**tomato** (n) A very attractive girl.

**top banana** (n) Headliner or primary comedian in a Burlesque show; anyone in the most prominent position.

**toss one's cookies** (v phr) To vomit.

**tough cookie** (n) Hard nosed person; a survivor.

**tough nut** (n) Very difficult person; hard to deal with.

**tripe** (n) Insincere, exaggerated, worthless talk.

**tub of lard** (n phr) A fat, flabby person.

**upchuck** (v) To vomit.

**vanilla** (adj) Caucasian; bland, unexceptional, dull.

**veggy** (n) A vegetarian.

**waffle** (v) To speak, write, or act equivocally or indecisively.

**waffle stompers** (n) Hiking boots.

**watering hole** (n) Bar or tavern.

**weenie (wiener)** (n) A penis; a cowardly or timid individual.

**well-oiled** (adj) Drunk.

**What's cookin'?** (phr) What's happening?

**What's eating you?** (phr) What's annoying or bothering you?

**whiskey tenor** (n) Hoarse-voiced individual.

**white bread** (adj) Dull, unexciting; lacking ethnic character. (see *vanilla*)

**white meat** (n) A Caucasian as an object of desire.

**wild mare's milk** (n) Whiskey.

# GAMES AND SPORTS

**ace** (v) To achieve a perfect score; to accomplish something without errors; to get an "A" on a test. (Cards, Tennis)

**ace buddy** (n) A good friend; one's best friend.

**ace-high** (adj) Successful; respected. (Cards)

**ace in the hole** (n phr) Information or advantages kept secret until required. (Cards)

**ace up one's sleeve** (n phr) A hidden asset. (Cards)

**across the board** (adj) All-inclusive; all the way. (Horse Racing)

**back to square one** (phr) Start over from the beginning. (Chess)

**ball game** (n) A situation. (Baseball)

**ball is in your court, the** (sent.) It is your turn to act. (Tennis)

**ballpark** (n) Certain limits; an intelligent approximation. (Baseball)

**ballpark** (v)  To estimate.

**barrel, in the** (phr)  Discharged or in imminent danger of being fired. (Shooting)

**behind the eight-ball** (phr)  In trouble. (Billards)

**bench warmer** (n)  Someone who is present but not active; a non-participant or bystander. (Baseball)

**bet your bottom dollar** (v phr)  To be absolutely sure. (Gambling)

**Bingo!** (interj)  Eureka! Aha! I found it! I won! You've got it!

**blue chip** (n phr)  The best quality; a high-priced stock. (Gambling)

**bush league** (adj)  Small time; of minor importance. (Baseball)

**card** (n)  A prankster or joker; an interesting personality. (Cards)

**cards, not in the** (phr)  Not destined or fated to happen. (Fortune telling)

**cash in one's chips** (v phr)  To die. (Poker)

**cheapskate** (n)  A stingy person; a tightwad. (Skating)

**chip in** (v phr)  To pay one's share; to contribute. (Poker)

**chips are down, the** (phr)  It's time to act or react. (Poker)

**clay pigeon** (n)  An easy to hit target; an easily victimized person. (Trap shooting)

**cueball** (n)  A bald person; a bald head. (Billiards)

**curve ball** (n)  A deceptive approach or proposition.

**deal from the bottom of the deck** (v phr)  To attempt to cheat someone. (Cards)

**deal someone a poor hand** (v phr)  To exploit or victimize someone. (Cards)

**desk jockey** (n)  Office worker. (Horse racing)

**deuce** (n)  A two-dollar bill; a powerful hot-rod. (Cards)

**dicey** (adj)  Risky; chancy. (Dice)

**dirty pool** (n phr)  Unfair, dishonest behavior. (Billiards)

**disc jockey** (n)  Radio announcer who plays records.(Horse racing)

**dive** (n)  A low-class bar or club; a feigned knock-out. (Boxing)

**down and out** (adj phr)  Penniless; out of luck. (Boxing)

**dust someone off** (v phr)  To beat up or kill someone. (Baseball)

**fan** (n)  An enthusiastic follower; a devotee.

**fancy footwork** (n)  Adroit evasion; clever maneuvering. (Boxing)

**fast shuffle, be given a** (v phr)  To be cheated; to have facts concealed from one. (Cards)

**feed bag, to strap on a** (v phr)  To eat a meal. (Horse racing)

**fish or cut bait** (phr)  Stop stalling; either finish the job or leave. (Fishing)

**fish story** (n)  An exaggerated tale. (Fishing)

**flash in the pan** (n phr)  Of momentary importance; of short endurance. (Riflery)

**fold** (v)  To go out of business. (Poker)

**foul ball** (n)  A useless or odd person. (Baseball)

**four-flusher** (n)  A cheater; a

bluffer; a faker. (Poker)

**full court press** (n phr) Applying great pressure against someone or something. (Basketball)

**fun and games** (n phr) Something most enjoyable (usually ironic).

**game plan** (n) Strategy.

**game time** (n) Time to do what has to be done.

**get to first base** (v phr) To make a successful initial step.

**give (get) a leg up** (v phr) To offer someone a helping hand. (Horse racing)

**glass jaw, have a** (v phr) To be easily knocked out; easily defeated. (Boxing)

**go to bat for someone** (v phr) To support or defend someone. (Baseball)

**go to the mat** (v phr) To fight. (Wrestling)

**good sport** (n phr) A person who accepts both victory and defeat graciously.

**grandstand** (v) To show off. (Baseball)

**grandstand play** (n) Means of gaining attention or sympathy. (Baseball)

**hard way, the** (n) Achieving something in the most difficult manner.

**hedge your bets** (v phr) To cover all possibilities. (Gambling)

**high as (higher than) a kite** (adj phr) Very drunk; stoned on drugs. (Kite flying)

**hit the bullseye** (v phr) To get something exactly right.

(Archery)

**hit the jackpot** (v phr) Strike it rich; win it all. (Gambling)

**hold one's cards close to one's chest (vest)** (v phr) Withhold information; be secretive. (Cards)

**home court advantage** (n phr) To play or operate in a friendly environment. (Basketball)

**home plate** (n) Landing strip; safe haven; an aircraft carrier. (Baseball)

**in the chips** (adj phr) Rich; affluent. (Poker)

**in spades** (adv phr) To the extreme; doubled. (Cards)

**in the ball park** (adv phr) In the region of; approximately. (Baseball)

**jockey** (v) To struggle for position; to taunt. (Horse racing)

**jockey** (n) Driver; pilot (e.g. cab jockey). (Horse racing)

**joker** (n) A negating element; an unfair chance. (Cards)

**jump the gun** (v phr) To make a false start; get ahead of oneself. (Racing)

**keep one's eye on the ball** (v phr) To be alert. (Baseball)

**kick off** (v phr) To begin; to die. (Football)

**knockout** (adj) A very attractive person or idea; a winner. (Boxing)

**know the score** (v phr) To be aware and well-informed.

**knuckle down** (v) To get down to work. (Marbles)

**level playing field** (n phr) Fair conditions.

**lightweight** (n)  A person not of great consequence in his/her field. (Boxing)

**long hitter** (n)  A heavy drinker. (Baseball)

**lose one's marbles** (v phr)  To go insane. (Marbles)

**lowball** (v phr)  To lower; reduce. (Poker)

**low blow** (n phr)  An unfair comment. (Boxing)

**luck of the draw** (n phr)  As fortune dictates. (Cards)

**major league** (n phr)  The top category; the "big time." (Baseball)

**major league player** (n phr)  Top player in any given field. (Baseball)

**make a pitch** (v phr)  To make a proposal; attempt to seduce a woman. (Baseball)

**make a play for** (v phr)  To attempt to gain or seduce.

**marathon** (n)  A long endurance contest or activity. (Running)

**Monday morning quarterback** (n phr)  Someone who knows what to say or do after the fact. (Football)

**name of the game, the** (n phr)  The important thing; the necessary element.

**no dice** (phr)  Absolutely not. (Dice)

**no-hitter** (n)  A losing proposition. (Baseball)

**no holds barred** (adj phr)  Without limits or inhibitions. (Wrestling)

**off-base** (adj)  Out of line; off the subject; beyond authority. (Baseball)

**off the pace** (adv phr)  Not performing in one's usual manner. (Racing)

**on the ball** (adv phr)  Skillful, alert.

**on a roll** (phr)  Enjoying a winning impetus; attaining momentum. (Dice)

**one-two punch** (n)  Adverse events in rapid sequence. (Boxing)

**out in left field** (adv phr)  Very unusual; bizarre. (Baseball)

**out of one's league** (adj phr)  In a situation where one's knowledge and ability fall short of the task. (Baseball)

**pack a punch** (v phr)  To possess great strength. (Boxing)

**parlay** (v)  To roll over winnings or profits into further gains. (Horse racing)

**pass the buck** (v phr)  To evade blame.

**ping (blip) jockey** (n)  One who monitors radar or electronic equipment. (Horse racing)

**play ball with** (v phr)  Cooperate with. (Baseball)

**play catch-up** (v phr)  Work hard to recover from a disadvantage.

**play dirty** (v phr)  To deceive or trick.

**play for keeps** (v phr)  To play hard.

**play games with** (v phr)  To manipulate.

**play hard ball** (v phr)  To act tough.

**play with a full deck, not** (v phr)

To be less than rational. (Cards)

**poker-faced** (adj) Expressionless; not betraying emotion. (Poker)

**pocket pool** (n) Masturbating with one's hands in pants pockets. (Pool)

**pull a fast one** (v phr) To attempt to deceive. (Possibly Poker)

**pull one's punches** (v phr) Avoid attacking. (Boxing)

**punching bag** (n phr) Someone others beat on; a scapegoat. (Boxing)

**punchy** (adj) Confused and battered.

**quarterback** (v) To manage or lead a group or organization. (Football)

**right off the bat** (adv phr) Instantly; primarily. (Baseball)

**roll with the punches** (v phr) Endure adversity and survive. (Boxing)

**saved by the bell** (adj phr) Saved at the last minute. (Boxing)

**score** (v) To steal; to cheat; to make a sexual conquest.

**sitting duck** (n) Easy to cheat. (Hunting)

**skate around** (v phr) To try to avoid one's obligations. (Ice skating)

**skate on thin ice** (v phr) To live dangerously; to take unnecessary chances; to come close to disaster.

**southpaw** (n) A left-handed person; someone whose actions are difficult to predict. (Baseball)

**spade** (n) An African-American. (derog.) (Cards)

**spike** (v) To destroy one's chances of success. (Baseball)

**sport** (n) A stylish person; a mocking way of addressing someone, similar to "big shot."

**stand pat** (v phr) To adhere firmly to a position or opinion. (Cards)

**step up to the plate** (v phr) To take action. (Baseball)

**strike out** (v phr) To fail com pletely. (Baseball)

**switch hitter** (n) Ambidextrous; versatile; doing several things well; bisexual. (Baseball)

**take a dive** (v phr) To lose deliberately. (Boxing)

**take it on the chin** (v phr) To stand up to a severe blow or unfortunate circumstances. (Boxing)

**take the gloves off** (v phr) To put delicacy aside. (Boxing)

**that's the ball game** (sent.) That's the end of the affair.

**that's the way the ball bounces** (sent.) That's life.

**three sheets to the wind** (adj) Drunk. (Sailing)

**three strikes and you are out** (sent.) You only get two chances.(Baseball)

**throw (toss) in the sponge (towel)** (v phr) To concede defeat; to quit. (Boxing)

**throw someone a curve** (v phr) To deceive. (Baseball)

**thumbs down** (n phr) Negative response. (Gladiators in ancient Rome)

**thumb one's nose at** (v phr) To

defy; to show disrespect.

**thumbs up** (n phr) Positive response; go ahead with something. (Gladiators in ancient Rome)

**touchdown** (n) A success; the achievement of a goal. (Football)

**tout** (v) To sell or promote. (Horseracing)

**turf** (n) One's territory or neighborhood. (Horse racing)

**Vatican roulette** (n) The rhythm method of birth control. (Roulette)

**wild pitch** (n) A botched attempt.

**win by a nose** (v phr) To barely win; succeed by a slim margin. (Horse racing)

**wing** (v) To wound instead of kill. (Hunting)

**wipe out** (v phr) To fail totally. (Surfing)

# HUMAN BODY, THE

## *Arms*

**arm and a leg, an** (n phr) A very high price.

**keep one at arm's length** (v phr) To keep one's distance from someone.

**long arm of the law, the** (n phr) A police officer; the long reach of the law.

**shot in the arm, a** (n phr) An encouragement; a boost.

**twist someone's arm** (v phr) To talk someone into doing something.

**welcome with open arms** (v phr) To receive someone with great enthusiasm.

## *Ass*

**ass backward** (adv phr) In a confused or stupid manner.

**ass on the line, put one's** (v phr) To risk one's reputation or job.

**asshole** (n) An idiot; an evil person.

**ass-kisser** (n) One who flatters a superior in order to get ahead.

**badass** (adj) Superfically tough or pugnacious.

**bet your sweet ass, you can** (v phr) To be absolutely sure.

**bug up one's ass, have a** (v phr) To be touchy; easily provoked.

**bust one's ass** (v phr) To work hard.

**cover your ass** (v phr) To provide or arrange excuses in advance.

**half-assed** (adj) Mediocre; ineffectual; incomplete.

**have one's ass in a sling** (v phr) To be in serious trouble.

**kick ass** (v phr) To assert power.

**pain in the ass** (n) An annoying, obnoxious person or thing.

**piece of ass** (n) A person regarded as a sexual object; sexual intercourse.

**smart-ass** (n) A know-it all.

**throw someone out on his/her ass** (v phr) Get rid of someone.

**tight-ass** (n phr) Tense and morally rigid person.

**wiseass** (n) A know-it-all person.

**work one's ass off** (v phr) To work extremely hard.

*Back*

**back-breaking** (adj) Physically challenging or difficult.

**get off my back** (v phr) Leave me alone; don't bother me.

**back off** (v) To stop annoying or harassing.

**back out** (v) To remove oneself from a situation or project.

**get one's back up** (v phr) To get extremely angry or hostile.

**get the monkey off one's back** (v phr) To break a narcotics habit.

**no skin off my back** (phr) No trouble to me.

**scratch my back, and I'll scratch yours** (phr) Returning a favor for a favor.

*Balls (Testicles)*

**ball** (v) To have sexual intercourse.

**ball-breaker** (n) A difficult person or task.

**balls** (n) Courage; nerve.

**balls to the wall** (adv phr) To the extreme; at full speed.

**ballsy** (adj) Brave; spunky.

**blue balls** (n phr) Sexual frustration.

**freeze one's balls off** (v phr) To experience extreme cold.

**have someone by the balls** (v phr) To have a tight grasp on someone.

**have the world by the balls** (v phr) To be in a very strong position.

*Belly*

**belly laugh** (n phr) Loud visceral laugh.

**belly up, go** (v phr) To fail or die.

**beer belly** (n) A protruding paunch.

**bellyache** (v) To complain or whine.

**potbelly** (n) A protruding paunch.

**yellowbelly** (n) A coward.

*Bodily Actions & Activities*

**bite off more than one can chew** (v phr) To tackle a job too large or complex for one's abilities

**(put the) bite on** (v phr) To vigorously ask someone for a loan; to blackmail.

**bite one's head off** (v phr) To respond quickly with great anger.

**bite your tongue** (v phr) Be very careful about what you are saying; don't say that.

**butt in** (v) To stick your nose into other people's business; to interject.

**butt heads** (v phr) To engage in conflict; to punish.

**chew one's ear off** (v phr) To talk too much.

**chew the fat** (v phr) To engage in casual conversation; to gossip.

**eat crow** (v phr) To be forced into a humiliating situation.

**eat dirt (shit)** (v phr) To be forced into an extremely degrading situation; to submit to insult.

**eat humble pie** (v phr) To be highly apologetic.

**eat like a horse** (v phr) To consume huge amounts of food.

**fart around** (v phr) To waste time.

**fart up a storm** (v phr) To engage in activity with no chance of success.

**kick** (n) A feeling of excitement.

**kick around** (v phr) To treat

roughly or neglectfully; to play with an idea.

**kick ass** (n) A subservient individual.

**kick ass** (v phr) To downgrade individuals as punishment for failure; motivate by browbeating.

**kickback** (n phr) Payment of a percentage of the profit for influencing the transaction.

**kick in** (v) To get started; to contribute one's share.

**kick in the guts** (n phr) An extreme or dangerous set-back.

**kick in the ass** (butt) (n phr) A serious set-back; a strong measure of encouragement..

**kick in the pants** (n phr) A set-back; a strong measure of encouragement.

**kick it** (v) To get rid of a habit or addiction.

**kick off** (v) To die; to start.

**kick over the traces** (v phr) To overcome disciplined self-control and indulge in unexpected activities; to suddenly change pattern.

**(get a) kick out of something or someone** (v phr) To get enjoyment or pleasure from an incident or an individual.

**kick someone out** (v phr) To dismiss; to eject.

**kick someone upstairs** (v phr) To promote someone to a position with prestige but no power.

**kick the habit** (v phr) To get rid of an addiction.

**kick the stuffing (out of someone)** (v phr) To beat up someone.

**kick the bucket** (v phr) To die.

**kick up a stink (storm)** (v phr) To stir up trouble.

**kick up daisies** (v phr) To die.

**kick up one's heels** (v phr) To cast off inhibitions; to enjoy oneself.

**(get your) kicks** (v phr) To experience excitement or pleasure.

**kicky** (adj) Intriguing; full of fun.

**(side-)kick** (n phr) A friend or buddy.

**kiss and make up** (v phr) To resolve a dispute or argument.

**kiss of death** (n phr) A superficially harmless act leading to ruinous consequences.

**kiss off** (n) A dismissal.

**kiss someone's ass** (v phr) To be obsequious; to fawn and flatter.

**kiss (bite) the dust** (v phr) To go down in defeat; to die.

**kiss up** (v) To fawn and flatter as a means of getting something in return.

**kisser** (n) The mouth; the face.

**(beat someone to the) punch** (v phr) To get there first; to launch an anticipatory attack.

**punch drunk** (adj phr) Acting dazed; suffering from repeated blows to the head.

**punchy** (adj) Groggy or dazed.

**read between the lines** (v phr) To infer from the overall content.

**run in** (n) A quarrel; an argument.

**run in** (v) To deliver.

**run into** (v) To have a chance encounter; to meet by chance.

**run out on** (v phr) To desert.

**run with the hare and hunt with the hounds** (v phr) To have it both ways; to take both sides.

**scratch** (n) Money

**scratch cat** (n) A bad tempered woman.

**(from) scratch** (adj) From the beginning; with little or no ingredients.

**scratch the surface** (v phr) To make a superficial investigation or analysis.

**(up to) scratch** (adj) Meeting minimum requirements.

**scratched** (adj) Eliminated; crossed out.

**scratcher** (n) A match.

**shuffle off this mortal coil** (v phr) To die (from Shakespeare's _Hamlet_).

**sight for sore eyes** (n phr) Something to be viewed with extreme pleasure.

**(out of) sight, out of mind** (v phr) Minimum contact leads to forgetting.

**slap and tickle** (n phr) Necking; sexual foreplay.

**slap-dash** (adj) Characterized by haste and carelessness.

**slaphappy** (adj) Groggy; dizzy; punch-drunk.

**sweet talk** (n phr) Conversation (often) deceitfully aimed at sexual or other conquests.

**talk big** (v phr) To brag or boast.

**talk funny** (v phr) To appear strange.

**talk (speak) of the devil** (v phr) We were just talking about you, and you suddenly appear.

**talk out of both sides of one's mouth** (v phr) To be hypo-critical.

**talk turkey** (v phr) To be frank, blunt, outspoken; to get down to business.

**talking heads** (n phr) Radio or TV talk show hosts, newscasters, or those in a similar position.

**talky** (adj) Talkative; loquacious.

**tickle your fancy** (v phr) To please by stimulating one's imagination and/or fantasies.

_Bones_

**bare bones** (n) The essential; the minimum.

**bone of contention** (n) A matter for argument.

**bone tired (weary)** (adj) Extremely tired; exhausted.

**bonehead** (n) Stupid person.

**boner** (n) An erect penis; a major mistake.

**bones** (n) Dice.

**cut to the bone** (v phr) To reduce to the bare minimum.

**feel in one's bones** (v phr) To have a strong intuition about something.

**have a bone to pick** (v phr) To have matter for a quarrel or complaint.

**make no bones about** (v phr) To admit freely; make no attempt to hide.

**skin and bones** (adj) Very thin, emaciated.

**to the bone** (adv phr) Thoroughly.

_Brain, Mind_

**beat one's brains out** (v phr) To think very hard to find the solution to a problem; a threat of bodily harm.

**blow one's mind** (v phr) To amaze;

to astound.

**brain** (n) A very smart person; a genius.

**brainchild** (n) An idea or project one has conceived all by oneself.

**brain dead** (adj) Stupid.

**brain drain** (n) A loss of talented individuals because they can get better opportunities elsewhere.

**brainstorm** (n) A sudden inspiration or insight.

**brainstorm** (v) To discuss a solution to a problem.

**brainwash** (v) To indoctrinate; impose one's will on someone.

**brainwave** (n phr) A sudden, useful idea.

**brainy** (adj) Smart; intelligent.

**bubble brain** (n phr) Stupid person.

**give someone a piece of one's mind** (v phr) Rebuke, tell someone off.

**have a good mind to** (v phr) To be intent on doing something.

**on the brain, have** (v phr) To think continuously about something; be fixated.

**pick someone's brains** (v phr) Ask someone for advice.

**shit for brains** (adj phr) Stupid; ineffectual; worthless.

*Breast, Bosom, Chest*

**bosom buddy** (n) A very close friend.

**breast** (n) While the male breast has given rise to practically no slang expressions, the female breast has received excessive attention in American slang. Slang names for the female breast are derived from the animal and the plant kingdom, from objects resembling the female breast, or simply from invented words derived from the word *breast*. For example: *tits, udders, melons, pears, jugs, boobs, bazooms, knockers, pineapples*, to mention only a few.

**get something off one's chest** (v phr) To reveal something one has previously suppressed.

**play close to the chest** (v phr) To be secretive.

*Cheek*

**cheek** (n) Impudence; arrogance.

**cheek by jowl** (n phr) Close together; familiar.

**cheeky** (adj) Impudent.

**tongue-in-cheek** (n) In jest; not literal.

**turn the other cheek** (v phr) Not to respond to an offensive action.

*Chin*

**keep one's chin up** (v phr) To hold up well under adversity.

**take it on the chin** (v phr) To accept disappointment or defeat.

*Ear*

**all ears** (adj) Attentive; listening.

**bend one's ear** (v phr) To talk incessantly to someone.

**chew one's ear off** (v phr) To talk to someone extensively and tediously.

**earful, give someone an** (v phr) To lecture or reprimand.

**play it by ear** (v phr) To improvise; act spontaneously.

**wet behind the ears** (adj) Young; inexperienced; naive.

*Elbow*

**at one's elbow** (phr) Very close; easy to reach.

**elbow bender** (n) A drinker.

**elbow grease** (n) Physical effort.

**elbow one's way in** (v phr) To push oneself in.

**elbow room** (n) Space enough to work and move around.

**elbow someone out** (v) To force someone out.

**not know one's ass from one's elbow** (v phr) Not to have a clue.

**rub elbows** (v phr) To associate with.

**up to the elbows** (adj phr) Deeply engaged.

*Eyes, Eyebrows, Eyelashes*

**bat an eyelash (eyelid), not** (v phr) Not to react.

**black eye** (n) A bad reputation; an adverse image.

**catch one's eye** (v phr) To get someone's attention.

**eye-opener** (n) Anything that informs or enlightens.

**eyeball** (v) To look over.

**feast one's eyes on** (v phr) To look at with enjoyment.

**for your eyes only** (n phr) Private; secret.

**four-eyes** (n) One who wears glasses.

**give someone the eye** (v phr) To look at in a flirtatious way.

**give someone the evil eye** (v phr) To put a malediction on someone.

**goo goo eyes** (n) Eyes expressing love; attraction.

**have eyes for** (v phr) To be preoccupied by; to be attracted to.

**Here's mud in your eye!** (phr) A drinking toast.

**highbrow** (adj) Educated; cultured.

**in a pig's eye** (n phr) Never; not at all.

**keep an eye on** (v phr) To watch steadily.

**make eyes at someone** (v phr) To communicate admiration through looks.

**My eye!** (interj) Exclamation of astonishment or doubt.

**red-eye, the** (n) A very early-morning train or plane.

**see eye to eye** (v phr) To be in agreement.

**shuteye** (n) Sleep.

*Face*

**baby face** (n) Innocent, childlike appearance.

**blue in the face, until one is** (adj phr) To the point of exhaustion.

**egg on one's face** (n phr) Embarrassment; humiliation.

**face-off** (n) Confrontation.

**face the music** (v phr) To accept the situation.

**feed one's face** (v phr) To eat.

**Get out of my face!** (phr) Keep away from me; leave me alone.

**in your face** (adj phr) Direct; confrontational.

**just another pretty face** (n phr) Nothing special; one of many.

**let's face it** (v phr) Acknowledge and accept a situation.

**poker face** (n) Expressionless; not betraying thought or emotions.

**suck face** (v phr) To kiss deeply and passionately.

**two-faced** (adj) Disloyal; dishonest.

### *Fingers*

**all thumbs** (adj phr) Clumsy.

**butterfingers** (n) A clumsy person; clumsiness.

**give the finger** (v phr) To make an obscene hand gesture.

**give me five** (phr) Shake (or slap) hands with me.

**give someone the finger** (v phr) To show contempt; treat unfairly.

**green thumb** (n) Gardening talent.

**high five** (n) Greeting involving the slapping of raised hands.

**lay a finger on someone** (v phr) To touch someone with harmful intent.

**put one's finger on** (v phr) To define exactly; to specify with precision.

**rule of thumb** (n) A general guideline; a truism.

**stick out like a sore thumb** (v phr) To be obviously different; to stand out.

**thumbs-up** (n) Approval.

### *Foot*

**drag one's feet** (v phr) To stall; delay.

**fancy footwork** (n) Adroit evasion; clever maneuvering.

**foot the bill** (v phr) To provide funds; absorb costs.

**get (have) cold feet** (v phr) To have second thoughts; back out.

**get one's feet wet** (v phr) To take the first step; test out a new experience.

**get a foot in the door** (v phr) To make an initial move; complete a first step.

**leadfoot** (n) A fast driver.

**one foot in the grave** (phr) Very ill; very old.

**play footsie with** (v phr) To cultivate a (too) close relationship with another person or party.

**put one's foot in one's mouth** (v phr) To make an embarrassing or stupid remark, usually without thinking.

**put one's feet to the fire** (v phr) To enter a high-risk situation.

**shoot oneself in the foot** (v phr) To get hurt through one's own ineptitude.

**take a load off one's feet** (v phr) To sit down; relax.

**two left feet, have** (v phr) To be clumsy; graceless.

**vote with one's feet** (v phr) To prove a point by walking away from or toward something.

### *Gut*

**bust a gut** (v phr) To make a great effort; to laugh heartily.

**gut feeling** (n) Instinct; intuition.

**gut reaction** (n) Automatic or instinctive response.

**gutless** (adj) Cowardly.

**guts** (n) Courage; internal parts.

**spill one's guts** (v phr) To tell everything one knows; to be frank.

**split a gut** (v phr) (see *bust a gut*)

### *Hair*

**get in someone's hair** (v phr) To

annoy; be in someone's way.

**hairy** (adj) Difficult or dangerous.

**have someone by the short hairs** (v phr) To have someone in a painful or difficult situation; to have control over.

**let one's hair down** (v phr) To relax; loosen up.

*Hand*

**catch someone red-handed** (v phr) To catch someone in a guilty or compromising position.

**give someone a hand** (v phr) To help out; to applaud.

**glad-hand** (v) To be effusive and gregarious.

**hand over fist** (adv phr) Energetically; persistently; rapidly.

**hand in glove** (phr) Very close to one another; conspiratorial.

**hand it to someone** (v phr) To compliment or praise; give credit.

**hand-me-down** (n) Something previously owned; second-hand.

**hand someone someone else's head** (v phr) To destroy someone's work or reputation.

**hands-down, to win** (v phr) Very easily; without an effort.

**hands-on** (adj phr) Direct involvement in something.

**handyman** (n) A person of several skills, a maintenance person.

**handy-dandy** (adj) Very useful.

**have one's hands full** (v phr) To be extremely busy.

**old hand** (n phr) An experienced person; an expert.

*Head*

**a hole in the head** (n) Anything that is irritatingly unnecessary.

**bite someone's head off** (v phr) To respond quickly and angrily.

**bonehead** (n) A stupid person.

**butthead** (n) A stupid person.

**give head** (v phr) To perform oral sex on someone.

**headshrinker** (n) A psychiatrist.

**headhunter** (n) A person hired to find someone to fill a company position.

**head in the clouds, to have one's** (v phr) To be a dreamer; an unrealistic person.

**head examined, should have one's** (v phr) Someone behaving strangely or doing strange things.

**heads will roll** (v phr) People will get into trouble, lose their jobs, etc.

**hit the nail on the head** (v phr) To be right; say the right thing.

**hothead** (n) An ill-tempered or impatient person.

**hand someone's his head** (v phr) To destroy someone's work or reputation.

**in over one's head** (adv phr) To get into something beyond one's ability.

**knucklehead** (n) A stupid or inept person.

**like a hole in the head, need something** (v phr) To get something you'd rather not have.

**off the top of one's head** (adv phr) Without much thinking; impromptu; spontaneously.

**over one's head** (phr) More than one can understand.

**shithead** (n) A stupid or inept person.

**skinhead** (n) Bald person; Marine recruit; Neo-Nazi.

**stand on one's head** (v phr) To make a great effort.

**talking head** (n) A television reporter.

**yell (scream) one's head off** (v phr) To shout very loudly.

### Heart

**all heart** (adj) Very kind person.

**bleeding-heart liberal** (adj phr) A person who is naively or ineffectually liberal.

**Have a heart!** (v phr) Be compassionate!

**heart of the matter** (n phr) The essence of something.

**heart to heart** (adj phr) A frank and open exchange.

### Heel

**close on one's heels** (adv phr) To follow someone closely.

**cool one's heels** (v phr) To wait; to be kept waiting.

**round heels** (n) A sexually available woman.

### Knee

**bring to one's knees** (v phr) To force to submit.

**cut someone off at the knees** (v phr) To deflate or reduce someone.

**knee-deep (in trouble)** (adj) In deep trouble.

**knee-jerk** (adj) Instinctive; automatic.

**knee slapper** (n) A very funny joke.

### Leg

**break a leg** (v phr) Good luck!

**get up on one's hind legs** (v phr) To assert oneself.

**give a leg up** (v phr) To help advance.

**have a leg on** (v phr) To have a good start on a project.

**last leg, be on one's** (v phr) To be near death; at the end of something.

**legwork** (n) Physical work related to a task.

**not have a leg to stand on** (v phr) To have no excuse or defense.

**pull one's leg** (v) To fool someone by playing on his credulity.

**shake a leg** (v phr) To hurry; to dance.

**stretch one's legs** (v phr) To get up after sitting for a long time

**take to one's legs** (v phr) To run away.

### Lip

**fat lip, give someone a** (v phr) To punch someone in the mouth.

**lip, give someone** (v phr) To protest or back-talk in an offensive way.

**lip** (n) Impudent talk; back-talk.

**lip service** (n) Talk that leads to no action.

**My lips are sealed** (v phr) A promise to keep a secret.

**stiff upper lip** (n) A stoic facade; calmness under pressure.

**tight-lipped** (adj) Untalkative; secretive.

**watch (read) my lips** (v phr) Listen to me carefully.

## Mouth

**all mouth** (adj) All talk and no action.

**badmouth** (v) To speak badly of.

**big mouth** (n) Big talker.

**diarrhea of the mouth** (n phr) In the habit of talking excessively.

**from the horse's mouth** (adv phr) From the source.

**loudmouth** (n) A loud and constant talker.

**mouth off** (v) To complain loudly.

**mouthful, a** (n) A large number of words spoken at once.

**put one's foot in one's mouth** (v phr) To embarrass oneself by making an unwarranted comment.

**run off at the mouth** (v phr) To talk more than one should.

**shoot one's mouth off** (v phr) To talk too much.

**talk from both ends (sides) of one's mouth** (v phr) To make contradictory statements.

**watch your mouth** (v phr) Be careful what you say.

## Nails

**fight someone tooth and nail** (v phr) To fight with everything one has.

**hang on by one's fingernails** (v phr) To cling on precariously; to be barely able to continue.

## Navel

**contemplate one's navel** (v phr) To sit around doing nothing.

## Neck

**neck** (v) To caress and kiss.

**get it in the neck** (v phr) To be hurt badly, physically or otherwise.

**pain in the neck** (adj phr) A real nuisance (genteel form of saying "pain in the ass.")

**stick one's neck out** (v phr) To take a chance.

## Nose

**brown nose** (n) A sycophant; ass kisser.

**have a nose for** (v phr) To have a good way of finding or doing certain things.

**no skin off my nose** (v phr) I have nothing to lose.

**nose up in the air, to have one's** (v phr) To be haughty, arrogant.

**nose job** (n) An operation to make one's nose look more attractive.

**nosy** (adj) Excessively curious.

**on the nose** (adj phr) Precisely.

**pay through the nose** (v phr) Pay excessively and forcibly.

**poke one's nose into something** (v phr) To intrude oneself into someone else's affairs.

**stick it up your nose** (v phr) Take it and don't bother me with it.

## Penis

**penis** (n) The male organ has many slang expressions, some descriptive, some fanciful. Examples: *dick, dork, cock, prick, peter,* etc., which take on additional meanings, mostly connoting a bad or unworthy person.

## Piss

**full of piss and vinegar** (adj phr) Full of energy; ready to go.

**pisser** (n) A very difficult job.

**pisshead** (n) A despicable person.

**piss in the wind** (v phr) To waste one's time and effort.

**piss off** (v) To make someone angry; get out of here.

**piss-poor** (adj) Of very low quality.

**pot to piss in, not have a** (v phr) To be very poor.

*Shit (Crap, Feces)*

**bad shit** (n phr) Bad luck; something bad in general.

**beat the crap out of someone** (v phr) To hurt someone physically; to beat someone in a game; to defeat.

**crock of shit** (n phr) Nonsense; lies and exaggerations.

**cut the crap** (v phr) Stop talking nonsense.

**full of shit** (adj phr) Lying; dishonest.

**good shit** (n) Good stuff.

**happy as a pig in shit** (adj phr) Extremely content.

**hot shit** (n phr) A very remarkable or attractive person.

**in deep shit** (adj phr) In deep trouble.

**not give a shit** (v phr) Not care at all.

**scare the shit out of someone** (v phr) To frighten someone to the point of losing control over one's bodily functions.

**shit** (n) Perhaps the most commonly used slang term in American English. Used in many and varied ways. Polite form: *Shoot.*

**Shit!** (interj) Stronger form of *damn* or *hell.*

**shit for brains** (n) A very stupid person.

**shit hits the fan, the** (v phr) Some big trouble starts.

**shithead** (n) Stupid person; bad person.

**shit or get off the pot** (v phr) Do what needs to be done or give it up.

**tough shit** (n) Too bad.

*Shoulder*

**carry the weight of the world on one's shoulders** (v phr) To walk around as though one is experiencing all the pain and trouble of the world.

**give someone the cold shoulder** (v phr) To treat someone with disdain; to ignore someone.

**put one's shoulder to the wheel** (v phr) To work vigorously.

**rub shoulders with** (v phr) To mingle with prominent people.

*Skeleton*

**have skeletons in one's closet** (v phr) To have deep dark secrets in one's life.

*Skin*

**by the skin of one's teeth** (adv phr) Barely getting by.

**get under someone's skin** (v phr) To anger or irritate someone.

**no skin off one's nose** (n phr) Does not affect one at all.

**pigskin** (n) The ball used in American football.

**save one's skin** (v phr) To avoid death or injury.

**skin** (n) Dollar bill; condom; hand

used for handshake.

**skin** (v)  To cheat; to defeat.

**skin flick** (n phr) A movie featuring nudity.

**skinhead** (n) A bald person; a Marine recruit; a Neo-Nazi.

**skinny-dip** (v) To swim naked.

**wolf in sheepskin (sheep's clothing)** (n phr) An aggressive person who pretends to be kind.

*Skull*

**out of one's skull** (adj phr) Crazy.

**thick skull** (n) Stupid.

*Stomach*

**cannot stomach something or someone** ( v phr) Not to be able to tolerate or stand.

**have the stomach for something** (v phr) To be able to stand something.

**turn one's stomach** (v phr) Make one feel ill.

*Throat*

**ram down one's throat** (v phr) To force something on someone.

**deep throat** (n phr) A secret contact.

*Toe*

**on one's toes** (adv phr) Alert.

**step on someone's toes** (v phr) To offend.

**toe the mark** (v phr) To behave properly.

**toe to toe, go** (v phr) To fight hard.

**turn one's toes up** (v phr) To die.

*Tongue*

**hold one's tongue** (v phr) To exert control over one's desire to speak up.

**on the tip of one's tongue** (adv phr) Something one almost remembers but not quite.

**tongue lashing** (n phr)  Verbal rebuke or abuse.

**tongue-tied** (adj phr) Unable to speak.

*Tooth*

**have teeth** (v phr) To show strength.

**in the teeth of** (n phr) Directly against.

**it has no teeth** (v phr) It has no enforcement power.

**show one's teeth** (v phr) Show strength; threaten.

**sink one's teeth into something** (v phr) To get involved in something with great enthusiasm.

**sweet tooth** (n phr) Weakness for candy and sweet food.

**tooth and nail, fight someone** (v phr) To fight ferociously, with all of one's means.

*Vagina, Female Genitals*

**cunt** (n) A woman; a whore; an evil woman. (extremely derog.)

**vagina** (n) There are many slang expressions for the female genitals, derived from the animal and plant kingdom, suggestive and derived terms. Examples: *bag, basket, bush, business, crack, cunt, fish pond, hog-eye, hole, hotbox, jewelry, monkey, muff, oatbin, pan, pussy, slot, snatch, tail, twat, cherry,* and many more.

*Whiskers*
**whiskers** (n) An old man.

# LEGAL, LAW ENFORCEMENT, AND CRIME

(*Note:* There is a vast underworld vernacular in American English, which is also true worldwide, since those who operate outside the law need special words to hide their intentions and activities. It is not our intention to delve into this kind of language. Only publicly known and well established underworld terms have been included.)

**ambulance chaser** (n phr) An unethical or over-aggressive lawyer.
**appoint oneself judge and jury** (v phr) To take complete charge.

**bail out** (v phr) To get someone out of trouble; to escape.
**ball and chain** (n) One's spouse.
**beat the rap** (v phr) To avoid punishment or retribution.
**blow the whistle** (v phr) To inform on someone; expose someone.

**con** (n) Convict; a swindle.
**con** (v) To cheat someone out of something; to put on.
**con man (con artist)** (n) Cheater.
**cop shop** (n) A police station.
**copper** (n) Police officer.

**day in court, have one's day** (v phr) To get one's turn to be heard.

**devil's advocate** (n) One who argues the dissenting side of an issue.
**D.O.A.** (Adj phr) Dead on Arrival (a body or an idea).
**don** (n) Mafia chief; big shot.

**federal case, make a** (v phr) To make a big issue out of something not so big.
**finger** (n) Police informer.
**finger** (v) To inform on someone.
**flatfoot** (n) Police officer.

**gander** (n) A criminal lookout.
**Gestapo techniques** (n) Brutality.
**get off someone's case** (v phr) To leave someone alone.
**get on someone's case** (v phr) To meddle; pay unwanted attention.
**G-man** (n) An FBI agent; government agent.
**goniff** (n) Thief.
**good time** (n phr) A prison term.
**gorilla** (n) A muscular criminal.
**gumball** (n) Light on top of a police car.
**gumshoe** (n) A police officer; detective.

**I rest my case** (v phr) I finished saying what I had to say.

**jailhouse lawyer** (n) One who always looks for loopholes.
**John Law** (n phr) A police officer.
**jury is out, the** (phr) No decision has been made.
**jury-rig** (v) To improvise a temporary repair or solution.

**kangaroo court** (n phr) A mock

court; a self-appointed punishing body.

**legal beagle** (n)  An astute and successful lawyer.

**legal eagle** (n) A cunning attorney.

**lifer** (n) Inmate serving a life sentence.

**Philadelphia lawyer** (n phr)  One who makes things unnecessarily complicated.

**pig** (n) Police officer. (derog.)

**plead (take) the fifth** (v phr)  To decline to answer any questions.

**police** (v) To clean up; to patrol; to maintain order.

**rabbi** (n)  A highly placed patron.

**rat** (n) An informer; a despicable person.

**rat** (v) To inform on someone.

**read the riot act** (v phr)  To reprove sternly.

**rip** (n)  Stolen goods.

**rip off** (v) To steal.

**ripoff** (n) A bad deal; too costly.

**ripoff artist** (n phr)  Thief; deceiver.

**sea lawyer** (n)  One who knows how to subvert the rules.

**smoking gun** (n phr) Concrete evidence.

**snitch** (v) To inform on someone.

**soldier** (n) A low-ranking Mafia member.

**stool pigeon** (n phr)  Police informer.

**third degree** (n) Prolonged intense questioning.

**throw the book at someone** (v phr) To give someone a severe punishment.

**walk** (v)  Be acquitted; set free.

# MEDICINE AND PHARMACEUTICALS

(*Note*: The so-called "drug culture," namely, the entire phenomenon of handling and using illicit drugs, has given rise to a huge slang vocabulary. It is not our intention to delve in great detail into this realm of American slang.)

**abortion** (n)  A complete failure.

**ambulance chaser** (n) An unethical or overly aggressive lawyer.

**aspirin** (n)  An inadequate or temporary solution to a problem.

**Band-Aid** (n) A temporary remedy.

**bite the bullet** (v phr) Face unpleasant facts.

**bitter pill** (n) A disappointment; an unfortunate occurrence.

**cancer** (n) An evil, destructive element or force.

**cancer stick** (n) A cigarette.

**coffin nails** (n)  Cigarettes.

**cough up** (v phr) To pay money or produce goods or information, usually reluctantly.

**D.O.A.** (phr) Dead on arrival; finished before it started.

**doc** (n)  A physician; an informal way of addressing someone.

**doctor** (n) A way of addressing someone of higher rank or education, not necessarily with a doctor's degree.

**doctor** (v) To add liquor to a drink; to alter dishonestly.

**Dr. Feelgood** (n phr) A physician or layperson who administers illicit or unhealthy means of feeling good.

**doctor's orders** (n phr) Something one is strongly advised to do.

**dope** (n) A stupid person.

**dope out** (v phr) To figure or work out.

**dosed** (adj) Infected with a venereal disease.

**drug on the market** (n phr) An unwanted commodity; a product which does not sell.

**drugstore cowboy** (n) An idler.

**German goiter** (n) A beer belly.

**goofballs** (n) Barbiturates.

**headache** (n) Trouble.

**Jewish Dristan** (n) Horseradish.

**Jewish penicillin** (n) Chicken soup.

**needle** (v) To tease someone.

**No-clap Medal** (n) Good conduct medal.

**O.D.** (v) To overdose; to overindulge.

**pill** (n) An obnoxious person.

**pill peddler** (n) A doctor.

**shot in the arm** (n phr) A boost.

**spin doctor** (n) One who interprets events to the advantage of one's employer.

**take one's medicine** (v phr) To accept adverse circumstances.

**use the needle** (v phr) To become a narcotics addict.

**verbal diarrhea** (n) Talking too much.

**what the doctor ordered, just** (n phr) The right thing.

# MILITARY

(*Note*: The use of military slang, which has been quite pervasive in American culture, has greatly dwindled since World War II, especially after the Vietnam War. Much of military slang has been absorbed by the general culture, especially by the business world.)

**A-1 (A-number-1)** (adj) Perfect; the best. (Navy)

**ammo, ammunition** (n) Any valuable information or argument useful in a debate, argument, or fight.

**ass in gear, get one's** (v phr) To get things together and ready.

**A.W.O.L.** (phr) Absent without permission.

**bail out** (v phr) To sell off; close out. (Air Force)

**balls to the wall** (adv phr) To the extreme; at full speed. (Air

Force)

**barracks lawyer** (n) Giver of unwanted advice. (Army)

**Batten down the hatches!** (interj) Get ready. Trouble is coming. (Navy)

**big gun** (n) A person in a position of high authority.

**big guns** (n) Persons, equipment, ideas, proposals, etc., capable of greatly affecting or changing a situation.

**bilge** (n) Worthless talk or writing. (Navy)

**blockbuster** (n) A great success. (WWII air bombing)

**bilgewater** (n) Nonsense. (Navy)

**blow out of the water** (v phr) To defeat utterly. (Navy)

**blitz** (v) To defeat soundly; to inundate with information.

**bomb** (n) A long direct pass in football; a complete failure, especially in the theater.

**bomb out** (v) To lose.

**bombard** (v) To inundate with information; to verbally assault someone, aggressively and continuously.

**bombshell** (n) A striking event; a very sexy woman.

**bounce off the wall** (v phr) To be in a very nervous state. (Army)

**brainwash** (v) To indoctrinate in an extreme way. (Korean War)

**brass (hat)** (n) Impudence; a military officer.

**buddy** (n) Close friend; comrade.

**buddy-buddy** (n) Close friend; (adj) too friendly for one's liking.

**buddy up to** (v phr) To become close to someone.

**by the numbers** (adv phr) Mechanically. (WWI)

**by the seat of one's pants, do something** (v phr) To act by instinct, not by clear instructions.

**call the shots** (v phr) To control the situation.

**cannonball** (n) A fast express train; a bundle of energy.

**commando** (n) Any aggressive person.

**co-pilots** (n) Amphetamines. (Air Force)

**dead soldier** (n) An empty bottle.

**Down the hatch!** (phr) A toast, followed by swallowing an entire drink.

**double, on the** (adj phr) At twice the normal speed.

**drill** (n) The accepted routine.

**drill sergeant** (n) A dictatorial and demanding supervisor.

**dud** (n) A failure.

**earn one's wings** (v phr) To pass required tests; to develop skills; to prove reliability. (Air Force)

**flagship** (n) The primary or lead ship, idea, company, or product of the line. (Navy)

**flak** (n) Troubles; problems; severe criticism. (Air Force)

**flak (flack)** (v) To act as a publicity agent. (Air Force)

**flak catcher** (n) A lower-ranking employee who acts as a shield between the boss and troublemakers.

**flash in the pan** (n phr) Of

momentary importance; of short endurance. (Army)

**flyboy** (n)  A combat pilot.

**fly off the handle** (v phr) To lose one's temper. (Air Force).

**fly right** (v phr)  Be honest. (Air Force)

**get on the stick** (v phr) To fall in with the routine; commit to the job. (Air Force)

**give it one's best shot** (v phr) To make one's best effort.

**give up the ship** (v phr)  Give up.

**gizmo** (n)  An unspecified object; something one does not know the exact name of (a "whatchamacall-it"). (Navy)

**glitch** (n)  Operating defect.

**go ballistic** (v phr)  Lose control, go crazy.

**go down in flames** (v phr) To fail spectacularly. (Air Force)

**good soldier** (n)  A cooperative underling;  one  who  follows orders (even doubtful ones).

**gun** (n)  A long surfboard.

**gung-ho** (adj) Enthusiastic.

**heavy artillery** (n)  (see *big guns*) (Army)

**hit the deck** (v phr) To get to work. (Navy)

**hold (down) the fort** (v phr) To remain behind to take care of things. (Army)

**jump the gun** (v phr) To act prematurely.

**latrine lawyer** (n phr)  An argumentative soldier.

**launch(ing) pad** (n)  A starting point.

**loose cannon** (n) An out-of-control or unpredictable person.

**map out** (v phr)  To make up advance plans.

**minefield** (n)  A dangerous place.

**nose dive** (n phr)  A sudden drop, as in the stock market.

**nuke** (v)  To destroy; to heat in a microwave.

**old Army game** (n)  A swindle. (Army)

**old soldier** (n)  Cigar or cigarette butt.

**on the beam** (adv phr)  On the right track.

**pistol** (n)  A lively or "fun" person.

**pull rank** (v phr)  To over-assert one's authority;  use authority arrogantly.

**second-in-command**  (n)  Next in authority after the top person.

**secret weapon** (n)  Hidden asset or ability.

**section 8** (n phr) discharge from military service on the grounds of insanity or unsuitability

**shoot** (v)  This verb is the source of a great deal of slang. Technically speaking, it comes from hunting, not the military, since a soldier fires, rather than shoots. The line of demarcation, however, has been blurred, to say the least. Examples:

**shoot down** (v) To put someone down, discredit.

**shoot from the hip** (v phr) To speak honestly.

**shoot oneself in the foot** (v phr) To get hurt through one's own ineptitude or words.

**shoot one's meal** (v phr) To vomit.

**shoot one's mouth off** (v phr) To brag; reveal secrets; talk too much.

**shoot one's wad** (v phr) To risk or give up everything.

**shoot-out** (n phr) An argument or fist fight.

**shoot the breeze** (v phr) To chat casually.

**shoot the works** (v phr) To do everything; bet all of one's money.

**shooting match, the whole** (n phr) The whole thing; everything.

**sky pilot** (n) A clergyman of any faith.

**SNAFU** (n) A large and obvious mistake; [Situation Normal, All Fucked Up]. (WWII)

**S.O.P. (Standard Operating Procedure)** (n) The usual operation.

**spike** (v) To destroy one's chances of success; to sabotage. (Army)

**squeeze gun** (n) A pressure riveter.

**straight shooter** (n) An honest, uncompromising person.

**submarine (sub)** (n) A sandwich on an oblong roll. (Navy)

**take no prisoners** (v phr) To kill everybody; do a thorough job.

**tell it to the Marines** (phr) An expression of extreme disbelief.

(Navy)

**top brass** (n) Persons with the highest office or position.

**topsider** (n) Person with a high government position.

**troops** (n) Lower echelon workers.

**wing it** (v phr) To improvise. (Air Force)

**whole nine yards** (n phr) The whole thing; the whole process. (Army and Navy)

**zap** (v) To hit or wound.

**zero in** (v phr) To concentrate; narrow one's focus.

## SENSES & FEELINGS

**boy (girl) smeller** (n) Young girl (boy) who spends a lot of time with the opposite sex.

**(cop a) feel** (v) To sneak a touch of a girl's body.

**feel cheap** (v phr) To feel worthless or degraded.

**feel for** (v phr) To be sympathetic; to feel affection for.

**feel funny** (v phr) To feel ill.

**feel like shit** (v phr) To feel lousy; to feel miserable.

**feel no pain** (v phr) To be drunk.

**feel one's oats** (v phr) To feel excitement about one's abilities and one's manhood or womanhood.

**feel rough** (v phr) To feel ill or unwell.

**feel something in one's bones** (v phr) To strongly sense that something (bad) is about to happen.

**feel up** (v) To use one's hands to make sexual advances.

**feel your own man** (v phr) To have a sense of being in control.

**feeler** (n) A tentative question or gesture.

**hear one out** (v phr) To test one's knowledge; to hear one's side of the story.

**(can't) hear oneself think** (v phr) There's too much noise.

**(never) hear the end of it** (v phr) To be blamed.

**see a man** (v phr) To go to the bathroom.

**see a man about a dog** (v phr) To go to the bathroom.

**see any flies on me?** (v phr) Do I look incapable of taking care of myself?

**see any green (on me)?** (v phr) Believe me, I am experienced.

**see how the land lies** (v phr) To look around; to analyze the situation.

**see off** (v) To reprimand (tell off); to say farewell to someone starting a journey.

**see one's aunt** (v phr) To go to the bathroom.

**see red** (v phr) To get angry.

**see stars** (v phr) To be knocked out.

**see the color of your money** (v phr) Put your bet on the table.

**see the devil** (v phr) Get drunk.

**see you!** (v) Goodbye!

**see you later, alligator!** (v phr) Goodbye!

**see what I mean?** (v phr) Do you understand?

**seeing is believing** (phr) Nothing is real unless you can touch it.

**seeing things** (phr) Having visions.

**(should have) seen it coming (a mile off)** (v phr) You are very gullible.

**short sighted** (adj phr) Lacking foresight.

**smell a rat** (v phr) To sense something is wrong.

**(sweet) smell of success** (n phr) Winning is wonderful.

**smeller** (n) Nose.

**(that) smells (stinks)** (v phr) That's highly offensive or abhorrent.

**smelly** (adj) Offensive; objectionable.

**stink** (n) A big fuss.

**stink bomb** (n phr) A mustard gas shell; a sudden offensive event.

**stink pot** (n phr) An unsavory individual.

**stinker** (n) A disgusting person; something very difficult.

**stinking** (adj) Drunk.

**stinking with money** (adj phr) Loaded with huge assets.

**stinko** (adj) Drunk.

**stinky** (adj) Lousy; objectionable.

**(bad) taste** (adj) Aesthetically inappropriate.

**tetched** (adj) Mentally unbalanced; touched.

**tetchy** (adj) Peevish; testy.

**touch** (v) To wheedle a loan.

**(in) touch** (adj) Making or maintaining contact.

**(out of) touch** (adj) Losing contact; ignorant.

**(Soft) touch (easy touch)** (n phr) A person easy to borrow from or solicit favors from.

**touch one for a loan** (v phr) To wheedle a loan.

**touch-and-go** (adj phr) Uncertain; insecure.

**touch bottom** (v phr) To reach the ultimate in degradation; to sink to a new low.

**touch of the tar brush** (adj phr) Having some negro ancestors.

**touch off** (v phr) To get something started.

**touch up** (v phr) To correct small defects; to improve appearance.

**touch wood** (v phr or interj) To avoid bad luck; to avoid the evil eye.

**touched** (adj) Mentally unbalanced; emotionally affected.

**touched by an angel** (v phr) Blessed; inspired.

**touched (in the head)** (v phr) Mentally unbalanced.

**touchy** (adj) Easily offended.

**touchy-feely** (adj) Sensitive.

## TRANSPORTATION

**ambulance chaser** (n) An unethical or overly aggressive lawyer.

**at a crossroads** (adv phr) To have several alternatives available.

**backseat driver** (n phr) Someone who tells the one in charge what to do.

**bandwagon, join (jump on, get on) the** (v phr) To join a current-ly popular cause.

**be in the same boat** (v phr) To be in the same situation or predicament.

**be off one's trolley** (v phr) To be crazy.

**big wheel** (n) An important person.

**bum steer** (n) Misdirection; bad advice.

**caboose** (n) The buttocks. (Railroad)

**charge one's batteries** (v phr) To be refreshed and re-energized.

**driver** (n) Airplane pilot.

**driver's seat, be in the** (v phr) To be in control; be in charge.

**fifth wheel** (n) A superfluous, useless person in a group. (Automotive)

**fly** (v) To drive fast.

**fly, it doesn't** (v phr) It does not work; it fails.

**give up the ship** (v phr) To give up hope.

**go into high gear** (v phr) To get going.

**hit the road** (v phr) To get going; leave.

**hot rod** (n phr) A fast car.

**jack up** (v phr) To raise the price excessively.

**jalopy** (n) Old and battered car.

**jerkwater** (adj) A small town. (Railroad)

**joy ride** (n phr) A ride taken for pleasure; a pleasant experience.

**joystick** (n phr) A control lever of an airplane, now also for computer games.

**jumpstart** (v) To stimulate; give impetus to. (Automotive)

**just off the boat** (adj phr) Naive; ignorant; easily victimized.

**keep on trucking** (phr) To continue on with what one is doing.

**locomotive** (n) An organized group cheer, starting slowly and softly and building up in intensity.

**middle of the road** (adj phr) Not given to extremes, especially in politics and lifestyle.

**mileage, get a lot of** (v phr) Get a lot of use out of something.

**miss the boat** (v phr) To lose an opportunity.

**Model-T** (n) Cheap, crude item.

**nosedive, take a** (v phr) To lose suddenly.

**on the wagon** (adj phr) To have given up alcohol.

**posh** (adj) Luxurious. (Cruise ship)

**put the cart before the horse** (v phr) To get ahead of oneself; get one's priorities wrong.

**railroad** (v) To convict someone on false or forged evidence; to force someone into an undesirable position.

**rock the boat** (v phr) To cause trouble; to unbalance a situation.

**saddle shoes** (n) Shoes with a contrasting colored instep.

**sail into** (v phr) To attack; criticize.

**ship comes home (in), when one's** (v phr) When one's fortune is made.

**space cadet** (n phr) Someone out of touch with reality.

**tailgate** (v) To follow closely and relentlessly. (Automotive)

**taken for a ride** (v phr) Swindled; deceived.

**third wheel** (n) (see *fifth wheel*) (Bicycling)

**trip** (n) A special experience.

**wheel and deal** (v phr) To make many and frequent business transactions.

**wheel man** (n) A skillful driver, especially of a getaway car.

**wheels** (n) A car; means of transportation.

## FORBIDDEN TERMINOLOGY — Derogatory Racial Terms

Readers who have followed the O.J. Simpson trial will remember numerous references to the "N-word." Occasionally, in the media, you may have encountered the word itself, namely *nigger,* an insulting word so inflammatory to African-Americans that the "N-word" had to be used as a euphemism. There are many such terms in the American language that are derogatory references to racial or religious background.

These terms have a long history, but are rarely openly used today. They are considered highly offensive to the individuals described or addressed, and hence not politically correct. Some are only mildly negative, but others are highly inflammatory and can be dangerous to use. It should be noted, however, that these words are sometimes used in jest between members of the same race or religion, much in the same way that a parent calls a child a *monkey* or a *little devil.* One common term not listed below is WASP (White, Anglo-Saxon Protestant). It may sometimes be mildly derogatory, but is usually used just to delineate an American ethnic division.

Some terms are simply abbreviations with a negative twist, but many have interesting histories. *Bohunk* is a shortened form of Bohemian-Hungarian. *Dago* probably comes from the Spanish name *Diego,* but primarily refers to Italians—obviously an etymological confusion. *Frog* and *Limey* refer to dietary habits. *Nigger* is a corruption of the term *Negro,* as pronounced by slave holders in the antebellum South. *Ofay* is Pig Latin for *foe.* *Slant* refers to the perceived shape of Asian eyelids. *Wog* is a sarcastic acronym for *Wily Oriental Gentleman.* And *Wop* may have originated as as an initialism for *WithOut Passport (or Papers).*

Because of their disparaging nature, these terms should never become part of one's active vocabulary. However, since they are words which you will periodically encounter, they should become part of a passive vocabulary and be rarely used but easily recognized.

| | | |
|---|---|---|
| **Bohunk** — Eastern European | **Jap** — Japanese | **Rusky** — Russian |
| **Chink** — Chinese | **Kike** — Jew | **Raghead** — Arab |
| **Dago** — Italian | **Kraut**—German | **Slant, Slope** — Asian |
| **Frog** — French | **Limey** — English | **Spade** — Black |
| **Gook** — Vietnamese | **Mick** — Irish | **Spick** — Hispanic |
| **Hebe** — Jew | **Nigger** — Black | **Wog** — Arab or East Indian |
| **Honkey** — Hungarian | **Nip**—Japanese | **Wop** — Italian |
| **Honky** — White | **Ofay** — White | **Yank**—American |
| **Hymie** — Jew | **Paddy**— Irish | |
| | **Polack**— Pole | |

## CONTRONYMS

This may seem amazing, but the fact is that there are over fifty words in American English which have two exactly opposite meanings. People who like to play with words call them *contronyms*, and a sampling of these words or expressions is given below:

**Bolt**: To fasten in place or to dash or break away. *Examples*: He bolted the two parts together; He bolted his political party.

**Below par**: Very good or very poor. *Examples*: He won the golf game with a below par score; His S.A.T. marks were below par.

**Critical**: Opposed to or necessary for. *Examples*: I am critical of your efforts; However, your work is critical to the success of this project.

**Impregnable**: Unable to be penetrated or able to be penetrated and impregnated. *Examples*: The army surrounded the fort, but found it impregnable; His wife had problems conceiving but, with medical assistance, she became impregnable.

**Out**: Visible or invisible. *Examples*: The moon will be out tonight; During the air raid, they turned the lights out.

**Overlook**: To look over or view or, alternatively, to fail to see. *Examples*: My high-floor apartment windows overlook the park; I received a citation because I overlooked a stop sign.

**Sanction**: To provide approval or to show disapproval by censuring. *Examples*: The union sanctioned the strike; The United Nations sanctioned Iraq.

**Seeded**: With seeds or without seeds. *Examples*: Two acres of land are seeded and ready to grow; Give me one pound of seeded raisins.

**Take**: To obtain or to provide. *Examples*: Do you mind if I take these?; Young children take cute photos.

**Trim**: To add things to or to cut something away. *Examples*: The week before Christmas, we trim the tree; The barber trims my mustache.

**Wear**: Endure or erode. *Examples*: Good quality cloth wears well; The tide slowly but surely wears away the sea wall.

**Wind up**: To start or to end. *Examples*: Wind the clock to get it started; It is getting late, so it is time to wind up this discussion.

More than 650 million people in the world speak English as either a first or second language. Do they all speak it identically? Not on your life. An American need only step over the border into Canada to realize just how widely varied the English language can be. In addition to Canadian English, there are Australian English, New Zealand English, South African English, Indian English, numerous varieties of pidgin-English, and of course, British English.

The two major groupings, however, are American English and British English. And the differences—believe it or not—can be huge. In fact, there are some cases where the same word or expression has totally opposite meanings in England and in the United States. When the U.S. House of Representatives *tables* a motion, they are shoving it off to the side, in effect killing it. When the British Parliament *tables* a motion, they are putting it on the table for prompt consideration. When an American judge *enjoins* a given action, he is forbidding the enjoined party from carrying out that action. When a British judge *enjoins* a given party, he is directing that party to carry out a specific act or action. In the theatre, if a London West End play is a *bomb*, it is a huge success. A Broadway play which *bombs* is an abject failure. And, of course, *public schools* in England would be considered *private schools* in the United States.

Obviously, not all terms have opposite meanings in our respective countries, but a tremendous number of words and phrases have different meanings or at least confusing (if not arcane) ones. Some of the differences involve changing a single letter, e.g. *tyre, manoeuver*, and *carcase* in England, versus *tire, maneuver*, and *carcass* in America. Some require changing only a single syllable, e.g. *aluminium* and *appendicectomy* in Britain versus *aluminum* and *appendectomy* in America. Many words ending in *-er* in America become *-re* in England, e.g. *centre* vs. *center*. Similarly, many words spelled with an *ou* in England use a simple *o* in America. The British *colour* and _labour_ become _color_ and _labor_ over here. The British are fond of shortening words and adding -_ers_ to the end in casual conversation. Champagne comes out as _champers_, and pregnant as _preggers_. A number of words are spelled the same but have different pronunciations. _Clerk_ is pronounced "clark," and _schedule_ is pronounced "shedule," not "skedule," in England. However, in most cases, as you will see from the following list, different words are needed to convey the same idea.

This section is divided into two parts—more or less mirror images of each other. The first consists of British terms, alphabetically arranged, coordinated with their American or U.S. equivalents. The second gives you alphabetically arranged American terminology, with "translations" into British English. As noted below, Canadians seem to have adopted (and adapted) large segments of both "languages."

Due to the ubiquitous nature of American movies and television, much more of the American variety of English is spoken worldwide. But there are many places, in particular England, Australia, New Zealand, and South Africa, where British terminology (though modified) still prevails. Canadians borrow a little from each area, often with amusing results. A sign frequently seen in Canada is _Tire Centre_, using the American spelling for tire and the British for center. At MIIS, where the Author taught, well over 90 percent of the T & I students knew American English, but were weak on British equivalents. It is hoped that the list below will close that gap.

One peculiarity should be noted. Probably due to movies and television, most Britons will recognize American terminology and sometimes use it. Unfortunately, the reverse is not true. Most Americans are no more skillful in recognizing British terms in the list below than are foreign students of English. Incidentally, many but not all of the following terms, particularly the casual ones, are used more frequently by middle class and lower economic class Britons than by their more literate and educated counterparts. Quite a few of these terms are colloquial and even slang, but they are frequently used on the streets of London and in English newspapers and periodicals.

There are several thousand terms where British terminology is different from American vernacular. About 2,500 of the more commonly used ones are listed below. In cases where there is some doubt as to whether a word or expression is used as a verb, noun, or other grammatical form, abbreviations such as (v), (n), (adj), and (adv) provide guidance.

Readers will note that quite a few British expressions originate with Hindi or other Indian languages, while more American expressions have American Indian or (in the Southwest) Mexican Spanish origins.

Since there are many terms for specialized automobile parts and for guidance while driving on English roads, a special section titled *Automotive, Aircraft, and Transportation* has been provided.

| BRITISH | U.S. | BRITISH | U.S. |
|---------|------|---------|------|
| about turn | about face | | machine |
| accident | | antenatal | prenatal |
|   department | emergency room | anti-clockwise | counter-clockwise |
| acclimatize | acclimate | anti-nuisance | |
| Admiralty | Department of the |   pill | tranquilizer |
| | Navy | appendicectomy | appendectomy |
| adopt | nominate | approved | |
| advance | |   school | reform school |
|   bookings | reservations | arrows | darts |
| afters | dessert | aquascutum | waterproof |
| agent (political) | campaign | | overcoat |
| | manager | argy-bargy | (n) an argument; |
| aggro | exasperation; | | (v) to argue |
| | violence | arm (of eye- | |
| agony aunt | advice columnist |   glasses) | temple; earpiece |
| | (e.g. Dear | arse | ass; buttocks |
| | Abby) | articled clerk | paralegal |
| air hostess | flight attendant | ash | cane |
| airy-fairy | delicate; unreal | assist the police | undergo police |
| A-levels | SATs | | questioning |
| Alf Garnett | Archie Bunker | assurance | insurance |
| All Fools Day | April Fool's Day | at a pinch | in a pinch |
| all-in | all-inclusive; | athlete | track and field |
| | without restric- | | person |
| | tions | athletics team | track team |
| all stations call | all-points bulletin | at the weekend | on the weekend |
| | (APB) | aubergine | eggplant |
| almoner | hospital social | Aunt Sally | scapegoat |
| | worker | au pair | live-in nanny |
| almshouse | poorhouse | Aussie | Australian |
| Alsatian | German shepherd | autocue | teleprompter |
| | dog | avenue | estate driveway |
| aluminium | aluminum | away day | day trip |
| amenity bed | private hospital | away team | visiting team |
| | room | | |
| amusements | carnival rides | back garden | backyard |
| ankle-biter | rug-rat | backhanders | kickbacks |
| anorak | parka; wind- | back of beyond | remote |
| | breaker | back of hill | ridge; crest |
| another | et al (legal) | backward | |
| ansaphone | answering |   thought | second thought |

| BRITISH | U.S. | BRITISH | U.S. |
|---------|------|---------|------|
| bad form | bad manners | bat | ping-pong paddle |
| bad patch | rough time | bate | rage |
| Bad show! | too bad; poor | bathe | swim |
| | performance | batman | officer's |
| bag (v) | catch; kill; claim | | manservant |
| bagman | tramp; traveling | bawdy house | cat house; |
| | salesman | | whorehouse |
| bags of... | loads of... | be a devil | take a chance |
| bag-wash | rough-dry laundry | beadle | ceremonial |
| bailiff | estate manager | | official |
| baker-legged | knock-kneed | beak | principal; school- |
| baking tray | cookie sheet | | master; judge |
| baksheesh | payoff; corruption | beaker | mug; cup |
| balls-up (n) | foul-up | bean | currency; coin |
| balloon went | | beastly | very unpleasant |
| up, the | trouble started | | or disagree- |
| banbury cake | small mincemeat | | able |
| | pie | beck | nod of the head |
| bangers | sausages | bedhead | headboard |
| bangers and | | bedmaker | chambermaid |
| mash | sausages and | bedside locker | nightstand |
| | mashed potatoes | bedsitter | studio apartment |
| bang on | exactly right; | beer from the | |
| | right on | wood | draft beer |
| bank holiday | public holiday | beetle crushers | heavy boots |
| bank note | dollar bill; paper | beetle off | get lost; scram |
| | money | before you can | |
| bankers order | instructions for | say knife | before you can |
| | bank to pay | | say Jack |
| | bills | | Robinson |
| bannock | a flat cake or bun | Belisha beacon | pedestrian |
| banting | dieting | | crossing |
| bap | hamburger bun | | signal |
| barmaid | waitress | bell | telephone call |
| barmy | weak-minded | bellpush | doorbell |
| barrack (v) | jeer | belt up! | shut up! |
| barrister | trial lawyer | be mother | pour tea or coffee |
| barrow | pushcart | bent | dishonest |
| bash (n) | attempt; try | bent copper | crooked police |
| basin | bowl | | officer |

| BRITISH | U.S. | BRITISH | U.S. |
|---|---|---|---|
| be on | be right; suitable | blimey! | damn! |
| berk | idiot; fool | blimp | pompous, stuffy person |
| bespoke | made to order | | |
| best end | rib chops; sirloin | bloater | smoked herring |
| betty | burglar's tool | block | large building |
| beyond the job | over the hill | block of flats | apartment house |
| biffin | red apple (cooked or baked) | bloke | fellow; guy |
| | | bloody | damned; fuckin' |
| big dipper | roller coaster | bloody-minded | stubborn; obstinate |
| biggen | make bigger | | |
| big wheel | ferris wheel | bloomer | error; blunder |
| bikkie (juvenile) | biscuit | bloomin' | damned |
| bill (restaurant) | check | blot one's copy- | |
| billingsgate | abusive language | book | spoil one's record |
| bin | wastebasket; trash can | blow the gaff | spill the beans |
| | | blower | telephone |
| bind | nuisance | blow-lamp | blow torch |
| bingle | long, curled bangs | bluebottle | police officer |
| | | blue-eyed boy | fair-haired boy |
| bint (derog.) | girl; woman | board | sign |
| bird | chick; girl | bobby | policeman |
| biro | ballpoint pen | bobbish | brisk |
| biscuit | cookie; cracker | bobby-dazzler | remarkable event or person |
| Bishop Barnaby | ladybug | | |
| bit of a lad | ladies' man | Bob's your | |
| bit of all right | pleasing; attractive | uncle! | There it is! |
| | | boffin | scientific researcher |
| bit of goods | pretty girl | | |
| bitter | draft beer | bogle | boogey man; scarecrow |
| bivvy | pup tent | | |
| black Maria | police wagon | boiled shirt | Tuxedo shirt |
| black or white? | cream in your coffee? | boiler | furnace |
| | | boiler suit | coveralls |
| blackguard | scoundrel | bollocks | balls; testicles |
| blackleg | scab (labor strike) | bolthole | escape hatch |
| blag | (n) violent rob- bery; (v) rob | bomb (v) | succeed |
| | | bone (v) | steal |
| blancmange | jelly pudding | boob (v) | err |
| bleeding | damned | bookstall | newsstand |
| blighter | uncouth, ob- noxious person | booking clerk | ticket seller |
| | | booking hall | ticket office |

| BRITISH | U.S. | BRITISH | U.S. |
|---|---|---|---|
| bootlace | shoestring | brimstone | sulfur |
| boots | shoe shiner | bring and buy | |
| bore (n) | well | sale | swap meet |
| Borstal | reform school | broad bean | lima bean |
| bosh | nonsense | broadcheck | checkered |
| boss-eyed | cross-eyed | brogues | clodhoppers; |
| bossy boots | bossy person | | bulky shoes |
| bother! | come on! damn! | brolly | umbrella |
| bottle | courage; guts | brown bread | whole wheat |
| bottom drawer | hope chest | | bread |
| botty | buttocks; rear end | brumous | foggy; rainy |
| bounce | cockiness | bub | boob; tit |
| boundary | limit | bubbly | champagne |
| bounder | uncouth, tactless | buck | boastful |
| | person | buck up | cheer up |
| bowler | derby hat | bucket (v) | rain heavily |
| box | street intersection | buffer | old duffer |
| box-room | hotel luggage | bug rake | comb |
| | storage | bugger all | nothing |
| box-up | bad mistake | bugger off | bug off; get lost |
| braces | suspenders | buggy | stroller |
| bracken | large fern | building | |
| brackets | parentheses; | society | savings and |
| | (square) brac- | | loan association |
| | kets | bum | buttocks; rear end |
| brain fag | mental exhaustion | bumble (v) | to make mistakes |
| brambles | blackberries | bummel | stroll; walk |
| brass | money | bunce | unexpected bonus |
| brass farthing | plugged nickel | bunch of fives | fist |
| braw | very good-looking | bunches (hair) | pigtails |
| brawn | head cheese | bung (n) | bribe |
| breaker's yard | junkyard | bung (v) | throw; toss |
| breaking up | end of (school) | bureau | desk with drawers |
| | semester | burgess | borough citizen |
| breast pin | tie pin; stick pin | burn | creek; river |
| breeze | loss of temper | bursar | college treasurer |
| breeze block | cinderblock | bursary | scholarship |
| brekkers | breakfast | busker | street performer |
| brew up | brew or make tea | bust | broken |
| brickie | bricklayer | butter bean | lima bean |
| bright | well | butter muslin | cheesecloth |

| BRITISH | U.S. | BRITISH | U.S. |
|---|---|---|---|
| buttered eggs | scrambled eggs | car boot sale | garage sale |
| buttery | snack bar | carcase | carcass |
| butties | sandwiches | cardies | cardigan sweaters |
| buttonhole | boutonniere | carr | bogs; wet marsh- |
| buy a pup | be tricked | | land |
| by election | special election | carriage | railway or subway |
| by half | too much | | car |
| | | carriage | |
| cab rank | taxi stand | forward | C.O.D. |
| caboose | galley | carriage paid | prepaid delivery |
| cad | uncouth person | carry-cot | infant carrier |
| caddle | confusion; | carry on | continue (doing or |
| | disorder | | talking) |
| cadge (v) | borrow or beg | cash desk | cashier; check-out |
| café (also *caff*) | snack bar | | counter |
| caird | gypsy; tramp | cash point | ATM (automatic |
| cakes and ale | fun and games | | teller machine) |
| cakewalk | easy task | cast | |
| call (v) | arrive; visit | nasturtiums | cast aspersions |
| call-box | telephone booth | castor sugar | refined granulated |
| call over | roll call | | sugar |
| Cambrian | Welshman | casual work | temporary work |
| came away | went away | casualty ward | emergency room |
| camiknickers | | catch it (v) | to be punished |
| (also *camis*) | women's under- | cater-corner | catty corner |
| | garments | catapult | slingshot |
| camp bed | cot | catch it | get into trouble |
| candyfloss | cotton candy | catch someone | |
| cannot for nuts | incompetent | out | catch one lying |
| canny | sly | catch you up | catch up with you |
| canoodling | cuddling; necking | catering corps | army cooks |
| Can that row! | shut up; be quiet | cause list | trial docket |
| can't...for nuts | worth beans; | chairperson | president |
| | incompetent | chairside | |
| canteen of | | assistant | dental assistant |
| cutlery | chest of | chalk and | |
| | silverware | cheese | day and night |
| cantrip | prank; trick | chamber maid | hotel maid |
| canty | cheerful; brisk | chambers | law offices |
| capsicum | bell pepper | champers | champagne |

| BRITISH | U.S. | BRITISH | U.S. |
|---------|------|---------|------|
| change | information; satisfaction | chip (v) | tease |
| chap | man; person | chip shop | fish and chip shop |
| chapel | any religion other than the Church of England | chips | French fries |
| | | chippy | fish and chip shop |
| | | chit | note; receipt |
| char (also *cha*) | tea | chivvy | keep after; harass |
| char (also *charlady*) | cleaning lady | chock a block | full up |
| | | chop | trademark; quality of brand |
| charge-hand | supervisor | chop box | picnic basket |
| charge-nurse | supervisor; head nurse | chronic | bad; severe |
| | | chuck it (v) | get rid of; quit |
| charge of costs | cost accounting | chucker-out | bouncer |
| Charlie | fool; victim | chuffed | pleased; delighted |
| chartered accountant | certified public accountant | clever dick | smart alec |
| | | chump | head; fool |
| chase up (v) | find; get | cinema | theater |
| chat show | talk show | Cinders | Cinderella |
| chat-up (v) | talk flirtatiously; seduce | circular tour | round trip |
| | | cistern | toilet tank |
| | | city, the | financial district |
| cheek | nerve; chutzpah | city centre | downtown |
| cheeky | impertinent | city editor | financial editor |
| cheerio | best wishes | city page | financial section (newspaper) |
| cheerie-bye | bye-bye | | |
| cheesed off | fed up; annoyed | civilised | civilized |
| Chelsea bun | currant bun | civil servant | government employee |
| chemist | druggist | | |
| cheque | bank check | claims assessor | claims adjuster |
| chequers | checkers | clanger | blunder |
| cheverel | kid; kid leather | clapped out | tired; exhausted |
| chicory | endive | claret | Bordeaux wine |
| chief constable | sheriff | clasp-knife | pocket knife |
| child-minder | babysitter | clean one's teeth | brush one's teeth |
| chimney | smokestack | | |
| chimney piece | mantelpiece; mantel | cleansing dept. | street cleaners |
| | | cleg | horsefly |
| chimney stack | line of chimneys | clerk | office worker (not a salesperson) |
| chinwag | conversation; chatter | | |

| BRITISH | U.S. | BRITISH | U.S. |
|---|---|---|---|
| clever dick | wise guy | cold store | freezer |
| climber | vine | collar stiffener | collar stay |
| clingfilm | plastic wrap | collar stud | collar button |
| clippie | female bus driver | collect (v) | pick someone up |
| | | collins | thank-you note |
| cloak room | check room | collop | portion of meat |
| cloak room attendant | hat-check girl | collywobbles | stomachache |
| | | colourways | range of colors |
| cloam oven | clay oven | come-day, go-day | happy-go-lucky |
| clobber | hit (v); gear (n) | come over queer | become dizzy; queasy |
| close down | shut down (radio, TV) | | |
| close on | nearly | come right across | come across |
| close season | closed season | come to stay | come for a brief visit |
| closet | small room (not a storage area) | come up | live in a college dormitory |
| clothes horse | drying rack | comforter | woollen scarf; (baby) pacifier |
| clothes peg | clothespin | coming up to | nearly |
| clotted cream | cream thickened by scalding | commercial traveller | traveling sales-person |
| coach | excursion bus | | |
| coat rail | clothes rack | commis boy | busboy |
| cob | adobe | commissionaire | hotel doorman |
| cock-a-hoop | excited | commons | shared meals |
| cock a snook | thumb one's nose | communication cord | emergency cord |
| cockshy (n) | target | conditionally discharged | put on probation |
| cock-up | foul-up | confidence trick | confidence game |
| cock won't fight, this | This dog won't hunt) | conker | horse chestnut |
| | | connexion | connection |
| cochineal | red food coloring | conserve | preserves (food) |
| coddle | overprotect | consignment note | bill of lading |
| codlin (n) | cooking apple | consultant | head of a hospital department |
| codswallop | nonsense | | |
| coffee bar | coffee house | | |
| coffee stall | moveable coffee bar | | |
| cold comfort | poor consolation | | |
| cold container | ice chest; cooler | | |

| BRITISH | U.S. | BRITISH | U.S. |
|---------|------|---------|------|
| contracts exchanged | real estate deal closed | counterfoil | housing check stub |
| cook (v) | tamper with | county town | county seat |
| cooker | stove | courgettes | zucchini |
| cookery book | cookbook | court card | face card |
| cop it (v) | die; get into trouble | court shoes | pumps |
| cop shop | police station | courtesy appearance | cameo appearance |
| copying pencil | indelible pencil | cove | guy; fellow |
| Cor! | exclamation of surprise | covered in | covered with |
| corn | cereal grain, e.g. wheat | covert coat | short, light overcoat |
| corn chandler | grain dealer | cowboy | incompetent or deceitful worker |
| cornet | ice cream cone | cow gum | rubber cement |
| cornflour | cornstarch | cow pat | cow pie; dung |
| cornstone | red and green limestone | crackers | crazy |
| corporation | municipal government | cravat | necktie |
| corrector of the press | proofreader | craved for | craved |
| cos lettuce | romaine lettuce | crawler board | repairer's dolly |
| cosh | blackjack (n); bludgeon (v) | cream crackers | soda crackers |
| costard | A variety of large apples | creamed potatoes | mashed potatoes with cream |
| costermonger | fruit/vegetable store or street vendor | creased | exhausted |
| costumier | costumer | credit account | charge account |
| cot case | bedridden patient | creepers | vines |
| cot-death | crib death (SIDS) | crepe bandage | gauze bandage |
| cottier | cottage resident | crinkle-crankle | full of twists and turns |
| cotton | thread | crisps | potato chips |
| cotton reel | spool of thread | croft | lot of arable land |
| cotton wool | absorbent cotton | crook drama | crime show |
| cotty | tangled; matted | cross, on the | on the bias |
| council house | subsidized | cross talk | discussion; repartee |
| | | cross wires | crosshairs (guns) |
| | | crossed cheque | bank check with red band protective mark |

| BRITISH | U.S. | BRITISH | U.S. |
|---|---|---|---|
| crotchet (also *crochet*) | quarter note (music) | daily | crazy housekeeper (non-live-in) |
| crown estate | federally owned land | damn all | nothing |
| cruet | salt and pepper shakers | dampen the clothes | sprinkle the clothes before ironing |
| crumbed cutlet | breaded cutlet | | |
| crystallised fruit | candied fruit | danger list (medical) | critical list |
| crumpet | English muffin | danger money | hazardous duty pay |
| culpable homicide | manslaughter | darbies | handcuffs |
| cul de sac | dead end street | dart (v) | tranquilize |
| cupboard | cabinet; cupboard | dash (n) | tip; gratuity |
| curate | vicar's assistant | Dash! | a mild curse |
| curate's egg | something both good and bad | davenport | drop-front desk with drawers |
| curd cheese | cottage cheese | davy | affidavit |
| curl down (with a book) | curl up (with a book) | daylight robbery | highway robbery |
| current account | checking account | day out | day off |
| current form | present behavior | day return | bargain rate roundtrip ticket |
| curtain rail | curtain rod | | |
| curtains | drapes | day trippers | people taking one-day outings |
| cut (v) | prepare; make | dead | totally; completely |
| cut-throat | straight razor | dead-men | empty bottles |
| cut to size | cut down to size | deaf aid | hearing aid |
| cutters | cookie cutters | deal together | get along together |
| cuttings | clippings (newspaper) | death duty | inheritance tax |
| CV (curriculum vitae) | resumé; list of qualifications | debit (v) | charge to |
| | | deed box | strong box; safe-deposit box |
| | | deed-poll | legal document of intention, e.g. change of name |
| D.J. | dinner jacket | | |
| dab hand | expert | | |
| dabs | fingerprints | dekko (n) | look |
| daft | foolish; silly; | delivery round | delivery route |

| BRITISH | U.S. | BRITISH | U.S. |
|---------|------|---------|------|
| demerara | raw brown sugar | dive entrance | basement entrance |
| demob (v) | be discharged | diversion | detour |
| | from armed | divvy | dividend |
| | services | D-notice | censorship (by |
| dene | seaside sand dune | | government) |
| deposit account | savings account | do | (v) arrange for |
| deputation | delegation | | or serve; (n) |
| despatch dept. | shipping dept. | | party; cele- |
| destructor | incinerator | | bration |
| devilry | mischief | do a bunk | run away |
| dialling tone | dial tone | do for | cook and clean for |
| diamanté | rhinestones | do oneself well | do well for |
| diary | day-book; date- | | oneself |
| | book | docket | ticket; sales slip |
| diary | | dodgy | risky; tricky |
| engagement | appointment | dog collar | clerical collar |
| dicky | shaky; unsound | dog-end | cigarette butt |
| did himself in | committed | dog tooth | houndstooth |
| | suicide | | (fabric pattern) |
| diddle (v) | cheat; gyp | dogsbody | servant; drudge |
| digestive biscuit | whole-wheat | doing the | |
| | cookie | shops | shopping |
| digger | Australian or | dole | welfare |
| | New Zealander | dolly-bird | bimbo |
| dig over (v) | weed | dolly mixture | multicolored |
| digs (also | | | candies |
| *diggings*) | furnished rooms | don | college fellow or |
| dim | stupid | | tutor |
| dinner's up | dinner's ready | done (v) | studied; cheated; |
| dinner suit | | | arrested |
| or jacket | tuxedo | done a runner | escaped |
| directly | immediately | done up | redecorated; |
| directory | | | repaired |
| enquiries | telephone | done with | used to advantage |
| | information | donkey's years | long time period |
| dirty weekend | weekend spent | door-knocker | door-to-door |
| | with lover | | salesperson |
| dishy | attractive; amiable | dormitory | |
| disorientated | disoriented | suburb | bedroom |
| district | precinct | | community |

| BRITISH | U.S. | BRITISH | U.S. |
|---------|------|---------|------|
| **Dorothy bag** | drawstring bag | **dry goods item** | any non-liquid |
| **dosser** | street person | **drying-up cloth** | dish towel |
| **dotty** | crazy; ditzy | **ducky** (also | |
| **double-barrelled** | hyphenated | *ducks*) | darling; dear |
| **double cream** | whipping cream | **dud cheque** | bad or bounced |
| **double Dutch** | nonsense | | check |
| **down deposit** | down payment | **duff** | (adj) worthless; |
| **downpipe** | downspout | | counterfeit; (n) |
| **down tools** (v) | quit work; strike | | boiled pudding |
| **down to me** | up to me | **duffer** | plodding; |
| **downs** | hills | | incompetent |
| **doxy** | prostitute | **Duff's up!** | Soup's on! |
| **dozy** | stupid; lazy | **dumb** | mute; speechless |
| **draper** | dry-goods store | **dummy** | pacifier for babies |
| **drainer** | drain board | **dummy run** | trial run |
| **draught** | | **dunny** | outhouse; privy |
|    **excluder** | weatherstripping | **dungarees** | overalls; coveralls |
| **draughts** | checkers | **dustbin** | garbage can |
| **drawing level** | minimum balance | **dust cart** | garbage truck |
| | (banking) | **duster** | dust ruffle |
| **drawing pin** | thumb tack | **dustman** | garbage collector |
| **dress** (v) | adorn; trim | **duvet** | comforter for bed |
| **dress a bed** | make the bed | **dynamo** | electrical |
| **dressing gown** | bathrobe | | generator |
| **drink mat** | coaster | | |
| **drinks counter** | store liquor | **each holidays** | every vacation |
| | department | **ear-basher** | bore |
| **drinks party** | cocktail party | **ear-biter** | frequent borrower |
| **drinks table** | bar | **ear-wig** (v) | eavesdrop |
| **drip-feed** | intravenous | **early days** | premature |
| | feeding | **earnest money** | deposit |
| **drippings** | dissolved fat from | **earth** | dirt |
| | meat | **earth closet** | outhouse |
| **drive** | driveway | **earthly, an** | a chance |
| **driver** (train) | engineer | **eat Yank way** | eat holding the |
| **drop a brick** | be tactless or | | fork in right |
| | indiscreet | | hand |
| **drove** (n) | old road used by | **edge** | pretensions |
| | drovers | **edge of the** | |
| **drum** | tiny shop |    **earth** | ends of the earth |
| **dry biscuit** | cracker | **effin' blind** (v) | curse |

| BRITISH | U.S. | BRITISH | U.S. |
|---|---|---|---|
| egg-flip | eggnog | excess | |
| eggs and | | (insurance) | deductible |
| soldiers | eggs and toast strips | excuse-me-dance | dance that allows cutting-in |
| egg-slice | spatula | | |
| eiderdown | feather-filled bed comforter | ex-directory | unlisted number |
| | | expect | assume; presume |
| elastic band | rubber band | extension lead | electrical exten- |
| elasticated | elastic; stretched | | sion cord |
| Elastoplast | Band-Aid | extractor fan | exhaust fan |
| elbows out | belligerent | | |
| electric fire | electric heater | face flannel | washcloth |
| electric torch | flashlight | facer | serious problem |
| elevenses | morning coffee break | faff | fuss |
| | | fag | gofer; cigarette |
| enclosed | cloistered | fag out (v) | do another's work |
| endless driven | | fagged | tired |
| belt | conveyor belt | faggots | meatballs or liver-balls |
| endorsements | traffic violation records | fair | (adv) quite; (v) make a clean |
| engaged | busy; occupied | | copy |
| engine driver | train engineer | fair cop | justified arrest |
| enkanlon | blueprint paper | fair on | fair to |
| enough on | | fair treat | attractive; |
| one's plate | all one can handle | | desirable |
| enquire | inquire | | |
| enquiry | information | fairy cake | cupcake |
| enquiry agent | private eye | fairy cycle | child's bicycle |
| estate | housing development | fairy floss | cotton candy |
| | | fallers | windfall fruit |
| estate agent | realtor; real estate agent | fancy (v) | imagine; want |
| | | fancy dress | masquerade |
| estate car | station wagon | fancy work | embroidery |
| evens | equal stakes in betting | fanny | vagina; backside |
| | | farrier | blacksmith |
| ever so (much) | extremely; very much | Father Christ-mas | Santa Claus |
| examination in | | faults | telephone repair |
| chief (legal) | direct examination | | service |
| | | feed on (v) | eat |

| BRITISH | U.S. | BRITISH | U.S. |
|---------|------|---------|------|
| feeder | child's bib | first-year | |
| feeding bottle | baby's bottle | college | |
| feel the wind | run out of money | student | freshman |
| fell | mountain; hill | firth | estuary |
| fell about (v) | laughed uncon- | fish eaters | fish-eating |
| | trollably | | utensils |
| fellow-mad | boy crazy | fish fingers | fishsticks |
| fen | boggy marsh land | fish slice | spatula |
| fetch | go for; bring | fishmonger | fish store |
| fête | fair | fit to tie | fit to be tied; |
| fiddle (v) | swindle; cheat | | angry |
| fiddler's green | heaven; bliss | fit up | frame up |
| fieldsman | fielder (sports) | fitments | fittings |
| fig roll | Fig Newton | fitted (v) | built-in |
| filing card | file card | fitted carpet | wall-to-wall |
| fill me out | fill me in | | carpet |
| fillet steak | boneless sirloin | five minutes to | |
| film | movie | midnight | almost too late |
| final reading | third step in | fiver | five pounds |
| | passing a law | flageolet | French kidney |
| find one's feet | learn one's way | | bean |
| | around | flagstaff | flagpole |
| findings | | flan | open pie; quiche |
| keepings | finders keepers | flannel | washcloth |
| finger of fate | hand of fate | flapjack | makeup compact |
| finish up | end up | flash (adj) | flashy; showy |
| finnan haddie | smoked haddock | flat | apartment |
| fir apple | pine cone | flat block | apartment house |
| fire brigade | fire department | flat spin | panic |
| fire office | fire insurance | flex | electric cord |
| | office | flick knife | switchblade |
| fire practice | fire drill | flicks | movies |
| fire raiser | arsonist | flip | short tour or flight |
| fireplace suite | fireplace tool set | flippin' (adj) | fuckin' |
| firing party | firing squad | | (euphemism) |
| first class | excellent | float | petty cash |
| first cost | | floater | mistake |
| (accounting) | direct labor and | flog | sell or peddle |
| | materials cost | flotation | going public |
| first floor | second floor | | (business) |

| BRITISH | U.S. | BRITISH | U.S. |
|---------|------|---------|------|
| flummery | flattering non-sense; dessert | fringe theatre | off-Broadway theater |
| flutter | small bet | frisson (n) | shiver |
| fly | sharp-witted; streetwise | from a child | since childhood |
| flyscreen | window screen | frowsty | musty |
| fly swat | fly swatter | fruit machine | slot machine |
| fog lamp | fog light | fruiterer | fruit store |
| folkweave | monkscloth | frypan | frying pan |
| foolscap | 12" x 18" paper | fug | stuffy, smoky air |
| football | soccer | fulham | crooked dice |
| footer | rugby or soccer | full age | legal age |
| for | going to | full marks | top grade; excellence |
| for it | in for a bad time | Full Monty | go all the way |
| forcing house | greenhouse | full stop | period (punctuation) |
| fork luncheon | buffet lunch | full stretch | to the limit of one's ability |
| form (school) | grade level; class | | |
| form master | classroom teacher | fun fair | carnival |
| fortnight | two weeks | funk | fear; panic |
| four, in a | double date | funnel | smokestack |
| four by two | two by four (lumber) | furnished apartments | furnished offices |
| four-post bed | four-poster bed | fused | shorted (electrical) |
| fourth-year | senior student | fuss of | fuss over |
| fox (v) | puzzle; baffle | | |
| foyer | lobby | | |
| franking machine | postage meter | G & T | gin and tonic |
| freaked (adj) | streaked; flecked | Gaelic coffee | Irish coffee |
| free house | pub selling many types of beer | gaff | public amusement area |
| freephone | toll-free number (800- or 888-) | gaffer | crew foreman; old man |
| freepost | postage paid at destination | gaga | senile |
| | | gallery | upper balcony tier |
| French beans | string beans | gallops | horse-training track |
| French letter | condom | game, on the | prostitution |
| fresh | new | games-mistress | female gym teacher |
| friendly society | benefit society | | |
| fringes (hair) | bangs | gammon | ham steak |

| BRITISH | U.S. | BRITISH | U.S. |
|---|---|---|---|
| gammy | lame; crippled | through to | call someone |
| gamp | umbrella | get-out clause | loophole |
| gangway | aisle; walkway | get shot of | get rid of |
| gaol | jail | get the chop | get fired |
| garden | yard | get stuffed! | go to Hell! |
| garden flat | basement | getting on at | nagging; scolding |
| | apartment | getting past it | getting up there |
| garden syringe | spray gun | get up one's | |
| gash (adj) | extra | nose | irritate; annoy |
| gasper | cigarette | | someone |
| gated | grounded | get up to | do |
| gaudy | festival | get your skates | |
| gauger | tax assessor; | on | get a move on; |
| | appraiser | | hurry up |
| gave in (v) | submitted; handed | geyser | gas water heater |
| | over | gherkins | pickles, sweet |
| Gawblimey! | God bless me! | ghoulies (also | |
| gazump (v) | outwit; swindle; | *goolies*) | testicles |
| | jack up price | gin and it | dry martini |
| gentlemen's | | ginger nut | gingersnap |
| relish | anchovy spread | gippo | soup; gravy |
| genteelism | use of snobbish | gippy tum | diarrhea |
| | euphemisms | Girl Guides | Girl Scouts |
| gentry | upper middle | giro | credit transfer |
| | class | | system |
| gents' cloaks | men's room | git | worthless person |
| get across | get to; annoy | give away (v) | give up |
| get along | move along | give it a miss | pass it up |
| get back (v) | recover; | give it a rest | cut it out |
| | transcribe | given in | |
| get cracking | get going; hurry | evidence | used as evidence |
| get knotted! | go to Hell! | give over | give up |
| get off it! | don't be | glass | mirror |
| | ridiculous! | glebe | church land |
| get one's feet | | go for (v) | attack |
| up | rest | go like a bomb | succeed |
| get one's | | go off | lose freshness; |
| monkey up | become angry | | spoil |
| get on with it | go ahead | go on a bit | talk a lot |
| get on or | | go sick | feel sick |

| BRITISH | U.S. | BRITISH | U.S. |
|---|---|---|---|
| **go-slow** | union work slow-down | | continue |
| **go to the** | | **got French** | speaks French |
| **country** | hold a general election | **got it in one** | right the first time |
| **go up on one's** | | **got up** | laundered; pressed |
| **lines** | forget one's lines (theater) | **governor** | prison warden |
| **gob** | mouth | **grab a pew** | take a seat |
| **gobsmacked** | startled; astonished | **graduand** | degree candidate |
| | | **graft** | legitimate work |
| **God spots** | televangelist shows | **grammar school** | high school |
| | | **gramophone** | record player |
| **goggle box** | TV set | **grass** | (n) police informer; |
| **going** (adj) | available at hand | | (v) to squeal |
| **going cold** | getting cold | **grave marks** | liver spots |
| **going up the** | | **greaseproof** | |
| **straight** | in the home stretch | **paper** | wax paper |
| | | **great majority** | the dead |
| **going spare** | available | **great toe** | big toe |
| **golf ball** | typewriter ball | **green fingers** | green thumb |
| **golf club** | country club | **green pepper** | bell pepper |
| **gone** | (adj) burned out; (v) 1. run; 2. gone past (time) | **greengrocer** | fruit and vegetable store |
| | | **griff** | reliable news |
| **gone hard** | dried out | **griller** | broiler |
| **gone missing** | has been missing | **grips** | bobby pins |
| **gone off** | lost interest in; became spoiled | **griskin** | lean pork or bacon |
| **good few, a** | a good many | **grog** | rum and water |
| **good show!** | well done! | **grotty** | dirty; ugly |
| **goods engine** | freight train locomotive | **ground floor** | first floor |
| | | **ground land-** | |
| **goods train** | freight train | **lord** | landowner |
| **goods waggon** | train box car | **ground rent** | rent building owner pays for leasing site |
| **gooseberry** | fifth wheel; unwelcome chaperon | **groundsman** | gardener |
| | | **groundage** | port tax on ships |
| **gormless** (adj) | not very bright | **grouse** | grumble; to grumble |
| **got beyond it** | became unable to | | |

| BRITISH | U.S. | BRITISH | U.S. |
|---|---|---|---|
| guard | railroad conductor | hangout | home; residence |
| gubbins | worthless; foolish | hard cheese | tough luck |
| guide dog | seeing-eye dog | hard done by | mistreated; |
| guinea seat | preferred seating | | abused |
| guiser | person in disguise | hard lines | bad luck |
| gully | large knife | hardware | housewares |
| gum | glue or paste | Harley Street | expert medical |
| gumboots | rubber boots | | advice |
| gummy | swollen | has no... | does not speak |
| gumstrip | flypaper | | (a foreign |
| gup | gossip | | language) |
| gym shoes | sneakers | haulier | trucker |
| | | have a go at | attempt; attack |
| haberdasher | notions store | have a tile loose | be feeble-minded |
| hack | work or riding | have a word | |
| | stable horse | with | talk to |
| had it away | | have him up | take someone to |
| with | had one's way | | court |
| | with; had sex | haven't long | |
| | with | had | have just had |
| had on (v) | been "had" or | haver (v) | talk nonsense |
| | tricked | having a bit on | |
| had up (v) | arrested | the side | being unfaithful |
| had you | had it with you | having it off | having sex |
| haircord | horsehair | having one on | putting one on |
| | upholstery | haycock | haystack |
| hair crack | hairline crack | headed paper | letterhead |
| hair grip | bobby pin | headmaster | |
| hairslide | barrette | (-mistress) | school principal |
| hair wash | shampoo | headphone | |
| half-round | half a sandwich | socket | headset jack |
| half term | mid-semester | health hydro | spa; health club |
| | break | Heath | |
| hall | large public room | Robinson | Rube Goldberg |
| hall porter | hotel bellman | heaps | large amounts |
| hallstand | hat rack | hell for leather | at top speed |
| hand | handwriting | helve | axe or pick handle |
| hand of pork | foreleg cut | herringbone | |
| hand in one's | | parlour | milking shed |
| pocket | always paying | Hessian | burlap; sacking |

| BRITISH | U.S. | BRITISH | U.S. |
|---------|------|---------|------|
| **Hey presto!** | Presto change-o! | **ice lolly** | popsicle |
| **hiccup** | hitch | **iced water** | ice water |
| **high** | tall | **ices** | ice cream cones |
| **High Street** | Main Street | **icing nozzle** | decorating tip |
| **high jump** | death or job loss | **icing sugar** | powdered sugar |
| **high rise block** | skyscraper | **identification** | |
| **high ropes** | high horse | **parade** | police line-up |
| **hip-bath** | portable tub | **industrial action** | strike or work |
| **hire purchase** | installment plan | | disruption |
| **hired** | rented | **immersion** | |
| **hoarding** | billboard | **heater** | electric water |
| **hogget** | yearling sheep | | heater |
| **hoggin** | gravel/clay | **in-built** | built in |
| | mixture | **in care** | in a foster home |
| **hogskin** | pigskin | **in credit** | in the black |
| **hoist** | steal; shoplift | **in-filling** | filling in |
| **holiday** | vacation | **in its thousands** | by the thousands |
| **holiday-maker** | vacationer | **in the club** | pregnant |
| **home and dry** | safe and sound | **in the hearth** | on the hearth |
| **homely** | homey; family | **in work** | employed |
| | oriented | **in your own** | |
| **hoodman blind** | blindman's bluff | **time** | on your own time |
| **hoover** (v) | vacuum | **incident room** | police interroga- |
| **hop it** | beat it; get out! | | tion room |
| **horse coper** | horse dealer | **indent** | on order |
| **horse float** | horse trailer | **Indian meal** | corn meal |
| **hosepipe** | garden hose | **Indiarubber** | pencil eraser |
| **hosiery** | underclothes; ac- | **industrial** | strike action |
| | cessories (men) | **infant's school** | kindergarten |
| **hot drawer** | warming oven | **inglenook** | chimney corner |
| **hotel note** | hotel bill | **ingrowing** | |
| **hot up** (v) | warm up | **toenail** | ingrown toenail |
| **house breaker** | building wrecker | **inheritance** | |
| **houseman** | resident physician | **powder** | arsenic |
| **humbug** | peppermint candy | **innings** | period of activity |
| **hump** | being depressed | **inside of** | less than |
| **humpty** | ottoman | **insurance pay-** | |
| **hunting box** | hunting lodge | **out** | insurance award |
| **hutment** | group of small | **intake** | reclaimed moor |
| | huts | | land |

| BRITISH | U.S. | BRITISH | U.S. |
|---|---|---|---|
| interval | intermission | jug | pitcher |
| interior sprung | | jug handles | protruding ears |
|   mattress | innerspring | jumble sale | "white elephant" |
| |   mattress | |   sale; rummage |
| inverted | | |   sale |
|   commas | quotation marks | jumped the | |
| invigilate | proctor a test |   queue | snuck in line; |
| Irish bridge | open stone drain; | |   butted in front |
| |   culvert | |   of |
| ironmonger | hardware store | jumped-up (n) | upstart |
| is nothing to | | jumper | pullover; sweater |
|   do with | has nothing to do | junior school | primary school |
| |   with | just so | expression of |
| issued with | issued | |   agreement |
| | | | |
| jab | shot; injection | kanga | sarong |
| Jack | laborer | kangaroo ball | pogo stick |
| Jack-box | lunch box | keel | flat-bottomed boat |
| jacket potato | baked potato | keep (v) | reside |
| jaffas | oranges | keeper | gamekeeper |
| jam tomorrow | pie in the sky | keltie | sheep dog |
| jammy | lucky | ken (v) | know; be aware |
| jar | glass of beer or | kentish fire | strong audience |
| |   liquor | |   reaction, usu. |
| jemmy (v) | jimmy; pry open | |   negative |
| jewellery | jewelry | kerfuffle | commotion; |
| jib (v) | balk | |   disorder |
| jiggery-pokery | hocus-pocus | kettle holder | pot holder |
| job centre | employment | kick one's heels | cool one's heels; |
| |   exchange | |   wait |
| John Collins | Tom Collins | kid (v) | deceive; trick |
| joiner | carpentry shop | kiosk | telephone booth |
| joint | meat roast | kip | bed; to sleep |
| jokey | ridiculous joke | kipper | smoked herring |
| jotter | small notebook | kirby grip | bobby pin |
| judder | wobble; shake; | kit | uniform |
| |   shudder | kit out (v) | renew one's |
| jugged hare | rabbit stew | |   wardrobe |
| juggernaut | very large truck | kitchen roll | paper towels |
| juggins | simpleton | kittle | ticklish; to tickle |

| BRITISH | U.S. | BRITISH | U.S. |
|---------|------|---------|------|
| kite | small airplane | **land up** (v) | end up |
| Kiwi | New Zealander | **landed** | okay; out of luck |
| knackered | exhausted | **language** | bad language |
| knave (cards) | jack | **larder** | pantry |
| knees-up | lively dance party | **larderette** | small pantry |
| knickers | underpants | **lashings** | lots |
|  | (women) | **last but one** | next to the last |
| knob | small lump of | **last post** | taps (military |
|  | material |  | tune) |
| knock back | eat or drink | **launderette** | laundromat |
|  | quickly | **lavatory** | toilet; restroom |
| knockers | breasts | **lavatory pan** | toilet bowl |
| knock-up | (n) tennis prac- | **law-hand** | handwriting for |
|  | tice; (v) awaken |  | legal documents |
|  | someone | **lay** | occupation; |
| knocking shop | brothel |  | business |
| knocking-up |  | **lay a charge** | file a police |
|   campaign | door-to-door |  | complaint |
|  | solicitation | **lay on** | provide services; |
| knuckle, close |  |  | cater (with |
|   to the | borderline |  | food) |
|  | indecency | **lead** | leash; electrical |
| knuckleduster | large ring |  | wire |
|  |  | **leader** | 1. editorial; |
| label | tag |  | 2. chief legal |
| labour |  |  | counsel |
|   exchange | employment | **leading** | pushing |
|  | office | **leant** (v) | leaned |
| lace | shoelace | **lease falls in** | lease runs out |
| lace-up (n) | walking shoe; | **lease of life** | lease on life |
|  | Oxfords | **leat** | flume |
| lacquer | hair spray | **leave the room** | go to the |
| ladies' fingers | okra |  | bathroom |
| lady-bird | ladybug | **leave well alone** | leave well enough |
| lag (v) | insulate; fall |  | alone |
|  | behind | **left luggage** | baggage check |
| lagging (n) | insulation |  | room |
| laid on | arranged for; | **leg-over** | sexual activity |
|  | provided | **leghold trap** | bear trap |
| laid on the shelf | pawned | **lending library** | public library |

| BRITISH | U.S. | BRITISH | U.S. |
|---------|------|---------|------|
| let (v) | rent out | live rough | live like the homeless |
| letter-box | mailbox | | |
| lettings | rental units | liver sausage | liverwurst |
| levant (v) | flee from creditors | livery man | stableman |
| | | living (n) | vicar's position |
| ley farming | rotating crops and grass | loads lift | freight elevator |
| | | local | neighborhood bar |
| library ticket | library card | locum | replacement doctor |
| licensed house | bar; pub | | |
| lido | public swimming pool | lodger | tenant |
| | | lolly | money; candy |
| lie doggo | play dead | lollypop lady | |
| lie in | sleep in; sleep late | (man) | school crossing guard |
| lie of the land | lay of the land | | |
| life assurance | life insurance | long arrived | just arrived |
| lift | elevator | long-case clock | grandfather clock |
| lift cage | elevator car | long chalk, | |
| liftman | elevator operator | by a | by a long shot |
| like one o'clock | energetically | long firm (n) | swindlers |
| like the | | long-headed | shrewd; wise |
| clappers | enthusiastically | long jump | broad jump |
| li-lo | air mattress | long-life milk | ultra-pasteurized milk |
| limbless (n) | amputee | | |
| limited (liability) | | long-lining | trawling for fish |
| company | corporation | long-sighted | far-sighted |
| lined | rich; well-off | long timber | lumber |
| linen bin | laundry basket | long vac | summer break |
| linen draper | dry goods trader | long-view | |
| line of country | field of expertise | window | picture window |
| linesman | railroad track walker | loo | toilet |
| | | look back (v) | come back later |
| lino | linoleum | look-in | brief visit |
| liquid paraffin | mineral oil | look over | look at |
| listed building | registered landmark | look slippy | hurry up |
| | | loose chippings | gravel |
| listening-in | listening | loose covers | furniture slip covers |
| litter bin | wastebasket; trash can | | |
| | | lose one's rag | lose one's temper |
| litterlout | litterbug | lose pat | lose one's train of thought |
| live at | live in | | |

| BRITISH | U.S. | BRITISH | U.S. |
|---------|------|---------|------|
| lost property | lost and found department | make a meal of | make a big production of |
| lot, the | everything | make do and | |
| lot of keys | set of keys | mend | make do; |
| loud-hailer | bullhorn | | economize |
| lounge | bed sitting room | make one's | |
| lounge suit | business suit | number | get in touch with |
| low water | financial problems | make the | |
| lucerne | alfalfa | running | take the lead |
| lucky dip | grab bag | malmsey | Madeira wine |
| luggage van | baggage car | Manchester | |
| lumber (v) | encumber | goods | cotton textiles |
| lumber room | storage room | mandoline | food slicer |
| luv | darling; dear | mangle (n) | clothes wringer; |
| lying open | standing open | | automatic |
| lying up | bed rest | | presser |
| | | manoeuver | maneuver |
| machining | using a sewing machine | manse | minister's home |
| macintosh (also | | mansion flat | condominium |
| mac) | raincoat | mark someone | |
| mad on | mad about; crazy about | off | set someone apart |
| made noises | suggested | market garden | truck garden |
| made to | custom made; fitted measure | marriage lines | marriage certificate |
| madly keen | extremely eager | marshalling | |
| mains | utility lines | yard | railroad yard |
| mains razor | electric razor | martini | dry vermouth |
| maize | corn (food) | mash | (n) mashed |
| maize cob | corn on the cob | | potatoes |
| maize flour | cornmeal | mass | |
| make a | | observation | poll; survey |
| balls-up | fuck up | masses (n) | numerous |
| make a long | | match | game; sporting |
| arm | reach for something beyond one's grasp | | event |
| | | matchboard | tongue-in-groove lumber |
| make a long | | mate | friend; pal |
| nose | thumb one's nose | matelot | sailor |

| BRITISH | U.S. | BRITISH | U.S. |
|---|---|---|---|
| matiness | friendliness | mince | chopped meat |
| maths | math | mincer | grinder |
| matron | head nurse | minerals | carbonated drinks |
| mattamore | cellar | miss off (v) | leave out |
| 'mazed up top | confused | mister | title for surgeon |
| meal table | dinner table | | or dentist |
| mean | stingy | mistress | girls' teacher |
| meat plate | platter | mixed with too | |
| Meccano set | Erector set | much water | not very smart |
| menaces, | | mockers | bad luck |
| demanding | | mog (moggy) | nickname for cats |
| money with | extortion | moke | donkey |
| mental | simple-minded | -monger | (suffix) dealer |
| merchant bank | investment bank | monkey | money; £500 |
| mercer | textile merchant | monkey-engine | pile driver |
| merchant | wholesaler; | monkey jacket | safety vest |
| | importer | monkey nuts | peanuts (in shell) |
| merry dancers | aurora borealis | monkey tricks | monkeyshines |
| merry-go-round | carousel | moor | open land; waste |
| merry thought | wishbone | | land |
| metal quarters | sole and heel taps | more on one's | |
| metals | train rails | plate | more to be done |
| meteorological | | Mothering Day | Mother's Day |
| office | weather bureau | mother's helper | nanny |
| meths | denatured alcohol | move house | change residence |
| mews | neighborhoods | moving stairs | escalator |
| | with cul-de-sacs | much joy | satisfaction; |
| mezzanine | seats just below | | success |
| | stage | muck about (v) | mess around; |
| midden | garbage dump; | | screw around |
| | landfill | mud-coloured | brown |
| middle article | short literary | mufti | civilian clothes |
| | essay | mug (v) | cram, study hard |
| mike (v) | shirk work | multi-storey | high rise |
| milkboiler | saucepan | multiple stores | chain stores |
| milk float | milk truck | music hall | vaudeville |
| milking parlour | milking shed | musical box | music box |
| milk-walk | delivery route | muslins | household linens |
| mill-board | clipboard | mutton | business |
| milliard | billion | muzzy | dull; drunk |

| BRITISH | U.S. | BRITISH | U.S. |
|---------|------|---------|------|
| **Naff off!** | | | (v) steal |
| (euphemism) | Fuck off! | **niffy** | stinky |
| **nail pad** | fingernail | **night sister** | night nurse |
| | buffer | **nil** | nothing; nought |
| **nail varnish** | nail polish | **nip (in, out,** | |
| **nancy; nancy** | | **up)** | move nimbly |
| **boy** | homosexual | **nipper** | child; kid |
| **nappies** | diapers | **nit** | fool; hair lice |
| **nasty piece of** | | **no distance** | not far |
| **work** | contemptible | **nob** | rich or socially |
| | person | | prominent |
| **natiform** | buttocks-like | | person |
| | shape | **nobble** | tamper with or fix |
| **national service** | military draft | **nobby** | stylish; elegant |
| **natter** | (n) aimless chatt- | **no joy** | no luck |
| | er; (v) grumble | **nominated** | |
| **natty** | fancy; flashy | **agent** | designated agent |
| **naturist** | nudist | **non-iron** | permanent press |
| **naught, nought** | zero; nothing | **non-U** | not characteris- |
| **naughts and** | | | tically upper |
| **crosses** | tick-tac-toe | | class |
| **navvy** | construction | **no oil painting** | no Marilyn |
| | worker | | Monroe |
| **near the** | | **normal price** | regular price |
| **knuckle** | indecent; off color | **nosh** | slap-together meal |
| **near thing** | narrow escape | **not a bit of it** | no way (emphatic |
| **neat** (liquor) | straight; without | | denial) |
| | ice | **not a sausage** | not a thing |
| **needle** | ill feeling | **not before time** | not a moment too |
| **needle nose** | lawyer | | soon |
| **nelly** | effeminate youth | **not cricket** | grossly unfair |
| **nesh** | soft; tender; | **not in the same** | |
| | vulnerable | **street** | not in the same |
| **never-never** | installment plan | | league |
| **newsagent** | newsstand | **not on** | not possible |
| **newsreader** | TV announcer | **not on your** | |
| **nice bit of** | | **nelly** | not on your life |
| **crumpet** | attractive woman | **not quite** | socially |
| **nice wash** | freshening up | | unacceptable |
| **nick** | (n) jail; prison; | **not so dusty** | fairly good |

| BRITISH | U.S. | BRITISH | U.S. |
|---|---|---|---|
| not to know | could not have known | | of address |
| note | paper money | on (adj) | (adj) acceptable; possible; (prep) at |
| notecase | billfold; wallet | | |
| nothing in it | nothing to it | on a good | |
| notice board | bulletin board | wicket | in a favorable position |
| notified | recorded; reported | on cost | business overhead; expense |
| noughts and crosses | tic tac toe | | |
| nowt | nothing | on heat | in heat |
| nuts on | crazy about | on its own | only |
| nutter (n) | eccentric or crazy person; weirdo | on license | 1. on parole; 2. licensed to sell alcoholic drinks |
| nylon tights | pantyhose | | |
| | | on my firm | with my company |
| oblique | slash mark (/) | on offer | for sale |
| obtaining by deception | fraud | on the boil | requiring immediate attention |
| occupier | occupant | on the cards | in the cards |
| odd, the | an occasional... | on the fiddle | swindling |
| odd done by | badly treated | on the knocker | door-to-door selling |
| odds and sods | miscellaneous people, etc. | one on her own | one of a kind |
| off | no longer interested in | one-room flat | efficiency apartment |
| off the back of a lorry | out the back of a truck; stolen | ongoings | goings-on |
| | | open access | library system allowing direct access to shelves |
| off colour | out of sorts | | |
| off-cut | remnant | | |
| off-license | liquor store | open cast mining | strip mining |
| off-load (v) | unload | | |
| off-putting | disconcerting | opening time | time when pubs can legally open |
| off-the-peg | off the rack | | |
| offer closes | sale ends | operating theatre | operating room |
| offer price | sale price | | |
| office block | office building | opportunity shop | thrift shop |
| oilskin | oilcloth | | |
| Old Bill, the | police | ordinary shares | common stock |
| old crock | affectionate form | organise | prepare; arrange |

| BRITISH | U.S. | BRITISH | U.S. |
|---------|------|---------|------|
| ostler | stable hand | paper blind | window shade |
| other half, the | wife/husband; better half | paper carrier | shopping bag |
| ourselves to ourselves | remaining aloof | paper handkerchief | tissue |
| out of oneself | not oneself; out of sorts; distracted | paper knife | letter opener |
| | | parade (n) | storefront; strip mall |
| out-college | off-campus | parade state | roll call |
| outfitter | men's clothing store | parading with placards | picketing |
| outgoings | costs after rent | paraffin oil | kerosene; coal oil |
| outhouse | outbuilding; farm building | paraffin burner | kerosene stove |
| | | parboiling | boiling |
| outside of enough | more than enough | parcel | package |
| | | parish lantern | the moon |
| oven gloves | pot holders; oven mitts | park | game preserve |
| | | parky | chilly |
| over the moon | in seventh heaven | part exchange | trade in |
| overall | smock; lab coat | parting | part in one's hair |
| overdress (n) | jumper | Pass the Parcel | Hot Potato (game) |
| overhead railway | elevated railroad | passage | hallway; corridor |
| overlooker | overseer | passing out (v) | graduating |
| overset (v) | upset | passing out parade | graduation ceremony |
| PC (police constable) | police officer | past one's work | past one's prime |
| pack it in | stop work | past praying for | beyond all hope |
| pack up (v) | die; pop off | pastoralist | cattle or sheep farmer |
| packed lunch | brown bag lunch | | |
| packet | a lot of money | pastry roller | rolling pin |
| package holiday | vacation package | pasty | potpie; turnover |
| paddy (n) | tantrum | patch (n) | beat; police patrol area |
| page | bellman | | |
| pair of steps | stepladder | Pater | Father |
| pan | toilet bowl | patty | pastry tart |
| Pancake Tuesday | Shrove Tuesday | paved garden | paved yard |
| | | pawpaw | papaya fruit |
| pants | men's undershorts | pay bed | hospital bed |
| pantechnicon | moving van | paying-in slip | bank deposit slip |

| BRITISH | U.S. | BRITISH | U.S. |
|---------|------|---------|------|
| | | | cider |
| payout | award; amount paid to lawsuit winner | persil white | 99 & 44% pure |
| | | peter (n) | safe; prison cell |
| pay-out | insurance settlement money | peterman | safecracker |
| | | physical jerks | exercises |
| pay packet | paycheck | phone through | telephone someone |
| pay round | terms for pay raise | | |
| | | pi (adj) | pious |
| paysheet | payroll | picked out | trimmed with |
| peach | tattle or report maliciously | picotee | variegated carnation |
| pea-souper | very heavy fog | pictures, the | movies |
| pebble glasses | thick eyeglass lenses | piece of goods | piece of work |
| | | piece of work | disreputable person |
| pecker | pluck; spirit; chin | | |
| peckish | slightly hungry | piece tin | lunchbox |
| peeler | police officer | pigs might fly | when pigs fly |
| peep-oh | peek-a-boo | pig's ear | failure; disbelief |
| peep-toe | open-toed shoe | pigeon pair | boy and girl twins |
| peg | clothespin | piggery | pigsty or farm |
| peg out (v) | die; hang out the wash | piling insult on top of injury | adding insult to injury |
| pelmet | valance | | |
| pen-friend | pen-pal | pillar box | mailbox |
| penman | forger | pinafore | apron |
| penny dropped, the | something became clear; the dawn broke | pinch-fisted | miserly; stingy |
| | | pink coat | hunting jacket |
| | | pinking | cutting scalloped edges on clothes |
| pension scheme | pension plan | | |
| pepperpot | pepper shaker | pinny | apron |
| peppercorn rent | small amount; token rent | pint | beer |
| | | pip | brief high-pitched sound; beep |
| perished (adj) | rotted; worn out | pips | fruit pits; seeds |
| permanent way | railway roadbed | piss off | go away; scram |
| Perpendicular Period | English Gothic architecture | pissed | drunk |
| | | pitch (n) | playing field |
| perry | fermented pear | pitcher | granite paving stone |

| BRITISH | U.S. | BRITISH | U.S. |
|---------|------|---------|------|
| plain as a pikestaff | obvious; unattractive | polling day | election day |
| | | polling station | voting place |
| plaits (hair) | braids | polka dots | chocolate chips |
| plantation | stand of planted trees or plants | poly bag | plastic bag |
| | | pommy (Aus.) | Englishman |
| plaster (n) | medical bandage (Band-Aid) | ponce | pimp; procurer |
| | | pong | stench; a stink |
| plasticated leather | vinyl upholstery | pontoon | blackjack (cards) |
| | | poof | Male homosexual |
| plate | gold- or silver-ware or plates | poop (n) | nobody; a fool |
| | | pop (v) | pawn |
| platebasket | silverware tray | pop off | leave or die unexpectedly |
| platelayer | railroad track layer | pop shop | pawn shop |
| | | pop-wallah | teetotaller |
| playing the goat | playing the fool | poppet | small child (usu. a girl) |
| play the game | play by the rules | | |
| play truant | play hookey | porridge | oatmeal |
| play up | cause problems; act up | portmanteau | suitcase |
| | | position | teller window; situation |
| pleader | advocate; lawyer | | |
| plimsolls | tennis shoes | post (v) | mail |
| plonk | house wine | post bag | mailbag |
| ploughman's lunch | simple pub lunch | post free | postpaid |
| | | post restante | general delivery |
| plug hole | sink or tub drain | post room | mail room |
| plummy | choice; rich | postcode | zip code |
| plus fours (men) | knickerbockers | posting | duty; assignment (military or diplomatic) |
| po-faced | humorless; solemn | | |
| | | postman (woman) | mail carrier |
| pocketbook | notebook; wallet | postman's knock | post office (teen kissing game) |
| pong | stink; smell | | |
| power point | electrical outlet | | |
| points | railroad switches | postoffice directory | telephone directory |
| policies | estate grounds | | |
| polish one's marble | make a good impression | postponement | raincheck |
| polishing shoes | shining shoes | potato crisps | potato chips |

| BRITISH | U.S. | BRITISH | U.S. |
|---|---|---|---|
| pother | fuss and bother | proofed | waterproofed |
| potted | abridged; drunk | propelling | |
| potter (v) | putter | pencil | mechanical pencil |
| prairie hare | jackrabbit | proper | complete; thor- |
| pram | baby carriage | | ough; authentic |
| pre-cooked | | property | |
| meal pack | frozen dinner | market | real estate |
| preference | | proprietary | |
| share | preferred stock | name | trademark |
| preggers | pregnant | proprietor | bar owner |
| prep | study hall period | provost | college president |
| presenter | news anchor; | pub | tavern; bar |
| | radio or TV | public call box | telephone booth |
| | host | publican | bar owner |
| press-button | push-button | public school | private school |
| press-fastener | snap fastener | pud | dessert |
| press stud | snap fastener | pudding basin | mixing bowl |
| press-cutting | | pudding club | pregnant |
| agency | clipping bureau | pull birds | pick up girls |
| press-on towel | sanitary napkin | pull-in | roadside |
| press-up | push-up | | restaurant |
| press man | reporter; | pull pints (v) | work as a |
| | journalist | | bartender |
| pressed (v) | rang | pull up your | |
| pricey | expensive | socks | perform better |
| pricking of | | pull a face | grimace; make a |
| thumbs | premonition of | | face |
| | danger | pulled about | roughly treated |
| primary school | elementary school | pullman restau- | |
| prise | pry; use a lever | rant car | train dining car |
| prison visitor | prison inspector | pump (n) | low-heeled shoe |
| private business | personal | Punch and | |
| | business | Judy show | puppet show |
| private address | home address | punch-up | fight; brawl |
| private enquiry | | punched card | punch card |
| agent | private detective | punnet | berry basket |
| private hire | taxi | punter | gambler; |
| programme | program | | customer |
| promise (v) | assure | purpose-built | made for a |
| prompt to time | right on time | | specific use |

| BRITISH | U.S. | BRITISH | U.S. |
|---|---|---|---|
| **push, given the** | fired; dismissed | **quick off the** | |
| **push-basket** | shopping cart | **mark** | quick to react |
| **push chair** | child's stroller | **quieten** | quiet down |
| **put a foot wrong** | start off on the | **quiff** | tuft of hair |
| | wrong foot | **quit** | acquit |
| **put a quart in** | | **quitted** | quit one's job |
| **a pint** | put a square peg | **quit of** | rid of |
| | in a round hole | **quod** | prison |
| **put about** | put out | | |
| **put down** (v) | 1. put (an animal) | **rabbit** | unathletic person |
| | to sleep; | **raceglasses** | binoculars |
| | 2. charge to a | **rachmanism** | exploitation by |
| | credit card) | | landlords |
| **put it down** | drink it | **racquets** | racketball |
| **put it to some-** | | **rag and bone** | |
| **one** | suggested | **man** | junk man |
| **put someone off** | cause to lose | **rag** | rag on; tease |
| | interest | **rag trade** | garment industry |
| **put someone's** | | **rail** | clothing rack |
| **name for-** | | **railings** | teeth |
| **ward** | nominate or | **railway halt** | flag stop |
| | recommend | **raise a finger** | signal a waiter |
| **put skates on** | hurry; get moving | **raise the wind** | raise money |
| **put a lid on it** | put a stop to it | **raising agents** | leavening (yeast |
| **putting off time** | killing time | | and baking |
| **putting the** | | | powder) |
| **black on** | blackmailing | **ramble** (v) | walk for pleasure; |
| **pylon** | utility pole | | take a stroll |
| | | **ramp** | swindle; racket |
| **quant** | punting pole | **randy** | horny; sexually |
| **quay** | wharf; pier | | aroused |
| **queer** | faint; giddy | **rasher** | slice of bacon |
| **Queer Street,** | | **rat** | quit or desert |
| **to be in** | have financial | **ratepayer** | taxpayer |
| | problems | **rates** | property taxes |
| **queue** (up) | stand or wait in | **rather** | 1. emphatic affir- |
| | line | | mation; 2. (adv) |
| **queue jumping** | getting in line out | | fairly |
| | of turn; butting | **rating** | ordinary seaman |
| | in | **ratty** | angry; irritable |

| BRITISH | U.S. | BRITISH | U.S. |
|---|---|---|---|
| rave (n) | dance party | renter | film distributor |
| rave about (v) | to praise | repair engineer | repairman |
| rawlplug | lead plug | repetition work | assembly line |
| razzle, on the | on a spree | | work |
| reach-me- | | return ticket | round-trip ticket |
| downs | hand-me-downs | reverse charge | |
| read | study a subject; | call | collect call |
| | take a course | rick (wrick) | strain or sprain |
| read out | read aloud | | ligaments |
| reader | proofreader | ride (n) | bridle path |
| reader's ticket | library card | right go at, | |
| readies (n) | cash-on-hand | have a | bawl someone out |
| ready, steady, | | righto | okay; all right |
| go! | get ready, get set, | rig out (v) | supply clothing; |
| | go! | | equip |
| reawoken | reawakened | ring (n) | racetrack betting |
| reception | hotel front desk | | area |
| reception clerk | room clerk | Ring-a-Ring- | |
| reckoning | | o'-Roses | Ring-Around-the- |
| machine | cash register | | Rosie (child's |
| recorded | | | song) |
| delivery | return receipt | ring pull | soda pop can's |
| | requested | | tab; pop-top |
| recordist | sound recorder | ring road | beltway |
| Red Indian | Native American; | ring up (v) | telephone |
| | American In- | ring wall | enclosure wall |
| | dian | rise in pay | raise in pay |
| red meat | dark meat | rising (v) | approaching |
| redcap | military police | rising damp | mildew |
| | officer | riveting | fascinating |
| redundant, | | roadie | manager for |
| made | discharged; laid | | traveling |
| | off | | entertainers |
| reel (of thread) | spool | rock | hard candy |
| regisseur | director of theater | rodent officer | rat catcher |
| | production | roger (v) | copulate; have sex |
| remission | time off for good | | with |
| | behavior | roll neck | turtleneck |
| removing | | romany | gypsy |
| cream | cleansing cream; | roofer | thank-you note |
| | cold cream | room | office |

| BRITISH | U.S. | BRITISH | U.S. |
|---|---|---|---|
| rootle (v) | uproot | running flush | |
| ropy | inferior; unsatis- | (cards) | straight flush |
| | factory | running knot | slip knot |
| rosy in the | | run down | dilapidated |
| garden | everything's | run down (v) | diminish; hunt |
| | coming up roses | | |
| rotter | uncouth or misbe- | sacked | fired; discharged |
| | haved person | safe as houses | very safe; fool- |
| rough grazing | pasture | | proof |
| round | sandwich | sailing boat | sailboat |
| round brackets | parentheses | salad cream | Miracle Whip; |
| round heels | easy girls | | mayonnaise |
| round the twist | crazy | sale of work | handicraft bazaar |
| rounders | baseball-like game | sale room | auction room |
| roundsman | delivery man | sales assistant | salesperson; clerk |
| routeing | routing | Sallies | Salvation Army |
| routemarch | long training | | members |
| | march | saloon carriage | train dining car; |
| row | rowhouses | | parlor car |
| rowing boat | rowboat | salt beef | corned beef |
| rowlock | oarlock | saltings, the | tideland; salt |
| rozzer | cop; police officer | | marsh |
| rubber | eraser | salt cellar (*salt* | |
| rubbish | 1. garbage; trash; | *pot*) | salt shaker |
| | 2. nonsense | sand-glass | egg-timer; hour- |
| rubbish tip | garbage dump | | glass |
| ruddy | damned | sand pit | children's sand- |
| rude parts | private parts; | | box |
| | genitals | sand shoe | tennis shoe |
| rug | blanket | sandstone | brownstone |
| rum | odd; strange; | sandwich cake | layer cake |
| | queer | sandwich tin | layer cake pan |
| rumble to | become aware of | sanitary towels | sanitary pads |
| rumbustious | rambunctious | sark | night shirt; night- |
| rump steak | sirloin; bottom | | gown; slip |
| | round; rump | sarky | sarcastic |
| | roast | Sassenach | Englishman |
| run a scheme | carry out a plan | sat (v) | served as an |
| run on the spot | run in place | | elected official |
| runner bean | string bean | satellite town | suburbs |

| BRITISH | U.S. | BRITISH | U.S. |
|---|---|---|---|
| satin paper | glossy paper | scug | ill-mannered |
| sauce boat | gravy boat | scullery | kitchen work- |
| sausage-dog | dachshund; | | room; back |
| | wiener dog | | kitchen |
| sausage roll | pig in a blanket | scupper | defeat |
| save-as-you- | | scurf | dandruff |
| earn | 401K plan | sea bank | sea wall |
| scarper | run away; flee | sealed | paved |
| scatteration | act of scattering | secateurs | garden shears |
| scatty | hare-brained; silly | second post | second mail |
| scent | perfume; | | delivery |
| | fragrance | secretary | writing desk |
| sceptical | skeptical | security snug | security blanket |
| scheduled | | see off (v) | force to leave |
| (building) | marked for | see over (v) | inspect |
| | preservation | see someone | |
| scheme | plan | right | do right by some- |
| schmutters | cheap clothes; | | one; ensure |
| | rags | | fair treatment |
| school attend- | | self-raising | self-rising (food) |
| ance officer | truant officer | self-service | |
| school break-up | end of the semes- | canteen | cafeteria |
| | ter; end of | sell a pup | cheat or deceive |
| | school year | Sellotape | Scotch tape |
| school dinner | lunch; lunch box | semidetached | duplex housing |
| schoolhouse | schoolteacher's | semiquaver | sixteenth note |
| | house | | (music) |
| schoolmaster | principal | semolina | cream of wheat |
| scoff (v) | eat greedily; scarf | send down (v) | expel or suspend |
| scran | spoiled leftovers | send up (v) | ridicule; spoof |
| scrape | smear of butter | sent to | |
| scribbling block | scratch pad | coventry | ostracized |
| scribbling | | servery | serving room or |
| paper | scratch paper | | area |
| scrounge, | | service flat | apartment with |
| on the | scrounging | | maid service |
| scrum | scrimmage; melee | service lift | dumbwaiter |
| scrummage | scrimmage | services | utilities |
| scrump | steal apples from | serviette | table napkin |
| | the tree | set fair (adj) | clear weather |

| BRITISH | U.S. | BRITISH | U.S. |
|---------|------|---------|------|
| set meal | fixed menu | | different color |
| set of apart- | | shoot (n) | hunting trip |
| ments | suite of rooms | shop | job |
| set on (v) | attacked by | shop assistant | sales clerk |
| set out | arrange; display | shop fitter | display designer |
| set the Thames | | shop gazing | window shopping |
| on fire | set the world on | shopkeeper | shop owner; |
| | fire | | manager |
| sett | stone paving | shop-soiled | shopworn |
| | block | shop-walker | floorwalker |
| settee | loveseat | shopper | shopping bag |
| shadow cabinet | minority leader- | shoppng centre | shopping mall |
| | ship | shopping | |
| shag (v) | copulate | parade | strip mall |
| shagged | exhausted | shopping | |
| shank's mare, | | precinct | cul-de-sac reserv- |
| ride a (v) | walk | | ed for shopping |
| shan't be a tick | I'll only be a | short commons | deprivation; short |
| | moment | | rations |
| shape | mold | shortcake | shortbread |
| share out (v) | divide equally | shortcrust | pie crust |
| share pusher | stockbroker who | shorthand | |
| | advertises | typist | stenographer |
| shares | investment stocks | shot in the | |
| sheep fold | sheep enclosure | locker | kept in reserve |
| sheep walk | sheep pasture | shot of | rid of |
| sheltered ac- | | shout | one's turn to pay |
| commodation | old age home | shouting the | |
| shin of beef | beef shank | odds | voicing one's |
| shingle | small round | | opinion |
| | pebbles | shovelboard | shuffleboard |
| ship chandler | marine equip- | shower room | bathroom |
| | ment supplier | shtoom | hush |
| shire | county | shufti (n) | look-see |
| shirty, get | lose one's | shy off (v) | shy away from |
| | temper | sideboard | buffet |
| shoeblack | shoeshine boy | sideboards | sideburns |
| shoesmith | blacksmith | side plate | bread plate |
| shoes, another | | sides | eyeglass temples |
| pair of | horse of a | | or earpieces |

| BRITISH | U.S. | BRITISH | U.S. |
|---------|------|---------|------|
| signal box | railroad signal tower | | heads |
| | | skint | broke; penniless |
| sign on | sign up | skip | trash dumpster |
| ex-directory number | unlisted number | skip rope (v) | jump rope |
| | | skirl | bagpipe sound |
| silent type-writer | noiseless type-writer | skirting board | baseboard |
| | | skive (v) | shirk |
| | | skivvy (n) | drudge |
| silly bugger | frivolous, foolish person | slag | sleazy girl; barfly |
| | | slag off (v) | slander |
| silly season | late summer | slane | spade for turf cutting |
| silver paper | tinfoil; aluminum foil | | |
| | | slanging match | abusive quarrel |
| silversides | rump roast | slap and cossy | theatre make-up and costume |
| sin-bin | dunce's corner | | |
| since | ago | slap-up | excellent; special |
| sing small (v) | be crestfallen | slash (n) | urination |
| single ticket | one-way ticket | slating | scolding |
| singlets | men's undershirts | sledge | sled |
| sippet | crouton | sleekit | sleek; smooth |
| sister | nurse | sleep rough | camp out; rough it |
| sit an exam | take a test | sleeping carriage | pullman; sleeping car |
| sit-upon (n) | buttocks; rear end | | |
| sitting member | incumbent | | |
| sitting room | living room | sleeping partner | silent partner |
| situation vacant | help wanted | sleevelink | cuff link |
| six over six | 20/20 vision | slide | barrette |
| sixth form | twelfth grade | slip carriage | detached railcar |
| skeleton in the cupboard | skeleton in the closet | slipper bath | portable tub |
| | | Sloane Ranger | yuppie |
| skelly-eyed | squint-eyed | slog | plod |
| sketching block | sketchbook | slops | unappetizing food |
| | | sloshed | drunk |
| skew-whiff | askew | slowcoach | slowpoke |
| skid-lid | crash helmet | slow off the mark | slow-witted |
| skiffle | guitar-rock music | | |
| skinheads | young working-class gangsters with shaved | slut's wool | fluff and dust |
| | | small beer | unimportant act or person |

| BRITISH | U.S. | BRITISH | U.S. |
|---|---|---|---|
| small-holding | small farm | sorel | fallow deer |
| smalls | underwear | sosatie | meat kabobs |
| smarm (v) | flatter insincerely; toady | spanner | monkey wrench |
| | | spare | angry; crazy |
| smarmy | oily; flattering | spatula | tongue depressor |
| smartish (adv) | quickly | speakers | on speaking terms |
| smashing | first-rate; A-1 | special area | depressed districts |
| smiled to | smiled at | special offers | sales |
| Snakes and Ladders | Chutes and Ladders | speciality | specialty |
| | | spectacles | eyeglasses |
| | | spend a penny | go to the toilet |
| snap check | spot check | spiky | touchy |
| sneak | tattler; rat; stool pigeon | spilt | spilled |
| | | spine-back | loose-leaf notebook |
| snip | bargain | | |
| snog (v) | neck | spinney | row of trees |
| snorker | sausage | spirits | alcohol and liquor |
| snort | tattler; rat; stool pigeon | spit | a spade-depth of earth |
| snowslip | avalanche | spiv | petty thief |
| snuff it | die; kick the bucket | splash (out) | spend money recklessly |
| snug (snuggery) | small bar room | split (n) | narc; police informer |
| soak (v) | pawn | | |
| soakaway | water drain pit | split new | brand new |
| social security | welfare | split on (v) | narc; betray |
| sock suspenders | men's garters | split pin | cotter pin |
| | | split pulse | split peas |
| sod | bastard (derog.) | split ring | spiral key ring |
| sod-all | nothing | splodge (v) | splotch; spot |
| sod off | scram; beat it | sponge bag | shaving kit; cosmetics bag |
| soft fruit | pitless fruit | | |
| soft furnishings | rugs, drapes, etc. | sponge-bag trousers | checked pants |
| soft sugar | brown sugar | | |
| solicitor | lawyer | spool | roll of film; cassette tape |
| solo mother | single mother | | |
| sootblacks | soot | sports mistress | girl's coach; gym teacher |
| sorbet | sherbet | | |
| sorbo rubber | hard sponge rubber | spot | dab; small amount |

| BRITISH | U.S. | BRITISH | U.S. |
|---|---|---|---|
| spot on | right on | standard lamp | floor lamp |
| spotted | polka-dotted | star prisoner | prisoner serving |
| spring greens | collard greens | | first jail term |
| spring onion | scallion | star turn | the main event |
| sprinting race | dash; sprint | starkers | naked; stark |
| spud bashing | peeling potatoes | | naked |
| spyhole | peephole | start (n) | scare |
| squails | Tiddly Winks | starter (food) | appetizer |
| | (child's game) | state school | public school |
| square | city block | stately home | luxury home open |
| squeeze-box | accordion | | to public |
| squew-eyed | squinting | statutory | |
| squib | firecracker | rights | consumers' rights |
| squiffer | concertina | stay-in strike | sit-in |
| squiffy | drunk | stay-press | permanent-press |
| squint, have a | be wall-eyed | steam-navvy | steam shovel |
| squit | twit; insignificant | step-in closet | walk-in closet |
| | person | stereogram | stereo |
| squitters | diarrhea | stewing steak | stew meat |
| S.R.N. | R.N. (registered | stick (n) | verbal abuse |
| | nurse) | stick it (v) | tolerate; endure |
| stable lad | stableman; stable | stick at trifles | nitpick |
| | boy | stick in his toes | dig in his heels |
| staff nurse | candy striper; | stick-jaw | caramel; taffy |
| | nurse's aide | stick no bills | post no bills |
| staging | greenhouse plant | stick of rock | hard candy stick |
| | shelves | sticking plaster | adhesive tape |
| stall (n) | booth (at a fair or | stickit minister | minister with |
| | trade show) | | license but no |
| stallage | rent for fair or | | pastorate |
| | trade show | sticky wicket | difficult situation |
| | booths | stiffener | alcoholic drink; |
| stalls | orchestra seats | | fortifier |
| stamp | stamp needed on | stirabout | porridge |
| | receipt | stirk | yearling calf |
| stand (v) | pay for | stock in (v) | stock up |
| stand (for | | stockist | supplier |
| office) | run for office | stodge (food) | heavy, starchy |
| stand down | step down; resign | | food |
| stand off (v) | lay off; leave | stone | fruit pit |
| | alone | stone-flagged | flagstoned |

| BRITISH | U.S. | BRITISH | U.S. |
|---------|------|---------|------|
| stood down | put something down | stump | checkbook stub |
| stook | shock (wheat, corn) | stump up (v) | pay up |
| | | sub | advance on salary |
| stop (v) | stay | sub-editor | copy reader |
| stop tap | last call; end of bar service | sub-fusc | dull or flat color |
| | | subject | citizen |
| stopped | docked pay | sugar basin | sugar bowl |
| stopping (n) | tooth filling | sugar/jam thermometer | candy thermometer |
| stopping train | milk train; local | | |
| stops late | stays late | sugar-soap | paint remover; stripper |
| store | storage or store-room | | |
| | | suiting | cloth for suits or coats |
| store cupboard | storage closet | | |
| stores | supplies; ware-house | sultanas | seedless white raisins |
| stout | strong, dark beer | summarised | summarized |
| straightaway | immediately | summer time | daylight saving time |
| strait-waistcoat | strait-jacket | | |
| strapping | bandages | sun-blind | awning |
| straw potatoes | julienne potatoes | sun-filter cream | sunscreen; suntan lotion |
| street piano | barrel organ | | |
| streets ahead | far superior | sun lounge | sun porch |
| strength, on the | on the payroll | sunbakers | sunbathers |
| striker | gun firing pin | sundowner | happy-hour drink |
| string-colour | off-white | sundriesman | dealer in sundries |
| string vest | mesh undershirt | sunshade | parasol |
| strip | team uniform | superannuation | retirement age; retirement fund payments and contributions |
| strip cartoon | comic strip | | |
| strip lighting | fluorescent lighting | | |
| strong room van | armored car | superintendent | police officer with rank above inspector |
| stroppy | bad tempered; belligerent | | |
| | | supply (n) | substitute teacher or clergy |
| struck on | infatuated; stuck on | | |
| | | surgery | doctor's office; clinic |
| stuck into | stuck with | | |
| stuff (v) | have sex | surgical spirits | rubbing alcohol |
| stumer | bad check | surname | last name |

| BRITISH | U.S. | BRITISH | U.S. |
|---|---|---|---|
| surround (n) | door and window frames; borders | Swiss bun | Danish |
| | | Swiss roll | jelly roll |
| suspenders | garters | switchback | roller-coaster |
| swagger cane | swagger stick | switched on | turned on; |
| swanning | goofing off | | knowledgeable |
| swatchways | channels between sandbanks | swizz (n) | swindle |
| | | swot (v) | study hard |
| swear oneself blind | insist adamantly | ta | thanks (informal) |
| sweat | (n) an old soldier; (v) sauté lightly | tabby | gossipy old maid |
| | | table (v) | put a motion on the table for consideration |
| sweater | sweatshirt | | |
| swede | turnip | | |
| sweet | dessert | tablet | pill |
| sweet biscuits | cookies | tablet of soap | bar of soap |
| sweet corn cobs | corn on the cob | tagged on (v) | tagged along |
| | | tags | aglets (aiglets) |
| sweet oil | olive or salad oil | tail male | entail (male heirs) |
| sweet kiosk | candy stall | tail of the eye | corner of the eye |
| sweet plates | dessert plates | take a decision | make a decision |
| sweet trade | confectionery business | take a fancy to | take a shine to |
| | | take-away place | take-out restaurant |
| sweet trolley | pastry cart | | |
| sweet wrappers | candy wrappers | take against | be against; oppose |
| sweetmeat | sweetened delicacy | take a pew | sit down |
| sweetshop | candy store | take a rise | get a rise out of |
| sweets (also *sweeties*) | candy | take a toss | admit failure |
| | | take in | subscribe |
| swill (v) | rinse thoroughly | take it as read | accept it as true |
| swill bins | trash cans | take it in turns | take turns |
| swimsuit | bathing suit | take it out of | take it out on |
| swimming-bath | swimming pool | take mass | conduct a religious service |
| swimming costume | bathing suit | take no harm | won't be damaged |
| swing door | swinging door | take one's point | accept someone's point of view; point taken |
| swing tickets | price tags on clothes | | |
| swingometer | applause meter | take tea | drink or have tea |
| swipes (n) | weak or light beer | take the biscuit | take the cake |
| swish (adj) | fashionable | take up | interrupt; arrest |

| BRITISH | U.S. | BRITISH | U.S. |
|---|---|---|---|
| take up a post | get a job | teds | hoodlums |
| taking the | | telephone box | pay phone |
| mickey out | | telephonist | operator |
| of someone | getting someone's | teleprinter | teletype |
| | goat | telly | TV |
| tallboy | highboy | ten-a-penny | dime a dozen |
| | (furniture) | ten by eight | eight by ten |
| tallow chandler | candlemaker; | | (measurement) |
| | merchant | tenner | ten-pound note |
| tally plan | installment plan | tenpins | bowling |
| tantalus | locked, glass | tenter | machinery |
| | liquor cabinet | | supervisor |
| tannoy | public address | terrace houses | row houses |
| | system (PA) | terylene | Dacron |
| tap | faucet | That horse | |
| taphouse | taproom | won't start | That dog won't |
| taped | fully understood | | hunt |
| ta-ra | ta-ta; goodbye | thatched roof | straw or reed roof |
| tariff | price list; list of | theatre porter | O.R. orderly |
| | fees | there it is | take it or leave it |
| tariff wall | national trade | thermionic | |
| | barrier | valve; valve | radio tube |
| tarted up | gussied up; | thermos flask | thermos bottle |
| | dressed up | thick as a plank | thick as a brick; |
| tat | junk | | dense |
| tattoo | outdoor military | thick on the | |
| | march or | ground | plentiful |
| | display | thin on the | |
| tattoo, devil's | finger-tapping | ground | scarce |
| tatty | shabby | throat, have a | have a sore throat |
| taxi rank | cab stand | throw a salute | salute |
| tea boy/girl | office boy/girl | throw up the | |
| tea cake | light sweet bun | sponge | throw in the towel |
| tea infuser | tea ball | thunderflash | noisy, smoking |
| teaching block | school building | | firecracker |
| teacloth | dish towel | thundering | huge |
| tearabout | juvenile misfit | tick | 1. a moment of |
| tearaway | young criminal | | time; 2. check |
| teddy boy | elegantly dressed | | mark |
| | rowdy | tick off (v) | tell off |

| BRITISH | U.S. | BRITISH | U.S. |
|---------|------|---------|------|
| tickety-boo | all right; terrific | to a degree | to a very high |
| tiddler | anything small, | | degree |
| | e.g. a minnow | tobacconist | tobacco store |
| tiddly | tipsy | today week | a week ago; a |
| tidy out | clean out | | week from |
| tied cottage | dwelling provided | | today |
| | by employer | toe-rag | tramp; hobo |
| tied house | brewery-affliated | toff | elegantly dressed |
| | pub | | person; dandy |
| tiffin | (n) lunch or after- | toffee | taffy; candy |
| | noon tea; (v) | toffee-nosed | stuck-up; snobby |
| | lunch | toffee shop | candy store |
| tig (also | | toil (n) | job |
| *tiggy*) | tag (child's game) | toilet | bathroom; |
| tights | pantyhose | | restroom |
| tike (also *tyke*) | mongrel | toilet-powder | talcum powder |
| till | cash register | tom (n) | prostitute; hooker |
| till all's blue | to the bitter end | Tom Tiddler's | |
| till receipt | cash register tape | Ground | gambling casino; |
| timber built | made of wood | | children's game |
| timetable | schedule | ton | 100 lbs; 100 mph |
| tread time (v) | mark the time | tonne | metric ton; 2,200 |
| tin opener | can opener | | lbs. |
| tinkle | (n) phone call; | too clever by | |
| | (v) phone | half | too smart for his |
| tinned | canned (food) | | own good |
| tintack | short tin-coated | too much in | |
| | nail | the window | overdressed; |
| tip | (n) garbage dump; | | showy |
| | (v) throw out | took a first | |
| tip one's lid | raise one's hat | class | graduated as class |
| tip the wink | warn | | valedictorian |
| tip-top | highest social | took his hook | went away |
| | class; the best | tooth comb | fine tooth comb |
| tip-up doors | overhead doors | tooth glass | glass for rinsing |
| tip-up seat | folding seat | | after brushing |
| tipple | alcoholic drink | | one's teeth |
| tipstaff | security guard | toothful | small sip of liquor |
| titbit | tidbit | toothsome | tasty; good- |
| titchy | tiny | | looking |
| titfer | hat | tootle | telephone call |

| BRITISH | U.S. | BRITISH | U.S. |
|---|---|---|---|
| top A (*or* C) | high A; high C (music) | traybake | sheet cake |
| top drawer | upper class; first class | treacle | molasses |
| top-hole | first rate | treacle sponge | gingerbread |
| top-liner | headliner; top banana | trick cyclist | psychiatrist |
| topping | excellent | tricky wicket | sticky situation |
| topside | rump roast | tried it on | attempted it |
| top up | fill up | tripper | tourist |
| tor | rocky peak; hill-top heap of rocks | trolley | cart (shopping, hospital, etc.) |
| torch | flashlight | trousers | pants; slacks |
| tosh | nonsense | trouser suit | women's pants suit |
| toss oars | raise oars in saluting | trout in the milk | smoking gun |
| tot | small alcoholic drink | truancy officer | truant officer |
| tot up | list and total | truckle bed | trundle bed |
| totter | junk man | trug | trough (gardening) |
| tour currier | tour guide | truncheon | nightstick |
| towel | (n) sanitary napkin; (v) thrash | trunk call | long distance call; toll call |
| towel rail | towel rack | trunks | long distance operator |
| towelling robe | terrycloth robe | tube of mints | roll of mints |
| tower block | skyscraper | tuck | snacks |
| towsing | rough treatment; abuse | tuck box | lunch box |
| trackway | beaten path | tuck shop | candy store near school |
| trade cycle | business cycle | tuck into | chow down |
| trades union | labor union | tucker | food |
| tradesman | storekeeper | tulle | lubricated surgical gauze |
| trading estate | industrial park | tumble drier | clothes dryer |
| training scheme | training course | tumble twist | shag carpet |
| trannie | transistor radio | tunny | tuna fish |
| transpire | custom house transfer permit | tup | ram (male sheep) |
| travel with rucksack | (v) backpack | turf accountant | bookie; book-maker |
| | | turf out | expel; dismiss |
| | | turfite | horse fanatic |

| BRITISH | U.S. | BRITISH | U.S. |
|---------|------|---------|------|
| turn | work shift; an act in a show | | clumsy |
| | | two for a pair | two of a kind |
| turn off | fire; discharge | | |
| turn out | clean thoroughly | umbrella | |
| turn over (v) | search a room | brigade | umbrella-carrying business professionals |
| turn someone up | make someone vomit | | |
| turn up for the books | out of nowhere; a surprise | un-unioned | non-union |
| | | unalike | unlike |
| | | unchancey | doomed |
| turn up trumps | turn out better than expected | uncome-at-able | inaccessible |
| turn-ups | cuffs (pants) | uncrushable | wrinkle-free |
| turn face to the wall | give up on life | under custody | in custody |
| | | under manager | assistant manager |
| turn queer | turn green | undercart | airplane under-carriage |
| turnip lantern | jack-o-lantern | | |
| turps | turpentine | undercut | beef tenderloin |
| tusser (also *tussore*) | course silk fabric; tussah | underdone | rare meat |
| | | undermentioned | mentioned below |
| twee | dainty; quaint | underpants | shorts (men); panties (women) |
| tweeny | between-floors maid | | |
| | | understrapper | subordinate; underling |
| twenty-tips | pack of cigarettes | | |
| twig (v) | catch on | unharbour | frighten deer from cover |
| twining plant | vine | | |
| twist | drink with two ingredients | unheaded stationery | without a letter-head |
| twister | liar; dishonest person | | |
| | | unit holder | stock holder |
| two-two | 22-caliber firearm | unit trust | mutual fund |
| two-up-two-down | inexpensive four-room duplex | unlicensed | not licensed to sell alcoholic drinks |
| two fingers (V-sign thrust upward) | the finger, i.e. fuck you | unobtainable | out of order |
| | | unrendered wall | unplastered wall |
| two-fisted | ambidextrous; | unsocial hours | overtime hours |
| | | up a gum tree | up a tree |

| BRITISH | U.S. | BRITISH | U.S. |
|---------|------|---------|------|
| **up all standing** | taken by surprise | **marrow** | squash |
| **up-and-downer** | violent quarrel | **verger** | sexton |
| **up on his toes** | showing anger | **vesta** | short match stick |
| **up one's nose** | irritating; annoying | **vest** | men's undergarment |
| **up sticks** | pulling up stakes; taking off | **vest** | men's undershirt |
| **up the spout** | pregnant; in serious trouble; hopeless | **victimization** | punishing someone for going on strike or for political reasons |
| **up to the knocker** | up to snuff; perfect | **victualler** | innkeeper |
| | | **view** | point of view |
| **uplift** | pick up; collect | **viewpoint** | scenic lookout |
| **upper circle** | first balcony tier | **villain** | crime suspect |
| **upper cut** | cut of beef | **vine** | vineyard |
| **upright chair** | straight chair | **vintner** | wine or liquor-store owner |
| **upsides with** | equivalent to | **votes blue** | votes conservative |
| **usher** | bailiff | | |
| **using language** | swearing | **voting paper** | ballot |
| **usquebaugh** | whiskey | | |
| **usual offices** | bathroom | **wage packet** | pay check |
| **utter barrister** | junior attorney | **wage round** | pay raise |
| | | **wages clerk** | bookkeeper; payroll clerk |
| **vac** | vacuum cleaner; vacation | **wages snatch** | payroll robbery |
| **vacant possession** | owning an empty house | **waistcoat** | vest |
| | | **waits** | Christmas carollers |
| **vacuum flask** | thermos bottle | **wake-up** (n) | alert individual |
| **vagabond** | hobo | **walk** | street vendor's route |
| **vagged** | arrested for vagrancy | **walk out with** | go out with; see someone |
| **valuer** | appraiser | | |
| **valve** (radio) | tube | **wall safe** | kitchen cupboard |
| **V.A.T.** | sales tax (value added tax) | **wallet** | briefcase |
| | | **wallop** | beer or liquor |
| **veal and hammer** | veal and ham pie | **wanker** | fool; masturbator |
| **vegetable** | | **wanted ringing back** | return call |

| BRITISH | U.S. | BRITISH | U.S. |
|---|---|---|---|
| warder | prison guard | whiskey | Irish or American whiskey |
| wardrobe | clothes closet | | |
| warehouse | | whisky | Scotch whiskey |
| store | discount store | white coffee | coffee with cream |
| warrant card | police badge | | |
| warn (n) | Miranda rights | white land | farming land |
| was in work | had a job | white night | sleepless night |
| wash one's | | white spirit | turpentine substitute |
| smalls | wash socks, underwear, etc. | white wax | paraffin |
| wash up (v) | do the dishes | Whitsun | Pentecost |
| washeteria | laundromat | wholemeal | whole wheat |
| washhand basin | wash bowl | whole time | full time |
| washing line | clothesline | wick, get on | |
| washing | | someone's | get on someone's nerves |
| powder | detergent | | |
| washing-up | | wide | shrewd; sneaky |
| liquid | dishwashing detergent | wide boy | one who cheats |
| | | wig | rebuke severely; dress down |
| washing-up | | | |
| machine | dishwasher | wilderness | politician's home after office |
| water closet | | | |
| (W.C.) | bathroom | William pear | Bartlett pear |
| way in | entrance | Wimpy bar | hamburger joint |
| way out | exit | wince | textile roller |
| wet weekend | sour-faced look | winceyette | flannelette |
| Wellingtons | | wind cheater | windbreaker |
| (also *wellies*) | waterproof boots | wind-up, put the | make someone nervous |
| whack | one's share | wind (somebody) | |
| whacked | exhausted; drunk | up (v) | to trick |
| whacking | huge | winder | watch stem |
| What's all this? | What's the trouble? | windows right | |
| | | down | windows wide open |
| What's going? | What's available? | wine gums | gummi candy |
| wheelhouse | pilot or deck house | wine bar | bar specializing in wine and food |
| whinge | whiner | wing game | game birds |
| whip-round | office collection for a gift | winkle out | extract |

| BRITISH | U.S. | BRITISH | U.S. |
|---|---|---|---|
| winkle-pickers | pointed-toe shoes | wrong'un | bad person |
| wipe over (v) | mop | | |
| wireless | radio | X-factor | overtime (pay) |
| wood straw | excelsior | | |
| works outing | company picnic | Y-fronts | men's briefs |
| work the oracle | use influence | Yard, the | Scotland Yard |
| work to rule | slow-down labor action | yarn | embroidery thread |
| | | year dot | forever; since day one |
| world and his wife | everybody and his brother (grand-mother) | yob (also *yobbo*) | boy (derog.) |
| | | yonks | very long time |
| wotcher! (n) | "what's up?" (greeting) | you lot | you guys |
| wound up | wound | | |
| wrapover | wrap-around skirt or dress | Zed (letter) | Z |
| | | Zimmer frame | walker (for the disabled) |
| wristlet watch | bracelet-style wristwatch | zip | zipper |
| writing block | writing pad | zip-fastener | zipper |

# AUTOMOTIVE, AIRCRAFT, AND TRANSPORTATION

For anyone who might be given an assignment in the automobile industry or who are involved with travel and tourism, this special section on British vs. American English should be particularly enlightening. When it comes to automobile parts and driving (motoring) information, there are probably more differences between British terminology and American than in any other area (with the possible exception of food).

For this reason the following words or expressions have been segregated from the general language section and given a separate category.

| BRITISH | U.S. |
|---|---|
| accommodation road | access road |
| accumulator | battery |
| actuator | switch; servo |
| aerial | antenna |
| aerodrome | airfield |
| aeroplane | airplane |
| angle-parking | diagonal parking |
| articulated lorry | tractor-trailer |
| arterial road | major highway |
| autodrome | racetrack |
| banned | have one's license suspended |
| bat (v) | rate of speed |
| baulk ring | synchro ring |
| Belisha beacon | crosswalk signal |
| black spot ahead | high auto accident area |

| BRITISH | U.S. |
|---|---|
| bonnet | hood |
| boot | trunk |
| bottom gear | low gear |
| box | street intersection |
| box spanner | lug wrench |
| bowser | gasoline refueling truck |
| brake | station wagon |
| breakdown van | tow truck |
| bulkhead | firewall |
| car hire | car rental |
| car park | parking lot; garage |
| car run | some distance |
| car smash | car crash |
| caravan | mobile home; trailer |
| carburettor | carburetor |
| carfax | crossroads |
| carriageway | freeway; highway |
| cat's eye | roadside reflector |
| central reservation | road divider; |

| BRITISH | U.S. | BRITISH | U.S. |
|---|---|---|---|
| charabanc | tour bus | driving license | driver's license |
| choke tube | venturi | driving mirror | rear-view mirror |
| Chunnel | English Channel tunnel | driving to the public danger | reckless driving |
| clamp | wheel lock for illegal parking | driving under the influence | DWI (driving while intoxicated) |
| circus | traffic circle | | |
| close | cul-de-sac; dead end | driving wheel | steering wheel |
| | | drop-head | convertible |
| clearway | highway with no intersections | dual carriageway | freeway |
| coach | long distance bus | dumpy screw- | |
| coach party | group of tourists | driver | short screwdriver |
| coachwork | automobile body | dynamo | generator |
| core plug | freeze plug | | |
| corniche road | coastal cliff road | | |
| courtesy light | interior dome light | earth | ground |
| | | estate car | station wagon |
| crawler lane | slow traffic lane | exhaust silencer | muffler |
| crocodile clip | alligator clip | | |
| crosshead; cross-ply | Phillips (screw-driver) | fascia (also *facia*) | dashboard |
| | | facia pocket | glove compartment |
| crown wheel | ring gear | | |
| | | fixed-head coupe | two-door coupe |
| damper | shock absorber | | |
| dangerous driving | reckless driving | flasher | turn signal |
| | | flat accumulator | dead battery |
| demister | defroster | | |
| deviation signal | turn signal | flyover | overpass |
| dip-switch | headlight dimmer | footway | sidewalk |
| dormobile | camper; small bus | footwell | leg room |
| double bend | S-curve on road | frogeye | bugeye |
| double-door saloon | four-door sedan | gas fitting | gas pipe |
| draft power | engine traction | gearbox | transmission |
| drink driving | drunk driving | gear change | shifting gears |
| drive shaft | axle shaft | gear lever | gear shift |
| drive-yourself car | rental car | ginnel | narrow alley |
| | | give way | yield |

| BRITISH | U.S. | BRITISH | U.S. |
|---|---|---|---|
| glove box | glove compart-ment | mini | compact car |
| | | monocoque | unibody |
| goods vehicle | delivery truck | mortuary van | hearse |
| gritting lorry | sand-spreading truck | motor (v) | drive |
| | | motor horn | car horn |
| gudgeon pin | wrist pin | motor spirit | fuel; gasoline |
| | | motoring | |
| hard standing | paved parking lot | offenses | traffic violations |
| head | roof of a car | motorist | driver |
| headline | roof upholstery | motorway | freeway; highway |
| hire car | rental car | mudguard (also | |
| hood | convertible roof | *mudwing*) | fender |
| hooter | horn | multiple smash | pile-up |
| horn ring | car horn; sound | | |
| | | nave plate | hubcap |
| number plates | license plates | nearside | passenger's side; |
| indicator light | turn signal | no through | no outlet; dead |
| inspection pit | grease pit | | end |
| | | no waiting | no parking |
| jointing | | nose | bumper |
| compound | gasket sealant | nose to tail | bumper to bumper |
| jumped a red | | number plate | license plate |
| light | ran a red light | | |
| | | off-side front | |
| kerb | curb | seat | driver's seat |
| | | overrider | bumper guard |
| lay-by | highway rest area | overtaking | passing |
| level crossing | railway crossing | over the road | across the street |
| lighting-up time | time of day when headlights are legally required | owner-driver | one driving his own car |
| lorry | truck | panda car | police patrol car |
| lorry pull-in | truck stop | panel beating | |
| low loader | flatbed truck | shop | body shop |
| | | paraffin | kerosene |
| made road (n) | paved and improved road | passenger light | dome light |
| | | patrol car | squad car |
| mascot | hood ornament | pavement | sidewalk |
| metal springs | sleeve clamps | pelican crossing | pedestrian operated traffic lights |
| metalled road | paved road | | |
| mileometer | odometer | | |

| BRITISH | U.S. | BRITISH | U.S. |
|---------|------|---------|------|
| petrol | gasoline; gas | roadman | road repairer |
| petrol garage | gas station | roadster | convertible |
| petrol gauge | gas gauge | road up (v phr) | street under |
| pillion | motorcycle's | | repair |
| | passenger seat | roadworks (n) | street under |
| pinking | knocking; pinging | | repair |
| point duty | traffic control | Roller | Rolls Royce |
| pointsman | traffic control | roundabout | traffic circle |
| | officer | run (v) | own and drive a |
| pot | pothole | | car |
| power-assisted | | run in | break in |
| steering | power-steering | running lights | parking lights |
| prang (v) | crash (a car or | | |
| | plane) | saloon | 2- or 4-door |
| precinct | no-traffic area | | sedan |
| prise (v) | pry | scuttle | cowl |
| propellor shaft | drive shaft | self-drive car | rental car |
| prop shaft | drive shaft | shooting brake | station wagon |
| proud | above; raised | shunt (v) | crash |
| puncture | flat tire | side curtains | removable side |
| push-start | starting car by | | windows |
| | pushing it | side lights | parking lights |
| put one's foot | | side turning | street corner; |
| down | put the pedal to | | crosswalk |
| | the metal | sill valance | rocker panel |
| | | sleeping | |
| quarterlight | vent window | policeman | speed bump |
| | | slip road | on- or off-ramp |
| refuse collection | | slow puncture | slow leak |
| vehicle | garbage truck | soft tyre | flat; flat tire |
| remold | retread | spanner | wrench |
| removal van | moving van | sparking plug | spark plug |
| rev counter | tachometer | speed cop | traffic cop |
| reversing lamps | back-up lights | speed merchant | speed demon |
| ring gear | flywheel gear; | speedo | speedometer |
| | starter gear | split pin | cotter pin |
| risk of | | sports car | convertible |
| grounding | bump in road | spring washer | lock washer |
| road | street | springing | car springs |
| road accident | car accident | squab seat | upholstered seat |

| BRITISH | U.S. | BRITISH | U.S. |
|---|---|---|---|
| starting handle | crank | | joint suspension |
| stop lamp | brake light | tube | subway |
| straight on | go straight ahead | turning | cross street |
| strangler | choke; throttle | turning over | engine running |
| street is up | street under repair | turnpike road | toll road |
| suction advance | vacuum advance | two stroke | twin cycle engine |
| subway | underpass; under-ground walkway | tyre | tire |
| sump | oil pan | unadopted road | private road |
| | | underground | subway |
| tail lamp | tail light | unmade track | dirt road |
| tail plane | stabilizer (aeronautics) | unmetalled track | unpaved road |
| tarmac | type of asphalt | urban clearway | high speed road prohibiting parking |
| tarred road | paved road | | |
| thumb a lift | hitch-hike | | |
| track | road; path; trail | van | panel truck |
| tram | street car; trolley | vehicle index | license plate registration |
| thrust bearing | throwout bearing | | |
| tickover (v) | idle | verges | shoulders |
| tip and run | hit and run | volte-face | about face |
| tipper | dump truck | | |
| toad crossing | similar to deer crossing | waggon | wagon |
| | | waiting | parking |
| top gear | high gear | warning cross | railroad crossing |
| top it up | fill it up | wheel nut | lug nut |
| torch | flashlight | windscreen | windshield |
| traffic offense notice | traffic ticket | wing | fender |
| | | wing mirror | sideview mirror |
| traffic warden | traffic cop | wrote off | totalled; wrecked |
| trafficator | turn signal | | |
| transport café | truck stop | Z - 2 miles | warning sign indi-cating sharp curves in road |
| tricar | three-wheeled automobile | | |
| trunnion | sliding or rotating | zebra crossing | crosswalk |

# AMERICAN VS. BRITISH ENGLISH

| U.S. | BRITISH | U.S. | BRITISH |
|---|---|---|---|
| abused | hard done by | apartment | flat |
| abusive | | apartment | |
|   language | Billingsgate |   house | block of flats |
| abusive quarrel | slanging match | appetizer | starter |
| acceptable | on | applause | |
| accessories | |   meter | swingometer |
|   (men) | hosiery | apple (type) | pippin; gauger |
| accordion | squeeze-box | appointment | diary engagement |
| act fairly | play the game | appraiser | valuer |
| adhesive tape | sticking plaster | approach | rising |
| advice | | April Fool's | |
|   columnist | agony aunt |   Day | All Fools' Day |
| advocate | pleader | apron | pinny |
| affidavit | davy | Archie Bunker | Alf Garnett |
| afternoon tea | tiffin | armored car | strong room van |
| a good many | a good few | arrest | take up |
| airplane, small | kite | arrested | had up; done |
| aisle (theater) | gangway | arrested for | |
| alcoholic drink | tipple; grog; |   vagrancy | vagged |
| | tot (small) | arsenic | inheritance |
| all one can | | | powder |
|   handle | enough on one's | arsonist | fire raiser |
| | plate | arthritis | screws |
| amaze (v) | knock-out | askew | skew-whiff |
| amazing person | knock-out | ass | bum; bottom; arse |
| ambidextrous | two-fisted | assignment | posting |
| American | | assistant | |
|   Indian | Red Indian |   manager | under manager |
| amorous | | astonished | gobsmacked |
|   amusement | slap and tickle | attack (v) | go for; have a go |
| amputee (n) | limbless | | at; try it on |
| amusement | | attacked | set upon |
|   park | gaff | attempt (v) | have a go at; try |
| anchor (TV; | | | it on |
|   radio) | presenter | at top speed | hell for leather |
| angry | ratty; spare | attractive | bit of all right; |
| annoy | get across | | dishy |
| annoyed | cheesed off | attractive | |
| annoying | up one's nose |   woman | nice bit of |
| antenna | aerial | | crumpet |

| U.S. | BRITISH | U.S. | BRITISH |
|------|---------|------|---------|
| auction room | sale room | ballot | voting paper |
| aurora borealis | merry dancers | **Band-Aid** | plaster; |
| authentic | dinkum | | Elastoplast |
| auto body shop | panel-beating | bandages | strapping |
| | shop | bangs (hair) | fringe |
| auto race track | autodrome | bar | licensed house |
| automobile | | barfly | slag |
| accident | road accident | bar of soap | tablet of soap |
| automobile | | bar owner | proprietor; |
| driver | motorist | | publican |
| automobile | | barber shop | hair dresser |
| horn | hooter | barrette | hairslide |
| automobile roof | hood | bargain | snip |
| available | | **Bartlett pear** | William pear |
| immediately | going | baseboard | skirting board |
| avalanche | snowslip | basement | |
| awaken (v) | knock-up | apartment | garden flat |
| awnings | sun blinds; blinds | bastard | sod |
| axle shaft | drive shaft | bath tub | bath |
| | | bathing suit | swimming |
| | | | costume |
| babble (v) | witter | bathrobe | dressing gown |
| baby carriage | pram | bathroom | shower room; |
| baby-sitter | child minder | | W.C. (water |
| backyard | back garden | | closet); loo |
| backpack | rucksack | bawl-out | |
| bad | chronic | someone (v) | have a right go at |
| bad check | dud cheque; | bazaar | suk; souk |
| | stumer | beat it | hop it |
| bad language | language | become aware | rumble to |
| bad manners | bad form | be crestfallen | sing small |
| bad person | wrong 'un | be deceived | buy a pup |
| bad tempered | stroppy | be injured | catch it |
| badge (police) | warrant card | beetle | chafer |
| baggage check | | bed | kip |
| room | left luggage | bed rest | |
| bailiff | tipstaff | (medical) | lying up |
| baked potato | jacket potato | bedroom | |
| balcony | | community | dormitory suburb |
| (theater) | gallery | beef shank | shin of beef |
| balk (v) | jib | | |

| U.S. | BRITISH | U.S. | BRITISH |
|---|---|---|---|
| beef tenderloin | undercut | booth (market | |
| beer | wallop; halves | or fair) | stall |
| | (small glass) | boots (water- | |
| beets | beetroot | proof) | Wellingtons; |
| bell pepper | capsicum | | wellies |
| belligerent | elbows out | Bordeaux wine | claret |
| bellman | hall porter; page | bore (n) | ear-basher |
| betray | split on | borrow (v) | cadge |
| bib (child) | feeder | bossy person | bossy boots |
| bicycle (child) | fairy cycle | bottom round | |
| bill of lading | consignment note | (steak) | rump steak |
| bill (currency) | bank note | bouillon spread | marmite |
| billboard | hoarding | bouncer | chucker-out |
| billfold | notecase | boutonniere | buttonhole |
| billion | milliard | bowling | tenpins |
| binoculars | raceglasses | box car (train) | covered goods- |
| blackberries | brambles | | wagon |
| blackjack | | box lunch | ploughman's |
| (cards) | pontoon | | lunch |
| blackjack (v) | cosh | boy crazy | fellow-mad |
| blacksmith | farrier; | bracelet | wristlet |
| | shoesmith | braids (hair) | plaits |
| blackmail (v) | put the black on | brawl | punch-up |
| blanket | rug | bread plate | side plate |
| blinders | | breaded cutlet | crumbed cutlet |
| (horse) | blinkers | break-up | |
| blindman's | | (laughing) (v) | fall about |
| bluff | hoodman blind | breakfast | brekkers |
| blow one's horn | parp one's hooter | bribe | baksheesh |
| blow torch | blow-lamp | bricklayer | brickie |
| blunder | bloomer; | bridal path | ride |
| | clanger | brief visit | look in |
| bobby pin | hair grip; kirby | briefcase | wallet |
| | grip | broad jump | long jump |
| bomb (v) | fail | broiler | griller |
| boneless sirloin | fillet steak | broke (money) | skint |
| boob | bub | brothel | knocking shop; |
| boogey man | bogle | | bawdy house |
| bookie | | brown bag | |
| (bookmaker) | turf accountant | lunch | packed lunch |

| U.S. | BRITISH | U.S. | BRITISH |
|------|---------|------|---------|
| brown sugar | soft sugar | candidacy | candidature |
| brownstone | sandstone | candied fruit | crystallized fruit |
| bubbly | champers | candlemaker | tallow chandler |
| buck (dollar) | quid (pound) | candy store | sweet shop |
| buffet | sideboard | canned (food) | tinned |
| buffet lunch | fork luncheon | car crash | car smash |
| bug off | bugger off; piss off | car rental | car hire |
| | | carbonated drinks | minerals |
| building (large) | block | caramels | stick-jaws |
| built-in | fitted; in-built | carnival | fun fair |
| bulletin board | notice board | carnival rides | amusements |
| bullhorn | loud hailer | carpenter | joiner |
| burglar's tool | betty | carpet (wall-to-wall) | fitted carpets |
| busboy | commis boy | cart | trolley |
| business cycle | trade cycle | cassette tape | spool |
| business suit | lounge suit | cash register | reckoning machine; till |
| bus stop | stance | | |
| busy | engaged | cash register tape | till receipt |
| butcher | flesher | cash cow | money spinner |
| butt (cigarette) | dog-end; fag-end | cash-on-hand | readies; ready |
| buttocks | bottom; arse; sit-upon; posterior | check-out (cashier) | cash desk |
| | | cast aspersions (v) | cast nasturtiums |
| by a long shot | by a long chalk | catch on (v) | twig to |
| | | cat | mog; moggy |
| cabinet | cupboard | cater (food) (v) | lay on |
| cad | blighter; rotter; bounder | catnip | catmint |
| | | cattlemen | pastoralists |
| cafeteria | self-service canteen | celebration | a do |
| | | certified public accountant (CPA) | chartered accountant |
| calf | stirk | | |
| call (n,v) | tinkle | | |
| cameo appearance | courtesy appearance | chain stores | multiple stores |
| | | chambermaid | bed maker |
| campaign manager | agent | champagne | champers; bubbly |
| camper (auto) | dormobile | | |
| can | tin | | |
| can opener | tin opener | | |
| can tab | ring pull | | |

| U.S. | BRITISH | U.S. | BRITISH |
|------|---------|------|---------|
| chance (n) | earthly | Chutes and | |
| change (in | | Ladders | |
| coins) | float | (game) | Snakes and |
| charge account | credit account | | Ladders |
| charge (v) | | chutzpah | cheek |
| (credit) | put down; enter | cigarette | gasper; fag |
| chatter | natter | cinder block | breeze block |
| cheap wine | plonk | Cinderella | Cinders |
| cheat (v) | fiddle; diddle; sell | cinnamon roll | Chelsea bun |
| | a pup | city block | square |
| cheated | done | civilian clothes | mufti; civvies |
| check | | clarify (soup | |
| (restaurant) | bill | or gravy) | run down |
| check mark | tick | class (school) | form |
| check room | cloak room; | clay oven | cloam oven |
| | cloaks | cleaning lady | daily |
| check stub | counterfoil | cleansing cream | removing cream |
| checked in | clocked in | clinic | surgery |
| checkers | draughts; | clipboard | millboard |
| | chequers | clippings | |
| checking | | (newspaper) | cuttings |
| account | current account | clodhoppers | brogues |
| cheerful | canty | cloistered | enclosed |
| cheer up | buck up | clothesline | washing line |
| cheesecloth | butter muslin | clothes rack | coat rail |
| cheesy | ropy | clothes presser | mangle |
| chest of | | clothespin | peg; clothes peg |
| silverware | canteen of cutlery | coal barge | keel |
| chick (girl) | bird | coal oil | paraffin oil |
| chicken wire | wire netting | coaster | drink mat |
| chilly | parky | coatroom | cloakroom |
| chimney | | cockiness | bounce |
| corner | inglenook | cocktail party | drinks party |
| chock-full | chock-a-block | coffee creamer | coffee whitener |
| chocolate chips | polka dots | coin (n) | bean |
| choice (adj) | plummy | collar button | collar stud |
| choke (auto) | strangler | collar stay | collar stiffener |
| chopped meat | mince | collect phone | |
| Christmas | | call | reverse charge |
| carollers | waits | | call |

| U.S. | BRITISH | U.S. | BRITISH |
|------|---------|------|---------|
| college president | provost | corridor | passage |
| college tutor | don | cost accounting | charge of cost |
| completely | dead | costumer | costumier |
| comb (n) | bug rake | cot | camp bed |
| come (v) | call | cottage cheese | curd cheese |
| comforter (bed) | eiderdown | cotter pin | split pin |
| comic strip | strip cartoon | cotton (absorbent) | cotton wool |
| company picnic | works outing | cotton candy | candyfloss |
| complete (adj) | proper | counter-clockwise | anti-clockwise |
| con man | illywhacker | counterfeit | duff |
| concertina | squiffer | country gentleman | squire |
| condominium | mansion flat | county | shire |
| condom | French letter | C.O.D. | carriage forward |
| confusion | caddle | county seat | county town |
| consolation, poor | cold comfort | court (v) | walk out with |
| conversation | chinwag | coveralls | boiler suit |
| convertible | sports car | cow dung | cow pat |
| conveyor belt | endless driven belt | cowcatcher (train) | plow |
| cookie sheet | baking tray | cowl (auto) | scuttle |
| cookies | sweet biscuits | crackers | biscuits; dry biscuits |
| cool one's heels | kick one's heels | cram (v) | (for a test) swot; mug |
| cop | rozzer | crank case (auto) | sump |
| copy reader | sub-editor | crazy | crackers; a nutter |
| corn (food) | maize | cream of wheat | semolina |
| corn meal | Indian meal | creek (n) | burn |
| corn on the cob | maize cob | crib death | cot-death |
| corned beef | salt beef | cricket player | bowler |
| corner (of the eye) | tail of the eye | cricket field | cricket pitch |
| corner cutter | wide boy | crime show | crook drama |
| cornstarch | cornflour | criticize (v) | bag |
| corp. | ltd; plc (private limited company) | crooked dice | Fulham |
| corporation | limited (liability) company | crooked police officer | bent copper |

| U.S. | BRITISH | U.S. | BRITISH |
|---|---|---|---|
| cross-eyed | boss-eyed | dead end | close; no through road |
| cross hairs (guns) | cross wires | dead letter office | returned letter office |
| cross street | turning | dealer | monger |
| crossing | side turning | deceive (v) | kid; sell a pup |
| crossing guard | lollipop lady (man) | deck house (boats) | wheelhouse |
| crossroads | carax | decorated cake | gateau |
| crosswalk | zebra crossing (striped) | decorating tip (food) | icing nozzle |
| crouton | sippet | deductible (insurance) | excess |
| crowd | scrum | deer crossing (auto) | toad crossing |
| cruddy | grotty | defroster (auto) | demister |
| cuddling | canoodling | delegation | deputation |
| cuff link | sleevelink | delivery route | delivery round; milk-walk |
| cuffs (pants) | turn-ups | deliveryman | roundsman |
| cunt | fanny | denatured alcohol | meths |
| cupcake (food) | fairy cake | dental assistant | chairside assistant |
| curb | kerb | deposit on purchases | earnest; earnest money |
| curse (v) | effin' blind | | |
| curtain rod | curtain rail | | |
| custom-made (clothes) | made to measure | depressed | humped |
| cutie | popsie | depressed districts | special areas |
| | | deprivation | short commons |
| Dacron | terylene | derby (hat) | bowler |
| dainty | twee | desk sergeant | station sergeant |
| damned | bloomin'; ruddy | desk (with drawers) | bureau |
| dance party | knees up; rave | | |
| dandruff | scurf | dessert | sweet; pud; pudding |
| Danish pastry | Swiss bun | | |
| dark beer | porter; stout; bitter | | |
| darts | arrows | | |
| dashboard (auto) | facia; parcel shelf | | |
| day student | out-college (adj) | | |
| daylight saving time | summer time | | |
| deadbeats | long firm | dessert plates | sweet plates |

| U.S. | BRITISH | U.S. | BRITISH |
|---|---|---|---|
| detour | diversion | distracted | out of oneself |
| diapers | nappies | divided high- | |
| diarrhea | gippy tum; squitters | way | dual carriageway |
| | | dividend | divvy |
| die (v) | pack it up; cop it; snuff it | doctor's office | surgery |
| | | dollars to | |
| dig in one's heels | stick in one's toes | doughnuts | Lombard Street to a China orange |
| dime a dozen | ten-a-penny | dolly (repair) | crawler board |
| dimmer | dipswitch | donkey | moke |
| dining car | saloon carriage | door-to-door | |
| dinner jacket | D.J. | selling | on the knocker |
| diplomat | diplomatist | doorbell | bellpush |
| direct examina- | | doorman | commissionaire |
| tion (legal) | examination in chief | | (hotel) |
| | | do the dishes | wash up |
| director | | double date | in a four |
| (theater) | regisseur | dour | po-faced |
| directory | | downpayment | down deposit |
| assistance | directory inquiries | downspout | downpipe |
| dirt | earth | draft beer | bitter; from the wood |
| dirt road | unmade track | | |
| dirty | grotty | draft (military) | (n) national ser- |
| disagreeable | beastly | | vice; (v) call up |
| disconcerting | off-putting | drapes | curtains |
| discount store | warehouse store | drawing paper | cartridge paper |
| discussion | cross talk | dressed up | tarted up |
| disheveled | grotty | dresser | chest of drawers |
| dish towel | drying-up cloth; tea cloth | dressing gown | undressing robe |
| | | dried out (adj) | gone hard |
| dishonest | bent | drink (v) | swallow |
| dishonest | | drink it | put it down |
| person | twister | drive (v) | motor |
| dishwasher | washing-up machine | driver | motorist |
| | | driveway | drive |
| disinterested | off | driving while | |
| dislike (v) | take against | intoxicated | driving under the influence |
| dismiss (v) | turf out | | |
| disoriented | disorientated | drop in | pop in |
| display installer | shop fitter | drudge (n) | skivvy; dogsbody |

| U.S. | BRITISH | U.S. | BRITISH |
|---|---|---|---|
| drug store | chemist's | elevated | |
| drunk | whacked; pissed; sloshed; squiffy; jaggering; potted | railroad | overhead railway |
| | | elevator | lift |
| | | elevator operator | liftman |
| dry goods store | draper | embroidery | fancy work |
| dry martini | gin and French | embroidery thread | yarn |
| dry vermouth | dry martini | | |
| dryer (clothes) | tumble dryer | emergency room | casualty |
| drying rack | clothes horse | | |
| dull | muzzy | employed | in work |
| dumbwaiter | service lift | employment exchange | job centre |
| dump (v) | tip | | |
| dumpster | skip | employment office | labour exchange |
| dump truck | tipper | empty bottles | dead-men |
| duplex | semi-detached; (four-room) two-up-two-down | end up (v) | land up; finish up |
| | | endive | chicory |
| dust balls | slut's wool | engineer (train) | driver; engine driver |
| | | enthusiastically | like the clappers |
| eat (v) | feed on | entrance | way in |
| eavesdrop (v) | ear-wig | equal stakes (betting) | evens |
| eccentric (n) | nutter | | |
| economize | make do and mend | equivalent to | upsides with |
| | | eraser | rubber |
| editorial | leader | Erector set | Meccano set |
| efficiency | one-room flat | escalator | moving stairs |
| eggnog | egg-flip | escape hatch | bolt hole |
| eggplant | aubergine | escaped (v) | done a runner; bolted |
| 800-number | freephone | | |
| election day | polling day | estuary | firth |
| electric cord | flex | everyone and his brother | the world and his wife |
| electric heater | electric fire | | |
| electric razor | mains razor | excellence | full marks |
| electrical generator | dynamo | excellent! | topping! |
| | | excelsior | wood straw |
| electrical wire | lead | excited | cock-a-hoop |
| elementary school | junior school | | |

| U.S. | BRITISH | U.S. | BRITISH |
|---|---|---|---|
| excommuni- | | felt hat (men) | trilby |
| cated | sent to coventry | fender (auto) | mudguard; wing; |
| exercises | physical jerks | | mudwing |
| exhaust fan | extractor fan | ferris wheel | big wheel |
| exhausted | whacked | festival | gaudy |
| exit | way out | fielder (sports) | fieldsman |
| expel | turf out; (from | field of | |
| | school) send | expertise | line of country |
| | down | Fig Newton | fig roll |
| expert | dab hand | fight (n) | punch-up |
| extortion | menaces | film distributor | renter |
| extra (adj) | gash | finalized | put paid to |
| extract (v) | winkle out | finally | for good and |
| eyeball (v) | measure or re- | | all |
| | view visually | financial | |
| | | district | the City |
| face card | | financial editor | city editor |
| (games) | court card | financial | |
| factory | works | section | city page |
| faculty (school) | staff | find (v) | chase up |
| fag; faggot | poof (derog.) | finders keepers | findings keepings |
| fail dismally | make a balls-up | fingernail | |
| faint | queer | buffer | nail pad |
| fair-haired boy | | fingerprints | dabs |
| (girl) | blue-eyed boy | fire drill | fire practice |
| | (girl) | firecracker | squib |
| family name | surname | fired | turned off |
| family room | sitting room | fireplace tool | |
| fancy | natty | set | fireplace suite |
| farsighted | long-sighted | firing pin (gun) | striker |
| fashionable | swish | first-rate | smashing; |
| Father | Pater | | top-hole |
| fear | funk | first balcony | |
| fed-up | cheesed-off; | (theater) | upper circle |
| | chocker | first floor | ground floor |
| feeble-minded | having a loose | fish sticks | fish fingers |
| | tile | fish store | fishmonger |
| feel sick (v) | go sick | fisherman | angler |
| feet of clay | heels of clay | flabbergasted | gobsmacked |
| fellow | bloke; cove | flag stop | railway halt |

| U.S. | BRITISH | U.S. | BRITISH |
|------|---------|------|---------|
| flashlight | torch; electric torch | four poster | four-post bed |
| flashy | natty | frame up | fit up |
| flagstone | stone-flagged | fraud | obtaining by deception |
| flatbed (truck) | low-loader | | |
| flat tire (auto) | puncture | freeway | motorway; dual carriageway |
| flatter insincerely | smarm | | |
| | | freezer | cold store |
| flattering nonsense | flummery | freight train | goods train |
| | | french fries | chips |
| flecked (adj) | freaked | French kidney bean | flageolet |
| flee | scarper | | |
| flight attendant | air hostess | fresh | cheeky (impudent) |
| | | friend | mate |
| flirt (v) | chat up | friendliness | matiness |
| fool | stirk | fringe benefits | perquisites |
| floor lamp | standard lamp | frivolous person | silly bugger |
| floorwalker | shop-walker | | |
| flower pot | bulb-bowl | front bumper (car) | nose |
| fluorescent lighting | strip lighting | | |
| | | fruit-ade | squash |
| fly swatter | flyswat | fruit store | fruiterer |
| flypaper | gumstrip | fuck off! | naff off! |
| flywheel gear (auto) | ring gear | fuckin' (adj) | flippin' |
| | | full-time | whole time |
| foggy | brumous | fun and games | cakes and ale |
| folding chair | tip-up seat | furnished offices | furnished apartments |
| food | tucker; stodge (heavy and starchy) | | |
| | | furnished apartment | digs; diggings |
| food slicer | mandoline | furniture | sticks |
| fool | (n) berk; (v) buy a pup; have on | fuss | faff |
| | | fuss and bother | pother |
| for rent | to let | | |
| for sale | on offer | galley | caboose |
| foreman | charge-hand; gaffer | galoshes | Wellingtons |
| | | game birds | wing game |
| forever | year dot | game preserve | park |
| forger | penman | game (n) | match |
| foul-up | balls-up; cock-up | garage sale | car boot sale |

| U.S. | BRITISH | U.S. | BRITISH |
|---|---|---|---|
| garbage can | swill bin; dust bin | ment | fascia box; glove box |
| garbage dump | rubbish tip | | |
| garden shears | secateurs | go away | bugger off; piss off |
| gardener | groundsman | | |
| garter belt | suspender belt | go to hell! | get stuffed!; get knotted! |
| garters | (men) sock suspenders; (women) suspenders | go to the bathroom | spend a penny |
| | | gofer | tea boy (girl) |
| gas gauge | petrol gauge | goodbye | cheery-bye |
| gas pipe | gas fitting | goof (v) | boob |
| gas station | petrol garage | goof off | swan |
| gasket sealant | jointing compound | gossip | gup |
| | | grab bag | lucky dip |
| gasoline (gas) | motor spirit; petrol | grade (level) | form |
| | | grade crossing | level crossing |
| gear shift | gear lever | graduate (v) | pass out |
| geezer | duffer | graduation exercise | passing out parade |
| general delivery | post restante | | |
| generator (electrical) | dynamo | grain | corn |
| | | grammar school | primary school |
| genitals | rude parts | | |
| German shepherd dog | Alsatian | grandfather clock | long-case clock |
| get fired | get the chop | granulated sugar | gran |
| get a job | take up a post | gratuity (tip) | dash |
| get into trouble | catch it | gravel | loose chippings |
| get rid of | get shot of | gravy | gippo |
| get someone's goat | take the mickey out of someone | gravy boat | sauce boat |
| | | green thumb | green fingers |
| | | greenhouse | glasshouse; forcing house |
| get under one's skin | get up one's nose | grimaced | pulled a face |
| | | ground (electrical) | earth |
| giddy | queer | grumble (v) | natter; grouse |
| gingersnap | ginger nut | guard rail (auto) | overrider |
| Girl Scouts | Girl Guides | | |
| given the boot | given the push | | |
| glass (beer) | jar | guided tour | packet holiday |
| glove compart- | | | |

| U.S. | BRITISH | U.S. | BRITISH |
|---|---|---|---|
| **guy** | bloke; cove | (furniture) | tall boy |
| **gyp** | diddle | **high gear** (auto) | top gear |
| **gypsy** | romany; caird | **high school** | grammar school |
| | | **high horse** | high ropes |
| **hairspray** | lacquer | **high A, high C** | |
| **ham** | gammon | (music) | top A, Top C, |
| **hamburger bun** | bap | | etc. |
| **hamburger** | | **highway** | dual carriageway |
|    **meat** | mince | **highway rest** | |
| **hammock** | pipe cot | **stop** | lay by |
| **hand of fate** | finger of fate | **highway** | |
| **hand organ** | street organ | **robbery** | daylight robbery |
| **handcuffs** | darbies | **hill** | fell; (*pl*) downs |
| **hand over** | give in | **hire** (v) | engage |
| **happy-go-lucky** | come-day, go-day | **hit and run** (n) | tip and run |
| **happy-hour** | sundowner | **hitch-hike** (v) | thumb a lift |
| **hard candy** | boiled sweets; | **hobo** | toe-rag |
| | rock | **hocus-pocus** | jiggery-pokery |
| **hardware store** | ironmonger | **hold a general** | |
| **hare-brained** | scatty | **election** | go to the country |
| **harassed** | chivvied | **home address** | private address |
| **harmonica** | mouth organ | **homeroom** | |
| **hat** | tile; titfer; lid | **teacher** | form-master |
| **hat rack** | hallstand | **homework** | prep |
| **haystack** | haycock | **homosexual** | nancy; nancy |
| **hazardous duty** | | | boy |
| **pay** | danger money | **hood** (auto) | bonnet |
| **head** | chump | **hood ornament** | mascot |
| **headboard** | bedboard | **hope chest** | bottom drawer |
| **headliner** | top-liner | **hopeless** | past praying for |
| **head nurse** | charge nurse; | **horny** | randy |
| | matron | **horse chestnut** | conker |
| **headset jack** | headphone socket | **horse of a dif-** | |
| **health farm** | health hydro | **ferent color** | another pair of |
| **heap** (n) | bing | | shoes |
| **hearing aid** | deaf aid | **horse trailer** | horse float |
| **hearse** | mortuary van | **horsefly** | kleg |
| **help wanted** | situations wanted | **horsehair** | |
| **hen** (gossip) | tabby | **upholstery** | haircord |
| **highboy** | | **hospital bed** | pay bed |

| U.S. | BRITISH | U.S. | BRITISH |
|------|---------|------|---------|
| hospital social worker | almoner | incinerator | destructor |
| hot dog bun | bridge roll | inclusive | all-in |
| hotel bellman | hall porter | incorporated | limited (liability) |
| hotel bill | account; hotel note | inc. | ltd; plc (private limited company) |
| hotel luggage storage | box-room | incumbent | sitting |
| houndstooth (pattern) | dog tooth | indelible pencil | copying pencil |
| hourglass | sand glass | industrial park | trading estate |
| house wine | plonk | information | enquiry |
| house plant | plant pot; pot plant | information (telephone) | directory inquiries |
| housewares | hardware | informant | split |
| housing development | estate | ingrown toenail | ingrowing toenail |
| hubcap | nave plate | inheritance tax | death duty |
| humorless | po-faced | innkeeper | victualler |
| hungry | peckish | inspect (v) | look over |
| hunky-dory | tickety-boo | installment plan | hire-purchase; tally plan; never-never |
| hunting trip | shoot | insulate (insulation) | lag |
| ice chest | cold container | insurance | assurance |
| ice cream | ices | insurance settlement | insurance pay-out |
| ice cream cone | cornet | intermission (theater) | interval |
| idiot | birk; berk | internal revenue | inland revenue |
| idle (auto) (v) | tickover | intravenous feeding | drip-feed |
| ill-omened | unchancey | investment bank | merchant bank |
| imagine (v) | fancy | Irish coffee | Gaelic coffee |
| immediately | directly; straightaway | IRS agent | inspector of taxes |
| impertinent | cheeky | It became clear | The penny dropped |
| in heat | on heat | | |
| in serious trouble | up the spout | itinerant worker | swagman (Aus.) |
| in the cards | on the cards | | |
| in the home stretch | go up the straight | | |
| inaccessible | uncome-at-able | | |

| U.S. | BRITISH | U.S. | BRITISH |
|------|---------|------|---------|
| **Jack** (cards) | knave | **lamb** | hogget |
| **jackrabbit** | prairie hare | **lame** | gammy |
| **jail** | nick; gaol | **landmark** | |
| **jam** (n) | conserve | **building** | listed building |
| **janitor** | caretaker; porter | **lane** | track |
| **jelly roll** | Swiss roll | **laundromat** | launderette; |
| **jerk** | twit | | washeteria |
| **jerk-off** (v) | wanker | **law offices** | chambers |
| **jimmy** (bur- | | **lawyer** | solicitor; pleader; |
| glar's tool) | jemmy | | barrister |
| **job loss** | high jump | **lay** (sex) | stuff; get a |
| **journalist** | press man | | legover |
| **julienne potato** | straw potato | **lay of the land** | lie of the hand |
| **jumper** | | **lazy** | dozy |
| (clothes) | overdress | **lease** (v) | let |
| **jump rope** | skipping rope | **lease runs out** | lease falls in |
| **junior attorney** | utter barrister | **leave** | |
| **junkman** | rag and bone man | **unexpectedly** | pop off |
| **junkyard** | breaker's yard | **legal age** | full age |
| **junk** | tat | **leg room** (auto) | footwell |
| | | **legal holiday** | bank holiday |
| **keep a low** | | **less than** | inside of |
| **profile** | keep your head | **letter opener** | paper knife |
| | down | **letterhead** | headed paper |
| **kerosene stove** | paraffin burner | **liar** | twister |
| **key ring** (spiral) | split ring | **library card** | reader's ticket |
| **kickbacks** | backhanders | **license plate** | |
| **kid leather** | cheverel | (index) | number-plate |
| **killed himself** | did himself in | **license plate** | |
| **kill time** | put off time | **registration** | vehicle index |
| **kitchen work** | | **license** | |
| **area** | scullery | **suspended** | banned |
| **knickers** (men) | plus-fours | **life insurance** | life assurance |
| | | **lima bean** | broad bean; |
| **lab coat** | overall | | butter bean |
| **labor union** | trades union | **linens** | muslin |
| **labor slowdown** | work to rule | **line up** (v) | queue; queue up |
| **ladies' man** | bit of a lad | **line-up** (police) | identification |
| **ladybug** | Bishop Barnaby; | | parade |
| | ladybird | **liquor** | spirits |

| U.S. | BRITISH | U.S. | BRITISH |
|---|---|---|---|
| liquor bottle | drink bottle | mail box | pillar box |
| liquor cabinet | drinks cabinet; cupboard | main event | star turn |
| | | Main street | High street |
| liquor store | off-license | major highway | arterial road |
| liquor store owner | vintner | major in (a subject) | read |
| list and total | tot up | make a good impression | polish one's marble |
| literary hacks | Grub Street | | |
| litterbug | litterlout | make tea (v) | brew up |
| live well (v) | do oneself well | make the bed | dress the bed |
| liver balls | faggots | mallet | bitel |
| liverwurst | liver sausage | manslaughter | culpable homicide |
| living room | sitting room | | |
| lobby | foyer | marine supplier | ship chandler |
| local train | stopping train | mark time (v) | tread time |
| locker room | changing room | marriage certificate | lines |
| long distance (toll) call | trunk call | | |
| look (n) | shufti; dekko | mashed potatoes | mash |
| lookout (scenic) | viewpoint | match stick | vesta |
| loose-leaf notebook | spine-back | math | maths |
| loose weave | wide weave | maximum capacity | at full stretch |
| lost interest | gone off | meat kabob | sosatie |
| lose one's temper | lose one's rag | meatballs | faggots |
| lots of | lashings | meat roast | joint |
| loveseat | settee | meat grinder | mincer |
| low gear (auto) | bottom gear | mechanical pencil | propelling pencil |
| lucky | jammy | median | central reservation; centre strip |
| lug wrench (auto) | box spanner | | |
| luggage storage (hotel) | box-room | mental exhaustion | brain fag |
| lumber | timber | mentioned below | undermentioned |
| lunch box | tuck box; piece tin; jack-box | menu | bill of fare; tariff; (fixed price) set meal |
| Madeira wine | malmsey | | |
| mail (v) | post | | |

| U.S. | BRITISH | U.S. | BRITISH |
|------|---------|------|---------|
| men's room | gents' cloaks | moving van | removal van |
| mesh shirt | string vest | muffin pan | bun tin |
| mess (n) | box-up | muffler (car) | silencer |
| mess around | muck about | mug | beaker |
| mezzanine | dress circle | municipal | |
| mid-term | | government | the corporation |
| vacation | half term | Musical Chairs | |
| midtown | city centre | (game) | General Post |
| military police | | musty | frowsty |
| officer | redcap | mutual fund | unit trust |
| milking shed | herringbone | | |
| | parlour | nag (v) | get on at |
| milkman | milk roundsman | nail (v) (sex) | roger |
| mineral oil | liquid paraffin | nail down | tape |
| minimum bal- | | nail polish | varnish; nail |
| ance (bank) | drawing level | | varnish |
| minority | | naked | starkers |
| leadership | shadow cabinet | narrow alley | ginnel |
| Miracle Whip | salad cream | necking | canoodling; |
| Miranda | | | snogging |
| rights (police) | warn (n) | necktie | cravat |
| mirror | glass | neighborhood | |
| mischief | devilry | bar | local |
| mistreated | hard done by | new | fresh |
| mixing bowl | pudding basin | newsstand | (indoors) news |
| mobile home | caravan | | agent; (out- |
| molasses | treacle | | doors) book- |
| moment (time) | tick | | stall |
| money | brass; ackers; | night shirt | sark |
| | monkey; lolly | nightgown | sark |
| mongrel | pyedog; tike; | nightstick | truncheon |
| | tyke | nightstand | bedside locker |
| monkey wrench | spanner | nod | beck |
| monkeyshines | monkey tricks | nominate | |
| mop (v) | wipe over | (political) | adopt |
| more to be | | non-union | un-unioned |
| done | more on one's | nonsense | bosh; tosh; |
| | plate | | rubbish; |
| mountain | fell | | codswallop |
| move along | get along | not kosher | not cricket |

| U.S. | BRITISH | U.S. | BRITISH |
|---|---|---|---|
| Not on your life! | Not on your nelly! | on the bias | on the cross |
| not really | not quite | on welfare | on the dole |
| not so bad | not so dusty | one of a kind | one on his (her) own |
| note | chit | one-armed bandit | fruit machine |
| notebook | pocketbook; (small) jotter | one-way ticket | single |
| notions store | haberdasher | only | on its own |
| nuisance | bind | open land | moor |
| nurse | sister | operating room | operating-theatre |
| nuts | dotty | O.R. nurse | theatre sister |
| | | O.R. orderly | theatre porter |
| oatmeal | porridge | orchestra seats (theater) | stalls |
| obnoxious person | blighter; rotter | ostracized | sent to coventry |
| obstinate | bloody-minded | ottoman | humpty |
| occupant | occupier | outclass (v) | be streets ahead |
| occupied | engaged | outfit (n) | kit |
| odd | rum | outlet (electric) | power point; point |
| odds and ends | odd-come-shorts | out of order (phone) | unobtainable |
| odometer | mileometer | out of sorts | off colour |
| off-Broadway | fringe (theatre) | outhouse | dunny; earth closet |
| off the rack (clothes) | off-the-peg | overalls | dungarees |
| office | room | overhead doors | tip-up doors |
| office building | house; office block | overhead (expense) | on cost |
| office worker | clerk | overpass (auto) | fly-over |
| oil pan | sump | oversee(r) | overlook(er) |
| oilcloth | oilskin | over the hill | beyond the job |
| oily (flattering) | smarmy | overtime | unsocial hours |
| O.K. | Righto | Oxfords (shoes) | lace-ups |
| okra | ladies' fingers | | |
| old fogey | buffer | pacifier | dummy; comforter |
| old port wine | vintage | | |
| olive oil | sweet oil | paddle (ping-pong) | bat |
| on credit | on the slate | paddy wagon | Black Maria |
| on order | indent | | |
| on parole | on license | | |
| on- (off-) ramp | slip road | | |

| U.S. | BRITISH | U.S. | BRITISH |
|---|---|---|---|
| **pal** | mate | **payroll clerk** | wages clerk |
| **panel truck** | van | **payroll savings** | |
| **panic** (n) | funk; flat spin | **plan** | save-as-you-earn |
| **pantry** | larder; lardette (small) | **peanuts** | monkey nuts |
| | | **peddle** (v) | flog |
| **pantsuit** | | **peek-a-boo** | peep-bo |
| (women) | trouser suit | **peephole** | spyhole |
| **pantyhose** | tights | **pen-pal** | pen-friend |
| **papaya** | pawpaw | **Pentecost** | Whitsun |
| **paraffin wax** | white wax | **pepper shaker** | pepper pot |
| **paralegal** | articled clerk | **perfect hap-** | |
| **parasol** | sunshade | **piness** | fiddler's green |
| **parentheses** | brackets; round brackets | **perform better** | pull up your socks |
| | | **perfume** | scent |
| **parka** | anorak | **period** | |
| **parking** | waiting | (punctuation) | full stop |
| **parking lights** | | **permanent** | |
| (auto) | running lights; side lights | **press** | stay-press |
| | | **person** | chap |
| **part** (hair) | parting | **petty thief** | spiv |
| **party** (n) | a do | **Phillips** | |
| **passing** (auto) | overtaking | **screwdriver** | crosshead; cross-ply |
| **paste** | gum | | |
| **pass it up** | give it a miss | **phone** (n,v) | tinkle |
| **pastry cart** | sweet trolley | **physician** | |
| **path** | track | (resident) | houseman |
| **paved** | sealed | **pick up** (v) | uplift (a thing); |
| **paved road** | tarred road | | collect (a |
| **pavement** | road | | person) |
| **paving block** | | **pick up women** | pull birds |
| (stone) | set | **picketing** | parading with |
| **paving stone** | | | placards |
| (granite) | pitcher | **pickles** | pickled cucumbers |
| **pawn shop** | popshop | **picnic basket** | chop box |
| **pawn** (v) | soak; pop | **picture window** | long-view window |
| **pawned** | laid on the shelf | **pie crust** | shortcrust |
| **pay for** (v) | stand | **pier** | quay |
| **pay phone** | telephone box | **pigheaded** | bloody-minded |
| **pay-off** | baksheesh | **pig in a** | |
| **payroll** | paysheet | **blanket** | sausage roll |

| U.S. | BRITISH | U.S. | BRITISH |
|---|---|---|---|
| pig sty | piggery | post no bills | stick no bills |
| pig's feet | trotters | postage meter | franking machine |
| pigskin | hogskin | postage paid | freepost |
| pigtails (hair) | bunches | postpaid | post free |
| piles of... | bags of... | pot holder | kettle holder; |
| pile-up (auto) | multiple smash | | oven gloves |
| pill | tablet | potato chips | crisps; potato |
| pimp | ponce | | crisps |
| pine cone | fir apple | pothole | pot |
| pious | pi | pot pie | raised pie |
| pit (fruit) | stone; pip | pour (rain) (v) | bucket |
| pitcher | jug | powdered sugar | icing sugar |
| pitless fruit | soft fruit | power source | mains |
| plain | homely | prank | cantrip |
| plant (factory) | works | prenatal | ante-natal |
| plastic bag | poly bag | precinct | district |
| plastic wrap | clingfilm | preferred stock | preference shares |
| platter | meat plate | premature | early days |
| play dead (v) | lie doggo | premonition of | |
| play hookey | play truant | danger | pricking of |
| playing field | pitch | | thumbs |
| pleasing thing | bit of all right | prepaid | |
| plentiful | thick on the | delivery | carriage paid |
| | ground | presto change-o | hey presto |
| plug | power point; point | pretensions | edge |
| pocket knife | clasp-knife | pretty girl | bit of goods |
| pogo stick | kangaroo ball | price tags | swing tickets |
| point of view | view | principal | schoolmaster |
| police (n) | Old Bill | prison | nick; |
| police station | cop shop | prison cell | peter |
| police informer | grass | prison guard | warder |
| police line-up | identification | prison | |
| | parade | inspector | prison visitor |
| police beat | patch | prison warden | governor |
| poorhouse | alms house | private eye | enquiry agent |
| popsicle | ice lolly | private | |
| porridge | stirabout | detective | private enquiry |
| port tax (ships) | groundage | | agent |
| port wine | vintage | private hospital | nursing home |
| possible | on | private school | public school |

| U.S. | BRITISH | U.S. | BRITISH |
|------|---------|------|---------|
| **problem** (serious) | facer | **quotation marks** | inverted commas |
| **produce vendor** | costermonger | | |
| **produce store** | greengrocer | **rack** | wire tray |
| **proofreader** | corrector of the press | **racket** (criminal) | ramp |
| **property taxes** | rates | **racketball** | racquets |
| **pry open** (v) | prise | **radio** | wireless |
| **pub owner** | proprietor; publican | **radio tube** | valve; thermionic valve |
| **public holiday** | bank holiday | **rage** | bate |
| **public stock issue** | flotation | **railroad car** | railway carriage |
| | | **railroad crossing** | warning cross |
| **public library** | lending library | | |
| **public school** | state school | **railroad station** | terminus |
| **pull-off** (road) | lay-by | **railroad yard** | marshalling yard |
| **pullman** | sleeping-car carriage | **rails** (train) | metals |
| | | **railway crossing** | level crossing |
| **pullover** | jumper | | |
| **pumps** (shoes) | court shoes | **rain check** | postponement |
| **punting pole** | quant | **raisins, seedless** | sultanas |
| **pup tent** | bivvy | **rambunctious** | rumbustious |
| **puppet show** | Punch and Judy show | **ring** (v) | press (a doorbell) |
| | | **rare** (food) | underdone |
| **push pin** | drawing pin | **rat catcher** | rodent officer |
| **push-up** | press-up | **rat** (informer) | sneak; grass |
| **pushcart** | barrow | **read aloud** | read out |
| **put an end to** | put paid to | **ready, set, go!** | ready, steady, go! |
| **put a motion on the table** | table (v) | **real estate** | property market |
| | | **real estate agent** | house agent |
| **put out** | put about | | |
| **putter** (v) | potter | **realtor** | estate agent |
| | | **receipt** | chit |
| **quarrel, violent** | up-and-downer | **recess** (school) | break; break-up |
| **quarter note** (music) | crotchet; crochet | **record player** | gramophone |
| | | **recording engineer** | recordist |
| **quickly** | smartish | | |
| **quiet down** | quieten | **redecorated** | done up |
| **quit** (v) | chuck it | **reform school** | Borstal; approved school |
| **quite** (adv) | fair | | |

| U.S. | BRITISH | U.S. | BRITISH |
|------|---------|------|---------|
| regular price | normal price | rinse | |
| religious TV | | thoroughly | swill |
| programs | God spots | river | burn |
| remnants | off-cuts | road divider | centre reservation |
| remote | back of beyond | road bump | risk of grounding |
| rent (v) | hire | roadside | |
| rental car | drive-yourself car; hire car | reflector | cat's eye |
| | | roadside | |
| rental units | lettings | restaurant | pull-up |
| rented | hired | rocker panel | |
| repaired | put right | (auto) | sill |
| repairman | repair engineer | rocks (in piles) | tor |
| reporter | press man | roll call | call over; parade state |
| reservations | advance bookings | | |
| reserve in | | roll of film | spool |
| advance | book | roll of mints | tube of mints |
| residence | hangout | roller (textile) | wince |
| resign | stand down | roller coaster | big dipper; switchback |
| rest (v) | get one's feet up | | |
| restroom | W.C. (water closet); loo; lavatory | rolling pin | pastry roller |
| | | Rolls Royce | Roller |
| | | romaine lettuce | cos lettuce |
| rest stop | | roof (auto) | head; (convertible) hood |
| (highway) | lay by | | |
| retailer | stockist | rooftops | backs of houses |
| retirement age | superannuation | room | apartment |
| retread (auto) | remould | room clerk | reception clerk |
| rhinestones | diamanté | room with bath | ensuite |
| rib chops | best end | roomer | lodger |
| rich (adj) | warm; lined | rotted (adj) | perished |
| ridge | back of hill | rough it | sleep rough |
| ridicule (v) | send up | rough | |
| right on | bang on | treatment | towsing |
| right on time | prompt to time | round of drinks | round |
| right the first | | round trip | circular tour |
| time | got it in one | round-trip | |
| Ring Around | | ticket | return ticket |
| the Rosie | Ring-a-Ring-o'-Roses | row houses | terrace houses |
| | | rubber boots | Wellingtons; wellies |
| ring (large) | knuckle-duster | | |

| U.S. | BRITISH | U.S. | BRITISH |
|---|---|---|---|
| rubber cement | cow gum | sausages | bangers; snorkers |
| rubber nipple | teat | saucepan | milkboiler |
| rubbing alcohol | surgical spirits | sauté lightly (v) | sweat |
| Rube Goldberg | Heath Robinson | savings account | deposit account |
| ruined | up the spout | Savings and | |
| rum and water | grog | Loan Assoc. | Building Society |
| rummage sale | jumble sale | sawbuck (ten- | |
| run for office | stand for office | dollar bill) | tenner (ten-pound |
| run in place (v) | run on the spot | | note) |
| running engine | | scab (labor | |
| (auto) | turning over | dispute) | blackleg |
| | | scallion | spring onion |
| safecracker | peterman | scarce | thin on the ground |
| safe-deposit box | deed box | scarf (woolen) | comforter |
| sailor | matelot; tar | schedule | time table |
| salad oil | sweet oil | schmeer (of | |
| salary advance | sub | butter) | scrape |
| salary | | scholarship | bursary |
| negotiations | pay round | school building | teaching block |
| sale price | offer price | school term end | breaking up |
| sales | (special) offers | Scotch whiskey | whisky |
| sales slip | docket | scoundrel | blackguard |
| sales tax | | scrambled eggs | buttered eggs |
| (equivalent) | V.A.T. (value- | scratch pad | scribbling block |
| | added tax) | scratch paper | scribbling |
| salesperson | sales (shop) | | paper |
| | assistant | screen door | wire screen |
| salt shaker | salt cellar; salt pot | screw (v) (sex) | shag |
| salt and pepper | | screwdriver | |
| set | cruet | (short) | dumpy |
| salute (v) | throw a salute | | screwdriver |
| sandbox | sandpit | sea wall | sea bank |
| sandwich (half) | half-round | seaman | rating |
| sanitary pads | sanitary towels | search a room | turn over |
| Santa Claus | Father Christmas | seat | bottom |
| sarong | kanga | seats, front row | |
| SAT (Schola- | | (theater) | mezzanine |
| stic Aptitude | | second balcony | |
| Test) | A-levels | (theater) | gallery |
| satisfaction | much joy | second floor | first floor |

| U.S. | BRITISH | U.S. | BRITISH |
|---|---|---|---|
| security blanket | security snug | heeled) | pumps |
| sedan, 2- or 4- | | shoelace | lace; bootlace |
| door | saloon | shoe-shine boy | boots; shoeblack |
| sedan, four- | | shop owner | shopkeeper |
| door | double-door | shopping | doing the shops |
| | saloon | shopping cart | trolley |
| seed | pip | shopping center | parade of shops |
| sell (v) | flog | shopping mall | hypermarket |
| senile | gaga | shopworn | shop-soiled |
| services, | | shortbread | shortcake |
| provide | lay on; do | shorted | |
| serving area | servery | (electrical) | fused |
| set of keys | lot of keys | shorts (men) | underpants; |
| set the world | | | Y-fronts |
| on fire | set the Thames | shot (medical | |
| | on fire | injection) | jab |
| sewing (by | | shoulder (road) | verge |
| machine) | machining | shrewd | canny, long- |
| sexton | verger | | headed (wise); |
| shabby | tatty | | wide (sneaky) |
| shades | blinds | Shrove Tuesday | Pancake Tuesday |
| shag carpet | tumble twist | shudder | judder |
| shaky | dicky | shuffleboard | shovelboard |
| shampoo | hair wash | sideburns | sideboards |
| sharp-witted | fly | sideview | |
| shaving kit | sponge bag | mirror | wing mirror |
| sheep pasture | sheep walk | sidewalk | pavement |
| sheep rancher | woolgrower; | sight-seeing bus | charabanc |
| | pastoralist | sign (n) | board |
| sherbet | ices; sorbet | signal a waiter | raise a finger |
| sheriff | chief constable | silent partner | sleeping partner |
| shipping | | silly | daft; scatty |
| department | dispatch | silly goose | silly bugger |
| | department | simple-minded | mental |
| shirk work (v) | mike | simpleton | juggins |
| shiver (n) | frisson | single mother | solo mother |
| shock (wheat, | | sit down | take a pew |
| corn) | stook | skeleton in the | |
| shock absorber | damper | closet | skeleton in the |
| shoes (low- | | | cupboard |

| U.S. | BRITISH | U.S. | BRITISH |
|---|---|---|---|
| sketchbook | sketching block | sneak in line | jump the queue |
| skyscraper | high rise block; tower block | soccer | football |
| | | soda crackers | cream crackers |
| slacks | kecks | soldier (old) | sweat (n) |
| slander (v) | slag off | soot | sootblacks |
| slash mark | | soup | gippo |
| (punctuation) | oblique | Soup's on! | Duff's up! |
| sled | sledge | spa | health hydro |
| sleep in | lie-in | spatula | |
| sleeve clamps | metal springs | (cooking) | fish slice; egg-slice |
| slingshot | catapult | | |
| slipcovers | | speaks French | has French |
| (furniture) | loose covers | special | slap-up |
| slip knot | running knot | special election | by election |
| slip | (evening dress) | spend (money) | |
| | opera top; (v) skite | recklessly | splash; splash out |
| slow-witted | slow off the mark | spill the beans | blow the gaff |
| slowpoke | slowcoach | split peas | split pulse |
| sly | canny | splotch (v) | splodge |
| small amount | spot | spoil (v) (food) | go off |
| small bet | flutter | spool (thread) | reel |
| small time | small beer | spool of thread | cotton reel |
| smart alec | clever dick | sporting event | match |
| smart cookie | long-headed | spot check | snap check |
| smash hit | bomb | sprats (food) | whitebait |
| smiled at | smiled to | spray gun | garden syringe |
| smock | overall | spring (auto) | springing |
| smoked herring | bloater | squash (food) | vegetable marrow |
| smoked | | | |
| haddock | finnan haddie | squeal (betray) | grass |
| smokestack | funnel; chimney | squint-eyed | skelly-eyed |
| smoking gun | trout in the milk | squinting | squew-eyed |
| snack bar | caff; buttery | stabilizer | |
| snacks (food) | tuck | (airplanes) | tail plane |
| sneakers | plimsolls; tennis shoes | stable hand | ostler |
| | | stand in line | queue; queue up |
| sneaky | wide | startled | gobsmacked |
| snorkel | | starving | clemmed |
| (submarine) | snort | station wagon | estate car |

| U.S. | BRITISH | U.S. | BRITISH |
|------|---------|------|---------|
| stay (v) | stop | sit-in | stay-in strike |
| steal (v) | bone | string beans | French beans; |
| steam shovel | steam-navvy | | runners |
| steel wool | wire wool | strip mining | open-cast mining |
| steering wheel | driving wheel | stroll | (v) ramble; (n) |
| stench (n) | pong | | bummel |
| stenographer | shorthand typist | stroller | buggy; push chair |
| step-ladder | pair of steps | strongbox | deed-box |
| sticker | label | stuck-up | toffee-nosed |
| stick it out | stick it | studio | |
| stingy | mean; pinch-fisted | apartment | bedsitter |
| stock up (v) | stock in | stuffed shirt | blimp |
| stocks | | subordinate | understrapper |
| (financial) | shares | subscribe (v) | take in |
| stolen (*hot*) | fell off the back | suburb | satellite town |
| | of a lorry | subway | tube; underground |
| stool pigeon | sneak; snort | suit (business) | lounge suit |
| storage room | lumber room | suitcase | portmanteau |
| storekeeper | tradesman | suite of rooms | set of apartments |
| stove (or *range*) | cooker | sulfur | brimstone |
| straight (drink) | neat | sun porch | sun lounge |
| straight flush | | sunscreen lotion | sun filter cream |
| (cards) | running flush | supplier | stockist |
| straight-jacket | straight-waistcoat | supplies | storage |
| straight razor | cut-throat | surplus | ex-army |
| strange | rum | | equipment |
| strapped (adj) | strappy | surprised | all standing |
| streaked (adj) | freaked | suspenders | braces |
| street | road | swap-meet | bring-and-buy sale |
| street car | tram | swear (v) | use language |
| street corner | side turning | swear on a | |
| street | | stack of | |
| entertainer | busker | bibles | swear blind |
| street | | sweater | woolly; cardy |
| intersection | box | sweatshirt | sweater |
| street | | swim (v) | bathe |
| performer | busker | swimming pool | swimming-baths |
| strike | (n) industrial acti- | swindle | (n) ramp; (v) |
| | on; (v) down | | fiddle |
| | tools | swindling | on the fiddle |

| U.S. | BRITISH | U.S. | BRITISH |
|---|---|---|---|
| swinging door | swing-door | team uniform | strip |
| switchblade | flick-knife | tease (v) | chip; have one on |
| swollen | gummy | teetotaller | pop-wallah |
|  |  | telephone (n) | blower |
| tachometer | rev (revolution) counter | telephone booth | kiosk; call-box |
| taffy | toffee; toffy | telephone call | bell; tootle; tinkle |
| tag | (game) tig; tiggy; (clothes) label | telephone directory | post office directory |
| tag along (v) | tag on | telephone |  |
| take a course | read | information | directory enquiry |
| take a loss | take a toss | telephone repair |  |
| take a seat | grab a pew | service | faults and service difficulties |
| take a test | sit an exam | teletype | teleprinter |
| Take it or leave it | There it is | tell someone off | tick someone off |
| take the cake | take the biscuit | teller | cashier |
| take the lead | make the running | tell on (v) | peach on |
| take turns | take it in turns | temple |  |
| take off (v) | up-stick | (eyeglasses) | arm |
| talcum powder | toilet-powder | temporary |  |
| talk |  | work | casual work |
| nonsensically | haver | tenant (renting) | lodger |
| talk show | chat show | tennis shoes | sand shoes |
| tall | high | terrycloth robe | towelling robe |
| tangled | cotty | textile |  |
| tantrum | paddy | merchant | mercer |
| taps | (song) last post; (shoes) metal quarters | the media |  |
|  |  | (journalism) | Fleet Street |
| ta-ta | ta-ra | thermos bottle | vacuum flask; thermos flask |
| target (n) | cockshy | thick fog | pea-souper |
| tavern | pub | thicket | spinney |
| tax assessor | gauger | third wheel | gooseberry |
| taxi | private hire | This dog won't |  |
| taxi stand | cab rank | hunt | This horse won't start; this cock won't fight |
| taxpayer | ratepayer |  |  |
| tea ball | tea infuser |  |  |
| teacher (girls' school) | mistress | thorough | proper |
|  |  | thrash (v) | towel |

| U.S. | BRITISH | U.S. | BRITISH |
|------|---------|------|---------|
| thread | cotton | touchy | spiky |
| thrift shop | opportunity shop | tough luck | hard cheese |
| thrifty | canny | tourist | tripper |
| throw | bung | tour group | coach party |
| throw out | turf out | tow truck | breakdown van |
| thumb one's | | towel rack | towel-rail |
| nose | cock a snook | track team | athletics team |
| thumbtack | drawing pin | track and field | athletics |
| tick-tack-toe | noughts and | tractor-trailer | arctic |
| | crosses | trade in | give in part |
| ticket office | booking-hall | | exchange |
| ticket seller | booking-clerk | trademark | proprietary name; |
| tidbit | titbit | | chop |
| tiddly winks | squails | traffic circle | circus; round- |
| tie pin | breast pin | | about |
| tight-fisted | pinch-fisted | traffic control | point duty |
| tightrope | | traffic cop | speedcop; traffic |
| walker | wire-walker | | warden; points- |
| tinfoil | silver paper | | man |
| tipsy | tiddly | traffic lane | |
| tissue | paper hand- | (slow) | crawler lane |
| | kerchief | traffic | |
| tobacco shop | tobacconist | violations | motoring offenses |
| toilet | lavatory; W.C., | traffic viola- | |
| | loo | tion records | endorsements |
| toilet bowl | pan; lavatory pan | training course | training scheme |
| toilet tank | cistern | tranquilizer | anti-nuisance pill |
| Tom Collins | John Collins | transcribe (v) | recover |
| tongue | | trash can | waste bin; litter |
| depressor | spatula | | bin |
| too much | by half | traveling | |
| tough luck | bad show | salesperson | commercial |
| tooth filling | stopping | | traveller |
| top (of a car) | hood | trawling | |
| top grade | full marks | (fishing) | long-lining |
| top notch | smashing | treated badly | odd done by |
| toss | bung | treated roughly | pulled about |
| to the limit | full stretch | trial run | dummy run |
| touchdown | | trial docket | cause-list |
| (sports) | try | trial lawyer | barrister |

| U.S. | BRITISH | U.S. | BRITISH |
|------|---------|------|---------|
| trick (v) | kid | understood | |
| trimmed with | picked out | fully | taped |
| troubled | shirty | under the | |
| truant officer | school attendance | doctor's | |
| | officer | care | under the doctor |
| truck | lorry | uniform (n) | kit |
| truck farm | market garden | unlike | unalike |
| truck stop | lorry pull-in | unlisted phone | |
| trucker | haulier | number | ex-directory |
| tuft of hair | quiff | | number |
| tuna fish (food) | tunny | unpleasant | beastly |
| turnip (yellow) | swede | unsanitary | insanitary |
| turnpike | motorway | unserviceable | U.S. |
| turtleneck | roll-neck | unsound | dicky |
| tuxedo | dinner jacket | up in arms | up on his toes |
| tuxedo shirt | boiled shirt | upper class | top drawer |
| TV | telly | upper crust | top drawer |
| 20/20 vision | Six over six | upper middle | |
| 22-caliber | | class | gentry |
| firearm | two-two | upset (v) | overset |
| twit | squit | upstart | jumped-up |
| two of a kind | two for a pair | up the creek | up a gum tree; |
| two by four | | | up the junction |
| (lumber) | four by two | utilities | services |
| two weeks | fortnight | utility pole | pylon |
| two-door coupe | fixed-head coupe | | |
| typewriter ball | golf ball | vacation | holiday; vac |
| | | vacationer | holiday-maker |
| ugly (shabby) | grotty | vacuum (v) | hoover |
| unable to play | unfit | vanilla pudding | blancmange |
| unathletic | rabbit | vaudeville | variety; music |
| underwear | | | hall |
| (men) | hosiery | vaudeville act | music-hall turn |
| underling | undersnapper | venturi (auto) | choke tube |
| underpants | | vermouth | martini |
| (women) | knickers | vest | waistcoat |
| underpass | subway | vine | climber; twining |
| underpants | | | plant; creeper |
| (men) | pants; Y-fronts | vinyl | |
| undershirt | vest | upholstery | plasticated leather |

| U.S. | BRITISH | U.S. | BRITISH |
|------|---------|------|---------|
| visiting team | away team | | torch |
| volleying | | welfare | the dole; social |
| (tennis) | knock-up | | security |
| vomit (v) | be sick | well (n) | bore |
| voting place | polling station | well done | good show |
| | | wharf | quay |
| wage control | wage restraint | What's | |
| wait in line (v) | queue; queue up | available? | What's going? |
| waitress (bar) | barmaid | wheelchair | invalid's chair; |
| walking | riding shank's | | bath chair; |
| | mare | | wheeled chair |
| walking shoes | brogues; lace-ups | while | whilst |
| wall-eyed | squinting | whipping | |
| wall-to-wall | | cream | double cream |
| carpet | fitted carpet | white elephant | |
| wallet | pocketbook | sale | jumble sale |
| want (v) | fancy | whole wheat | |
| warden (prison) | governor | bread | wholemeal bread |
| warehouse | storage | whorehouse | knocking-shop; |
| warm up (v) | hot up | | bawdy-house |
| warming oven | hot drawer | windbreaker | windcheater |
| wash bowl | wash-basin | window crank | window winder |
| washcloth | (face) flannel | window screen | flyscreen; wire |
| wash up | wash oneself | | mesh |
| wastebasket | bin; litter bin | window shade | paper blind |
| watch stem | winder | window | |
| water heater | calorifier | shopping | window-gazing |
| waterproofed | proofed | windshield | windscreen |
| waxed paper | grease-proof | wire (v) | telegraph |
| | paper | wise | long-headed |
| weak beer | swipes | witness stand | witness-box |
| weak-minded | barmy | wonderful | wizard |
| weatherstrip- | | woods | wolds |
| ping | draught excluder | work shift | turn |
| weather bureau | meteorological | wrap-around | |
| | office | (clothes) | wrap-over |
| weed (v) | dig over | wrecking ball | house breaker |
| weenie | winkie | wrench | spanner |
| weigh (v) | weigh up | wrinkle-free | uncrushable |
| welding torch | oxyacetylene | writing pad | writing block |

| U.S. | BRITISH | U.S. | BRITISH |
|------|---------|------|---------|
| **writing desk** | secretary | **zealous** | madly keen |
| | | **zero** | nought |
| **yard** | garden | **zip code** | post-code |
| **yarn** | wool | **zipper** | zip; zip fastener |
| **year one** | year dot | **zucchini** | courgettes |
| **yield** (v) | give way | **Z** (alphabet) | Zed |

# U.S.-BRITISH EMBARRASSMENTS

Words in one language often sound like words with embarrassing meanings in a second language. These embarrassments are often (but not always) of a sexual nature. One uses a word or phrase in one's own language, only to be greeted with an uncomfortable silence or a nervous titter from foreign speakers.

The most obvious examples involve differences between American English and its British counterpart. One famous old story involves an English lass staying at the home of some American friends. As she headed for her room the first night, she innocently asked her host, "Please *knock me up* at 8 a.m.," only to be greeted with peals of laughter. She thought she was asking for a wake-up knock on her bedroom door, and was deeply embarrassed when she learned that, in American English, to be *knocked up* is to become *pregnant*.

Another troublesome phrase for Americans visiting England is, "She fell on her *fanny.*" The Americans mean to indicate that a woman had fallen on her rump or behind, and are stunned to learn that, in England, a *fanny* is a vagina. Kind of difficult to fall on. *Fag* and *faggot* are also troublesome words. In American English, both are terms for a homosexual. In England, one often sees advertisements for *faggots*, another name for meatballs. And a *fag* is a junior boy at school made to perform menial tasks for upper level students. So if an Englishman tells you that "John Burns was my *fag* at Eton," don't think that he is coming out of the closet (i.e. declaring himself a homosexual). Along the same lines, if an Englishman, while saying goodbye, tells you to "Keep your pecker up," he is not referring to anything anatomical. What he is trying to tell you, in American terminology, is to "Keep your chin up," or "Keep your spirits high."

On a non-sexual level, probably the most misunderstood word between our two cultures is *sandwich*. To the Englishman who has never visited America, the term *sandwich re*fers to what Americans call *finger sandwiches,* small, thin rectangular white bread sandwiches with the crusts removed. When an English lady visits a coffee shop in New York and asks for some cheese sandwiches and some chicken sandwiches, the waiter will promptly ask, "How many?" If she replies, "Oh, about six or eight," boy, is she in for a surprise!

# Chapter Seven

# WORLDWIDE ENGLISH

As noted earlier in this book, over 300 million people in the world speak English as their primary language. At least an equal number speak English as a second or third language. The largest English-speaking populations are of course in the United States and Great Britain. However, English is the first language of additional millions of people in Australia, Canada, India, Ireland, New Zealand and South Africa.

In general, we all understand each other but, as you have seen in the previous chapter on American and British English, there are substantial differences. The same can be said of the English used in the other countries listed above. With a few exceptions, Canadian English consists of a blending of American and British English, but the other English-speaking countries have all developed their own unique and distinctive expressions (including slang and colloquialisms).

The number of these expressions runs into the thousands or tens of thousands, but we have attempted to gather in this chapter some of the more frequently used local terms. Some expressions will already be familiar to readers, since they have found their way into literature and the cinema, and eventually into American and British dictionaries. Most of the terms listed below, however, will be more obscure or arcane and, consequently, this chapter should be very useful to interpreters and especially translators who periodically find a need for worldwide English terminology.

## AUSTRALIAN & NEW ZEALAND ENGLISH

| | |
|---|---|
| **Anzacs** (n) | Australian & New Zealand Army Corps |
| **aspro** (n) | aspirin |
| **Aussie** (n) | Australian |
| **barbie** (n) | barbecue |
| **bastard** (n) | a term of affection |
| **battler** (n) | one striving for livelihood |
| **be bushed** (v phr) | to lose one's bearings |
| **big smoke** (n) | the city |
| **billabong** (n) | a dry stream bed |
| **billy(can)** (n) | a can or camper's cooking pot |
| **bloody beaut** (adj phr) | swell; fantastic |
| **bloke** (n) | a fellow; one's love |
| **boilover** (n) | unexpected result |
| **bonkers** (adj) | crazy |
| **bruce** (n) | (my) man; bloke |
| **bush** (n) | area away from settlements |
| **bush telegraph** (n phr) | word of mouth |
| **cheesed off** (adj phr) | angry; irritated |
| **choppers** (n) | teeth |
| **ciggies** (n) | cigarettes |
| **cob** (v) | take a liking to |
| **cobber** (n) | friend; buddy |
| **cockatoos (cockies)** (n) | settlers on small land areas |
| **cockeyed bobs** (n phr) | squalls |
| **coldie** (n) | a can of beer |

| | |
|---|---|
| **come again!** (v phr) | please repeat what you said |
| **crook** (adj) | ill; sick |
| **digger** (n) | friend; buddy |
| **dinkum** (adj) | genuine; fair; honest |
| **dob (someone)** (v) | to inform on |
| **dog tied up** (n phr) | an unpaid bill |
| **dog's disease** (n phr) | influenza |
| **domain** (n) | well-tended park |
| **doona** (n) | quilt |
| **drongo** (n) | an inept person; a fool |
| **drunk as chloe** (adj phr) | extremely drunk |
| **dubro** (n) | a stupid person |
| **duffer** (n) | worthless mining claim |
| **esky** (n) | portable cooler |
| **fair dinkum** (adj phr) | honest; true |
| **feeling crook** (v phr) | feeling sick |
| **flicks** (n) | movies |
| **fossick** (v) | to rummage; to search for gold overlooked by others |
| **galah** (adj) | stupid person |
| **get one's issue** (v phr) | to be killed |
| **gibber** (n) | a stone |
| **go for a burn** (v phr) | take a fast drive |
| **gonce** (n) | money |
| **good on yer** (adv phr) | good for you |
| **gumboots** (n) | rubber boots |

| | |
|---|---|
| **jackeroo** (n) | a tenderfoot |
| **joey** (n) | baby kangaroo |
| **jumper** (n) | sweater; pullover |
| **Kiwi** (n) | a New Zealander |
| **knobtwister** (n) | a bookie |
| **larrikin** (n) | a young hooligan |
| **layby** (n) | a time payment |
| **lurk** (n) | a regular job |
| **make a blue** (v phr) | to blunder |
| **mate** (n) | partner; buddy |
| **motza** (n) | a large amount |
| **moz (mozzle)** (n) | luck |
| **mozzies** (n) | mosquitos |
| **muck** (n) | ballads |
| **muckin' around (about)** (v phr) | fooling around |
| **not worth a bob or two** (adj phr) | an expression of contempt |
| **ocker** (n) | an aggressive person of limited abilities |
| **on the outer** (v phr) | be in a less favored position |
| **out in the mulga** (adj phr) | away from the city |
| **outback** (n) | vast, relatively unsettled areas of Australia |
| **paddock** (n) | field |
| **peckish** (adj) | a little hungry |
| **pick a blue** (v phr) | to quarrel; to pick a fight |

| | |
|---|---|
| **piss off!** (v phr) | get lost! |
| **Pommies** (n) | Englishmen |
| **prang** (n) | car or bicycle accident |
| **push bike** (n) | a bicycle |
| **rort** (n) | party; racket |
| **rough end of the pineapple** (n phr) | sharp end of the stick |
| **sand shoes** (n) | sneakers; tennis shoes |
| **sarvo** (n) | this afternoon |
| **sealed road** (n phr) | paved road |
| **sheila** (n) | (my) woman; babe; chick |
| **she'll be right** (v phr) | everything will turn out OK |
| **shikkered** (adj) | drunk |
| **shicer** (n) | swindler |
| **shinplaster** (n) | homemade check |
| **shypoo** (n) | liquor |
| **sickie** (n) | a day's leave |
| **smooge** (v) | to smooch; to neck or pet |
| **spunky** (adj) | attractive to the opposite sex |
| **squatters** (n) | people living off the land |
| **station** (n) | large land holding |
| **stirrer** (n) | troublemaker; joker |
| **swagman** (n) | tramp; hobo |
| **take to the mallee** (v phr) | to leave quickly |
| **tramping** (n) | hiking |

| | |
|---|---|
| **tucker** (n) | food |
| **tucker bag** (n phr) | pack for food or belongings |
| **turn doc** (v phr) | to betray |
| **twang** (n) | opium |
| **up a gum tree** (adv phr) | up the creek |
| **waddy** (n) | a stick |
| **walla(h)** (n) | an Australian |
| **walloper** (n) | policeman |
| **waltzing Matilda** (n phr) | bag or pack at the end of a stick |
| **winge** (v) | to whine |
| **winger** (n) | constant complainer |
| **within cooee** (adv) | close by |
| **woolies** (n) | long underwear |
| **wowser** (n) | a sourpuss; pessimist |
| **yakker** (n) | hard work |
| **Yank tank** (n phr) | large American car |

## INDIAN ENGLISH

| | |
|---|---|
| **alinda** (n) | veranda |
| **amah** (n) | a wet nurse |
| **arrack** (n) | liquor similar to anisette |
| **ashram** (n) | a retreat, usually for the study of yoga |
| **ayah** (n) | nursemaid |
| **baba** (n) | an old man |
| **begum** (n) | courtesy title for women |
| **bhang** (n) | Indian hemp |
| **bhisti** (n) | water carrier |
| **Bodhisattva** (n) | enlightened one |
| **brahmin** (n) | highest caste |
| **catamaran** (n) | log raft |
| **chadar** (n) | clothing made of sheets |
| **chai** (n) | tea |
| **chapati** (n) | unleavened bread |
| **charca** (n) | spinning wheel |
| **choli** (n) | blouse |
| **crewel** (n) | chain stitching |
| **daal** (n) | lentils |
| **dahi** (n) | yogurt |
| **dervish** (n) | member of a Muslim brotherhood dedicated to poverty |
| **devi** (n) | a goddess |
| **dharma** (n) | moral or religious duty |
| **dhoti** (n) | loose loin cloth worn by some Indian men |
| **dosai** (n) | thin pancakes |
| **fakir** (n) | Muslim religious practicing beggar |
| **ganesh** (n) | elephant god |
| **ganja** (n) | marijuana |
| **garuda** (n) | mythical eagle divinity |
| **ghee** (n) | clarified butter |
| **godown** (n) | a warehouse |
| **guru** (n) | religious teacher |
| **halwa** (n) | sweet made from nuts and sesame seeds |
| **hookah** (n) | a bubbly; a water-cooled pipe |
| **kali** (n) | angry dark Hindu god |

**kanga** (n)       a comb
**karma** (n)       fate; destiny
**kebab** (n)       small pieces of meat
                    grilled on a spit
**khave khana**
   (n phr)          a tea shop
**kofta** (n)       meat balls
**kumar** (n)       a young man
**lakh** (n)        100,000
**lama** (n)        a Buddhist priest
**lassi** (n)       an iced milk drink
**lathi** (n)       a bamboo billy club
                    or nightstick
**mahal** (n)       a palace
**maharajah**
   (n)              great king
**maharishi** (n)   great teacher
**mahout** (n)      elephant driver
**mantra** (n)      a meditational
                    chant
**maya** (n)        an illusion
**memsahib** (n)    title of respect for a
                    woman
**mithai** (n)      Indian sweets
**nawob** (n)       prince; figure of
                    great wealth and
                    prestige
**nirvana** (n)     enlightenment
**Parsi** (n)       a member of a
                    Zoroastrian
                    religious sect
**patel** (n)       a village headman
**pukka** (adj)     reliable; solid;
                    worthy of respect
**purdah** (n)      the curtained sur-
                    roundings where
                    Muslim women
                    live and the un-
                    revealing clothes
                    they wear
**raj** (n)         rule; government
**rajah** (n)       ruler of a raj
**rani** (n)        queen; wife of the
                    rajah
**rupee** (n)       unit of Indian
                    currency
**sahib** (n)       a term of respect
                    for a man; sir
**shish** (n)       a skewer or spit
                    used in cooking
**sitar** (n)       stringed Indian
                    musical instru-
                    ment with a long
                    neck and gourd
                    body
**sri** (n)         a title of respect
**stele** (n)       a gravestone
**sufi** (n)        a Muslim mystic
**swami** (n)       a holy man
**thali** (n)       a vegetarian meal
**thug** (n)        a rough, brutal
                    hoodlum or
                    gangster
**tiffin** (n)      a light meal,
                    usually including
                    tea
**tikka** (n)       barbecued small
                    pieces of meat or
                    chicken
**Vishnu** (n)      main Hindu god
**yoga** (n)        Hindu discipline
                    aimed at spiritual
                    tranquility
**yoni** (n)        female fertility
                    symbol

## IRISH ENGLISH

(The number of Irish English words is unusually large for a specific reason. Many of the words given below are regional, more common in certain locations than in others. But they arc all recognizable, ie part of the passive vocabulary, of almost all English-speaking Irish people. A complete dictionary of Irish-English would be voluminous, so the examples given below constitute only the most commonly used terms.)

**acushla** (adj)    darling; sweetheart

**Adam's ale**
  (n phr)    plain drinking water

**agra(w)** (n)    my love

**airy** (adj)    haunted; ghostly

**all to** (prep)    except

**amadaun** (n)    a foolish person

**amplush** (n)    a fix; having a problem

**aroon** (n)    my love; my dear

**avoureen** (n)    a sweetheart

**ballyhooley**
  (n)    loud criticism; a tongue lashing

**banshee** (n)    a female fairy

**beknownst**
  (adj)    known

**black fellow**
  **(man)** (n)    a surly, vindictive person

**blarney** (n)    smooth, plausible deceptive talk

**blather(skite)**
  (n)    foolish boaster or his boasts

**blaze (blazes)**
  (adj)    hurried; excessive

**blind alley**
  (n phr)    dead end

**bold** (adj)    impudent; brash

**boreen** (n)    a narrow road

**bother** (adj)    troublesome; annoying;

**box and dice**
  (n phr)    everything

**brablins** (n)    a rabble; crowd of children

**braddach** (adj) mischievous

**break** (v)    to fire or discharge an employee

**brief** (adj)    prevalent

**brogue** (n)    an Irish accent; a type of shoe

**broken** (adj)    bankrupt

**broth (of a boy)** (adj)    manly; brave

**buff** (n)    the skin

**cabin-hunting**
  (n)    gossiping at house after house

**cadge** (v)    door-to-door sales

**cailey** (n)    evening visit for a chat or to gossip

**canny** (adj)    discreet; knowing

**carn** (n)    a mound; a pile of stones

**carry** (v)    to lead or drive

**cat of a kind**
  (n phr)    two of the same kind (negative implication)

**(bad) cess** (n)    bad luck

**chanter** (v)    to find fault; to grumble

**chaw** (v or n)    to chew; a chew

**Christian** (n)    a human being

**clabber (clobber)** (n)    thick milk

**clout** (n)  a blow with the hand; a small rag

**cog** (v)  to crib; plagiarize

**colleen** (n)  a girl

**commons** (n)  land held jointly by a community, eg village green

**cooleen** (n)  a fair-haired girl

**cot** (n)  a small boat

**cracked** (adj)  crazed; mad

**cracklins** (n)  lard renderings

**craw-sick** (adj)  hungover

**croaked** (adj)  doomed to death

**cugger-mugger** (n)  whispering; quiet gossiping

**current** (adj)  in good health

**cushlamo-chree** (n)  my love; my heart throb

**devil's needle** (n phr)  a dragonfly

**diddy** (n)  a titty; a woman's breast or nipple

**dido** (n)  a ridiculously overdressed girl

**dollop** (v)  to adulterate

**drad** (n)  a grin; a grimace

**dundeen** (n)  a chunk of bread without butter

**dunner** (v)  to knock loudly

**earnest** (adj)  really and truly

**elegant** (adj)  excellent (not necessarily fancy)

**(doing) finely** (adv)  improving in health

**flipper** (n)  an untidy person

**fluke** (n)  tiny; nothing at all

**forby** (prep)  beside; next to

**fox** (v)  to deceive

**Gael** (n)  Irish Celt

**gaffer** (n)  a young lad

**gahela** (n)  a little girl

**galoot** (n)  a clownish fellow

**gawk** (n)  a tall clumsy fellow

**girsha** (n)  a little girl

**glunter** (n)  a stupid person

**gob** (n)  mouth

**going on** (v phr)  bantering; teasing

**gorsoon (gossoon)** (n)  servant boy; lad

**grawvar** (adj)  loving; affectionate

**greet** (v)  to weep

**ginder** (n)  a brightly colored silk scarf

**gubbalagh** (n)  a mouthful

**gulpin** (n)  an uncouth person

**half a one** (n phr)  half a glass of whiskey

**half joke and whole earnest** (adj phr)  jokingly; half in earnest

**hand's turn** (n)  occasional odd job

**(the) hard word** (n phr)  a tip-off; a hint

**harvest** (n)  autumn

**haverel** (n)  a rough, ignorant boor

**ho** (n)  equal to (in a negative sense)

**holy show** (adj)  r i d i c u l o u s looking

**hugger-mugger** (n)  whispering or quiet gossiping

**hot foot** (adv) immediately
**hurley** (n) hurling
**huzho (husho)**
  (n) a lullaby
**jaw** (n) impudent talk
**(on his)**
  **keeping** (n) hiding from the
      police
**kemp** (v) to compete
**keowt** (n) a contemptible
      person
**kink** (n) a fit of coughing or
      laughing
**kishtha** (n) hidden treasure
**kitterdy** (n) a fool
**kybosh** (n) a defeat; a set-back
**lad** (n) a mischievous,
      tricky person
**larrup** (v) to wallop; to beat
      thoroughly
**lashings** (n) plenty
**leather** (v) to beat
**leprechaun**
  (n) a kind of Irish fairy
**(as) lief** (adv) rather; willing
**light** (adj) slightly crazy
**likely** (adj) good-looking
**lob** (n) a substantial
      quantity
**lone** (adj) unmarried; single
**long family**
  (n phr) a large family
**loose leg** (adj) footloose and fancy
      free
**lybe** (adj) a lazy individual
**made** (adj) fortunate
**man above**
  **(upstairs)** (a) God
**mannam** (n) my soul
**(too) many**
  (adj) too much for;
      overmatched

**mau-galore**
  (adj) nearly drunk
**mavoureen** (n) dear; darling; my
      love
**miscaun** (n) a lump of butter
**mitch** (v) to play truant
**molly** (n) an effeminate man
**mooch** (n & v) a slow, stupid
      person; to move
      like one
**naboclesh** (v) never mind; don't
      bother
**nicely** (adv) satisfactorily
**offer** (n) an attempt
**overright** (adj) the opposite
**pannican** (n) a small tin cup
**piper's**
  **invitation**
  (adj phr) uninvited
**plaumase** (n) soft, flattering,
      insincere talk
**pooka** (n) a mischievous
      goblin
**pookeen** (n) blindman's buff (a
      children's game)
**pottheen** (n) illegal whiskey
**power** (n) a large quantity; a
      great deal of
**puke** (n) a puny, sickly
      looking person
**quality** (n) gentry; the upper
      classes
**queer (and)**
  (adv) extremely; very
**rack** (n) a comb
**rag on every**
  **bush**
  (n phr) a womanizer
**rawney** (n) a delicate or sickly
      looking person
**redden** (v) to light (fire or
      pipe)

**right or wrong**
  (adv phr)         earnestly
**rip** (n)         a coarse woman; a
                    scold
**rocket** (n)      a little girl's dress
**Roman** (n)       a Catholic person
**rookaun** (n)     noisy merriment
**sapples** (n)     soap suds
**scalded** (v)     annoyed; vexed;
                    mortified
**sconce** (v)      to banter; to treat
                    lightly
**scout** (n)       an overly bold and
                    aggressive girl
**scrab** (v)       to scratch
**screenge** (v)    to search for
**set** (v)         to rent out or let
**shamrock** (n)    the Irish national
                    flower
**sheebeen** (n)    an unlicensed bar
**sheep's eyes**
  (n phr)           adoring looks at a
                    lover
**shillelagh** (n)  an oak walking
                    stick; a club
**shuggy-shoo**
  (n)               see-saw (a child's
                    game)
**skree** (n)       lots of small things
**slug** (n)        a drink; a quick
                    drink
**slugabed** (n)    a lazy lout; a
                    sluggard
**snaggle-tooth**
  (n)               a person with
                    crooked or
                    gapped teeth
**something like**
  (adj)             excellent
**sonsy** (adj)     fortunate; healthy

**stag** (n)        a selfish woman;

                    an informer
**stim (stime)**
  (n)               a tiny quantity
**straddy** (n)     a street person
**strap** (n)       a bold, overly
                    forward girl
**stravage** (v)    to roam about idly
**streel** (n)      a slattern; a lazy,
                    untidy woman
**strong** (adj)    healthy (not
                    necessarily
                    muscular)
**stroop** (n)      a kettle spout
**strum** (n)       a sulky, silent
                    person
**sup** (n)         a sip; one mouthful
                    of liquid
**towards**
  (phr)             as compared to
**trake** (n)       a trek; a long,
                    tiresome walk
**turf** (n)        peat used for fuel
**venom** (n)       energy
**watch-pot** (n)   a freeloader at
                    meal-times
**whisht** (n or v) silence; be silent
**whiteheaded**
  **boy** (n)       fair-haired boy
**why for?**
  (v phr)           for what?
**wicked** (adj)    cross; angry;
                    severe
**widow-man**
  (n)               widower
**widow-woman**
  (n)               widow
**wire (in)** (v)   to begin strenuous
                    work; to join a
                    fight
**wit** (n)         common sense
**wish** (n)        friendship; esteem

## SCOTTISH ENGLISH

**agley** (adv)   awry; badly
**bailie** (n)   an alderman
**braw** (adj)   top-notch; pretty; well-dressed
**breeks** (n)   pants; trousers
**cairngorm** (n)   a Scottish semi-precious stone
**Caledonian** (adj)   a native of Scotland
**cantrip** (n)   magic trick; witches spell
**clan** (n)   a group of families claiming common ancestry
**cockaleekie** (n)   a Scottish soup of chicken and leeks
**corbie** (n)   raven; crow
**coronach** (n)   sad bagpipe tune
**cuddy** (n)   donkey
**curling** (n)   Scottish game played on ice
**cutty** (adj)   very short
**eightsome** (n)   eight person Scottish dance
**eldritch** (adj)   weird; uncanny
**Erse** (n)   Gaelic
**factor** (n)   estate manager
**finnoc** (n)   kind of white trout
**flite** (v)   to quarrel; scold
**forby (forbed)** (adv)   next to; past; nearby
**Free Church** (n phr)   Scottish Presbyterian Church
**Gael** (n)   Scottish Celt
**gillie** (n)   outdoor servant; hunt assistant

**goodman** (n)   husband; householder
**gowan** (n)   daisy
**haggis** (n)   traditional Scottish dish of meat and herbs cooked in a sheep's stomach
**highland fling** (n)   Scottish dance
**hodden** (n)   coarse woollen cloth
**hodden grey** (n)   cloth of mixed black and white wool
**hogmanay** (n)   New Year's Eve and associated festivities
**hunkers** (n)   buttocks
**keek** (n)   peep
**kilt** (n)   traditional tartan skirt worn by Scotsmen
**kirk** (n)   church
**kittle** (adj)   to be handled with care
**laddie** (n)   boy; lad
**laird** (n)   estate owner
**landloper** (n)   bum; vagrant; tramp
**leal** (adj)   true; loyal
**loch** (n)   lake
**loon** (n)   fool; boor
**mail** (n)   rent; tax; tribute
**mickle** (adj)   great; large
**muckle** (n)   large quantity
**on one's hunkers** (adj)   squatting
**overly** (adv)   too much
**pirn** (n)   fishing reel; bobbin

| | |
|---|---|
| **provost** (n) | chief magistrate of a borough |
| **randy** (adj) | rowdy; horny |
| **reel** (n) | lively Scottish dance |
| **sawney** (n) | fool |
| **Scotty** (n) | Scotsman; Scottish terrier |
| **sonsy** (adj) | buxom; handsome; sweet-natured |
| **southron** (adj) | characteristic of an Englishman |
| **sporran** (n) | purse or pouch worn in front of a kilt |
| **tawse** (n) | leather strap |
| **wee** (adj) | small |

## SOUTH AFRICAN ENGLISH

NOTE: Many of the following words or phrases are Afrikaans (modified old Dutch) or of Afrikaans origin. However, most of them are frequently used by English speaking South Africans. Many appear regularly in advertising, on shop signs and on traffic signs, and consequently have become part of local English.

| | |
|---|---|
| **aandete** (n) | dinner |
| **Afrikaans** (n) | S African language of white minority made up of old Dutch mixed with English |
| **afslag** (n) | discount |
| **apteek** (n) | pharmacist; drug-store |
| **baai** (n) | bay |
| **baba; babatjie** (n) | baby |
| **babelas** (n) | hangover |
| **bad** (n) | bath |
| **badkamer** (n) | bathroom |
| **bakkie** (n) | pick-up truck |
| **bedank** (v) | thanks |
| **beesvies** (n) | beef |
| **berg** (n) | mountain |
| **beseerde** (n) | injuries |
| **besoeker** (n) | visitor |
| **bespreek** (v & n) | to book; reservation |
| **betyds** (adv) | on time |
| **bier** (n) | beer |
| **bioskoop** (n) | cinema |
| **blixem** (adj) | cheeky; nervy |
| **blom** (n) | flower |
| **bok** (n) | antelope |
| **boom** (n) | tree |
| **bottle store** (n phr) | liquor store |
| **braal** (n & v) | barbecue |
| **brandstof** (n) | fire |
| **brief** (n) | letter |
| **brood** (n) | bread |
| **burg** (n) | town |
| **dagga** (n) | marijuana |
| **dame** (n) | ladies (toilet) |
| **dankle** (v) | thank you |
| **dom** (adj) | stupid |
| **dorp** (n) | town |
| **Engels** (n) | English |
| **fooit jai** (n) | tip |
| **getroud** (adj) | married |
| **gratis** (adj) | free |
| **hoeveel** (n) | how much? |
| **hold your thumbs** (v phr) | cross your fingers |

| | | | |
|---|---|---|---|
| **howzit?** | | **parkering** | |
| (v phr) | how are you? | (n & adj) | parking |
| **huurmotor** | | **pos** (n) | mail |
| (n) | taxi | **posgeld** (n) | postage |
| **inkopies** (n) | shopping | **poskaart** (n) | post card |
| **inligting** (n) | information | **poskantoor** | |
| **izit?** (v phr) | really? | (n) | post office |
| **ja** (adv) | yes | **pronk** (n & v) | show off |
| **ja-nee** (adj) | sure | **rank** (n) | bus stop; taxi |
| **jol** (n) | a party | | stand |
| **just now** | | **robot** (n) | traffic light |
| (adv) | soon; recently | **rock up** | |
| **Kaap** (n) | Capetown | (v phr) | to show up |
| **kaas** (n) | cheese | **roomys** (n) | ice cream |
| **kerk** (n) | church | **sambreev** (n) | umbrella |
| **koop** (v) | to buy | **shame** (adj) | how cute |
| **kopffie** (n) | coffee | **sis** (adj) | gross; disgusting |
| **kraal** (n) | homestead | **skakel** (v) | ring up; contact |
| **kueldrank** (n) | cold drink | **smaak** (n) | taste; snack |
| **laan** (n) | street; avenue | **snelveg** (n) | highway |
| **lekker** (adj) | nice | **spoorveg** (n) | train; railroad |
| **lief** (n & v) | love | **stad** (n) | town |
| **lugpos** (n) | airmail | **stasie** (n) | station |
| **mark** (n) | market | **strand** (n) | beach |
| **meer** (n) | lake | **suiker** (n) | sugar |
| **meisie** (n) | girlfriend | **tafel** (n) | table |
| **meneer** (adj) | Mr | **take-away** | |
| **middstad** (n) | city center | (adj phr) | takeout |
| **motor** (n) | automobile | **takkie** (n) | sneaker |
| **motorfiets** (n) | motorcycle | **te koop** | |
| **nag** (n) | night | (adj phr) | for sale |
| **nagklub** (n) | nightclub | **tee** (n) | tea |
| **nee dankie** | | **varsity** (n) | university |
| (v phr) | no thanks | **veld** (n) | open countryside |
| **oke** (n) | fellow; chap | **voetsak!** | |
| **ontbyt** (n) | breakfast | (v phr) | get lost! scram! |
| **oop** (adj) | open | **vrymal** (n) | freeway |
| **ouens** (n) | guys | **welkom** | |
| **pad** (n) | path | (v and adj) | welcome |
| | | **winkel** (n) | shop |

# Chapter Eight

# FOREIGN WORDS AND PHRASES FREQUENTLY USED IN ENGLISH

The author's wife is Japanese, so it is not uncommon for American friends to ask him, "Do you speak any Japanese?" My answer is invariably, "I know about as many Japanese words as you do." They all deny knowing any Japanese, so I offer to wager each of them that they know at least ten Japanese words. **I have never lost this bet.** Almost all educated Americans know: *Mikado, geisha, kimono, kamikaze, harakiri, samurai, sake, sayonara, sumo, karate, judo,* and *jiujitsu.* Many more know: *obi, sushi, sashimi, tempura, shoji, tatami, futon, bonsai, ikebana,* and *origami.*

Since English is spoken frequently in many countries and since both England and America have had millions of emigrants from many places, it should be no surprise that thousands of foreign words and phrases have become an integral part of the English language. English is an Anglo-Saxon language with roots in Latin, the Romance languages, and German. This means most, if not all, English words are variations of foreign words, and such words have legitimately entered the language. Those are not the words or phrases which will be covered in this section.

This chapter covers foreign words which for the most part have retained their original foreign meanings and have not turned into English words, but are still frequently used for special purposes or for emphasis in English writing. Such words or phrases often appear in "quotes" or more frequently in *italics* when interspersed with English words. Many of them can be found with great frequency in specialized vocabularies. Latin, for example, is very common in legal briefs. Singers and people in the music business use many Italian words. Interior decorators and antique dealers know the meanings of many French expressions. Those involved with martial arts use a variety of Japanese and Chinese terms. And international cooks use food terms from most of these languages.

Three brief notes: Yiddish is a language brought by Jews from Europe. It includes many German words or variations of these. Consequently, there may be some confusion about certain words or expressions which could be in either the German or the Yiddish list. The author has attempted to divide them in accordance with the way they entered the United States. Those coming directly from Germany have been put in the German list. The bottom line is that it makes no difference as regards their use in English.

Second, a special problem exists with Spanish words. So many of these have been used for a long time in the American Southwest — Texas, Arizona, New Mexico, and Southern California—that they have become part of Southwestern English. It is often difficult to ascertain whether these words are still Spanish or whether they are now English words of Spanish origin. The author has done his best to make this separation.

Finally, it should be noted that the meanings of these words, as used in the United States, may vary from the meanings in their country of origin. An excellent example is *voir dire,* which in French means *to see (or look into)* and *to say (or tell)* but in the U.S. describes a legal procedure for selecting a jury. Such examples are infrequent, but they do exist. Most expressions, however, hew to their original meanings.

Literally thousands of foreign words and expressions find frequent use in the American Language. The lists below cover more than 400 of the more popular ones. It is not intended to be all inclusive. While foreign words and phrases from more than a dozen languages have found their way into American usage, the vast bulk of terms used here are from seven of these. Included are Latin, French, Italian, German, Spanish, Japanese, and Yiddish.

# LATIN

**a fortiori**  All the more so

**a posteriori**  Based on reasoning from known facts

**a priori**  Based on former knowledge

**ab initio**  From the beginning

**ab ovo**  From the beginning

**absente reo**  In absence of the defendant

**actus dei**  An act of God

**ad astra per aspera**  To the stars through bolts and bars

**ad extremum**  At last; finally

**ad hoc**  As to this (only for a specific purpose)

**ad hominem**  Argument based on the person addressed

**ad infinitum**  Without limits

**ad lib (ad libitum)**  Speaking without a text ("playing it by ear")

**ad litem**  In accordance with the law suit

**ad nauseam**  To a disgusting degree

**ad valorem**  A tax based on value

**Adeste Fideles**  Come all ye faithful

**Agnus Dei**  Lamb of God

**alma mater**  One's school or college

**alter ego**  One's other identity

**alter idem**  Another of the same kind

**alumnus** (*fem.* **alumna**)  College graduate

**amicus curiae**  A friend of the court

**amor omnia vincit**  Love conquers all

**amor patriae**  Love of one's country

**Anno Domini  (A.D.)**  In a specific year of the Christian Era

**ante bellum**  Prior to the Civil War

**aqua pura**  Water

**aqua fortis**  Nitric acid

**aqua regia**  A mixture of nitric and hydrochloric acids

**ars gratia artis**  Art for the sake of art

**aurora borealis**  The "northern lights"

**ave atque vale**  Hail and farewell!

**Ave Maria**  "Hail Mary" (Roman Catholic prayer)

**bona fide**  In good faith

**casus belli**  An act that justifies war

**causa mortis**  In view of a death

**cave canem**  Beware the dog

**caveat emptor**  Let the buyer beware

**certiorari**  Legal writ transferring a case to higher courts

**Corpus Christi**  A Catholic festival

**corpus delicti**  Body of the offense

**corpus juris**  Comprehensive body of all state or country laws

**cui bona?**  Who benefits?

**cum grano salis**  With a grain of salt; dubiously

**cum laude**  With honors (refers to academic degrees)

**curriculum vitae** (CV) resume

**de facto**  In fact; by right;actually exercising power
**de gustibus (non disputandum est)**  Each to his own taste
**de jure**  According to the law
**dementia praecox**  Schizophrenia; mental withdrawal from reality
**de minimus**  To the smallest degree
**de novo**  Anew; afresh
**de profundis**  From the depths (of sorrow)
**dei gratia**  By the grace of God
**deo volente**  God willing
**deus ex machina**  In Greek or Roman plays, a god who intervenes to achieve a satisfactory conclusion
**Dies Irae**  Day of judgment
**disjecta membra**  Fragments, as of an author's writings
**duces tecum**  A subpoena requiring production of certain documents
**dulce et decorum (est pro patria mori)**  It is sweet and fitting to die for one's country

**e pluribus unum**  One entity assembled from many parts
**elixir vitae**  Water of life; panacea
**ergo**  Therefore
**et aliae (et al)**  And others
**et cetera (etc.)**  And other things
**et tu, Brute?**  You also, Brutus? (said to one who betrays)
**ex cathedra**  With authority
**ex curia**  From the court
**ex libris**  From the library of...
**ex officio**  By virtue of his office

**ex parte**  A one-sided legal action
**ex post facto**  A law having a retroactive effect
**extempore**  Without forethought; off-the-cuff
**excelsior**  Upward and onward!
**exempli gratia (e.g.)**  For example

**flagrante delicto, in**  Caught in the act (often used sexually)

**genus homo**  The human race
**gluteus maximus**  Buttocks; ass; behind
**gratis**  Free of charge

**habeas corpus**  A legal writ demanding the release of an illegal detainee
**hic jacet**  Here lies
**hominus est errarum**  To make a mistake is human
**homo sapiens**  Man (species)
**horribile dictu**  Terrible to relate

**ibidem (ibid.)**  In the same place. (Refers to a book, page, etc. cited just before)
**id est (i.e.)**  That is
**idem**  The same as the previous one
**in camera**  In chambers; secretly
**in extremis**  At the point of death
**in loc. cit.**  In the place cited
**in loco parentis**  In the place of a parent
**in perpetuum**  Forever
**in posse**  Potentially
**in propia persona**  In one's own person or right
**in re**  Lawsuit regarding an object
**in situ**  In place; on site

**in terrorem** An intimidation clause in a will

**in utero** In the uterus

**in vino veritas** In wine, there is truth

**in vitro** In an artificial environment; in a test tube

**incognito** In disguise

**inter alia** Among other things or people

**inter alios** Among other persons

**ipso facto** As a necessary consequence of the act

**labor omnia vincit** Work overcomes all

**lapsus linguae** A slip of the tongue

**lares et penates** Esteemed household possessions

**lingua franca** A hybrid language; one used internationally

**lux et veritas** Light and truth

**Magna Carta** The Great Charter of English liberties

**magna cum laude** With high honors (see *cum laude*)

**magnum opus** The greatest work of an artist or writer

**mala fide** In bad faith

**mare nostrum** Mediterranean Sea

**materia medica** Study and source of pharmaceuticals

**mea (maxima) culpa** I am (grievously) at fault

**mens sana in corpore sano** A sound mind in a sound body

**mirabile dictu** Miraculous to relate

**modus operandi** Method of operating

**modus vivendi** Way of life

**mutatis mutandi** With necessary changes in details (legal)

**ne plus ultra** Point of highest achievement

**nil desperandum** Never despair

**nolo contendere** Plea in criminal cases where defendant does not admit or deny guilt

**(non) compos mentis** (Not) of sound mind; insane

**non sequitur** It does not follow

**nota bene (N.B.)** Note well; take particular notice

**nunc pro tunc** A legal decision made now but dated earlier

**obiter dictum** A peripheral judicial opinion

**opere citato (op. cit.)** In the work cited

**o tempora, o mores!** My, how times have changed

**Pater Noster** The Lord's Prayer

**paterfamilias** Head of the household

**Pax Romana** Enforced peace - originally by Rome

**peccavi** Confession of sin

**per annum** Per year

**per capita** Per person

**per curium** By the court

**per diem** Per day

**per mensum** By the month

**per stirpes** By the number of families (legal)

**persona non grata** An unwelcome person; out of favor

**post mortem** Examination of a body after death

**placebo** An innocuous medication used for medical research
**post partum** Period after childbirth
**prima-facie** Apparent evidence
**pro bono (publico)** Free legal services
**pro Deo et patria** For God and country
**pro forma** As a matter of form
**pro rata** In proportion
**pro tanto** To that extent
**pro tempore** For the time being
**putto** Plump young male angel

**qua** As
**quantum meruit** Lawsuit for payment for part of work
**quid pro quo** An equal exchange
**quo jure?** By what right?
**Quo modo?** In what manner?
**quo vadis?** Where are you going?

**re** With reference to
**res gestae** Facts attending the act in question
**res ipsa loquitor** It speaks for itself
**res judicata** A point already judicially decided
**rigor mortis** Stiffening after death
**R.I.P. (Requiescat in Pace)** Rest in peace

**sanctum sanctorum** Holy of Holies; place of total privacy
**sine die** (Adjourned) indefinitely
**sine qua non** An essential element or condition

**Spiritus Sanctum** The Holy Ghost
**S.P.Q.R.** The Senate and the people of Rome
**stare decisis** A legal point already binding
**status quo** The existing situation
**sui generis** Unique; one of a kind
**summa cum laude** With the highest honors (degree)

**tabula rasa** A clean slate
**Te Deum** A Latin religious hymn
**tempus fugit** Time flies
**terra firma** Solid ground

**ultra vires** Beyond (corporate) authority
**Ursa Major** The Big Dipper

**vade mecum** A portable guidebook
**veni, vidi, vici** I came, I saw, I conquered
**verbatim** Word for word
**verbum sat sapienti** A word to the wise is sufficient
**veritas** Truth
**via** By way of
**vice versa** The contrary
**vide** See; refer to
**vide ante** See before
**vide infra** See below
**videlicet** That is; namely
**virgo intacta** Virginal
**viva voce** By word of mouth
**vox populi** The voice of the people

# FRENCH

**à bas** Down with...!
**à bientôt** So long!
**à bon marché** At a good price
**à cheval** On horseback; straddling (an issue)
**à deux** For two; intimate
**à la bonne heure** Well done!
**à la carte** As itemized on the menu
**à la française** In the French manner
**à la mode** According to fashion; with ice cream
**à propos** By the way; incidentally
**à votre santé** To your health (a drinking toast)
**affaire d'amour** Love affair
**affaire de coeur** Love affair
**affaire d'honneur** An affair of honor
**agent provocateur** A secret agent tasked with sabotage
**aide-de-camp** A military officer acting as an executive secretary
**ami** (_fem._ **amie**) Friend; lover
**amour propre** Self esteem; vanity
**ancien régime** Old Order (in France, before the Revolution)
**appliqué** A small decorative piece applied to a larger surace, often on clothing
**après moi le déluge** After I leave, there will be chaos
**arrière pensée** Ulterior motive
**art nouveau** A decorative style which began in the 1890's
**au contraire** On the contrary

**au courant** Up-to-date
**au gratin** With cheese
**au jus** With gravy
**au pair** Equal exchange (e.g. a mother's helper or a housekeeper for room and board)
**au revoir** Until we meet again
**avant-garde** Ahead of the times

**bas relief** Relief sculpture with figures projecting slightly
**beaux-arts** The fine arts
**belle dame sans merci, La** The beautiful woman without mercy; death
**belles lettres** Literature showing aesthetic values
**bête noire** A person to be avoided
**bon appétit** Have a good appetite
**bon marché** Cheap; a bargain
**bon mot** A clever saying
**bon vivant** A person who enjoys good living, e.g. food
**bon voyage!** Enjoy your trip!
**bonjour** Good day; hello
**bonsoir** Good evening
**bouillabaisse** Fish chowder
**buffet** Self-serve meal
**bustier** Strapless wide brassiere

**café au lait** Coffee with milk
**café filtre** Filtered coffee
**carte blanche** A free hand
**cause célèbre** An issue arousing heated public debate
**ça va sans dire** It goes without saying

**c'est la vie** Well, that's life

**chaise-longue (lounge)** A reclining chair with room for one's legs

**chanterelle** A type of mushroom

**chanteuse** A female singer

**chargé d'affaires** Embassy official replacing the minister or the ambassador

**chef-d'oeuvre** Masterpiece

**cherchez la femme** Find the woman (often when searching for a motive in a crime)

**chez nous** At our place

**concierge** Bellman; hall porter

**connaisseur** Expert; one who knows

**coq-au-vin** Chicken cooked in red wine

**coquette** A flirtatious woman

**coquille St. Jacques** Creamed scallops served in their shell

**cordon bleu** Blue ribbon; master chef

**cordon sanitaire** A chain of buffer states between enemy nations

**corps de ballet** Ballet chorus line

**coup d'état** Overthrow of a state by a rebellious group

**coup de grâce** Killing stroke

**coup de main** Surprise attack

**coup de maître** A master-stroke

**coup d'oeil** Quick glance

**crème de la crème** The very best

**croissant** A crescent shaped roll

**croix de guerre** A French military award

**cul-de-sac** A dead-end street

**danse macabre** Dance of death

**de jour** Of the day (*soup de jour*: today's soup)

**de rigueur** Socially obligatory

**de trop** Excessive; superfluous

**début** First appearance; coming out

**débutante** Young woman having a party as a rite of passage

**déjà vu** Illusion of having experienced an event before

**demimonde** Underclass; those living in near respectability

**demitasse** A small cup of strong black coffee; a small cup

**dernier cri** The latest word or style

**déshabillé** Naked or semi-dressed

**double entendre** A pun, word, or expression with double meaning

**droit du Seigneur** Royal right to first night with new brides

**eau-de-vie** Brandy made of fruit soaked in alcohol

**éclat** Brilliant success

**école** School

**émeute** A popular uprising

**eminence grise** Man behind the throne

**en arrière** In the rear

**en avant** Forward

**en bloc** All together

**en brochette** On a skewer

**en garde** Fencer's opening position

**en masse** Acting as a group

**en papillotes** Cooked while wrapped in paper

**en passant** In passing

**en route** On route; along the way

**enfant terrible** A spoiled, misbehaving child or an adult acting like one

**éngagé** Committed to a cause

**entre nous** Just between us

**entrecôte** A rib steak

**écritoire** A writing desk

**espadrille** Canvas shoes

**espalier** Ornamental tree or bush trained to hug a wall

**esprit de corps** Devotion and loyalty within a group

**esprit d'escalier** Witty or intelligent comment you forgot to make at a gathering

**étagère** A bric-a-brac cabinet with open shelves

**fait accompli** A completed act, now irreversible

**faux ami** A word whose obvious translation is wrong

**faux pas** A social blunder

**femme fatale** A dangerous, seductive woman

**fille de joie** A prostitute

**fin de siècle** Characteristic of the late 19th century

**flambé** Served with liquor set on fire

**fleur-de-lys** A heraldic device shaped like a three-petalled iris

**force majeure** An uncontrolled event, e.g. a flood or earthquake

**franc** Basic coin of France

**gaga** Doddering; crazy

**gourmet** A food expert; a discerning eater

**gourmand** One who delights in hearty eating

**grande dame** Woman of queenly bearing; one who puts on airs

**grand mal** Major epileptic fit with loss of consciousness

**grand monde** High society

**Grand Prix** International road races

**haute couture** High fashion and design

**haute cuisine** Gourmet cooking

**honni soit qui mal y pense** Shame unto him who thinks evil

**hors de combat** Out of action; disabled

**hors d'oeuvre** Small appetizers

**idée fixe** A fixed idea; obsession

**ingénue** Actress playing an innocent young girl

**je ne sais quoi** An unidentified item; a thing-a-ma-bob

**joie de vivre** The joy of living

**laissez-faire** Doctrine that government should not interfere with commerce

**laissez-passer** A pass used in lieu of a passport

**la vie en rose** High life in full bloom

**lèse majesté** Overstepping authority

**ma chérie** My sweet one; my dear

**madeleine** Small shell-shaped cake

**mademoiselle** Miss or Ms.

**maître d'hôtel (Maitre D')** Restaurant head steward

**mal de mer** Sea sickness
**Mardi Gras** Shrove Tuesday;
 Carnival
**masseur** Male massage expert
**masseuse** Female massage expert
**ménage à trois** Sex between
 three people (usually a man and
 two women); three living
 together
**meunière** Fried in flour & butter
**millefeuille** Flaky pastry
**mise en scène** Setting or staging
**mot juste** The precise word

**Nez Percé** American Indian tribe
**noblesse oblige** Honorable
 behavior, an obligation of noble
 birth
**nom de guerre** A temporary
 pseudonym
**nom de plume** A writer's
 pseudonym
**nonpareil** Incomparable;
 matchless
**nouvelle cuisine** Modern French
 cooking, with lighter sauces
**nouveau riche** A recent
 millionaire who lives
 ostentatiously

**objet d'art** Valuable art object
**outré** Exaggerated, far-out

**papier mâché** Items made of
 molded paper pulp
**par avion** Via air mail
**par excellence** Of the highest
 degree
**parvenu** An upstart
**pas de deux** Ballet routine for
 two
**pâté de foie gras** Pressed goose-
liver paste
**petit-fours** Small, rich pastries
**petit mal, Le** A minor epileptic
 fit
**petits pois** Small green peas
**pied-à-terre** A small secondary
 apartment or house
**pièce de resistance** Most
 important component
**pissoir** Public men's urinal
**piste** Ski run of hard-packed
 snow
**plafond** A decorated ceiling
**plage** A beach
**plat du jour** Blue plate special
**porte cochère** Carriage entrance
 or a covered driveway
**pot-au-feu** Boiled meat and
 vegetables dish
**prix fixe** Fixed price; a complete
 dinner menu

**quelque chose** A trifle
**qui vive** On the alert; vigilant

**raison d'être** Justification for
 existing
**rechauffé** Reheated leftovers
**rendez-vous** An appointment or
 a meeting place
**rentier** Person with income from
 real estate, bonds etc.
**répondez s'il vous plaît**
 **(R.S.V.P.)** Please reply
**ris de veau** Calf's sweetbreads
 (food)
**roman à clef** A novel based on
 actual people and events

**sang-froid** Composure; coolness
**sans souci** Carefree; easygoing
**santé!** To your health! (A toast)

**savoir-faire** Tact; adroitness

**savoir-vivre** Good breeding; good manners

**succès de scandale** Notoriety gained from a shocking performance

**succès d'estime** Gaining acclaim from critics

**succès fou** Extraordinary success, mainly financial

**table d'hôte** A full-course meal

**tête-a-tête** Intimate; private

**ton** Style; vogue

**tout de suite** Immediately

**trompe-l'oeil** That which fools the eye; an optical illusion

**tutu** A short ballet skirt

**vichyssoise** Potato and leek soup (usually cold)

**vis-à-vis** With regard to; face-to-face

**voilà!** There you are; there it is; aha! (exclamation)

**voir dire** Jury selection procedure

**vol-au-vent** A light pastry shell, often filled with meat or chicken

# GERMAN

**Angst** Anxiety; dread
**auf Wiedersehen** Until we meet again

**Bauhaus** German school of architecture.
**blitz** To bombard someone with information, etc.
**Blitzkrieg** Lightning war
**Brauhaus** Brewery; beer cellar

**Dachshund** Short-legged dog
**Der Mensch denkt, Gott lenkt** The best laid plans often go astray; (man thinks, God directs)

**ersatz** Fake; substitute

**Festschrift** Collection of writings in honor of a scholar
**flak** Bursting shells from anti-aircraft artillery; excessive criticism
**Frau** Mrs.
**Fräulein** Miss
**Führer** A (ruthless) leader.

**Gemütlichkeit** Feelings of warmth; coziness
**Gestalt** Shape or form; total picture; more than the sum of its parts
**Gestapo** Nazi German secret police
**Gesundheit!** (in response to a sneeze) To your health; God bless you!
**Götterdämmerung** Twilight of the Gods

**Gott mit uns** God is with us

**Heil! (Sieg heil!)** Used as a greeting in Nazi Germany
**Herr** Mr.

**Kaffeeklatsch** An informal gathering (originally of women during the day) to chat
**kaput** Spoiled; ruined; dead
**Kinderspiel** Child's play
**Kitsch** Shallow, pretentious art or writing
**Kriegspiel** Chess variation with neither player seeing the other's moves
**Küche, Kirche, und Kinder** Cooking, church, and children ("a woman's place")
**Kultur** Culture
**Kulturkampf** Conflict between state and church

**Landstrum** General draft; the force drafted
**Lebensraum** One's environment; living space
**Leberwurst** Liverwurst (sausage)
**Lebkuchen** A chewy cookie made with fruit and honey
**Leitmotiv** A dominant theme or motive force
**Lieder** Songs
**Liederkranz** Strong flavored soft cheese
**Linzertorte** A jam-topped cookie
**Luftmensch** A person with no aim in life; one who appears to live on air

**Luftwaffe** Nazi air force
**Lumpen(proletariat)** The poorest elements of the proletariat

**Mein Kampf** Adolph Hitler's book outlining his aims

**Nazi** Member of Hitler's National Socialist German Workers' Party
**nix** *(from* **nichts**) No, nothing; to nullify

**Panzer** Tank
**Poltergeist** A ghost who makes noises and rapping sounds
**Prosit!** To health! (a toast)
**Putsch** Sudden political uprising

**Sachertorte** A chocolate and raspberry layer cake
**Sauerbraten** A sweet and sour pot roast
**Schadenfreude** Malicious enjoyment of another's misfortune
**Schlagsahne (schlag)** Whipped cream
**Schnapps** Strong spirits
**Schnitzel** Veal cutlet
**Schwarzwälder Kirschtorte**
Black Forest cherry cake
**Spiel** Play; speech; sales pitch
**Stein** Beer mug
**Streusel** Topping for a coffee cake
**Sturm und Drang** Storm and stress; sound and fury

**Übermensch** Superman
**Umlaut** A punctuation mark indicating vowel sound change, e.g. ö or ü

**Verboten** Forbidden

**Wanderlust** Passion or urge to travel
**Wehrmacht** Nazi armed forces
**Wiener schnitzel** Breaded veal cutlet
**Wie geht's?** How is it going?
**Weltanschauung** World view
**Weltschmerz** World weariness
**wunderbar** Wonderful; marvelous
**Wunderkind** A child prodigy
**Wurst** Sausage (cooking)

**Yodel** Singing with falsetto interjections

**Zeitgeist** Spirit of the times

## ITALIAN

**a cappella** Singing without instrumental accompaniment
**adagio** Slow musical tempo
**aggioramento** Updating the policies, rules, etc.
**agitato** Fast; with excitement
**al dente** Cooked lightly so as to be firm when eaten (e.g., pasta)
**al fresco** Taking place outdoors
**allegro** Lively, cheerful tempo
**andante** Slow musical tempo
**andiamo** Let's go
**antipasto** Appetizer served before the main course
**aria** An operatic solo
**autostrada** Expressway

**bambino, bambina** Young boy, young girl
**bel canto** Opera style with smooth, artistic vocal technique
**bravo!** Well done
**bravissimo!** Very well done
**buffo (basso)** Comical opera singer, usually a bass
**buon giorno** Good day

**cacciatore** Hunter-style cooking
**cannelloni** Rolls of pasta filled with meat or cheese
**Ciao!** Hello! Cheers! Good-bye!
**corso** A fashionable street
**Cosa Nostra** The Mafia
**così fan tutte** That's the way of the world

**diva** An operatic prima donna
**Don** A high-ranking member of the mafia; a title of respect
**donna** Lady

**Duce, Il** Leader; usually refers to Mussolini

**falsetto** Artificial way of high-pitched singing
**fettuccine** Long, flat ribbon-like pasta
**furioso** Passionate musical tempo
**forte** Musically loud and forceful
**fortissimo** Extremely loud (music)

**gelato** Italian ice cream
**glissando** Smoothly sliding one musical tone into the next
**gnocchi** Small dumplings made with flour and potatoes
**grappa** Strong grape liquor

**imbroglio** Confused, tangled situation
**in flagrante** Caught in the act; caught red-handed (mostly refers to sexual misconduct)
**impresario** Organizer or manager of a performing company
**intermezzo** Short musical movement, e.g., between the acts of an opera

**la donna è mobile** The lady is fickle
**la dolce vita** High living, indolent and luxurious
**linguine** Flat pasta with oval cross-section

**madrigal** An a capella song involving two or more singers

**maestro** Master in any art; particularily a music conductor

**mafia** Italian organized crime gang

**mafioso** Mafia member

**Mamma mia!** My goodness!

**ma non troppo** With moderation (music)

**mezzo forte** Moderately loud (music)

**mezzo piano** Moderately soft (music)

**moderato** Moderate musical tempo

**molto** Rapid musical tempo

**mozzarella** White Italian cheese

**osso buco** Veal with marrowbone stewed in wine

**pace in terra** Peace on earth

**paisan** Compatriot (mostly an Italian one)

**palazzo** A palatial mansion

**paparazzi** celebrity-pursuing photographers

**pianissimo** Very soft and quiet

**piano** Softly; quietly

**piazza** Public square

**pizza** Tomato and cheese pie

**pizzicato** Music made by plucking the strings

**presto** Rapid musical tempo

**prima donna** A temperamental and conceited performer

**ravioli** Pasta shaped like small pockets with meat or cheese filling

**salto** Leap (circus)

**sotto voce** Softly; in an undertone

**terza rima** Italian verse form of three lines rhyming aba, bcb, cdc, etc.

**tessitura** Average pitch of a vocal composition

**tiramisù** An Italian dessert made with devil's food cake, liquor, and chocolate

**tortellini** Squares of pasta stuffed with meat

**traduttore traditore** Translators are traitors

**virtuoso** A master in one's field

# JAPANESE

**Banzai!** Shout of supreme joy, often patriotic

**bonsai** Art of growing dwarf ornamental trees

**bushido** Spiritual code of the Japanese warrior

**cho-cho** Butterfly

**futon** Sleeping mat; convertible sofa bed

**gaijin** Foreigner (non-Japanese)

**geisha** Traditional female entertainers providing singing, dancing, and conversation

**Ginza** Shopping and entertainment district in Tokyo

**go** A chess-like game played with black and white stones

**Haiku** Formal poem of three lines and seventeen syllables

**hara-kiri (hari-kiri)** Ritual suicide by disembowelment

**honcho** U.S. slang for "big chief"

**ikebana** Floral arrangement

**issei** Japanese immigrant to America ("first generation")

**judo** A martial art stressing agile motions, not strength

**kabuki** One of three major classical theaters in Japan

**kamikaze** Suicide pilot

**kanji** Ideographs (Chinese characters) used in writing

**karate** Hand-to-hand self-defense

**Keiretsu** Powerful Japanese financial and industrial combine

**kendo** Japanese art of fencing and swordplay

**kimono** Traditional Japanese dress

**mama san** Chief hostess at a bar or club

**mikado** The emperor of Japan

**miso** Bean paste (soup or broth)

**netsuke** Miniature carvings, usually in ivory, and in an artistic fashion

**Nippon; Nihon** Alternative word for Japan

**nisei** Generation of Japanese Americans born in the U.S. ("second generation")

**no(h)** Oldest form of traditional Japanese dance-drama

**obi** Kimono sash

**origami** The art of paper folding

**ramen** Chinese wheat noodles

**sake** Rice wine

**-san** Japanese honorific suffix added to names

**sansei** Second generation of American-born Japanese ("third generation")

**sashimi** Fresh raw fish pieces served with soy sauce

**sayonara** Good-bye

**Sensei** teacher (title)

**shamisen** Three-stringed, plucked musical instrument

**shinkansen** High-speed passenger railroad system

**shogun** Top military dictator

**shoji** Sliding screen room dividers

**skosh** (abbr. *sukoshi*) A little.

**soba** Buckwheat flour noodles

**suki-yaki** Thinly sliced beef, tofu, vegetables, and soy broth often cooked at the table

**sumo** Traditional Japanese wrestling

**sushi** Vinegared rice with raw fish or seafood topping

**tatami** Traditional Japanese floor mats

**tempura** Deep-fried fish or vegetables dipped in batter

**tofu** Soy bean curd

**tsunami** A tidal wave

**udon** Japanese wheat noodles

**wasabi** Green horseradish

**yakitori** Chicken grilled on bamboo skewers

**yen** Japanese currency

# SPANISH

**adios** Good-bye; farewell
**aficionado** Fan, enthusiastic follower
**aguardiente** "Fire water"; hard liquor
**alcalde** Mayor
**alforja** Saddlebag
**altiplano** A high plateau
**amigo** Friend
**ándele!** Come on; hurry up
**armada** Large military force, mainly naval
**arriba!** Hurrah!
**arroyo** Deep gully or gulch, frequently dry
**arroz con pollo** Chicken and rice dish
**asado** Roast meat, barbecue
**auto de fe** Burning of heretics at the stake
**ayuntamiento** Town council

**bandido** Bandit; robber; cunning
**barrio** Neighborhood (esp. Mexican-American)
**bésame mucho** Kiss me again and again
**bodega** Wine store; grocery
**bravo!** Excellent! Well done!
**buenos días** Good morning; hello
**burrito** Tortilla filled with meat or cheese
**burro** Donkey

**caballero** Gentleman; sir; horseman
**cacique** Chief
**café con leche** Coffee and cream
**camino Real** King's highway

**cantina** Canteen; snack bar
**casa** House
**castañetas** Castanets
**caudillo** Leader
**chaparral** Thicket of shrubs
**chicano** Mexican American
**chico(a)** Little one; boy (girl)
**chile con carne** A spicy meat, red pepper and bean dish
**chile relleno** Stuffed peppers
**chiquita** Kid; child; cute one
**churrasco** Argentinian steak
**chorizo** Spicy sausage
**conquistador** Conquerer
**corazón** Heart, darling
**cordillera** Mountain range
**corrida (de toros)** Bullfight
**costa** Coast
**Cuba Libre** Rum and Coke drink
**cucaracha** Cockroach; a Mexican dance

**dinero** Money
**don** Sir
**Don Juan** Lady chaser; womanizer
**doña** Madam, Mrs.

**empanada** Meat or fruit pie
**enchilada** A rolled tortilla stuffed with meat and cheese

**fiesta** Religious feast or holiday
**flamenco** Spanish gypsy style of dance and music
**flan** Baked custard
**flotilla** Small fleet
**frijoles** Beans, usually black beans

**garbanzo** Chickpea

**gaucho** Argentinian cowboy

**gracias a Dios** By the grace of God; thank God

**grande** Great

**gringo** A foreigner, usually American or British

**guacamole** Avocado dish

**hacienda** Ranch

**hasta la vista** Until we meet again

**hidalgo** Spanish nobleman; one resembling such a nobleman

**hola** Hello

**hombre** A man

**hot tamale!** An exclamation of surprise

**huevos rancheros** Mexican fried egg dish with chorizos and beans

**junta** Military ruling group

**linda** Beautiful (woman)

**loco** Crazy

**machete** Long curved hacking knife

**macho** A he-man

**machismo** He-man philosophy (mostly pejorative)

**madre** Mother

**Madre de Dios** Mother of God

**mañana** Tomorrow (also used to convey the idea of putting something off indefinitely)

**mano a mano** Hand to hand

**mantilla** Spanish scarf, usually lace

**margarita** Mexican cocktail made of tequila and lime juice

**mariachi** Mexican singing band

**mesa** Table land on a hill top

**mescal** Cactus liquor; hallucinogenic cactus substance

**mi casa es su casa** My home is your home

**nada** Nothing

**número uno** Number one

**olé!** Bravo! Here, here! We approve!

**padre** Priest

**paella** A casserole dish of rice, chicken, seafood, and chorizo

**pan** Bread

**paseo** A leisurely walk; a strolling lane or street

**paso doble** A two-step dance to music often heard at bullfights

**patio** Inner court

**pensión** Boarding house

**peseta** Spain's currency

**peso** Mexican currency

**picador** A horseman in a bullfight who weakens the bull by piercing his neck muscles

**piñata** Overhead decoration filled with small toys and candy to be opened by children

**plaza de toros** Bullfighting arena

**poco a poco** Little by little

**politico** Politician

**poncho** Blanket-like cloak

**por favor** Please

**pueblo** Town or village

**pulque** Mexican drink, made from agave

**qué tal?** How's it going?

**que será será** What will be will be

**quesadilla** Corn meal pie with cheese; cheesecake
**quién sabe?** Who knows?

**raza** "The Race" (Hispanic Americans in general; specifically Mexican-Americans)
**río** River
**Ropa Vieja** Cuban stew dish

**salsa** Sauce, often spicy hot; music and dance form
**salud!** To your health! (Toast)
**señor** Mister
**señora** Mrs.
**señorita** Miss
**sierra** Mountain range
**siesta** A nap
**sombrero** Mexican broad-brimmed hat

**taco** Tortilla folded around a meat or cheese filling

**tamale** Corn meal with chicken or meat wrapped in corn husk or banana leaves
**tapas** Spanish appetizers
**tequila** Liquor distilled from cactus juice

**tonto** Foolish person
**torero** Toreador; bullfighter
**tortilla** Thin unleavened corn bread
**tostada** Toast; fried tortilla

**vaquero** Central America cowboy
**vaya con Dios** Go with God
**verónica** Cape maneuver in bullfighting
**vigilante** Individual enforcing law without legal authority
**vino** Wine
**viva!** To life! We applaud!

# YIDDISH

**aha! (Hoo-ha!)** Eureka!; I see!; Now you understand

**alrightnik** A boasting successful man; nouveau riche

**A.K.** *Alte kocker*; a failing old man; an old fart

**Ashkenazi** Jews from Germany, Poland, or Russia

**bagel** A boiled and baked dough-nut shaped roll

**balabusteh** An exemplary home-maker and hostess

**Bar Mitzvah** Jewish confirm-ation of a thirteen-year-old boy

**Bat (or Bas) Mitzvah** Jewish confirmation of a thirteen-year-old girl

**bialy** A floured onion roll

**blintz** A cheese-filled crepe

**borscht** Beet soup

**boychik** A young boy

**bris** Circumcision ceremony

**bubaleh** Little grandmother or an affectionate term for a child

**cabbalah** A Jewish mystic movement of Rabbinic origin

**challah** A braided white egg bread

**cholent** A bean and meat dish similar to a French Cassoulet

**Chanukah** Festival of Lights (also spelled *Hanukkah*)

**chutzpah** Extreme nerve; unmitigated gall

**dreck** Crap; trash

**dybbuk** An evil spirit claiming the body of a living person

**feh!** An exclamation of disgust

**finif (Fin)** A five-dollar bill

**gefilte fish** A fish loaf made of chopped fish

**gelt** Money

**gesundheit!** To your health! (Often used after one sneezes)

**glick** (Good) luck

**glitch** Error; slide or slip

**golem** A robot; lifeless figure

**goniff** Thief

**goy** A non-Jew

**gut yontiff** Happy holiday

**gut shabbos** Good Sabbath

**Hadassah** Women's Zionist organization dedicated to health care

**halvah** Candy made of sesame seeds and honey

**Hamantash** A three-cornered poppyseed cake

**Hanukkah** See *Chanukah*

**hassid** Member of a pious Jewish religious sect

**Hatikvah** Israel's national anthem

**kaddish** A prayer for the dead

**kasha** Cooked cereal; groats

**kibitz** To offer unwanted advice while watching a game or listening to an argument

**kibbutz** A co-op farm

**kichel** A small, plain cookie

**kinder** Children

**kineh horah** Beware the evil eye

**kishka** Stuffed derma; guts

**klutz** A clumsy bungler

**knish** A small dumpling, normally filled with potatoes

**kosher** Ritually clean; acceptable; legal

**kreplach** A triangular dumpling filled with cheese or meat

**kugel** Potato or noodle pudding

**kurveh** (also *curveh*) A prostitute

**kvell** To gloat; show great pride and pleasure

**kvetch** To intensely gripe or complain

**latkes** Potato pancakes

**l'chaim!** To your health! To life! (A drinking toast)

**loshen horah** The evil tongue; gossip

**matzoh** Unleavened bread

**mavin** A real expert; a connoisseur

**mazel** Good luck

**mazel tov!** Congratulations

**medinah** Country or state

**megillah** An overly long story with too many details

**mench** A decent human being

**menorah** A candelabrum with seven or eight branches

**meshuggeh** Crazy; wild

**mezuzah** A small box containing a scrolled Biblical passage, usually mounted on the home entrance

**mikvah** A ritual bath

**mishpocheh** Family

**mohel** A circumciser

**momzer** A bastard; a shrewd person

**naches** Extreme pride and pleasure from a child

**no-goodnick** An unethical person; a bum

**nu?** Well? What's cooking?

**nudnik** A pest; a real nuisance

**oy!** (**Oy-oy-oy! Oy veh!**) An all-purpose word expressing worry, dismay, surprise, etc.

**parnoseh** Livelihood

**Pesach** The feast of Passover

**pisher** A pisser; a young squirt

**putz** A jerk; simpleton; fool

**rebbe** A learned Rabbi

**Rosh Hashanah** Jewish New Year

**Seder** Passover banquet and religious service

**Sephardi** Jews from Spain, Portugal, and the Middle East

*(Note: most of the following words beginning with "sh" are often spelled with "sch")*

**shalom** Peace; hello; good-bye

**shamus** Synagogue sexton; a "private eye"

**schav** Sorrel or spinach soup

**shaygetz** A non-Jewish male

**shikker** Drunk

**shiksa** A non-Jewish female

**shlemiel** A fool; a social misfit

**shlepp** To drag or pull behind

**shlimazel** A hard luck person

**shlock** Shoddy, cheaply made

**shlong** Penis

**shloomp** Stupid; dishevelled

**shmaltz** Chicken fat; excessive sentimentality; bathos

shmatte  Rag; a cheap dress

shmeck  A taste

shmeer  To smear or to bribe

shmegeggy  Stupid person

shmo  A boob; a clumsy jerk

shmooze  Friendly talk or gossip

shmuck  Contemptuous term for a nasty dope or jerk; a penis

shnorrer  A beggar or a chiseler

shnook  A pathetic but likeable "sad sack"

shnoz (shnozzle)  A nose, usually very big

shofar  A ram's horn trumpet

shpritz  A touch of; a spray

shtarker  A strong person

shtetl  A small town

shtik  A piece; a devious trick; contrived act or device

shtunk  An ungrateful person; a mean stinker

shtup  To push or press; to have sex or fornicate

shul  A synogogue

shvartze  A black person (derog.)

shvitzer  A braggart; a show-off

talis  Prayer shawl

Talmud  A compendium of Jewish law, based on the Bible

tokhes (tochis, tush, tushy)  One's behind or buttocks; tush or tushy used for children or lovers only

Torah  The first five books of the Old Testament

tsimmes  Candied carrots; a big deal

tsuris  Trouble

tummler  Entertainer; inciter

tzaddik  A righteous person

yarmulke  A skullcap

yenta  A gossip; a shrew

yeshiva  A Rabbinical Seminary

yid  An offensive term for a Jew

Yom Kippur  The Day of Atonement; highest Jewish holiday

zaftig  Juicy; well-rounded; buxom

---

## A BILINGUAL PALINDROME

**English:** Anger? 'tis safe never. Bar it! Use love.
**Latin:** Evoles ut ira breve nefas sit; regna.

The palindrome of the English expression, when read in Latin, has exactly the same meaning. Try your hand at creating palindromes in your own language.

### EMBARRASSING CROSS-CULTURAL MOMENTS

Red faces can result from confusion between other languages and American English. There are two restaurants in New York called *Chin Chin*. The first is owned by two Chinese brothers named Chin; the second uses that name because *Chin chin* in Italy is a drinking toast, much like *Cheers!* or *Santé!* If you see a group of young Japanese girls giggling uproariously while looking up at this name on one of the restaurant canopies, don't be confused. *Chin chin* in Japanese is an informal word for a little boy's penis, equivalent to the term *weewee* in the American language.

Another word for jam in the United States is *preserves,* a term widely used in England. Consequently, American/Spanish translators missing the precise word sometimes guess at *preservativos.* American/French translators similarly err and use *priservatifs* for jam. To their embarrassment, such translators find that these two terms refer to *condoms. Mermelada* and *confiture* are the proper words for jam in Spanish and French, respectively.

A friend of mine as a young man emigrated to America from Poland. When he arrived, speaking virtually no English, he was picked up by some friends and driven to Connecticut. All along the way, he kept gazing out of the car window and mumbling under his breath that America is a terrible country. His friends told him in Polish that he was crazy, that America was a wonderful country. What was troubling him? His reply—which further confused his friends—was, "Well, we have these things in Poland too, but we don't advertise it all over the place." My friend was referring to roadside signs saying *Curve.* In Polish, as in Spanish and Japanese, every letter is pronounced. *Curwa* (pronounced *Curvah* in Polish) means prostitute. Along similar lines, Louisa May Alcott's book *Little Women,* when published in France, must use a different title. *Little Women* in colloquial French also concerns prostitutes.

# Chapter Nine

# ACRONYMS, ABBREVIATIONS, AND INITIALISMS

Acronyms are words formed from the initial letters of a name or phrase (e.g., AIDS for Acquired ImmunoDeficiency Syndrome) or by combining parts of a series of words (e.g., "Nabisco" for NAtional BIScuit COmpany). Note that the acronym must end up as a natural word, i.e., it must be able to be pronounced as a single word. While these are the general rules, many liberties are taken. For the sake of convenience and brevity, letter combinations (initialisms) which cannot logically be considered a single word are slurred so as to invent acronyms which more or less sound like the letter combination. An example is "Fannie Mae" (Federal National Mortgage Association) based on the initialism FNMA. "Fannie Mae" is much easier to say than "ef-en-em-ay." In the computer field, another example is "scuzzy" for SCSI (Small Computer System Interface). Other pseudo-acronyms combine an entire short word with one or more letters from another word, e.g. "e-mail" for Electronic MAIL. In the list of acronyms given below, when necessary, actual pronunciations are given in (parentheses) immediately following the acronym.

Abbreviations are shortened forms of actual words. Examples are "etc." for *et cetera* and "Inc." for Incorporated. To simplify your search, the abbreviations list below has been divided into a number of categories covering the fields from which the abbreviated words spring. Initialisms (often erroneously termed "abbreviations") are shortened versions of names or phrases formed from initial letters or by combining portions of the name or phrase. Initialisms are almost always shown in capital letters, while abbreviations may be either upper or lower case or a combination thereof. It is important to note that initialisms differ from acronyms in that they do not form an actual *word,* but are pronounced as a group of individual letters, e.g. I.B.M. ("eye-bee-em") for International Business Machines or T&I

("tee & eye") for Translation and Interpretation. Published lists of acronyms frequently include expressions which are really initialisms; a recent article in the *ATA Chronicle* showed this type of confusion. It was not a grievous error, and except to linguistic purists, it is of little practical consequence.

There are, in fact, many expressions which can be read both ways. VAT (Value Added Tax), for example, is sometimes pronounced as a single word (rhyming with *cat*). On other occasions, you will hear the same expression enunciated as distinct letters, namely "vee-ay-tee." Another good one is IHOP (International House Of Pancakes) — "eye-hop" or "I-H-O-P." Then there are letter combinations which could be pronounced as a single word but never are in practice. The AMA (American Medical Association) and SOP (Standard Operating Procedure) are typical examples. How does one know which is the conventional pronunciation? Pretty much the same way you know which nouns in West European languages are masculine or feminine. You commit them to memory.

Abbreviations are almost always used in writing rather than in speech. Acronyms and initialisms, however, may be used both in speech and writing. There are literally tens of thousands of acronyms, abbreviations, and initialisms, with a number of dictionaries or compilations listing most of them. Our list of about 100 acronyms given below has culled only those which writers, editors, and translators are likely to encounter with any frequency.

No attempt has been made to suggest exactly how to translate the following. In the case of many international businesses, such as I.B.M., these shortened forms have frequently found international use. There are many other cases, however, where the foreign equivalent of the name or organization has totally different initial letters, and consequently, the acronyms and initialisms would also be totally different. In the following list, a few examples are given of European language equivalents for internationally used English acronyms. MATIF, for example, refers to the Paris Futures Market, whose French name is *Marché À Terme International de France*. As regards abbreviations, of course, every language has its own.

Please note that some abbreviations are followed by a period and some initialisms are separated by periods. The current trend is to drop the periods (e.g., U.S.A. becomes USA; N.A.F.T.A. is known as NAFTA).

A caveat regarding possible confusion with both acronyms and initialisms. If you leaf through one of the voluminous dictionaries on this subject listed in the Bibliography of this book, you will find that many acronyms—and particularly many initialisms—have more than one meaning, since they may derive from subjects or organizations whose initial letters are the same, but whose meanings are entirely different. This can be embarrassing, even dangerous. For example, the acronym or initialism JIFA is used for both the Japan-Israel Friendship Association and, by a strange coincidence, The Japan Islamic Friendship Association.

Noting that the computer industry probably uses more acronyms than any other field, and that there is a huge amount of work for translators and interpreters in this industry, a special chapter of computer-related acronyms, abbreviations, initialisms and specialized communications terminology follows this one.

Acronyms can sometimes be humorous. For example, when the wife of the publisher is asked about her profession, she says that she is a CEO of an HMO in DC (Chief Executive Officer of a Health Maintenance Organization in the District of Columbia). The author's wife thinks that he should carry a card saying 'M.R. AKA A.K.' (decipher this one if you can!)

# ACRONYMS

| | |
|---|---|
| AARP | American Association of Retired Persons |
| AID | Agency for International Development |
| | Fr. ADI (*Agence pour la Développment International*) |
| AIDS | Acquired ImmunoDeficiency Syndrome |
| ALCOA | ALuminum COmpany Of America |
| ALTA | American Literary Translation Association |
| AMEX | AMerican Express; AMerican (Stock) EXchange |
| AMOCO | AMerican Oil COrporation |
| AMTRAK | AMerican TRAcK |
| ANSI | American National Standards Institute |
| APEC | Asia Pacific Economic Cooperation |
| ARAMCO | ARabian-AMerican (oil) COmpany |
| ARCO | Atlantic Richfield COmpany |
| ASAP | As Soon As Possible |
| ASCAP | American Society of Composers, Authors & Publishers |
| ASEAN | Association of SouthEast Asian Nations |
| | |
| BIS | Bank for International Settlements |
| | Ge. BIZ (*Bank für Internationalen Zahlungsausgleich*) |
| | Fr. BRI (*Banque des Règlements Internationaux*) |
| | Sp. BPI (*Banco de Pagos Internacionales*) |
| | |
| CARE | Cooperative for American Remittances Everywhere |
| CAT (SCAN) | Computerized Axial Tomography |
| COLA | Cost Of Living Adjustment |
| COSTCO | COST COmpany |
| CUSIP | Committee on Uniform Securities Identification Procedures |
| | |
| DINK (DINC) | Double Income, No Kids |
| | |
| EBIT | Earnings Before Interest, Taxes, [depreciation, and amortization] |

| | |
|---|---|
| ECU | European Currency Unit |
| | Sp. UCE (*Unidad de Cuenta Europea*) |
| EFTA | European Free Trade Association |
| | Fr. AELE (*Association Européenne de Libre-Échange*) |
| | Sp. AELI (*Asociación Europea de Libre Intercambio*) |
| EMI | European Monetary Institute |
| | Ge. EWI (*Europäisches WährungsInstitut*) |
| ERA | Earned Run Average |
| ESOP | Employee Stock Ownership Plan |
| ESSO | Standard Oil |
| | |
| FAX | FACSimile |
| FEMA | Federal Emergency Management Agency |
| FIFO | First In, First Out |
| | Fr. PEPS (*Premier Entré, Premier Sorti*) |
| | Sp. PEPS (*Primero Entrar, Primero Salir*) |
| FLAK | FLieger Abwehr Kanone  (Ge.) |
| FNMA | (Pronounced "Fanny Mae") Federal National Mortgage Association |
| | |
| GAAP | Generally Accepted Accounting Principles |
| | Fr. PCGA (*Principes Comptable Généralment Admis*) |
| | Sp. PCGA (*Principios de Contabilidad Generalmente Aceptados*) |
| GAAS | Generally Accepted Auditing Standards |
| | Fr. NVGR (*Normes de Vérification Généralmente Reconnues*) |
| GATT | General Agreement on Tariffs and Trade |
| GESTAPO | GEheime STAatPOlizei |
| GIGO | Garbage In, Garbage Out |
| | |
| HUD | (U.S. Department of) Housing and Urban Development |
| | |
| IHOP | International House Of Pancakes |

| | |
|---|---|
| INTERCOM | INTER-COMmunication |
| INTERNET | INTERnational NETwork |
| INTERPOL | INTERnational criminal POLice organization |
| IRA | Individual Retirement Account |
| | Fr. PEP (*Plan d'Épargne Populaire*) |
| ISO | International Standardization Organization |
| | |
| JAC | Foreign Exchange Administration Board |
| | Sp. JAC (*Junta de Administración Cambiaria*) |
| JETRO | Japan External TRade Organization |
| | |
| LASER | Light Application by Stimulated Emission of Radiation |
| LIBOR | London InterBank Offered Rate |
| LIFO | Last In, First Out |
| | Fr. DEPS (*Dernier Entré, Premier Sorti*) |
| | Sp. UEPS (*Último Entrar, Primero Salir*) |
| | |
| MAD | Mutually Assured Destruction |
| MADD | Mothers Against Drunk Driving |
| M.A.S.H. | Mobile Army Surgical Hospital |
| MATIF | Paris Futures Market (*Marché À Terme International de France*) |
| MEFF | Madrid Futures Market (*MErcado de Futuros Financieros*) |
| MIIS | Monterey Institute of International Studies |
| MIRV | Multiple Independently (targeted) Re-entry Vehicles |
| MITI | Ministry of International Trade and Industry |
| MYACO | MYA COmpany |
| | |
| NABISCO | NAtional BIScuit COmpany |
| NAFTA | North American Free Trade Agreement |
| | Fr. ALENA (*Accord de Libre-Échange Nord Américain*) |
| | Sp. TLC (*Tratado de libre comercio*) |
| NASA | National Aeronautics and Space Administration |
| NATO | North Atlantic Treaty Organization |

| | |
|---|---|
| NAV | Net Asset Value |
| | Fr. VAN (Valeur Actualisée Nette) |
| | Sp. VAN (Valor de Activo Neto) |
| NIES | Newly Industrializing EconomieS |
| NIMBY | Not In My Back Yard |
| NOW | National Organization for Women |
| NYFE | New York Futures Exchange |
| NYMEX | New York Mercantile EXchange |
| NYNEX | New York New England eXchange |
| NYSE | New York Stock Exchange |
| | |
| OPEC | Organization of Petroleum Exporting Countries |
| | Ge. OPEC (_Organisation der Öl-Exportierenden Länder_) |
| | Fr. OPEP (_Organisation de Pays Exportateurs de Pétrol_) |
| | Sp. OPEP (_Organizacion de paises exportadores de petroleo_) |
| OSHA | Occupational Safety and Health Administration |
| | |
| PFLAG | (Pronounced "pee-flag") Parents and Friends of Lesbians And Gays |
| PIN | Personal Identification Number |
| POSH | Port Out, Starboard Home |
| POSSLQ | Person of the Opposite Sex Sharing Living Quarters |
| | |
| RADAR | RAdio Detection And Ranging |
| REM | Rapid Eye Movement |
| | |
| SAC | Strategic Air Command |
| SALT | Strategic Arms Limitation Treaty |
| SAM | Surface-to-Air Missile |
| SCUBA | Self-Contained Underwater Breathing Apparatus |
| SCUD | Subsonic Cruise Unarmed Decoy (missile) |
| SLMA | (Pronounced "Sallie Mae") Student Loan Marketing Association |
| SNCC | (Pronounced "Snick") Student Nonviolent Coordinating Committee |

| | |
|---|---|
| SONAR | SOund Navigation And Ranging |
| START | STrategic Arms Reduction Talks (Treaty) |
| SUNOCO | SUN Oil COmpany |
| | |
| TEXACO | TEXAs (oil) Company |
| TIP | To Insure Promptings |
| | |
| UCITS | Undertaking for Collective Investment in Transferable Securities<br>Fr. OPCVM (*Organisme de Placements Collectifs en Valeurs Mobilières*) |
| UNEP | United Nations Environmental Program |
| UNESCO | United Nations Educational, Scientific, and Cultural Organization |
| UNICEF | United Nations International Children's Emergency Fund |
| UNOCAL | UNion Oil (Company) of CALifornia |
| UNRRA | United Nations Relief and Rehabilitation Administration |
| UNSCOM | United Nations Special Commission |
| | |
| VAT | Value Added Tax<br>Fr. TVA (*Taxe sur la Valeur Ajoutée*)<br>Ge. MwST (*MehrwertSTeuer*)<br>Sp. IVA (*Impuesto de Valor Añadido [Agregado]*) |
| | |
| WAC | Women's Army Corps |
| WAF | Women in the Air Force |
| WASP | White Anglo-Saxon Protestant |
| WAVES | Women Accepted for Volunteer Emergency Service |
| | |
| YUPPIE | Young Urban Professional |
| | |
| ZIP | Zone Improvement Plan |

# ABBREVIATIONS AND INITIALISMS

## Clothing Sizes and Colors

| | |
|---|---|
| bl. | black; blue |
| gr. | green |
| L | large |
| M | medium |
| P | petite |
| S | small |
| tlr. | tailor |
| XL | extra large |
| XS | extra small |
| XXL | double extra large |
| wh. | white |
| yel. | yellow |

## Streets and Roads

| | |
|---|---|
| Ave. | avenue |
| Cr.(Ci) | circle |
| Ct. | court |
| Cyn. | canyon |
| Hwy. | highway |
| Is. | island |
| Jct. | junction |
| Ln. | lane |
| Ped. | pedestrian |
| Rd. | road |
| Rte. | route |
| St. | street |
| Ter. | terrace |
| Tpk. | turnpike |
| Twp. | township |
| Xing | crossing |
| Xway | expressway |

## Times and Dates

*Units of Time*

| | |
|---|---|
| sec. | second |
| min. | minute |
| hr. | hour |
| wk. | week |
| wkly. | weekly |
| mo. | month |
| yr. | year |
| c. | century |

*Time Clarifiers*

| | |
|---|---|
| A.M. | Also *a.m.*; before noon |
| P.M. | Also *p.m.*; after noon |
| A.D. | *Anno Domini* (In the year of our Lord; since the birth of Christ) |
| B.C. | before the birth of Christ |
| B.C.E. | before the common era |

*Time Zones*

| | |
|---|---|
| EST | Eastern Standard Time |
| CST | Central Standard Time |
| GMT | Greenwich Mean Time |
| MST | Mountain Standard Time |
| PST | Pacific Standard Time |

*Days of the Week*

| | |
|---|---|
| Mon. | Monday |
| Tues. | Tuesday |
| Wed. | Wednesday |
| Thu. | Thursday |
| Fri. | Friday |

| | | | |
|---|---|---|---|
| Sat. | Saturday | ENT | ear, nose, and throat |
| Sun. | Sunday | HIV | human immuno-deficiency virus |

*Months of the Year*

| | | | |
|---|---|---|---|
| Jan. | January | HMO | health maintenance organization |
| Feb. | February | ICU | intensive care unit |
| Mar. | March | ID | inside diameter; intra-dermal |
| Apr. | April | | |
| *(Note: May is not abbreviated)* | | K | kelvin |
| Jun. | June | liq. | liquid |
| Jul. | July | log | logarithm |
| Aug. | August | LSD | lysergic acid diethylamide; "acid" |
| Sept. | September | | |
| Oct. | October | max. | maximum |
| Nov. | November | min. | minimum |
| Dec. | December | mol.wt. | molecular weight |
| | | mp | melting point |
| | | neg. | negative |

## Medical, Science, and Math

| | | | |
|---|---|---|---|
| | | neut. | neutral |
| b.i.d. | *bis in die*; twice daily | NTP | normal temperature and pressure |
| bp | boiling point; base pair | | |
| BPH | benign peristaltic hyperplasia | o.d. | outside diameter |
| | | O.D. | Doctor of Optometry |
| BTU | British thermal unit | o/d | overdose |
| C. | celsius; centigrade; carbon | PMS | pre-menstrual syndrome |
| cal | calories | PMT | pre-menstrual tension |
| CAT | computerized axial tomography | pos. | positive |
| | | PSA | prostate specific antigen |
| CPR | cardiac pulmonary resuscitation | rev. | revolution; reverse |
| | | RF | radio frequency |
| dc | direct current | rms | root mean square |
| DIMCAP | | RNA | ribonucleic acid |
| | diminished capacity | RPM | reliability performance measure |
| DNA | deoxyribonucleic acid | | |
| DTs | delirium tremens | R.P.S. | revolutions per second |
| EEG | electroencephalogram | Rx | prescription |
| ECG | electrocardiogram | sci. | science; scientific |

std     standard
STD     sexually transmitted disease
STP     standard temperature and pressure
TB     tuberculosis
temp.     temperature
t.i.d.     (*tir in die*) three times daily
tinct.     tincture
TM     transcendental meditation
t.s.     temperature switch; tensile strength
vac.     vacuum
VD     venereal disease
VTOL     vertical takeoff and landing (aircraft)

## Radio and Television

ABC     American Broadcasting Corporation
a.m.     amplitude modulation
BBC     British Broadcasting Corporation
CBS     Columbia Broadcasting System
CNN     Cable News Network
f.m.     frequency modulation
NBC     National Broadcasting Corporation
NPR     National Public Radio
UHF     ultrahigh frequency
VHF     very high frequency
VLF     very low frequency

## Weights and Measures

bsk.     (Also bskt.) basket
bu.     (Also bush.) bushel
bx.     box
c.     cup
cc     cubic centimeter
cl     centiliter
cm     centimeter
$cm^3$     cubic centimeter
cwt.     hundredweight
dl     deciliter
dm     decimeter
F     Fahrenheit
F.P.S.     feet per second
ft     foot
$ft^2$     square foot
G.P.M.     gallons per minute
gal.     gallon
gm     gram
ID     inside diameter
in     inch
$in^2$     square inch
kc     kilocycle
kcal     kilocalorie
kg     kilogram
km     kilometer
kt.     karat
kW     kilowatt
kWh     (also kW h) kilowatt hour
l     liter
lb     pound
m     meter
mA     milliampere
mg     milligram
mi.     mile
ml     milliliter

| | |
|---|---|
| mm | millimeter |
| mph | miles per hour |
| mV | millivolt |
| o.d. | outer diameter |
| oz | ounce |
| pt. | pint |
| qt | quart |
| rm. | ream |
| sq ft | square feet |
| sq. | square |
| tbs. | (Also tbsp.) tablespoon |
| tsp. | teaspoon |
| W h | watt hour |
| wt. | weight |
| yd | yard |

## Degrees and Titles

| | |
|---|---|
| AB | (*Artium Baccalaureus*) Bachelor of Arts |
| BA | Bachelor of Arts |
| BBA | Bachelor of Business Administration |
| BCE | Bachelor of Chemical Engineering; Bachelor of Civil Engineering |
| BE | Bachelor of Education; Bachelor of Economics; Bachelor of Engineering |
| BFA | Bachelor of Fine Arts |
| BLA | Bachelor of Liberal Arts; Bachelor of Landscape Architecture |
| BM | Bachelor of Medicine |
| BME | Bachelor of Mechanical Engineering; Bachelor of Music Education |
| BMus | Bachelor of Music |
| BP | (also Bpharm) Bachelor of Pharmacy. (Also Bphil) Bachelor of Philosophy |
| BPE | (also BPEd) Bachelor of Physical Education |
| BPharm | Bachelor of Pharmacy |
| BPhil | Bachelor of Philosophy |
| BS | (Also BSc) Bachelor of Science; Bachelor of Surgery |
| BScA | Bachelor of Science in Agriculture |
| CE | civil or chemical engineer |
| CEO | Chief Executive Officer |
| CFO | Chief Financial Officer |
| chmn | (Also chm. or Chm.) chairman |
| Cmdr. | Commander |
| CO | Commanding Officer |
| COO | Chief Operating Officer |
| CPA | Certified Public Accountant |
| CPO | Chief Petty Officer |
| D.A. | District Attorney |

| | | | |
|---|---|---|---|
| DD | Doctor of Divinity | MC | Master of Ceremonies |
| DDS | Doctor of Dental Surgery; (Also DDSc) Doctor of Dental Science | M.D. | Doctor of Medicine |
| | | MFA | Master of Fine Arts |
| | | Mgr. | Manager |
| | | Mlle. | Mademoiselle (Miss) |
| | | Mme. | Madame (Missus) |
| EE | electrical engineer(ing) | MP | Military Police |
| | | MPA | Master of Public Administration |
| Esq. | esquire (usually a legal title) | Mr. | Mister; Master |
| Gov. | governor | Mrs. | Missus (a married woman) |
| G.P. | general practitioner | | |
| JD | Doctor of Laws *or* Jurisprudence | Ms. | (Any woman) |
| | | MSW | Master of Social Work |
| j.g. | junior grade | MusB | Bachelor of Music |
| J.P. | Justice of the Peace | MusD | Doctor of Music |
| Jr. | (Also Junr) junior | NCO | noncommissioned officer |
| Jwlr. | jeweler | | |
| LLB | Bachelor of Laws | N.P. | Notary Public |
| LLD | Doctor of Laws | O.B.E. | Officer of the Order of the British Empire |
| Lt. | Lieutenant | | |
| Lt.Col. | Lieutenant-Colonel | PhD | Doctor of Philosophy |
| Lt.Com. | Lieutenant-Commander | P.M. | Prime Minister; Postmaster |
| Lt.Gen. | Lieutenant-General | Pres. | President. (Also Presb.) Presbyterian |
| Lt.Gov. | Lieutenant-Governor | | |
| M. | Master | Prof. | Professor |
| MA | Master of Arts | R.N. | Registered Nurse |
| MACI | Master of Arts in Conference Interpretation | SB | Bachelor of Science |
| | | Secy. | secretary |
| | | Sen. | Senator; Senior |
| MAT | Master of Arts in Translation | soph. | sophomore |
| | | Sr. | Senior; Señor; Sir; Sister (nun) |
| MATI | Master of Arts in Translation and Interpretation | | |
| | | Sra. | Señora |
| | | Srta. | Señorita |
| MBA | Master of Business Administration | tchr. | teacher |
| | | treas. | treasurer |

| V.Adm. | Vice-Admiral |
| V.C. | Vice-Chairman; Vice-Consul |
| V.P. | Also (V.Pres.) Vice-President. Vice-Principal |
| WO | Warrant Officer |

## Geography

| AK | Alaska |
| AL | (Also Ala.) Alabama |
| Alg. | Algeria |
| AR | (Also Ark.) Arkansas |
| Arg. | Argentina |
| Aus. | Austria; Australia |
| AZ | (Also Ariz.) Arizona |
| Bol. | Bolivia |
| Braz. | Brazil |
| CA | (Also Calif.) California; Central America |
| Can. | Canada |
| Ch. | (Also Chi.) Chicago; China |
| CO | (Also Colo.) Colorado |
| Col. | Colombia |
| CT | (Also Conn.) Connecticut |
| DC | District of Columbia |
| DE | (Also Del.) Delaware |
| Eg. | Egypt |
| FL | (Also Fla.) Florida |
| Fr. | France |
| GA | (Also Ga.) Georgia |
| G.B. | Great Britain |
| Ger. | Germany |

| Guat. | Guatemala |
| HI | Hawaii |
| IA | Iowa |
| ID | Idaho |
| IN | (Also Ind.) Indiana |
| Ind. | India; Indiana |
| Ire. | Ireland |
| Ital. | Italy |
| Jpn. | Japan |
| JFK | John F. Kennedy Airport (in New York) |
| KS | (Also Kan.) Kansas |
| KY | (Also Ky.) Kentucky |
| L. | Lake |
| LA | (Also La.) Lousiana |
| L.A. | Los Angeles; Latin America |
| L.A.X. | Los Angeles International Airport |
| L.I. | Long Island, New York |
| MA | (Also Mass.) Massachusetts |
| MD | (Also Md.) Maryland |
| ME | Maine; Middle East |
| Mex. | Mexico |
| MI | (Also Mich.) Michigan |
| MN | (Also Minn.) Minnesota |
| MO | (Also Mo.) Missouri |
| Mor. | Morocco |
| MS | (Also Miss.) Mississippi |
| Mt. | mount; mountain |
| MT | (Also Mont.) Montana |
| N.A. | North America |
| NC | (Also N.C.) North Carolina |

| | | | |
|---|---|---|---|
| ND | (Also N.D.) North Dakota | SD | (Also S.D.) South Dakota |
| NE | (Also Neb.) Nebraska | SE | southeast |
| N.E. | (Also N. Eng.) New England; northeast | Sp. | Spain |
| | | Sw. | (Also Swed.) Sweden |
| NH | (Also N.H.) New Hampshire | SW | southwest |
| | | Switz. | Switzerland |
| NJ | (Also N.J.) New Jersey | TN | (Also Tenn.) Tennessee; true north |
| NM | (Also N.M.) New Mexico | | |
| | | trop. | tropic; tropical |
| Nor. | (Also No.) Norway | TX | Texas |
| NV | (Also Nev.) Nevada | UAE | United Arab Emirates |
| NW | northwest | UAR | United Arab Republic |
| NY | (Also N.Y.) New York | U.K. | United Kingdom |
| | | U.S. | United States |
| N.Y.C. | New York City | USA | United States of America |
| NZ | (Also N. Zeal.) New Zealand | | |
| | | USSR | Union of Soviet Socialist Republics |
| Oc. | ocean | | |
| OH | Ohio | UT | Utah |
| OK | (Also Okla.) Oklahoma | VA | (Also Va.) Virginia |
| | | Ven. | Venezuela; Venice |
| OR | (Also Ore.) Oregon | VI | Virgin Islands; Vancouver Island |
| PA | (Also Pa.) Pennsylvania | | |
| | | VT | (Also Vt.) Vermont |
| Par. | Paraguay | WA | (Also Wash.) Washington |
| P.I. | (Also Phil. Is.) Philippine Islands | | |
| | | WI | (Also Wis.)Wisconsin |
| PR | Puerto Rico | WV | (Also W.Va.) West Virginia |
| RI | (Also R.I.) Rhode Island | | |
| | | WY | (Also Wyo.)Wyoming |
| S.A. | South America; South Africa; Saudi Arabia | | |
| SC | (Also S.C.) South Carolina | | |
| Scot. | Scotland | | |

## Businesses & Organizations

| | |
|---|---|
| AA | Alcoholics Anonymous |
| AAA | American Automobile Association |
| A&P | Atlantic & Pacific Tea Co. |
| AARP | American Association of Retired Persons |
| ACLU | American Civil Liberties Union |
| ADA | Americans for Democratic Action; American Dental Association |
| ALTA | American Literary Translators Assoc. |
| AMA | American Medical Association |
| AP | Associated Press |
| ATA | American Translators Association |
| BBB | Better Business Bureau |
| BPOE | Benevolent & Protective Order of Elks |
| CIA | Central Intelligence Agency |
| CB | (*seabee*) Construction Battalion (military) |
| DAR | Daughters of the American Revolution |
| DEA | Drug Enforcement Agency |
| DOA | US Department of Agriculture; Dead on Arrival |
| DoD | US Department of Defense |
| DOE | US Department of Energy |
| DOL | US Department of Labor |
| DOJ | US Department of Justice |
| DOT | US Department of Transportation |
| FAA | Federal Aviation Administration |
| FBI | Federal Bureau of Investigation |
| FCC | Federal Communications Commission |
| FDA | Food & Drug Administration |
| FHA | Federal Housing Administration |
| FIT | International Fed. of Translators |
| FTC | Federal Trade Commission |
| GOP | Grand Old Party (Republican party) |
| IBM | International Business Machines Corp. |
| IEEE | Institute of Electrical and Electronics Engineers |
| ILA | International Long-shoremen's Assoc. |
| IMF | International Monetary Fund |

INS    International News
Service; Immigration and Naturalization Service

IRA    Individual Retirement
Account; Irish Republican Army

IRS    Internal Revenue
Service

IWW    Industrial Workers of
the World

KKK    Ku Klux Klan

MGM    Metro Goldwyn
Mayer

NCR    National Cash
Register

NAJIT  National Association
of Judiciary Interpreters and Translators

NEA    National Education
Association;
National Endowment for the Arts

NFL    National Football
League

NHL    National Hockey
League

NIH    National Institutes of
Health

NLRB   National Labor
Relations Board

NRA    National Recovery
Administration

N.S.P.C.A.
National Society for
the Prevention of
Cruelty to Animals

OAS    Organization of
American
States

OCS    Officer Candidate
School

OPA    Office of Price
Administration

OTC    Officers' Training
Corps

PTA    Parent-Teacher
Association

PWA    Public Works Authority

RC     Red Cross; Reformed
Church

ROTC   Reserve    Officers'
Training Corps

SBA    Small Business
Administration

SP     shore patrol

SPC    Society for the
Prevention of Crime

S.P.C.A.
Society for the
Prevention of Cruelty
to Animals

S.P.C.C.
Society for the
Prevention of Cruelty
to Children

S.P.Q.R.
(*Senatus Populusque
Romanus*) the Senate
and the People of
Rome

SSA    Social Security
Administration

TVA    Tennessee Valley
Authority

| | |
|---|---|
| TWA | Trans-World Airlines |
| UA | (Also *UAL*) United Airlines; United Artists |
| UAW | United Automobile Workers |
| UMT | universal military training |
| UMW | United Mine Workers |
| UN | United Nations |
| UPS | United Parcel Service |
| USAF | United States Air Force |
| USCG | United States Coast Guard |
| USDA | US Department of Agriculture |
| USMC | United States Marine Corps |
| USN | United States Navy |
| USO | United Service Organization |
| USPS | United States Postal Service |
| VFW | Veterans of Foreign Wars |
| W.C.T.U. | Women's Christian Temperance Union |
| WPA | Work Projects (*or* Progress) Administration (1935-1943) |
| Y.M.C.A. | Young Men's Christian Association |
| Y.M.H.A. | Young Men's Hebrew Association |
| Y.W.C.A. | Young Women's Christian Association |
| Y.W.H.A. | Young Women's Hebrew Association |

## Commerce and Education

| | |
|---|---|
| ADR | American Depository Receipt |
| advt. | advertisement |
| A/P | Accounts Payable |
| APR | Annual Percentage Rate |
| A/R | Accounts Receivable |
| aka | also known as |
| ATM | Automated Teller Machine |
| a.v. | (*Ad valorem*) according to value |
| bkpt. | (Also bkrpt.) bankrupt |
| b/p | bills payable |
| c.c. | carbon copy; copies |
| c.f. | (Also c/f) carried forward; cost and freight |
| c.i.f. | (Also CIF) cost, insurance, and freight (contract) |
| CMO | Collateralized Mortgage-backed Obligation |
| Co. | company |
| c.o.d. | (Also COD) cash on delivery |

| | | | |
|---|---|---|---|
| CPA | Certified Public Accountant | IDB | InterAmerican Development Bank |
| CPI | Consumer Price Index | IFB | Invitation For Bid |
| Corp. | corporation | IMF | International Monetary Fund |
| d.b.a. | doing business as *or* at | | |
| dup. | duplicate | Inc. | Incorporated |
| EBIT | earnings before interest and taxes | IPO | initial public offering |
| | | IRR | internal rate of return |
| EBITDA | | LBO | leveraged buyout |
| | earnings before interest,taxes, depreciation, and amortization | L/C | (Also l/c) letter of credit |
| | | Ltd. | Limited (liability) |
| | | MBO | management buyout |
| ECU | European Currency Unit | mfg. | manufacturing |
| | | mfr. | manufacturer |
| EEC | European Economic Community (*or* The Common Market) | NPV | net present value |
| | | NYSE | New York Stock Exchange |
| EMCOF | European Monetary Cooperation Fund | o/c | overcharge |
| | | o/d | on demand; overdraft |
| EMS | European Monetary System | O/s | out of stock |
| | | OTC | over the counter |
| e.p.s. | earnings per share | p.a. | per annum |
| ERM | Exchange Rate Mechanism | pat. | patent(ed) |
| | | P/A | power of attorney |
| EU | European Union | P/C | (Also p/c) petty cash; prices current |
| FOB | (Also f.o.b.) free on board | | |
| | | pct. | per cent |
| FRN | floating-rate note | pd. | paid |
| FX | (Also f.x.) foreign exchange | p.d. | per diem (daily) |
| | | P.O. | purchase order |
| GDP | gross domestic product | P.O.E. | port of entry |
| gds | goods | P.P. | parcel post |
| GNP | gross national product | p.t. | pro tempore |
| IBRD | International Bank for Reconstruction and Development (the World Bank) | QC | quality control |
| | | rcd. | (Also recd) received |
| | | rcpt. | (Also rept) receipt |
| | | req. | requisition; request |

| | | | |
|---|---|---|---|
| RFP | request for proposal | whs. | (Also whse.) warehouse |
| RFQ | request for quotation | whsle. | wholesale |
| ROA | return on assets | wrnt. | warrant |
| ROE | return on equity | | |
| ROI | return on investment | **Grammar, Literature,** | |
| rpt. | report; reprint | **and Writing** | |
| S.A.T. | scholastic assessment | | |
| | test | abbrev. | (Also abbr.) |
| sch. | school | | abbreviation |
| SDR | special drawing rights | adj. | adjective |
| SEC | Securities and Ex- | adv. | adverb |
| | change Commission | ant. | antonym |
| sld. | sold | Bib. | biblical |
| SOP | standard operating | clm. | column |
| | procedure | c/o | (in) care of |
| spec. | specification | conj. | conjunction |
| Sr. | Senior | Cont. | continue; continued |
| steno. | stenography | e.g. | (*exempli gratia*) for |
| St. Ex. | Stock Exchange | | example. (*ejusdem* |
| stge. | storage | | *generis*) of a like kind |
| teleg. | telegram | et. al. | (*et alia*) and others |
| tel. (no.) | telephone (number) | etc. | (*et cetera*) and other |
| telex | teleprinter exchange | | things |
| temp. | temporary (employee) | fem. | feminine |
| tfr. | transfer | ibid. | (*ibidem*) referenced in |
| TP | equity loans | | the same place |
| trans. | transaction; transfer | id. | (*idem*) the same |
| treas. | treasurer | | (reference) |
| tripl. | triplicate | i.e. | (*id est*) that is |
| UCITS | Undertakings for | interj. | interjection |
| | Collective | ital. | italics |
| | Investment in | L. | (Also Lat.) Latin |
| | Transferable | lang. | language |
| | Securities | l.c. | lower case |
| unan. | unanimous | lex. | lexicon |
| univ. | university | masc. | (Also mas.) masculine |
| W/B | waybill | MT | Machine Translation |
| w.p.m. | words per minute | n. | noun |

| | | | |
|---|---|---|---|
| n.b. | (*nota bene*) note well | var. | variant; variable |
| obj. | object(ive) | vbl. | verbal |
| objn. | objection | ver. | verse |
| o.p. | out of print | viz. | namely |
| opp. | opposite | vocab. | vocabulary |
| p. | page; paragraph; participle; part | vs. | (Also v.) versus |
| | | vv. | verbs; verses |
| phr. | phrase | v.v. | vice versa |
| pl. | plural | | |
| pp. | pages | | **General Use** |
| p.p. | past participle | | |
| pref. | prefix; preface | ABC | American-born Chinese |
| prep. | preposition | ABCs | the alphabet |
| pron. | pronoun; pronunciation | APO | Army Post Office |
| | | ASAP | as soon as possible |
| ptg. | printing | bis. | twice; encore |
| p.t.o. | please turn over | D-Day | 6 June 1944 - Allied |
| QED | (*quod erat demonstr-andum*) which was to be proven | | invasion of Europe, aka: *Disembark-ation Day*) |
| re | in reference to; revised edition | DDT | A highly toxic insecticide (dichlorodiphenyltri-chloro-ethane) |
| ref. | reference | | |
| RSVP | (*répondez s'il vous plait*) please reply | DFC | Distinguished Flying Cross |
| sic | read as it stands | DMZ | demilitarized zone |
| sing. | singular | DOA | dead on arrival |
| stet | retain; nullify correction | el. | elevated railway |
| | | ERA | Equal Rights Amendment |
| subj. | Also (sub.) subject(ive) | | |
| suf. | suffix | ESP | Extrasensory perception |
| supp. | (Also sup.) supplement(ary) | ETA | estimated time of arrival |
| | | ETD | estimated time of departure |
| sym. | symbol | | |
| syn. | synonym | ex | former husband or wife |
| u.c. | upper case | FPO | fleet post office |
| v. | (Also vb.) verb(al); versus | | |

| | | | |
|---|---|---|---|
| GI | general *or* government issue; enlisted soldier | pwr | power |
| | | qlty | quality |
| | | q.t. | quietly; in secret |
| G-man | government-man; FBI agent | qty. | quantity |
| | | R.B.I. | run(s) batted in |
| GPO | General Post Office; Government Printing Office | rel. | religion; relative(ly) |
| | | ret. | return; retired; retained |
| | | RFD | rural free delivery |
| ICBM | intercontinental ballistic missile | RIP | (*requiescat in pace*) rest in peace |
| IOU | I owe you; loan receipt | RR | railroad |
| IQ | intelligence quotient | rm. | room |
| IUD | intrauterine (contraceptive) device | rt. | right |
| | | sgd. | signed |
| | | sig. | signature; signal |
| KO | knockout | s.o.b. | son of a bitch |
| KP | kitchen patrol | sop. | soprano |
| Lib. | Liberal | SOP | standard operating procedure |
| LP | long-playing (record) | | |
| MIA | missing in action | SOS | save our souls; help! |
| MP | military police | S.R.O. | standing room only |
| mkt | market | S.S. | steamship |
| N/A | not applicable | stad. | stadium |
| n.g. | no good; not given | S.U.V. | sport utility vehicle |
| OK | okay; all correct; fine | ten. | tenor |
| P.A. | public address (system) | TKO | technical knock-out |
| | | TLC | tender loving care |
| PC | politically correct | TNT | Trinitrotoluene explosive |
| PDA | public display of affection | | |
| | | ult. | ultimate(ly) |
| PDQ | pretty damn quick; please deliver quickly; immediately | vet. | military veteran |
| | | veter. | veterinarian |
| | | VIP | very important person |
| | | W.C. | water closet; toilet |
| pkg. | also *pkge*; package | wmk. | watermark |
| POW | prisoner of war | WWI | World War I |
| PR | public relations | WWII | World War II |
| PT | patrol torpedo boat | ZPG | zero population growth |

# Chapter Ten

# ACRONYMS, ABBREVIATIONS, AND INITIALISMS IN THE COMPUTER, INTERNET AND COMMUNICATIONS INDUSTRIES

As noted earlier, the computer industry probably uses more acronyms than any other field. Since there is a huge amount of work for writers and translators in this industry, an special list of approximately 90 computer-related acronyms is supplied. The computer industry is so saturated with acronyms that there is even a title for all computer acronyms. The initialism TLA (three-letter acronyms) is often used to refer to the terms listed below, even though only slightly more than half consist of three letters.

A second list of over 100 abbreviations and initialisms is also provided. Finally a brief glossary of additional terms is given. These are commonly used short words and phrases which are not acronyms, abbreviations or intitialisms, but which might confront translators and interpreters in this field.

## ACRONYMS

| | |
|---|---|
| ALU | Arithmetic Logic Unit |
| ANSI | American National Standards Institute |
| ASCII | (Pronounced "Ass-key") American Standard Code for Information Interchange |
| | |
| BASIC | Beginner's All-purpose Symbolic Instruction Code |
| BIT | Binary digIT |
| BLOBS | Binary Large ObjectS |
| | |
| CAD | Computer Aided Design |
| CALL | Computer-Aided Learning Language |

| | |
|---|---|
| CASE | Computer Aided Software Engineering |
| CD-ROM | Compact Disc — Read Only Memory |
| CISC | Complex Instruction Set Computer |
| COBOL | COmmon Business Oriented Language |
| COM | COMmand |
| | |
| DAT | Digital AudioTape |
| DOS | Disc Operating System |
| DRAM | Dynamic Random Access Memory |
| | |
| EBCDIC | (Pronounced "Ebb-see-dick") Extended Binary Coded Decimal Interchange Code |
| EISA | Extended Industry Standard Architecture |
| E-MAIL | Electronic MAIL |
| ESDI | Enhanced Small Device Interface |
| | |
| FAQ | (Pronounced "Fack") Frequently Asked Questions |
| FLOPS | FLoating-point Operations Per Second |
| FORTRAN | FORmula plus TRANslation language |
| FUD | Fear, Uncertainty, Doubt |
| | |
| GIF | (Pronounced "Giff") Graphic Interchange Format |
| GUI | (Pronounced "Gooey") Graphical User Interface |
| | |
| IMHO | In My Humble Opinion |
| IMO | In My Opinion |
| INTERNET | INTERnational NETwork |
| ISA | Industry Standard Architecture |
| | |
| LAN | Local-Area Network |
| LAT | Lovely And Talented |
| LED | Light-Emitting Diode |
| LIM | Lotus, Intel, Microsoft (expanded memory specification) |
| LOL | Laughing Out Loud |
| | |
| MCA | Micro Channel Architecture |
| MIDI | Musical Instrument Digital Interface |

| MIME | Multiple Internet Mail Extensions |
|------|-----------------------------------|
| MIPS | Millions of Instructions Per Second |
| MIS | Manager of Information Services |
| MO | Magneto-Optical (discs) |
| MODEM | MOdulator/DEModulator |
| MOO | Multiple-Object Oriented |
| MPEG | (Pronounced "Em-peg") Moving Picture Experts Group |
| MUD | Multiple-User Dungeon |
| | |
| NASDAQ | (Pronounced "Nazz-dack") National Association of Securities Dealers Automated Quotations (system) |
| NAV | National Anti-Virus program |
| NIC | (Pronounced "Nice") Network-Interface Card |
| | |
| OLE | (Pronounced "Oh-lay") Object Linking and Embedding |
| OOP | Object-Oriented Programming |
| OTOH | On The Other Hand |
| | |
| PARC | Palo Alto Research Center |
| PIC | Personal Intelligent Communicator |
| POP | Point Of Presence |
| POS | Point Of Sale |
| POST | Power-On Self Test |
| POTS | Plain Old Telephone Service |
| | |
| QBE | (Pronounced "Cue-bee") Query By Example |
| QDOS | Quick and Dirty Operating System |
| QWERTY | (Pronounced "Kwer-tee") Standard computer keyboard (First six letters at keyboard top left spell "QWERTY") |
| | |
| RAID | Redundant Array of Inexpensive Discs |
| RAM | Random Access Memory |
| RBOC | (Pronounced "R-bock") Regional Bell Operating Company |

| | |
|---|---|
| RISC | (Pronounced "Risk") Reduced Instruction Set Computer(ing) |
| ROFL | Rolling On the Floor Laughing |
| ROM | Read-Only Memory |
| | |
| SCSI | (Pronounced "Scuzzy") Small Computer System Interface |
| SEQUEL | Standard English QUEry Language |
| SLIP | Serial Line Internet Protocol |
| SVGA | Super Video Graphics Array (also SUGA) |
| SYSOP | SYStems OPerator (ions) |
| | |
| TIFF | Tagged Image File Format |
| | |
| UI | (Pronounced "ooey") User Interface |
| URL | Uniform Resource Locator |
| | |
| VAR | Value-Added Reseller |
| VIGA | (Pronounced "Vee-ga") VIdeo Graphics Array (also VGA) |
| VRML | (Pronounced "Ver-mule") Virtual Reality Modeling Language |
| | |
| WADR | (Pronounced "Wad-R") With All Due Respect |
| WAIS | (Pronounced "Ways") Wide-Area Information Servers |
| WAN | Wide-Area Network |
| WIBNI | Wouldn't It Be Nice If... |
| WIMP | Window, Icon, Menu, Pull-Down Menu |
| WIN | WINdows |
| WOMBAT | Waste Of Money, Brains And Time |
| WORM | Write Once, Read Many |
| WYSIWYG | ("Wizz-ee-wigg") What You See Is What You Get |

## COMPUTERS, INTERNET AND COMMUNICATIONS ABBREVIATIONS AND INITIALISMS

| | |
|---|---|
| AMS | Account Management System |
| ANS | Advanced Network Services |
| AOL | America Online |
| ATM | Asynchronous Transfer Mode; Automated Teller Machine |
| ASCII | American Standard Code for Information Exchange |
| | |
| BBS | Bulletin Board System |
| BCD | Binary Coded Decimal (system) |
| BPS | Bits Per Second |
| BTW | By The Way |
| B$^2$TW | Balls To The Wall (measurement of speed) |
| | |
| CC | carbon copy |
| CCITT | Consultative Committee on International Telegraphy and Telephony |
| CD | Carrier Detect; Compact Disc |
| CD-I | Compact Disc Interactive |
| CGA | Color Graphics Adapter |
| CGI | Common Gateway Interface |
| CIS | Contact Image Sensor; Compuserve Information Service |
| CMYK | Cyan, Magenta, Yellow, blacK |
| CP/M | Control Program for Microcomputers |
| CPM | Customer Premise Management; Critical Path Method |
| CPU | Central Processing Unit |
| CRT | Cathode Ray Tube |
| | |
| DBMS | DataBase Management Systems |
| DDE | Dynamic Data Exchange |
| DES | Data Encryption Standard |
| DNS | Domain Naming System |
| DPI | Dots Per Inch |

| | |
|---|---|
| DSS | Direct Station Select; Decision Support Systems; Digital Satellite System |
| DTP | Desk Top Publishing |
| DVD | Digital Video Disk |
| | |
| EDI | Electronic Data Interchange |
| EGA | Enhanced Graphics Adapter |
| E-Mail | Electronic Mail |
| EMS | Expanded Memory Specification; Enterprise Messaging Server |
| | |
| FAQ | Frequently Asked Questions |
| FDD | Floppy Disk Drive |
| FPS | Fast Packet Switching; Frames Per Second |
| FTP | File Transfer Protocol |
| | |
| GB | Giga Bytes |
| GIF | Graphics Interchange Format |
| GIGO | Garbage In, Garbage Out |
| GPS | Global Positioning System (satellite) |
| | |
| HDTV | High Definition TeleVision |
| HTML | HyperText Markup Language |
| HTTP | HyperText Transfer Protocol |
| | |
| IDE | Integrated Drive Electronics; Integrated Development Environment |
| IEEE | Institute of Electrical and Electronic Engineers |
| IMHO | In My Humble Opinion |
| IOW | In Other Words |
| IP | Internet Protocol |
| IPO | Initial Public Offering |
| IRC | International Record Carrier; Internet Relay Chat |
| IRL | In Real Life |
| ISDN | Integrated Services Digital Network ("I Still Don't Know") |
| ISP | Internet Service Pro-vider |
| IT | Information Tech-nology |

| | |
|---|---|
| ITU | International Telecommunications Union |
| JADP | Just Another Data Point |
| JPEG | Joint Photographic Experts Group |
| KB | KiloBytes |
| LCD | Liquid Crystal Display |
| LED | Light-Emitting Diode |
| LOL | Laughing Out Loud |
| MB | MegaBytes |
| MDT | Mean Down Time |
| MHz | MegaHertz |
| MIS | Management Information System |
| MO | Magneto Optical (drive) |
| MRP | Material Requiring Planning |
| MSN | MicroSoft Network |
| MT | Machine Translation |
| NIC | Network Interface Card |
| NNTP | Network News Transfer Protocol |
| NNRP | Network News Reading Protocol |
| NSF | National Science Foundation |
| OCE | Open Collaboration Environment |
| OCR | Optical Character Recognition (Reader); Outgoing Call Restriction |
| OCS | Optical Character Scanner |
| OEM | Original Equipment Manufacturer; Operations Enterprise Model |
| OOC | Out of Character |
| OOP | Object-Oriented Programming |
| PC | Personal Computer; Peg Count; Printed Circuit |
| PCI | Peripheral Component Interconnect |
| PCMCIA | Personal Computer Memory Card International Association |

| | |
|---|---|
| PDA | Personal Digital Assistant |
| PGP | Pretty Good Privacy |
| PKZIP | A file compression program |
| PNG | Portable Network Graphics |
| POP | Post Office Protocol |
| POS(T) | Point-of-Sale (Terminal) |
| PPP | Point-To-Point Protocol |
| | |
| RBOC | Regional Bell Operating Company |
| RDBMS | Relational DataBase Management System |
| RGB | Red, Green, Blue |
| RL | Real Life |
| ROTFL | Rolling On The Floor Laughing |
| RR | Road Runner |
| RSI | Repetitive Strain Injury |
| RTFM | Read The Fucking Manual |
| | |
| SDLC | Synchronous Data Link Control |
| SGML | Standard Generalized Markup Language |
| SMTP | Simple Mail Transfer Protocol |
| SQL | Structured Query Language |
| SSL | Secure Sockets Layer |
| | |
| TB | Tera Bytes |
| TCP/IP | Transmission Control Protocol/Internet Protocol |
| 3-D | Three-Dimensional (spreadsheets) |
| TLA | Three-Letter Acronym |
| TMOT | Trust Me On This |
| TPTB | The Powers That Be |
| TTYTT | To Tell You The Truth |
| | |
| UI | (pronounced "ooey") User Interface |
| URL | Uniform Resource Locator |
| | |
| VAR | Value-Added Re-seller |
| | |
| W3C | World Wide Web Consortium |
| WTFIGO | What The Fuck Is Going On |

XGA          eXtended Graphics Array

XLBR        Chinese word-processing software
XML          Extensible Markup Language
XMS          eXtended Memory Specification

YOYOW     You Own Your Own Words
Y2K          2000 A.D.


## GLOSSARY OF SPECIAL TERMS

BAND WIDTH    Capacity of Internet transmission lines to carry
                       electronic traffic.

BROWSER         Software which enables browsing on the world
                       wide web.

COAX TV
    CABLE      Coaxial cables with enough capacity to enable
                       wide band width transmission over
                       extended distances.

CYBERSPACE    The entire universe of all interconnected
                       computers.

DOMAIN NAME  Name registered as an Internet address.

DOWNLOAD    Transferring computer information from other
                       computers to your own.

E-MAIL           Internet transmitted messages between
                       computer users

FAVORITE
    FOLDER     A storage area for most frequently used Web
                       pages and addresses.

HEADEND        Centralized equipment in the main office of
                       the cable service provider, where cable
                       signals are received and/or sent.

HUB              A connecting device for attaching multiple cables to the modem.

HYPERTEXT    Documentary text with links which enable rapid jumps to connect with other textual material.

INTERNET     A system of interconnected networks for use in computer communications worldwide.

IP ADDRESS  An Internet address equivalent to a Domain Name, but expressed by a four-part number separated by dots. (All Internet computers have an IP address.)

JAVA          A programming language which permits games, animation and other computer applications to be transferred between computer stations on the world wide web.

NETIQUETTE  Internet etiquette.

NEWSGROUP  A community public bulletin board which permits Internet users to post messages electronically.

SEARCH
   ENGINE     An Internet system which enables you to search for and find specific subject matter by entering key words. The search engine then provides a list of areas and IP addresses which include the key words.

SUBNET       A network subdivision, enabling rapid connection to a subset within an IP address.

SURF THE NET  To browse through multiple Internet information sources, using browser software.

USENET       An electronic bulletin board (see NEWSGROUP).

# Chapter Eleven

# THE BIRDS AND THE TREES

The following are lists dealing with the vocabulary of nature, colors and baby talk in English and in some foreign languages. As with previous sections, no claim is being made that the lists are all-inclusive. Only four European languages and two Asian languages are included. The list of animal groupings, on the other hand, is perhaps too complete. Many of the terms are today rarely used. They harken back to times when America and England were almost totally agricultural societies.

Regarding animal sounds, there is a basic problem in transliteration between the sounds we actually hear and the letters we put on paper. Perhaps this is the reason that there is not too much in the library covering this area. It is certainly the reason that animals seem to be sounding off or speaking different languages in different countries. The author finds this thought amusing.

The author and various contributors have done their best to provide an accurate replica of the precise sounds, but as in so many areas in translation, judgment must be exercised. (Reader corrections or additions to the following tables are welcome.)

The point was made in the introduction that words and phrases in this book add spice to the American Language. Nowhere is this more true than in this section. We hope that all those interested in the American Language will find this chapter entertaining and enlightening.

## ANIMAL KINGDOM TERMINOLOGY

| GENERAL NAME | MALE | FEMALE | OFFSPRING | GROUP |
|---|---|---|---|---|
| **bear** | bear | she-bear | cub | sloth |
| **bird** | male bird | female bird | chick | flock; (*in air*) flight |
| **cat** | tom | kitty; cat | kitten | (*newborn*) litter; kindle |
| **chicken** | rooster; cock; (*castrated*) capon | hen | chick | brood |
| **cow** | (*breeding*) bull; (*castrated*) ox | cow | calf | herd |
| **deer** | buck; hart; stag | doe; hind | fawn; calf | herd; (*female*) bevy |
| **dog** | dog | bitch | puppy | pack |

## ANIMAL KINGDOM TERMINOLOGY
### (Continued)

| GENERAL NAME | MALE | FEMALE | OFFSPRING | GROUP |
|---|---|---|---|---|
| duck | drake | duck | duckling | (on water) paddling |
| elephant | bull | cow | calf | herd |
| fish | male fish | female fish | | school; shoal |
| fox | fox | vixen; bitch | cub | skulk |
| goat | billy goat | nanny goat | kid | flock; herd |
| goose | gander | goose | gosling | gaggle; (in air) skein |
| horse | stallion; (castrated) gelding | mare | foal; (male) colt; (female) filly | herd |
| lion | lion | lioness | cub | pride |

## ANIMAL KINGDOM TERMINOLOGY
(Continued)

| GENERAL NAME | MALE | FEMALE | CHILD | GROUP |
|---|---|---|---|---|
| peacock | peacock | peahen | chick | muster; ostentation |
| pheasant | grouse | hen | chick | nide |
| pig (hog; swine) | boar | sow | piglet | herd |
| sheep | ram | ewe | lamb | flock |
| swan | cob | pen | cygnet | wedge |
| tiger | tiger | tigress | cub | (newborn) litter* |
| turkey | turkey-cock | turkey-hen | chick; poult | flock |
| whale | bull | cow | calf | school; herd; pod; gam |
| wolf | wolf | bitch | cub | pack |

* Tigers are solitary creatures, thus no term for a group exists

## ADDITIONAL ANIMAL GROUPS

| Animal | Group | Animal | Group |
|---|---|---|---|
| ant | swarm; colony | jay | party |
| antelope | herd | jellyfish | smack |
| badger | cete | kangaroo | troop |
| bee | swarm | lark | bevy |
| boar | | mallard | sord |
| buffalo | herd | mole | labor |
| coot | covert | monkey (ape) | shrewdness |
| elk | herd | moose | herd; gang |
| game bird | covey | nightingale | watch |
| hawk | cast | owl | parliament |
| insect | swarm | parrot | company |

## ADDITIONAL ANIMAL GROUPS

| Animal | Group | Animal | Group |
|---|---|---|---|
| penguin | colony | sparrow | host |
| plover | congregation | squirrel | dray |
| pony | string | starling | murmuration |
| porpoise | shoal | stork | mustering |
| quail | bevy | teal | spring |
| rabbit | warren | turtledove | pittying |
| raven | unkindness | wasp | swarm |
| rhinoceros | crash | woodcock | fall |
| seal | pod | woodpecker | descent |
| snipe | wisp | zebra | herd |

| ANIMAL SOUNDS (English) | | |
|---|---|---|
| **Animal** | **Sound (v)** | **Rendition** |
| **bird** | sing; chirp | tweet-tweet; chirp-chirp; cheep-cheep |
| **nightingale** | warble | |
| **crow** | caw | caw-caw |
| **owl** | hoot | whoo |
| **cat** | meow | meow |
| **chicken** | cluck | cluck-cluck |
| **rooster** | crow | cock-a-doodle-doo |
| **hen** | cluck;cackle | cluck-cluck |
| **chick** | peep | peep-peep |
| **cow** | low | moo |
| **bull** | bellow | |
| **dog** | bark | bow-wow; woof; arf |
| **dove** | coo | cooo |
| **duck** | quack | quack-quack |
| **goose** | honk | honk-honk |
| **goat** | bleat | nyaaah |
| **horse** | neigh; whinny | nyaaay |
| **lion** | roar | rooaaar |
| **pig** | squeal; oink | oink-oink |
| **sheep** | bleat | baaa; baa-baa |
| **swan** | trumpet | wooo |
| **turkey** | gobble | gobble-gobble |

| ANIMAL SOUNDS (Foreign Languages) | | | | | | |
|---|---|---|---|---|---|---|
| Animal | French | Spanish | German | Japanese | Korean | Chinese |
| bird | cui-cui | pio-pio | tschirp-tschirp | chun-chun chi-chi | chaek-chaek | jio-jio jiji |
| crow | croâ croâ | | krah-krah | kâ -kâ | kak-kak | ya-ya-ya |
| owl | | | uhhuhh-uhhuhh | hô-hô | boo-ung boo-ung | g-ru, g-ru |
| cat | miaou | miau | miau | nyâ-o; nyâ-nyâ; (*purr*) goro-goro | yaong-yaong | meow |
| chicken rooster hen chick | cocorico piou-piou | ki-kiri-ki cloc-cloc pio-pio | kickeriki gag-gag piep-piep | kokekokkô kokekokkô piyo-piyo | kokodaek kokodaek piyak-piak | gu-gu-gu go-go-ge jio-jio |
| cow | meuh | mu | muh | mô-mô | eummae-eummae | moo |
| dog | ouah-ouah | guau-guau | wau-wau | wan-wan; kyan-kyan | meong-meong | wong-wong |
| dove | roucrou-roucrou | mnn-cucurucu | rugedigu | kukkû-kukkû | goo-goo | ku-ku-ku |
| duck | coin-coin | cua-cua | quak-quak | gâ-gâ | quak-quak | gâ-gâ |

## ANIMAL SOUNDS
### (Foreign Languages - Continued)

| Animal | French | Spanish | German | Japanese | Korean | Chinese |
|---|---|---|---|---|---|---|
| goose | can-can | ohn-ohn | gwag-gwag | | | goâ-goâ |
| goat | behh | beee | määh | mê-mê | mem-mem | naaa |
| horse | hihihi-hahaha | hiiiii | wihii | hi-hin | hihing-hihing | si-si-si |
| lion | rroarrr-oarrr | grrr | grraauu | ga-ô | euheung | hao-u |
| pig | grroank | no-no | grunz-grunz | boo-boo | kul-kul | gon-gon |
| sheep | meh | beee | määh | mê-mê | mem-mem | mei-mei |
| turkey | glou-glou | | gluck-gluck | | | |

## FLOWERS

| English | French | German | Italian | Spanish | Chinese | Japanese |
|---|---|---|---|---|---|---|
| anemone | anémone | Anemone | anemone | anémona | 秋牡丹 | アネモネ |
| azalea | azalée | Azalee | azalea | azalea | 杜鵑花 | ツツジ |
| bougain-villea | Bougain-villée | Bougainvillea | buganvillea | buganvilla | 九重葛 | ブーゲンビリヤ |
| crocus | crocus; safran | Krokus | croco | azafrán | 番紅花 | クロッカス |
| daffodil | narcisse des bois | Narzisse | trombone; giunchiglia | narciso atrompetado | 黄水仙 | ラッパスイセン |
| daisy | marguerite | Gänseblümchen | margherita | margarita | 雛菊 | ヒナギク |
| dandelion | pissenlit | Löwenzahn | dente di leone | diente de león | 蒲公英 | タンポポ |
| dogwood | cornouiller | Hartriegel; Hornstrauch | sanguinella | cornejo | 山茱萸 | ハナミズキ |

**FLOWERS**
(Continued)

| English | French | German | Italian | Spanish | Chinese | Japanese |
|---|---|---|---|---|---|---|
| geranium | géranium | Geranie | geranio | geranio | 天竺葵 | ゼラニウム |
| hibiscus | hibiscus | Hibiskus; Eibisch | ibisco | hibisco | 芙蓉 | ハイビスカス |
| hyacinth | jacinthe | Hyazinthe | giancinto | jacinto | 風信子 | ヒヤシンス |
| hydrangea | hortensia | Hortensie | ortensia | hortensia | 繡球花 | アジサイ |
| jasmine | jasmin | Jasmin | geisomino | jazmín | 茉莉花 | ジャスミン |
| lilac | lilas | Flieder | lilla | lila | 紫丁香 | ライラック |
| lily of the valley | muguet | Maiglöckchen | giglio | lirio | 百合 | ユリ |
| narcissus | narcisse | Narzisse | narciso | narciso | 水仙花 | 水仙 |

**FLOWERS**
(Continued)

| English | French | German | Italian | Spanish | Chinese | Japanese |
|---------|--------|--------|---------|---------|---------|----------|
| pansy | pensée | Stiefmütter- chen | viola del pensiero | pensamiento | 三色紫羅蘭 | パンジー |
| pinks (carnation) | oeillet (incarnat) | Gartennelke; Nelke | garofano | clavel; clavellina | 石竹 | ナデシコ |
| rose | rose | Rose | rosa | rosa | 玫瑰 | バラ |
| snapdragon | muflier; gueule-de-loup | Löwenmaul | bocca di leone | conejito; boca de dragón | 金魚草 | キンギョソウ |
| sunflower | tournesol; soleil | Sonnenblume | girasole | girasol; mirasol | 向日葵 | ヒマワリ |
| sweetpea | pois de senteur | Gartenwicke | pisello odoroso | guisante de olor | 香豌豆花 | スイートピー |
| tulip | tulipe | Tulpe | tulipano | tulipán | 鬱金香 | チューリッツ |

## BIRDS

| English | French | German | Italian | Spanish | Chinese | Japanese |
|---|---|---|---|---|---|---|
| blackbird | merle | Amsel | merlo | mirlo | 燕八哥 | ムクドリモドキ |
| canary | canari | Kanarien-vogel | canarino | canario | 金絲雀 | カナリヤ |
| crow | corneille | Krähe | cornacchia | cuervo | 烏鴉 | カラス |
| cuckoo | coucou | Kuckuck | cucu; cucolu | cuco | 布穀鳥 | カッコウ |
| dove | colombe | Taube | columbo(a) | paloma; pichón | 鴿子 | ハト |
| eagle | aigle | Adler | aquila | águila | 老鷹 | ワシ |
| finch | pinson | Fink | fringuèllo | pinzón | 金翅雀 | アトリ科の小鳥 |
| gull (seagull) | mouette; gogo | Möwe | gabbiano | gaviota | 海鷗 | カモメ |
| hawk (falcon) | faucon | Habicht | falco | halcón | 鷹 | タカ |

## BIRDS
(Continued)

| English | French | German | Italian | Spanish | Chinese | Japanese |
|---|---|---|---|---|---|---|
| humming-bird | oiseau-mouche colibri | Kolibri | colibri | colibrí | 蜂鳥 | 蜂鳥 |
| jay (magpie) | (*jay*) geai; (*magpie*) pie | Elster | ghiandaia | arrendajo | 鴬鵲 | カケス |
| mocking-bird | moqueur | Spott-drossel | mimo poliglotta | sinsonte | 模仿鳥 | マネシツグミ |
| owl | hibou | Eule | gufo | búho; lechuza | 貓頭鷹 | フクロウ |
| parakeet | perruche | Sittich | parracchetto | periquito; perico | 鸚哥 | インコ |
| parrot | perroquet | Papagei | pappagallo | papagayo; loro; cotorra | 鸚鵡 | オウム |
| pigeon | pigeon | Taube | piccione | paloma | 鴿子 | ハト |
| raven | corbeau | Rabe | corvo | cuervo | 大烏鴉 | ワタリガラス |

**BIRDS**
(Continued)

| English | French | German | Italian | Spanish | Chinese | Japanese |
|---|---|---|---|---|---|---|
| robin | rouge-gorge | Rotkehlchen | pettiroso | petirrojo | 知更鳥 | コマドリ |
| sparrow | moineau | Sperling | passero | gorrión | 麻雀 | スズメ |
| swallow | hirondelle | Schwalbe | rondine | golondrina | 燕子 | ツバメ |
| tanager | tangara | Tangara; Tanagra | tanagra | tanagra | 鶏 | フウキンチョウ |
| thrush | grive | Drossel | tórdo | zorzal | 鶫 | ツグミ |
| vulture | vautour | Geier | avvoltoio | buitre | 禿鷹 | ハゲタカ |
| warbler | fauvette | Grassmücke | canterino | silvido; curruca | 刺嘴鶯 | 鳴鳥(めいちょう) |
| woodpecker | pic; pivert | Specht | picchio | pájaro carpintero | 啄木鳥 | キツツキ |
| wren | roitelet | Zaunkönig | scricciolo | reyezuelo | 鷦鷯 | ミソサザイ |

## FISH

| English | French | German | Italian | Spanish | Chinese | Japanese |
|---------|--------|--------|---------|---------|---------|----------|
| bass (sea bass) | bar; loup de mer | Barsch | pesce persico (spigola) | róbalo | 鱸魚 | スズキ |
| bluefish | tassergal | Blaufisch | pesce serra | pomátomo | 綠鱈 | アミキリ |
| carp | carpe | Karpfen | carpa | carpa | 鯉魚 | 鯉 |
| catfish | poisson-chat | Wels | pesce gatto | bagre | 鯰魚 | ナマズ |
| cod | cabillaud; morue | Kabeljau | merluzzo | bacalao | 鱈魚 | タラ |
| eel | anguille | Aal | anguilla | anguila | 鰻魚 | ウナギ |
| flounder | flet | Flunder | passera de mar | platija; lenguado | 比目魚 | カレイ |

## FISH
(Continued)

| English | French | German | Italian | Spanish | Chinese | Japanese |
|---|---|---|---|---|---|---|
| herring | hareng | Hering | aringa | arenque | 鯡魚 | ニシン |
| mackerel | maquereau | Makrele | sgombro | caballa | 鯖魚 | サバ |
| pike | brochet | Hecht | luccio | lucio | 梭子魚 | カワカマス |
| pompano | pompano | Pompano | | pámpano; pampanito | 鯧魚 | コバンアジ |
| salmon | saumon | Lachs | salmone | salmón | 鮭魚 | 鮭 |
| sardine | sardine | Sardine | sardina | sardina | 沙丁魚 | イワシ |
| smelt | éperlan | Stint | sperlano | eperlano | 胡瓜魚 | シシャモ |

## FISH
(Continued)

| English | French | German | Italian | Spanish | Chinese | Japanese |
|---------|--------|--------|---------|---------|---------|----------|
| snapper (red snapper) | lutjanidé (vivaneau) | Schnapper | pesce ballerino | cubera; pargo | 真鯛 | フエダイ |
| sole | sole | Seezunge | sogliola | lenguado | 鯷 | シタビラメ |
| sturgeon | esturgeon | Stör | storione | esturion | 鱘魚 | チョウザメ |
| swordfish | espadon | Schwertfisch | pesce spada | pez espada | 劍魚 | メカジキ |
| trout | truite | Forelle | trota | trucha | 鱒魚 | マス |
| tuna | thon | Thunfisch | tonno | atún | 鮪魚 | マグロ |
| turbot | turbot | Steinbutt | rómbo gigante | rodaballo | 菱魚 | ホシダルマガレイ |

## TREES

| English | French | German | Italian | Spanish | Chinese | Japanese |
|---|---|---|---|---|---|---|
| apple | pommier | Apfel | melo | manzano | 蘋果 | リンゴの木 |
| beech | hêtre | Buche | faggio | haya | 山毛棒 | ブナ |
| birch | bouleau | Birke | betulla | abedul | 樺樹 | シラカバ |
| cedar | cèdre | Zeder | cedro | cedro | 杉樹 | ヒマラヤスギ |
| cherry | cerisier | Kirschbaum | ciliegio | cerezo | 樱桃 | サクラ |
| chestnut | châtaignier; marronier | Kastanienbaum | castagno | castaño | 栗樹 | クリの木 |
| elm | orme | Ulme | olmo | olmo | 榆樹 | ニレ |
| fir | sapin | Fichte | abete | abeto | 冷杉 | モミ |
| hickory | hickory; noyer-blanc | Hickorybaum | hickory | nopal americano | 山核桃 | ヒッコリー |
| mahogany | acajou | Mahagani | mogano | caoba | 紅木 | マホガニー |
| maple | érable | Ahorn | acero | arce | 楓樹 | カエデ |

## TREES
(Continued)

| English | French | German | Italian | Spanish | Chinese | Japanese |
|---|---|---|---|---|---|---|
| oak | chêne | Eiche | quercia | roble | 橡樹 | オーク |
| pecan | pacanier | Pecanbaum | noce americano | pacana | 美洲山核桃 | ペカン |
| pine | pin | Fichte | pino | pino | 松樹 | マツ |
| poplar | peuplier | Pappel | pioppo | alamo | 白楊樹 | ポプラ |
| redwood | sequoia | Redwood | sequoia | secoya | 紅杉樹 | セコイア |
| walnut | noyer | Walnuss | noce | nogal | 胡桃樹 | クルミの木 |
| willow | saule | Weide | salice | sauce | 柳樹 | ヤナギ |
| yew | if | Eibe | tasso | tejo | 紫杉樹 | イチイ |

# COLORS – COULEURS – COLORES – FARBEN

Translation of words for different colors presents another challenge to T & I professionals. This is an area which, at first sight, appears relatively simple, i.e. until you delve further into the problem. It seems simple because all languages have words for the primary languages – red, yellow, green and blue – and for the achromatic pair, black and white. All other colors result from blending these, either as pigments or a light wavelengths.

Primary blends, such as orange, purple, pink and brown, as well as grey (gray) achieved by blending black and white, also provide few translation difficulties. These too are recognized in virtually all languages. Were these all the colors translators had to deal with, life would be simple. However, the U.S. National Bureau of Standards system for defining colors recognizes 267 different colors, shades and hues. Translating most of these is not so simple.

Let us start with one sub-category, color names, which in English do not include the basic color as part of the name. Nor are they directly connected with the colors of fruits, flowers, metals, etc. Some of these specialized color words are aquamarine, crimson, cyan, magenta, mauve, and taupe. Since most of these terms were derived from Romance languages or from Latin, direct translations are usually available into the FIGS languages. For example, aquamarine is *aguamarina* in Spanish; magenta is *magenta* in French and *magenta* in Spanish; crimson is *cramoisi* in French, *carmesí* in Spanish and *karmasin* in Italian. Other languages, particularly those of the Far East, do not find such obvious translations easily available.

Another category which provides problems consists of colors of fruits, vegetables and other foods. The color of metals such as brass or of animals, such as the fawn, also fit into this group. In English you can say orange-colored or plum-colored, but are more likely to economize on words and just say orange or plum. That is not necessarily true in other languages. In Spanish, for example, the orange fruit is called *naranja*, but the color orange is more likely expressed as *anaranjado* or *naranjado*. Sometimes, alternative translations are acceptable. A case in point – in German, cream or cream colored can be translated as *cremefarben* or simply as *creme*. There are no rules, and most dictionaries are of little help. They frequently do not distinguish between the fruit as a noun or its color as an adjective, leaving the translator to wonder what is the *mot juste*. To complicate matters, there exist some English words directly referring to fruit colors, but different from the words for the fruit itself. Cerise, for instance, means cherry red, which is identical to its German translation *Kirschrot*. Lacking a precise term in the target language, one could always use a literal translation, e.g. the "color of persimmon," but this would be inelegant.

Then there is another problem. Colors referring to bodily appearances are frequently different than the same or similar colors describing paint or cloth. In English we use the word *tan* for both the color of the sunbather's skin and for the color of his or her clothes. Not so with many other languages. The color of a Spanish woman's tan skirt would be *café claro* but, if she tans at the beach, her skin color is described as *bronceado*. Hair colors too provide many distinctions; these will be described later. Finally, there are those composite color terms, e.g. powder blue, emerald green and brick red, or confusing ones such as baby blue. Do exact translations exist?

Further complicating your translation is the fact that many colors are preceded by modifiers such as *light, medium, dark* or *very dark*. Or, there are variants such as *brilliant, pale* or *strong*, all of which can sometimes be translated literally, but sometimes cannot. Are there equivalent words in the target language for *grayish, yellowish* or *purplish*? Maybe.

Do you still think that accurately translating color terms is simple? Perhaps the following tables may be of some help, but note that even these are missing translations for colors such as Apricot, Avocado, Burlap, Cranberry, Cyan, Heather, Persimmon, Putty and Topaz.

| COLOR | FRENCH | SPANISH | ITALIAN | GERMAN | JAPANESE | CHINESE |
|---|---|---|---|---|---|---|
| AQUAMARINE | Aigue-marine | Aguamarina | Acquamarina | Aquamarin | 淡青碧色 | 杏黄色 |
| BLACK | Noir(e) | Negro(a) | Nero(a) | Schwarz | 黒 | 黑色 |
| BLUE | Bleu(e) | Azul | Azzuro; Blu | Blau | 青 | 藍色 |
| Baby BLUE | Bleu clair | Celeste | Celeste | Babyblau | 水色；空色 | 嬰兒藍 |
| Cobalt BLUE | Bleu de cobalt | Azul de cobalto | Blu cobalto | Kobaltblau | コバルトブルー | 鈷藍 |
| Navy BLUE | Bleu marine | Marino (de mar) | Blu scuro | Marineblau | 紺 | 藏青色 |
| Powder BLUE | Bleu pastel | Azul claro | Grigio azzuro | Taubenblau | 淡青灰色 | 粉藍色 |
| Sky BLUE | Bleu ciel; Azur | Celeste; Azul de cielo | Celeste | Himmelblau | 空色；水色 | 天藍色 |

| *COLOR* | FRENCH | SPANISH | ITALIAN | GERMAN | JAPANESE | CHINESE |
|---|---|---|---|---|---|---|
| BONE | | De color hueso | Color osso | Eierschalenfarbig | 骨白色 | 骨白色 |
| BRONZE | Couleur de bronze; Bronze | Color de bronce | Bronzeo(a) | Bronze | ブロンズ色 | 古銅色 |
| BROWN | Marron | Color de café; Marrón | Marrone | Braun | 茶色 | 棕色 |
| BURGUNDY | Lie-de-vin | Color de vino | Rosso vino | Burgundrot | | 紫紅色 |
| CARROT | Carotte | Color zanahoria | Color carota | Karottengelb | | 胡蘿蔔色 |
| CERISE | Cerise | Color de cereza | Rosso ciliegia | Kirschrot | サクランボ色 | 鮮紅色 |
| CHALK | Crayeux | Color de tiza | Bianco gesso | kreidefarben | 白亜色 | 白堊色 |

| COLOR | FRENCH | SPANISH | ITALIAN | GERMAN | JAPANESE | CHINESE |
|---|---|---|---|---|---|---|
| **CHARCOAL** | Charbon gris; Gris anthracite; Gris foncé | Gris marengo | Grigio scuro | Schwarzgrau | チャコールグレー | 碳黑色 |
| **CHARTREUSE** | Chartreuse | Amarillo verdoso | Verde pallido | Chartreuxgrau | 黄色がかった薄緑色 | 蘋果綠色 |
| **CHOCOLATE** | Chocolat | Chocolate | Cioccolato | Schokoladen-braun | チョコレート色 | 深褐色 |
| **COPPER** | Cuivré | Cobrizo(a) | Ramato(a); Rame | Kupferrot | 銅色 | 紫銅色 |
| **CREAM** | Crème | Color crema | Panna | Cremefarben; Creme | クリーム色 | 奶油色 |
| **CRIMSON** | Cramoisi | Carmesi | Cremisi | Purpurn; Purpurrot | えんじ色 | 深紅色 |
| **ECRU** | Ecru | Color crudo | Ecru | Naturfarben, ekrü | 淡褐色 | 淡褐色 |
| **FAWN** | Fauve | Pardo; De cervato | Marroncino(a) | Beige | 淡黄褐色 | 淡黄褐色 |

| COLOR | FRENCH | SPANISH | ITALIAN | GERMAN | JAPANESE | CHINESE |
|-------|--------|---------|---------|--------|----------|---------|
| FLESH | Couleur chair; Carnation | Color de cutis | Color carne | Hautfarben | 肌色 | 肉色 |
| FUCHSIA | Fuchsia | Fuscia | Fucsia | Fuchsienrot | 赤紫色 | 紫紅色 |
| GINGER | Dans les tons roux | | Fulvo | Kupferrot (hair only) | しょうが色 | 薑黄色 |
| GOLD | D'or; Doré | Dorado | Dorato(a) | Gold, golden | 金色 | 金色 |
| GREEN | Vert | Verde | Verde | Grün | 綠 | 綠色 |
| Blue-GREEN | Bleu-vert | Azul verdoso | Verde blu | Blaugrün | 青緑色 | 藍綠色 |
| Emerald GREEN | Émeraude | Esmeralda | Verde smeraldo | Smaragdgrün | エメラルドグリーン | 翡翠綠 |

| COLOR | FRENCH | SPANISH | ITALIAN | GERMAN | JAPANESE | CHINESE |
|---|---|---|---|---|---|---|
| Olive GREEN | Vert olive; Olive | Verde oliva | Verde oliva | Olivgrün | | 橄欖綠 |
| Sage (GREEN) | Vert cendré | Verde salvia; Verde seco | Verde salvia | Graugrün | 灰緑色 | 灰綠色 |
| Sea GREEN | Glauque | Verde mar | Verde mare | Meergrün | 海緑色 | 海綠色 |
| GREY (GRAY) | Gris | Gris | Grigio | Grau | 灰色 | 灰色 |
| HONEY | Couleur de miel | Color de miel | Color miele | Honigfarben | 蜂蜜色 | 蜜黃色 |
| INDIGO | Indigo | Añil | Indaco | Indigo | 藍色 | 靛藍色 |
| IVORY | Ivoire | Color marfil | Avorio | Elfenbeinfarben | アイボリー | 乳白色 |
| KHAKI | Kaki | Caqui | Cachi | K(h)akibraun; K(h)akifarben | カーキ色 | 土黃色 |

| COLOR | FRENCH | SPANISH | ITALIAN | GERMAN | JAPANESE | CHINESE |
|---|---|---|---|---|---|---|
| LILAC | Couleur de lilas | De color de lila | Lilla | Fliederfarben, zartlila | ライラック色 | 淡紫色 |
| MAGENTA | Magenta | Color magenta | Magenta | Magenta, tiefrot | 紫紅色 | 品紅色 |
| MAROON | Bordeau | Color de vino | Bordeau | Kastanienbraun; Rötlichbraun | 栗色 | 紫醬色 |
| MAUVE | Mauve | Malva | Malva | Malvenfarben; mauve | 藤色 | 淡紫色 |
| OATMEAL | Beige; Grège | Avena | Beige | Hellbeige | 灰色がかった黄色 | 米灰色 |
| OCHRE (OCHER) | Ocre | Ocre | Ocra | Ockerfarben | 黄土色 | 黄褐色 |
| ORANGE | Orange; Orangé | Anaranjado(a) | Arancione | Orange | だいだい色 | 橘黄色 |

| COLOR | FRENCH | SPANISH | ITALIAN | GERMAN | JAPANESE | CHINESE |
|---|---|---|---|---|---|---|
| PEACH | Pêche; De pêche | Color de melocotón | Pesca | Pfirschfarben | ピーチ色 | 桃色 |
| PEARL | Nacré | Nacarado(a) | Grigio perla | Grauweiß; perlmuttfarben | 真珠色 | 藍灰色 |
| PINK | Rose | Rosa | Rosa | Rosa; rosafarben; rosarot; pink | ピンク色 | 粉紅色 |
| PLUM | Prune; Lie-de-vin | Color ciruela | Prugna | Pflaumenblau | 暗紫色 | 紫紅色 |
| PUCE | Puce | Color pardo rojizo | Color pulce | Braunrot | 暗褐色 | 紫褐色 |
| PURPLE | Violet | Purpureo; Morado | Viola | Purpurn; violett | 紫色 | 紫色 |
| RED | Rouge | Rojo; Pelirrojo(a) | Rosso | Rot | 赤 | 紅色 |
| Brick RED | Brique | Color ladrillo | Rosso mattone | Ziegelrot | 赤煉瓦色 | 褐紅色 |

| COLOR | FRENCH | SPANISH | ITALIAN | GERMAN | JAPANESE | CHINESE |
|-------|--------|---------|---------|--------|----------|---------|
| Ruby RED | Couleur rubis | Color rubí | Rosso rubino | Rubinrot | ルビー色 | 深紅色 |
| ROSE | Couleur de rose; Rose | Rosa | Rosa | Rosarot; Rosenrot | ばら色 | 玫瑰紅 |
| SALT & PEPPER | Chiné noir | | Sale e pepe | Pfeffer-und-Salz | 胡麻塩 | 黑白混合 |
| SAND | Couleur de sable | Color de arena | Color sabbia | Sandfarben | 砂色 | 沙土色 |
| SILVER | Argenté | Plateado(a) | Argenteo(a) | Silber | 銀色 | 銀白色 |
| STRAW | Paille | Color de paja; Pajizo | Color paglia | Strohblond (hair only) | わら色 | 淡黄色 |
| TAN | Brun roux; Doré | Marrón; Café claro | Marrone chiaro | Hellbraun | 黄褐色 | 棕褐色 |

| COLOR | FRENCH | SPANISH | ITALIAN | GERMAN | JAPANESE | CHINESE |
|---|---|---|---|---|---|---|
| Sun TAN | Bronzée | Bronceado | Abbronzato | Sonnenbräune | 小麦色 | 棕褐色 |
| TANGERINE | Mandarine | Mandarina | Mandarino (arancione) | Stark orange; Rötlich orange | 蜜柑色 | 橘紅色 |
| TAUPE | Taupe | Gris oscuro | Grigio talpa | Taupe, braungrau | 褐色がかった濃暗灰色 | 褐灰色 |
| TURQUOISE | Turquoise | Turquesa | Turchese | Türkis | 青緑色 | 青綠色 |
| VERMILION | Vermillon | Bermellón; De color rojo vivo | Vermiglio | Zinnoberrot | 朱色 | 朱紅色 |
| VIOLET | Violet | Violeta | Viola | Violett | すみれ色 | 紫色 |

| COLOR | FRENCH | SPANISH | ITALIAN | GERMAN | JAPANESE | CHINESE |
|---|---|---|---|---|---|---|
| WATER-MELON | Couleur de Pastèque | Color de sandía | Rosso anguria | Wassermelon-enfarben | ピンクがかった赤 | 淡紅色 |
| WHITE | Blanc | Blanco(a) | Bianco | Weiß | 白 | 白色 |
| Off-WHITE | Blanc cassé | Blanquecino(a); De color hueso | Bianco sporco | Gebrochen-weiß | オフホワイト | 灰白色 |
| WINE | Lie-de-vin | Color de vino | Color vino | Burgund | ワインカラー | 深紅色 |
| YELLOW | Jaune | Amarillo | Giallo(a) | Gelb | 黄色 | 黄色 |
| Lemon YELLOW | Jaune de citron | Amarillo limón | Giallo limone | Zitronengelb | レモン色 | 檸檬色 |

## FOOTNOTE ON COLORS

There is another fascinating aspect of translating and interpreting colors, namely the use of colors to designate pornographic material or sexual hoopla. In the United States and the United Kingdom, the use of the color *blue* is associated with obscene and pornographic material, or unacceptable behavior. We have *blue movies* to indicate X-rated cinema and *blue laws* involving what activities are allowed and what stores may be open on Sundays and high holidays. Boston and Scotland were once famous for their blue laws.

In most Spanish speaking countries, however, the color *green* is associated with such actions. A popular Spanish expression is *un viejo verde*, which literally translates as *a green man*. A more accurate translation into English would be *a dirty old man*. In Mexico, the pornographic color is *red*, so the expression would be *un viejo rojo*.

In Japan, *pink* is the controlling color for actions verging on the pornographic. A well known (and very entertaining) book on the history and culture of Japanese sexual mores is entitled *The Pink Samurai*.

## HAIR COLORATION

Don't ask why, but, unlike in English, color names for hair in many languages are different from names for the same colors used to describe other items. In English there are names like *blond, brunette* and *strawberry blond*. Otherwise, standard color terms are used for hair color, though we might combine words, as in *redhead*, or use nicknames such as *blondy* or *gingey*. Of course, as with the other color words, just to keep Translators busy, there are modifiers such as *light* and *dark* and, naturally, *bleached*. As you can see from the following table, when it comes to hair colors, foreign languages seem to have many more specialized words:

| HAIR COLOR | FRENCH | SPANISH | ITALIAN | GERMAN | JAPANESE | CHINESE |
|---|---|---|---|---|---|---|
| AUBURN | Châtain roux | Castaño rojizo | Ramato(a); Color rame | Rotbraun; rostrot | とび色 | 茶褐色 |
| BLOND | Blond(e) | Blondo(a); Rubio(a) | Biondo(a) | Blondine (person); Blond (hair color) | 金髪 | 金黄色 |
| Platinum BLOND | Blond(e) platiné(e) | Pelo rubio; Platino | Biondo(a) platinato(a) | Platinblond | プラチナブロンド | 淡金黄色 |
| Strawberry BLOND | Blond(e) Vénitien(ne) | Bermejo(a) | Biondo tizianesco | Rotblond | 赤みがかったブロンド | 草莓紅 |
| BROWN | Brun(e); Châtain(e) | Castaño | Bruno | Braun | 茶色 | 棕色 |
| BRUNETTE | Brunet(te) | Morena; Trigueña | Bruna | Brünett | ブルネット | 淺黑色 |
| CARROT | Carotte | Pelirrojo(a) | Pel de(i) carota | Kupferrot | 赤毛 | 棕紅色 |
| GINGER | Roux (rousse) Rouquin | Pelirrojo(a) | Rossiccio(a) | Kupferrot | 赤毛 | 薑黄色 |

| HAIR COLOR | FRENCH | SPANISH | ITALIAN | GERMAN | JAPANESE | CHINESE |
|---|---|---|---|---|---|---|
| GOLDEN | D'or; Doré | Rubio(a) | Biondo oro | Goldblond | 金髪 | 金黄色 |
| GREY (GRAY) | Grisonnant; Au cheveux gris | Canoso(a) | Diventare; Grigio | Grau(haarig) | 白髪 | 灰色 |
| RED | Roux | Pelirrojo(a) | Rossiccio(a); Roso(a) | Rot(haarig) | 赤毛 | 紅色 |
| SALT & PEPPER | Poivre et sel | | Brizzolato | Pfeffer-und-Salz | 白髪まじり | 黑白混合 |
| SANDY | Blond(e) roux | Rubio(a) | Biondo(a) cenere | Rotblond | | 沙土色 |
| SILVER | Argenté(e) | Plateado(a) | Dai capelli argentei; Grigio argenteo | Silbergrau | 銀髪 | 銀灰色 |
| WHITE | Blanc(he) | Blanco | Bianco | Weißhaarig | 白髪 | 白色 |

## BABY TALK

This book is dedicated to areas of language which are rarely taught in language or T & I schools. Many words or expressions in these areas are also difficult to look up in dictionaries. Baby Talk is a typical example. Unfortunately, there are no language dictionaries for infants or toddlers. Worse yet, it is fruitless to ask others for help unless (1) they have been fluent in their language since childhood, and (2) they have raised young children. Such people are hard to find when you need them.

To complicate matters, terms used with young children seem to vary, even in the same language. Diapers in the United States are often referred to as *didies*, while in England they use *nappies*, since their term for diapers is napkins. Spanish-speaking friends from Argentina tell me that they use *Número uno* and *Número dos* with young children undergoing toilet training. This is equivalent to the American terms Number One and Number Two used to tell children the difference between peeing and defecating. In Spain, however, these terms are never used. Similar to the French, they use *Hacer pipi* and *Hacer caca* for these bodily functions.

Readers may be able to fill in with additional terms but, after much research, we have come up with the following:

| WORD OR EXPRESSION | ENGLISH | FRENCH | SPANISH | ITALIAN | GERMAN | JAPANESE | CHINESE |
|---|---|---|---|---|---|---|---|
| Baby's Ass | Tush; Tushy | Petites fesses | Cola; Culito | Culetto | Popo | | 屁股 |
| Little Boy's Penis | Wee wee; Pee pee | Pipi; Zizi | Pito | Ucellino | Pippi | ちんちん | 雞雞 |
| Urinate | Number one; Pee pee; Wee wee | Faire pipi | Hacer pipi Número uno | Urinare | Pipi machen; klein machen; Pinkeln | しーずる、ちーずる、しーレーする | 尿尿 |
| Defecate (shit) | Number two; Poo poo | Faire caca | Hacer caca; Número dos | Cacare | Kacka machen; groß machen | うーんずる、うんちずる、うんずる。 | 便便 |
| Diapers | Didies | Couche; Pampers | Pañalitos | Pannolino | Windeln | おむたん | 尿片 |
| Feces (shit) | Ca ca; Poo poo | Caca | Caca | Cacca | Kacka | | 便便 |
| Baby's First Words | Mamama; Dadada | Mamama; Papapa | Mamama; Papapa | Mamama; Papapa | Mama; Papa | まんま、んま、まーま、ば、ぱ。 | 媽媽；爸爸 |
| Terms of Affection for Children | Baby; Sweety; Little Monkey; Honey | Mon petit chou; cher; gosse | Pichón; Pichona; Chico(a); Niño(a); Muchacho(a) | Piccoletti; Creature; Carusi | Süßer; Süße; mein Kleiner; meine Kleine; mein Schatz; mein kleiner Engel; Spatz | ～ちゃん、～た ん、～しゃん | 寶寶：好；甜甜：心心 |

# Chapter Twelve

# ODDS AND ENDS

## FROM WHERE DO YOU HAIL?

If you come from New York, you are called a *New Yorker.* If from Hawaii, an *Hawaiian.* People from Denmark are called *Danes,* and from Norway come *Norwegians.* Those hailing from Tokyo are dubbed *Tokyoites.*

All of which creates problems for writers, editors, translators, and interpreters. There are some rules and many exceptions. If the name of the place ends in a consonant, one usually (but not always) adds -*er* to indicate the individual coming from that place. Four other possible endings are -*i*, -*iac*, -*ite* and -*ese.* For places whose names end with an "a" one usually (but not always) adds an -*n* or an -*ian.* For state and city names ending in a "y," the "y" is usually dropped and -*ian* substituted. Names ending in "poli" or "polis" frequently have this changed to -*politan.* Then there are cases where the name for the individual is a shortened form of the name for the place; examples are *Danes* from Denmark or *Finns* from Finland.

Some names have historical backgrounds. For example, people from Glasgow are called *Glaswegians,* probably because Vikings from Norway frequently raided Scotland, leaving behind red-headed children and names that rhyme with *Norwegian.* Residents of Los Angeles are called *Angelinos* and those from Indiana, affectionately (or sometimes maliciously), *Hoosiers.* Maine residents are called *Down Easters.* Residents of Rio de Janeiro have an odd monicker, namely *Cariocans.* Another important element is that the name be smooth sounding, not rough on the ears.

This is all, therefore, a linguist's nightmare. And one must be careful: you would soon find yourself in trouble if you called someone from Paris a *Parisite,* or someone from Maine a *Maniac.* People from Crete would be offended if called *Cretins,* as would Michigan residents if they knew a little Yiddish and you called them *Meshug-geners*. The bottom line is that you can pay attention to the rules given above but, for the most part, the only solution is to commit these names to memory. The following list of over 500 names, while certainly not all inclusive, may provide some assistance. For resident names ending in -*man*, -*woman* can also be used.

Note: Where appropriate, place names are followed by the country or American State abbreviation in parentheses.

| PLACE | RESIDENT | PLACE | RESIDENT |
|---|---|---|---|
| **Aberdeen (Scotland)** | | **Atlanta (GA)** | Atlantan |
| | Aberdonian | **Augusta (GA)** | Augustan |
| **Abilene (TX)** | Abilenian | **Austin (TX)** | Austinite |
| **Accident (MD)** | Accidental | **Australia** | Australian |
| **Afghanistan** | Afghanistani | **Austria** | Austrian |
| **Africa** | African | **Avon (UK)** | Avonian |
| **Alabama** | Alabaman | **Azores** | Azorean |
| **Alaska** | Alaskan | | |
| **Albania** | Albanian | **Baghdad (Iraq)** | Baghdadi |
| **Albert Lea (MN)** | Albert Lean | **Baltimore (MD)** | Baltimorean |
| **Alexandria (Egypt)** | | **Bangladesh** | Bangladeshi; |
| | Alexandrian | | Bengali |
| **Algeria** | Algerian | **Baraboo (WI)** | Barabooian |
| **Allentown (PA)** | Allentonian | **Barcelona (Spain)** | |
| **Amarillo (TX)** | Amarilloan | | Barcelonian |
| **Ames (IA)** | Amesite | **Bay City (TX)** | Bay Citian |
| **Amsterdam (Netherlands)** | | **Beatrice (NE)** | Beatrician |
| | Amsterdammer | **Beijing (China)** | Beijinger |
| **Amsterdam (NY)** | Amsterdamian | **Beirut (Lebanon)** | |
| **Anchorage (AK)** | Anchorageite | | Beiruti |
| **Angola** | Angolan | **Belarus** | Belarussian |
| **Annapolis (MD)** | Annapolitan | **Belgium** | Belgian |
| **Arabia** | Arabian | **Berlin (Germany)** | |
| **Argentina** | Argentinian | | Berliner |
| **Arkansas** | Arkansan | **Berkshire (UK)** | Berkshireman |
| **Armenia** | Armenian | **Bermuda** | Bermudan; |
| **Asia** | Asian | | Bermudian |
| **Aspen (CO)** | Aspenite | **Biarritz (France)** | |
| **Athens (Greece)** | Athenian | | Biarrot |

| PLACE | RESIDENT | PLACE | RESIDENT |
|---|---|---|---|
| Billings (MT) | Billingsite | Carthage (Africa) | |
| Birmingham (UK) | | | Carthaginian |
| | Brummie | Casablanca (Morocco) | |
| Bolivia | Bolivian | | Casablancan |
| Bordeaux (France) | | Cedar Rapids (IA) | |
| | Bordelaise | | Cedar Rapidian |
| Boston (MA) | Bostonian | Ceylon (Sri Lanka) | |
| Brazil | Brazilian | | Ceylonese |
| Bridgeport (CT) | Bridgeporter | Charleston (SC) | Charlestonian |
| Bronx (NY) | Bronxite | Charlestown (MA) | |
| Brooklyn (NY) | Brooklynite | | Townie |
| Brussels (Belgium) | | Cheshire (UK) | Cestrian |
| | Bruxellois | Chester (UK) | Cestrian |
| Buckinghamshire (UK) | | Chester (PA) | Chesterite |
| | Bucksian | Chicago (IL) | Chicagoan |
| Budapest (Hungary) | | Chichester (UK) | Cisestrian |
| | Budapestiek | Chico (CA) | Chican |
| Buenos Aries (Argentina) | | Chile | Chilean |
| | Porteño | China | Chinese |
| Buffalo (NY) | Buffalonian | Cleveland (OH) | Clevelander |
| Bulgaria | Bulgarian | Clinton (NJ) | Clintonian |
| Burkina Faso | Burkinabe | Cohoes (NY) | Cohosier |
| Burma (Myanmar) | | Colombia | Colombian |
| | Burmese | Columbus (MI) | Columbian |
| | | Columbus (OH) | Columbusite |
| Cairo (Egypt) | Cairene | Colorado | Coloradan |
| Calabria (Italy) | Calabrese | Concord (NH) | Concordite |
| California | Californian | Concordia (KS) | Concordian |
| Cambodia | Cambodian | Copenhagen (Denmark) | |
| Cambridge (UK) | Cantabrigian | | Copenhagener |
| Cambridge (MA) | Cantab | Cork (Ireland) | Corkonian |
| Canada | Canadian | Cornwall (Canada) | |
| Canal Zone | Zonian | | Cornwallite |
| Canton (OH) | Cantonian | Cornwall (UK) | Cornishman |
| Cape Town (South Africa) | | Corpus Christi (TX) | |
| | Capetonian | | Corpus |
| Caracas (Venezuela) | | Christian | |
| | Caraqueño | Corsica (France) | Corsican |
| Carolina (N & S) | Carolinian | Corvallis (OR) | Corvallisian |
| Carmel (CA) | Carmelite | Costa Rica | Costa Rican |

| PLACE | RESIDENT | PLACE | RESIDENT |
|---|---|---|---|
| Covington (KY) | Covingtonian | Egypt | Egyptian |
| Crete | Cretan | El Paso (TX) | El Pasoan |
| Croatia | Croat | El Salvador | Salvadoran |
| Cuba | Cuban | England | Englishman |
| Cumberland (MD) | | Erie (PA) | Erieite |
| | Cumberlander | Escondido (CA) | Escondidan |
| Cumberland (UK) | | Ethiopia | Ethiopian |
| | Cumbrian | Europe | European |
| Cyprus | Cypriot | Evansville (IN) | Evansvillian |
| Czech Republic | Czech | Exeter (UK) | Exonian |
| | | | |
| Dakota (N & S) | Dakotan | Fargo (ND) | Fargoan |
| Dallas (TX) | Dallasite | Fergus Falls (MN) | |
| Dalmatia (Croatia) | | | Fergusite |
| | Dalmatian | Fife (Scotland) | Man of Fife |
| Damascus (Syria) | | Finland | Finn |
| | Damascan | Flanders (Belgium) | |
| Danbury (CT) | Danburian | | Flemish |
| Danzig (Poland) | Danziger | Flint (MI) | Flintite |
| Del Mar (CA) | Del Martian | Florence (Italy) | Florentine |
| Denmark | Dane | Florida | Floridian |
| Denver (CO) | Denverite | France | Frenchman |
| Derbyshire (UK) | Darbian | Frankfurt (Germany) | |
| Detroit (MI) | Detroiter | | Frankfurter |
| Devon (UK) | Devonian | Frederick (MD) | Frederictonian |
| Dijon (France) | Dijonese | Fresno (CA) | Fresnan |
| Dodge City (Kansas) | | | |
| | Dodge Citian | Gabon | Gabonese |
| Dominican Republic | | Galena (IL) | Galenian |
| | Dominican | Galilee (Israel) | Galilean |
| Dubuque (IA) | Dubuquer | Galloway (Scotland) | |
| Duluth (MN) | Duluthian | | Gallovidian; |
| Dundee (Scotland) | | | Galwegian |
| | Dundonian | Galway (Ireland) | |
| Düsseldorf (Germany) | | | Galwayman |
| | Düsseldorfer | Genoa (Italy) | Genovese |
| | | Georgia | Georgian |
| Ecuador | Ecuadorian | Germany | German |
| Edinburgh (Scotland) | | Glasgow (Scotland) | |
| | Edinburgher | | Glaswegian |

| PLACE | RESIDENT | PLACE | RESIDENT |
|-------|----------|-------|----------|
| Glendale (CA) | Glendalian | India | Indian |
| Goa (India) | Goan; Goanese | Indiana | Hoosier |
| Grand Island (LA) | | Indianapolis | Indianapolitan |
| | Grand Islander | Indonesia | Indonesian |
| Great Britain | British(er); | Iowa | Iowan |
| | Briton | Iran | Iranian |
| Greece | Greek | Iraq | Iraqi |
| Greensboro (NC) | | Ireland | Irish; Irishman |
| | Greensburgher | Iron Mountain (MI) | |
| Guam | Guamanian | | Mountaineer |
| Guatemala | Guatemalan | Israel | Israeli |
| | | Istanbul (Turkey) | |
| Hackensack (NJ) | | | Istanbullu |
| | Hackensackite | Italy | Italian |
| Hague, The (Netherlands) | | Ivory Coast | Ivorian |
| | Hagenaar | | |
| Haiti | Haitian | Jacksonville (FL) | |
| Halifax (Canada) | Haligonian | | Jacksonvillian |
| Hamburg (Germany) | | Jamaica | Jamaican |
| | Hamburger | Japan | Japanese |
| Hamilton (Canada) | | Jeffersontown (KY) | |
| | Hambletonian | | Jeffersonian |
| Hampshire (UK) | Hantsian | Jersey (UK) | Jerseyman |
| Hartford (CT) | Hartforder | Jerusalem (Israel) | |
| Herkimer (NY) | Herkimerite | | Jerusalemite |
| Hibbing (MT) | Hibbingite | Johnson City (TN) | |
| Hickory (ND) | Hickorite | | Johnson Citian |
| Hoboken (NJ) | Hobokenite | Jordan | Jordanian |
| Holland | Hollander; | Juneau (AK) | Juneauite |
| | Dutch | | |
| Honduras | Honduran | Kalamazoo (MI) | Kalamazooan |
| Hong Kong (China) | | Kannapolis (NC) | Kannapolitan |
| | Hong Konger | Kansas | Kansan |
| Honolulu (HI) | Honolulan | Kauai (HI) | Kauaian |
| Hungary | Hungarian | Kentucky | Kentuckian |
| | | Kenya | Kenyan |
| Iceland | Icelander | Kerrville (TX) | Kerrvillian |
| Illinois | Illinoisian | Key West (FL) | Keywester |
| Independence (MO) | | Knoxville (TN) | Knoxvillian |
| | Independent | Korea | Korean |

| PLACE | RESIDENT |
|---|---|
| **Kuwait** | Kuwaiti |
| **Lake Placid (NY)** | Lake Placidian |
| **Lancashire (UK)** | Lancastrian |
| **Laos** | Laotian |
| **Lapland** | Lapp; Laplander |
| **Las Cruces (NM)** | Crucen |
| **Las Vegas (NV)** | Las Vegan |
| **Latvia** | Latvian |
| **Lausanne (Switzerland)** | Lausanoise |
| **Laval (Canada)** | Lavallois |
| **Lawrence (KS)** | Lawrentian |
| **Lawrence (MA)** | Lawrencian |
| **Leavenworth (KS)** | Leavenworthean |
| **Lebanon** | Lebanese |
| **Lebanon (PA)** | Lebanonian |
| **Liberia** | Liberian |
| **Libya** | Libyan |
| **Liechtenstein** | Liechtensteiner |
| **Lille (France)** | Lillois |
| **Lima (Peru)** | Limeño |
| **Limoges (France)** | Limougeaud |
| **Lincolnshire (UK)** | Lindunian; Lincolnian |
| **Lisbon (Portugal)** | Lisboan |
| **Little Rock (AR)** | Little Rockian |
| **Liverpool (UK)** | Liverpudlian; Scouser |
| **London (UK)** | Londoner |
| **Long Beach (CA)** | Long Beacher |

| PLACE | RESIDENT |
|---|---|
| **Long Island (NY)** | Long Islander |
| **Los Altos (CA)** | Los Altan |
| **Los Angeles (CA)** | Angeleno |
| **Louisiana** | Louisianan (ian) |
| **Lyons (France)** | Lyonnais |
| **Macau (China)** | Macanese |
| **Macon (GA)** | Maconite |
| **Madagascar** | Malagasy |
| **Madras (India)** | Madrasi |
| **Madrid (Spain)** | Madrileño; Madrilenian |
| **Maine** | Mainer |
| **Majorca (Spain)** | Majorcan; Mallorquan |
| **Malaysia** | Malaysian; Malay |
| **Maldives** | Maldivian |
| **Mali** | Malian |
| **Malta** | Maltese |
| **Man, Isle of (UK)** | Manxman |
| **Manchester (CT)** | Manchesterite |
| **Manchester (UK)** | Mancunian |
| **Manchuria (China)** | Manchurian |
| **Manhattan (NY)** | Manhattanite |
| **Manila (Philippines)** | Manilite |
| **Manitou Springs (CO)** | Manitoids |
| **Mariel (Cuba)** | Marielitos |
| **Maritime Provinces (Canada)** | Maritimer |

| PLACE | RESIDENT | PLACE | RESIDENT |
|---|---|---|---|
| **Marseilles (France)** | | **Montevideo (Uruguay)** | |
| | Marseillais | | Montevidean |
| **Marshall (TX)** | Marshallite | **Montreal (Canada)** | |
| **Marshall Islands** | Marshallese | | Montrealer |
| **Martha's Vineyard (MA)** | | **Moose Jaw (Canada)** | |
| | Vineyarder | | Moose Javian |
| **Martinique** | Martiniquais | **Morocco** | Moroccan |
| **Maryland** | Marylander | **Morristown (NJ)** | Morristonian |
| **Massachusetts** | Bay Stater | **Moscow (ID)** | Moscowite |
| **Maunch Chunk (PA)** | | **Moscow (Russia)** | |
| | Chunker | | Muscovite |
| **Maui (HI)** | Mauian | **Mozambique** | Mozambican |
| **Mauritius** | Mauritanian | | |
| **Medicine Hat (Canada)** | | **Nairobi (Kenya)** | Nairobian |
| | Hatter | **Naples (Italy)** | Neapolitan |
| **Melbourne (Australia)** | | **Natchez (MI)** | Natchezian |
| | Melburnian; | **Naxalbari (India)** | |
| | Melbournite | | Naxalite |
| **Memphis (TN)** | Memphian | **Nazareth (Israel)** | |
| **Meriden (CT)** | Meridenite | | Nazarene |
| **Metz (France)** | Messin | **Nepal** | Nepalese |
| **Mexico** | Mexican | **Netherlands** | Dutch |
| **Mexico City** | Chilango | **Nevada** | Nevadan |
| **Miama (FL)** | Miamian | **New Delhi (India)** | |
| **Michigan** | Michigander; | | Delhite |
| | Michiganian | **New England** | New Englander |
| **Milan (Italy)** | Milanese | **New Haven (CT)** | New Havenite |
| **Minneapolis (MN)** | | **New Jersey** | New Jerseyite |
| | Minneapolitan | **New Orleans (LA)** | |
| **Minnesota** | Minnesotan | | Orleanian |
| **Mississippi** | Mississippian | **New South Wales (Australia)** | |
| **Modesto (CA)** | Modestan | | New South |
| **Moline (IL)** | Moliner | | Welshman |
| **Monaco** | Monacan; | **New York** | New Yorker |
| | Monagasque | **New York City** | Gothamite; |
| **Mongolia** | Mongolian | | New Yorker |
| **Montenegro** | Montenegrin | **New Zealand** | New Zealander |
| **Monterey (CA)** | Montereyan | **Newark (NJ)** | Newarker |
| **Monterrey (Mexico)** | | **Newcastle (Australia)** | |
| | Regiomontano | | Novocastrian |

| PLACE | RESIDENT | PLACE | RESIDENT |
|-------|----------|-------|----------|
| **Newcastle-Upon-Tyne (UK)** | Tynesider; Geordie | **Paducah (KY)** | Paducahan |
| | | **Pakistan** | Pakistani |
| **Newfoundland** | Newfoundlander | **Palm Beach (FL)** | Palm Beacher |
| **Newport (RI)** | Newporter | **Palo Alto (CA)** | Palo Altan |
| **Niagara Falls (NY)** | Niagran | **Panama** | Panamanian |
| | | **Paris (France)** | Parisian |
| **Nicaragua** | Nicaraguan | **Paraguay** | Paraguayan |
| **Nice (France)** | Niçois | **Pasadena (CA)** | Pasadenan |
| **Niger** | Nigerien | **Passaic (NJ)** | Passaicite |
| **Nigeria** | Nigerian | **Pau (France)** | Palois |
| **Nogales (AZ)** | Nogalian | **Pecos (TX)** | Pecosite |
| **Norfolk (NE)** | Norfolkan | **Peloponnesia** | Peloponnesian |
| **Norfolk (VA)** | Norfolkian | **Pennsylvania** | Pennsylvanian |
| **Norfolk (UK)** | North Anglian | **Pensacola (FL)** | Pensacolian |
| **Norfolk Island** | Norfolk Islander | **Peoria (IL)** | Peorian |
| **North Carolina** | North Carolinian | **Peru** | Peruvian |
| **North Slope (AK)** | North Sloper | **Philadelphia (PA)** | Philadelphian |
| **Northumberland (UK)** | Northumbrian | **Philippines** | Filipino |
| | | **Phoenix (AZ)** | Phoenician |
| **Norway** | Norwegian | **Pierre (SD)** | Pierrite |
| **Nyack (NY)** | Nyacker | **Pine Bluff (AR)** | Pine Bluffian |
| | | **Piqua (OH)** | Piquard |
| **Oaxaca (Mexico)** | Oaxacan | **Pitcairn Island** | Pitcairn Islander |
| **Ohio** | Ohioan | **Pittsburgh (PA)** | Pittsburgher |
| **Oklahoma** | Oklahoman | **Plains (GA)** | Plainsman |
| **Olean (NY)** | Oleander | **Plymouth (MA)** | Plymouthian |
| **Oman** | Omani | **Plymouth (PA)** | Plymouthite |
| **Opelika (AL)** | Opelikian | **Poland** | Pole |
| **Oregon** | Oregonian | **Portland (ME)** | Portlander |
| **Orkney Islands (UK)** | Orcadian | **Portugal** | Portuguese |
| **Osaka (Japan)** | Osakan | **Poughkeepsie (NY)** | Poukeepsian |
| **Oslo (Norway)** | Osloer | **Providence (RI)** | Providentian |
| **Owensboro (KY)** | Owensboroan | **Puebla (Mexico)** | Poblano |
| **Oxford (UK)** | Oxonian | **Puebla (CO)** | Puebloan |
| **Ozark Mountains** | Ozarkian | **Puerto Rico** | Puerto Rican |
| | | **Punxsatawney (PA)** | Punxyite |

| PLACE | RESIDENT | PLACE | RESIDENT |
|-------|----------|-------|----------|
| **Qatar** | Qatari | **Saint Louis (MO)** | |
| **Quebec (Canada)** | | | Saint Louisian |
| | Québecois; | **Saint-Malo (France)** | |
| | Quebecker | | Malouïn |
| **Queens (NY)** | Queensite | **Saint Paul (MN)** | Saint Paulite |
| **Queensland (Australia)** | | **Saipan** | Saipanese |
| | Queenslander | **Salem (MA)** | Salemite |
| **Quincy (IL)** | Quincyan | **Salinas (CA)** | Salinan |
| **Quito (Ecuador)** | Quiteño | **Salt Lake City (UT)** | |
| | | | Salt Laker |
| **Ramona (CA)** | Ramonaite | **San Antonio (TX)** | |
| **Red Bank (NJ)** | Red Banker | | San Antonian |
| **Regina (Canada)** | Reginan | **San Francisco (CA)** | |
| **Reno (NV)** | Renoite | | San Franciscan |
| **Rhode Island** | Rhode Islander | **San Juan (PR)** | San Juanero |
| **Richmond (IN)** | Richmondite | **San Marino** | Sammarinese |
| **Richmond (VA)** | Richmonder | **San Paulo (Brazil)** | |
| **Rio de Janeiro (Brazil)** | | | Paulisto |
| | Carioca | **Santa Ana (CA)** | Santa Anan |
| **Rochester (NY)** | Rochesterian | **Santa Barbara (CA)** | |
| **Romania** | Romanian | | Santa Barbaran; |
| **Rome (Italy)** | Roman | | Barbareno |
| **Rouen (France)** | Rouennais | **Santa Fe (NM)** | Santa Fean |
| **Royal Oak (MI)** | Royal Oaker | **Santiago (Chile)** | Santiagan |
| **Russia** | Russian | **Saratoga Springs (NY)** | |
| **Rutland (VT)** | Rutlander | | Saratogian |
| | | **Saskatoon (Canada)** | |
| **Saginaw (MI)** | Saginawian | | Sakatonian |
| **Saint Augustine (FL)** | | **Saudi Arabia** | Saudi |
| | Saint | **Saugus (MA)** | Saugonian |
| | Augustinian | **Sault Sainte Marie (MI)** | |
| **Saint-Cloud (France)** | | | Sooite |
| | Clodoaldien | **Savannah (GA)** | Savannahian |
| **Saint Croix (France)** | | **Scandinavia** | Scandinavian |
| | Cruzan | **Schenectady (NY)** | |
| **Saint-Dié (France)** | | | Schenectadian |
| | Déodatien | **Scotland (UK)** | Scot; Scotsman |
| **Saint Joseph (MI)** | | **Seattle (WA)** | Seattleite |
| | Saint Josephite | **Selma (AL)** | Selmian |
| **Saint Kitts** | Kittitian | **Senegal** | Senegalese |

| PLACE | RESIDENT | PLACE | RESIDENT |
|-------|----------|-------|----------|
| **Serbia** | Serb; Serbian | **Sudan** | Sudanese |
| **Seychelles** | Seychellois | **Sumatra** | Sumatran |
| **Shanghai (China)** | | **Summit (NJ)** | Summitite |
| | Shanghailander | **Superior (WI)** | Superiorite |
| **Sheboygan (WI)** | Sheboygander | **Suriname** | Surinamese |
| **Sherbrooke (Canada)** | | **Swaziland** | Swazi |
| | Sherbrookois | **Sweden** | Swede |
| **Shreveport (LA)** | Shreveporter | **Switzerland** | Swiss |
| **Shropshire (UK)** | Salopian | **Sydney (Australia)** | |
| **Sicily (Italy)** | Sicilian | | Sydneysider |
| **Singapore** | Singaporean | **Syracuse (NY)** | Syracusan |
| **Sioux City (IA)** | Sioux Cityan | **Syria** | Syrian |
| **Slovakia** | Slovak | **Szechuan (China)** | |
| **Slovenia** | Slovenian | | Szechuanese |
| **Somalia** | Somali | | |
| **South Africa** | South African | **Tacoma (WA)** | Tacoman |
| **South America** | South American | **Taiwan** | Taiwanese |
| **South Bend (IN)** | Michinian | **Tajikistan** | Tajik |
| **Soweto (South Africa)** | | **Tangier (Morocco)** | |
| | Sowetan | | Tangerine |
| **Spain** | Spaniard | **Tanzania** | Tanzanian |
| **Spokane (WA)** | Spokanite | **Taos (NM)** | Taoseno |
| **Springfield (MA)** | | **Tasmania (Australia)** | |
| | Springfielder | | Tasmanian; |
| **Springfield (MO)** | | | Taswegian |
| | Springfieldian | **Taunton (MA)** | Tauntonian |
| **Sri Lanka** | Sri Lankan | **Tehran (Iran)** | Tehrani |
| **Stockholm (Sweden)** | | **Tel Aviv (Israel)** | Tel Avivian |
| | Stockholmer | **Tennessee** | Tennessean |
| **Stockton (CA)** | Stocktonian | **Texarkarna (AR)** | |
| **St. Petersburg (FL)** | | | Texarkanian |
| | Saint | **Texas** | Texan |
| | Petersburgite | **Thailand** | Thai |
| **St. Petersburg (Russia)** | | **Togo** | Togolese |
| | Saint | **Tokyo (Japan)** | Tokyoite |
| | Petersburger | **Toledo (OH)** | Toledan |
| **Stratford (Canada)** | | **Topeka (KS)** | Topekan |
| | Stratfordian | **Toronto (Canada)** | |
| **Stratford-Upon-Avon (UK)** | | | Torontonian |
| | Stratfordian | **Torrance (CA)** | Torrancite |

| PLACE | RESIDENT | PLACE | RESIDENT |
|---|---|---|---|
| **Toulouse (France)** | | **Victoria (Canada)** | |
| | Toulousain | | Victorian |
| **Trinidad** | Trinidadian | **Vienna (Austria)** | |
| **Trinidad (CO)** | Trinidadan | | Viennese |
| **Tripoli (Libya)** | Tripolitan | **Vietnam** | Vietnamese |
| **Trois-Rivières (Canada)** | | **Virginia** | Virginian |
| | Trifluvien | **Virgin Island** | Virgin Islander |
| **Troy (NY)** | Trojan | | |
| **Tucson (AZ)** | Tucsonan | **Waco (TX)** | Wacoite |
| **Tunisia** | Tunisian | **Wales (UK)** | Welshman |
| **Turkey** | Turk | **Wallis Island** | Wallisian |
| **Turkmenistan** | Turkmen | **Waltham (MA)** | Walthamite |
| **Tyrol (Austria)** | Tyrolean; | **Washington, D.C.** | |
| | Tyrolese | | Washingtonian |
| | | **Waterbury (CT)** | Waterburian |
| **Uganda** | Ugandan | **Watson Lake (Canada)** | |
| **Ukraine** | Ukrainian | | Watson Laker |
| **Ulster (Ireland)** | Ulsterman | **West Virginia** | West Virginian |
| **United Arab Emirates** | | **Wichita (KS)** | Wichitan |
| | Emirian | **Wight, Isle of (UK)** | |
| **United Kingdom** | British(er); | | Vectian |
| | Briton | **Winnipeg (Canada)** | |
| **Urbana (IL)** | Urbanan | | Winnipegger |
| **Uruguay** | Uruguayan | **Wisconsin** | Wisconsinite |
| **USA** | American | **Wooster (OH)** | Woosterite |
| **Utah** | Utahn | **Worcester (MA)** | Worcesterite |
| **Utica (NY)** | Utican | **Wymore (NE)** | Wymorean |
| **Uzbekistan** | Uzbek | **Wyoming** | Wyomingite |
| | | | |
| **Vail (CO)** | Vailite | **Yakima (WA)** | Yakiman |
| **Valdosta (GA)** | Valdostan | **Yap (Micronesia)** | |
| **Valparaiso (Chile)** | | | Yapese |
| | Valparaisan | **Yarmouth (Canada)** | |
| **Vancouver (Canada)** | | | Yarmouthian |
| | Vancouverite | **Yemen** | Yemeni |
| **Venezuela** | Venezuelan | **Yonkers (NY)** | Yonkersite |
| **Venice (Italy)** | Venetian | **York (PA)** | Yorker |
| **Veracruz (Mexico)** | | **Yorkshire (UK)** | Yorkshireman |
| | Jarocho | **Youngstown (OH)** | |
| **Vermont** | Vermonter | | Youngstowner |

| PLACE | RESIDENT | PLACE | RESIDENT |
|-------|----------|-------|----------|
| **Ypsilanti (MI)** | Ypsilantian | **Zambia** | Zambian |
| **Yucatan (Mexico)** | | **Zimbabwe** | Zimbabwean |
| | Yucatocan | **Zurich (Switzerland)** | |
| **Yugoslavia** | Yugoslavian | | Züricher |

## NICKNAMES AND SPECIAL DESIGNATIONS

For historical reasons, many places have special nicknames for their
residents. Outsiders also coin special words – often mildly derogatory
– for neighbors who amuse them or with whom they find fault. A
number of these are offered below, divided into two parts: (1)
nicknames for residents of many of the states in the U.S.A., and (2)
a few special designations which have become popular over the years.

### STATE NICKNAMES

| STATE | NICKNAME | STATE | NICKNAME |
|-------|----------|-------|----------|
| **Alaska** | Sourdough | | Sunflower |
| **Arizona** | Zonie | **Kentucky** | Bear; Blue |
| **Arkansas** | Goober Grabber; | | Grasser |
| | Josh | **Louisiana** | Pelican |
| **California** | Gold Coaster | **Maine** | Fox; Logger; |
| **Colorado** | Centennial; | | Down Easter |
| | Rover; | **Maryland** | Cockader; |
| | Silverine | | Crawthumper |
| **Connecticut** | Wooden Nutmeg | **Massachusetts** | Bay Stater; |
| **Delaware** | Blue Hen | | Puritan |
| **Florida** | Gator; | **Michigan** | Wolverine |
| | Everglader | **Minnesota** | Gopher |
| **Georgia** | Buzzard; | **Mississippi** | Border Eagle; |
| | Sandhiller | | Mud Cat |
| **Indiana** | Hoosier | **Missouri** | Piker |
| **Iowa** | Hawkeye | **Nebraska** | Antelope; |
| **Kansas** | Jayhawker; | | Cornhusker |

| STATE | NICKNAME | STATE | NICKNAME |
|---|---|---|---|
| **Nevada** | Digger; Miner; | | Leatherhead |
| | Sage Hen; | **Rhode Island** | Gun Flint |
| | Silver Stater | **South Carolina** | Clay Eater; |
| **New Jersey** | Blue | | Rice Bird; |
| **New York** | Knickerbocker | | Sandlapper |
| **North Carolina** | | **Tennessee** | Big Bender; |
| | Tar Heel: Tucko | | Hardhead |
| **North Dakota** | Flickertail | **Texas** | Cowboy; Long |
| **Ohio** | Buckeye | | Horn; Ranger |
| **Oklahoma** | Sooner | **Virginia** | Cavalier; |
| **Oregon** | Beaver; | | Soreback |
| | Hard Case; | **West Virginia** | Panhandler; |
| | Webfoot | | Snake |
| **Pennsylvania** | Coal Miner; | **Wyoming** | Sheepherder |

## SPECIAL DESIGNATIONS

| | |
|---|---|
| Angelino | Los Angeles |
| Anzac | Australia & New Zealand |
| Aussie | Australia |
| Brit | Great Britain; United Kingdom |
| Brummy | Birmingham, U.K. |
| Canuck* | Canada |
| Carioca | Rio de Janeiro |
| Cockney | East End, London, U.K. |
| Digger | Australia |
| Down Easter | Maine |
| Frog* | France |
| Geordie | North East England |
| Kiwi | New Zealand |
| Limey* | England |
| Pommy* | England |
| Rosbeef* | England |
| Scouse | Liverpool, U.K. |
| Yank* | United States |

(Note: terms marked * are mildly derogatory)

# A PRONOUNCED DIFFERENCE

## A MARE'S NEST OF ENGLISH SPELLING & PUNCTUATION

Of all the languages in the world, English is probably the most difficult in the area of spelling and pronunciation. However, "difficult" may be the wrong word. *Absurd* might be more accurate. George Bernard Shaw wrote and commented extensively on this subject. One of his favorite examples concerned the pronunciation of a word he invented, GHOTI. Shaw opined that it should be pronounced FISH. How come? Well, if you pronounce the GH as you would in the word LAUGHTER, and you pronounce the O as in the word WOMEN, and you pronounced the TI as in the word NATION – what do you get? The answer, of course, is FISH. Ridiculous, isn't it?

A more complete picture of the craziness of English spelling and pronunciation is given in an excerpt from the following poem, which has been floating around for years. Read it out loud. If you can pronounce each word correctly, you will have no problem with English translation and interpretation. You will prove that you know the language better than ninety percent of American (or British) native speakers. And, if the differences in pronunciation of some of these words stumps you, what a great opportunity to improve your English speaking and understanding ability.

> Dearest creature in creation,
> Study English pronunciation.
> I will teach you in my verse
> Sounds like corpse, corps, horse, and worse.
> I will keep you, Suzy, busy,
> Make your head with heat grow dizzy.
> Tear in eye, your dress will tear,
> So shall I! Oh hear my prayer.
>
> Just compare heart, beard, and heard,
> Dies and diet, lord and word,
> Sword and sward, retain and Britain.

(Mind the latter, how it's written.)
Now I surely will not plague you
With such words as plaque and ague.
But be careful how you speak:
Say break and steak, but bleak and streak;
Cloven, oven, how and low,
Script, receipt, show, poem, and toe.

Hear me say, devoid of trickery,
Daughter, laughter, and terpsichore,
Typhoid, measles, topsails, aisles,
Exiles, similes, and reviles;
Scholar, vicar, and cigar,
Solar, mica, war and far;
One, anemone, Balmoral,
Kitchen, lichen, laundry, laurel;
Gertrude, German, wind and mind,
Scene, Melpomene, mankind.

Billet does not rhyme with ballet,
Bouquet, wallet, mallet, chalet.
Blood and flood are not like food,
Nor is mould like should and would.
Viscous, viscount, load and broad,
Toward, to forward, to reward.
And your pronunciation's OK
When you correctly say croquet,
Rounded, wounded, grieve and sieve,
Friend and fiend, alive and live...

*– Author Unknown*

To confirm this extraordinary environment of pronunciation, here is a series of sentences in which two words are spelled exactly the same, but their pronunciations differ. For example, in the first sentence, the *pol* in the initial word *polish* is pronounced the same as in the word *doll*. The *pol* in the second word *Polish* is pronounced the same as the word *pole*. Should you reverse the pronunciations and, with a heavy accent, ask in a bookstore for a book on how to Polish your English, the bookseller might tell you that your English is Polish enough already.

The same problem occurs in all the succeeding sentences, where two words with the same spelling have totally different pronunciations. *Caveat orator.*

- We must polish the Polish furniture

- He could lead if he would get the lead out.

- The farm was used to produce produce.

- The dump was so full that it had to refuse more refuse.

- The soldier decided to desert in the desert.

- This was a good time to present the present.

- A bass was painted on the head of the bass drum.

- I did not object to the object.

- The insurance was invalid for the invalid.

- The bandage was wound around the wound.

- They were too close to the door to close it.

- The buck does funny things when the does are present.

- To help with planting, the farmer taught his sow to sow.

- After a number of injections, my jaw got number.

- Upon seeing the tear in my clothes, I shed a tear.

- I had to subject the subject to a series of tests.

- How can I intimate this to my most intimate friend?

## The Vocabulary of Punctuation

| | | | |
|---|---|---|---|
| . | period | # | pound sign; hatch mark |
| , | comma | % | percent sign |
| ' | apostrophe | ¢ | cent sign |
| : | colon | $ | dollar sign |
| ; | semicolon | ç | cedilla |
| ? | question mark | ~ | tilde |
| ! | exclamation point | ´ | accent acute |
| — | dash | ` | accent grave |
| - | hyphen | ^ | accent circumflex |
| " " | quotation marks | ¨ | umlaut |
| ' ' | single quotes | ‾ | macron |
| ( ) | parentheses | ˘ | breve |
| [ ] | brackets | ^ | caret |
| { } | braces | oö | dieresis |
| / | forward slash | @ | at sign |
| & | ampersand | = | equal sign |
| * | asterisk | + | plus sign |

# POSTSCRIPT

An afterthought to an afterthought. The postscript to our first edition was intended to apologize for any mistakes we might have made. It also appealed to our readers to write to us whenever they uncovered such mistakes. The penultimate paragraph in this Postscript renews that appeal. In between, please allow us to repeat much of the original so that we can *kvetch* about the trials and tribulations of preparing this book.

In Marc Antony's famous speech after the assassination of Julius Caesar, he orates, "The evil that men do lives after them. The good is oft interred with their bones." I fear that is also the case with published dictionaries and compendiums such as this.

The "good," of course, is the huge amount of work and effort that goes into writing and assembling a book of this type. Thousands of hours in the library and at the computer, some of it fun but much of it drudgery, were required before this book could reach your desk or library shelves. The "evil" is that, with the voluminous amount of words and expressions covered and the infinite detail to be explored, mistakes are bound to creep in. Some are simple typos. Misspellings occur, particularly when transmuting into a language other than English. Then there are questions of judgement, e.g. whether an expression is an acronym or an initialism or whether two proverbs have the same or similar meaning, or only express similar thoughts.

Instead of claiming that, "We don't make **misteaks**," the author, his wife, the publisher, and several editors have meticulously gone over the text in an attempt to minimize or, if possible, eliminate any errors. We are virtually certain that we have failed and that there still have been oversights. Our only excuse is identical to one used in Rome 2,000 years ago: *Errare humanum est.* To make a mistake is human. We apologize for being human.

This Postscript, however, has a different purpose than a simple apology, which could have been done in far fewer words. The author is not asking the reader to overlook errors — in fact, quite the contrary. The publisher and I would be delighted to receive from any and all users of this revised second edition of the Compendium details on any errors or mistakes in judgment we have made, or of any failure to correct mistakes in the first edition. In that way, when (*in'sha'allah*) the third expanded edition of this book appears, there will be greater precision and fewer bloopers.

Thank you in advance for your cooperation.

# BIBLIOGRAPHY

## ENGLISH & WORLDWIDE ENGLISH

**Acronyms, Initialisms, and Abbreviations Dictionary**, ed. by Mossman, Jenifer. 19th ed. 3 vol. (Part I: A-F; Part 2: G-O; Part 3: P-Z), Gale Research, Inc., Washington D.C., 1995.

**American English — English American**, ed. by Bickerton, Anthea. Abson Books, Abson, England, 1977.

**American Idioms**, by Makkai, Adam. 2nd ed. Barron's Educational Series, Inc., Hauppauge, NY, 1994.

**Amo, Amas, Amat, and More**, by Ehrlich, Eugene H. Harper and Row, New York, 1985.

**Black English**, by Dillard, J.L. Vintage Books Edition. Random House, New York, 1973.

**British/American Language Dictionary**, by Moss, Norman. Passport Books, New York, 1984.

**British English A to Zed**, by Schur, Norman. HarperPerennial, New York, 1991.

**British English for American Readers**, by Grote, David. Greenwood Press, Westport, CT, 1992.

**Britishisms,** ed. by Holofcener, Lawrence. Partners Press, Princeton, NJ, 1981.

**Concise Dictionary of English Slang**, A, by Freeman, William. Philosophical Library, New York, 1956.

**Crazy English,** by Lederer, Richard. Pocket Books, Division of Simon and Schuster, New York, 1990.

**Dictionary of American Proverbs**, A, ed. by Mieder, Wolfgang. Oxford University Press, New York, 1992.

**Dictionary of American Slang**, compiled by Wentworth, Harold and Stuart Berg Flexner. Thomas Y. Crowell, New York, 1975.

**Dictionary of Appropriate Adjectives**, by Mikhael, E.H. 2nd ed. Cassell, London, 1995.

**Dictionary of Foreign Phrases and Abbreviations**, by Guinagh, Kevin. 3rd ed. H. W. Wilson Co., New York, 1983.

**Dictionary of Foreign Terms**, by Mawson, C.O. Sylvester. Updated by Charles Berlitz. 2nd ed. Thomas Y. Crowell Co., New York, 1972.

**Dictionary of Proverbs, Maxims, and Famous Classical Phrases of the Chinese, Japanese, and Korean — Wisdom of the Far East,** by Yoo, Young H. Far Eastern Research and Publications Center (FERPC), 1972.

**Dictionary of Similes**, A, by Wilstach, Frank. Bonanza Books, New York, 1924.

**Dictionary of Slang and Unconventional English**, by Partridge, Eric and ed. by Paul Beale. 8th ed. Macmillan, New York, 1985.

**English as We Speak It in Ireland**, by Joyce, P.W. Wolfhound Press, Dublin, Ireland, 1997.

**Exaltation of Larks, An,** by Lipton, James. Viking Penguin, New York, 1986.

**Exploring Australia,** by Ivory, Michael. Fodor's Travel Publications, Inc., New York, NY, 1998.

**Glossary of Colloquial Anglo-Indian Words and Phrases, A,** by Yule, Henry and Burnell, A.C. Curzon Press, Richmond, Surrey, U.K., 1995.

**Guide to South Africa,** by Briggs, Philip. Globe Pequot Press, Inc., USA, 1997.

**Hacker's Dictionary, The,** compiled by Steele, Guy L. Jr. et al. Harper and Row, New York, 1983.

**Historical Dictionary of American Slang,** by Lightner, J.E. Vol. 1 (A-G) 1994; Vol. 2 (H-O) 1997; Vol. 3 (P-Z) is scheduled to be released in 2000. Random House, New York.

**India,** by Honan, Mark et al. Lonely Planet Publications, Oakland, CA, 1999.

**Fodor's India,** edited by Mills, Anastasia Redmond. Fodor's Travel Publications, Inc (Div. Of Random House), New York, NY, 1998.

**Joys of Yiddish, The,** by Rosten, Leo. McGraw-Hill Book Co., New York, 1968.

**Labels for Locals,** by Dickson, Paul. Merriam-Webster, Springfield, MA, 1997.

**Let's Go South Africa,** edited by Dovey, Lindine. St. Martins Press, New York, NY, 2000.

**Lexicon of Black English,** by Dillard, J.D. Seabury Press, New York, 1977.

**NTA's Dictionary of Acronyms and Abbreviations,** compiled and translated by Kleindler, Steven Racek. NTC Publishing Group, Lincolnwood, IL, 1993.

**NTC's American Idioms Dictionary,** by Spears, Richard A., Ph.D. NTC Pub. Group, Lincolnwood, IL, 1995.

**NTC Dictionary of Everyday American English Expressions,** by Spears, Richard A., PhD. NTC Pub. Group, Lincolnwood, IL.

**Oxford Dictionary of Abbreviations, The,** Clarendon Press, Oxford, 1992.

**Oxford Dictionary of English Proverbs, The,** compiled by Smith, William G. 3rd ed., Clarendon Press, Oxford, 1970.

**Quick Brown Fox; Using Australian English, The,** by Devine, Frank. Duffy and Snellgrove, Potts Point, N.S.W., 1998.

**Shorter Oxford Dictionary, The.** Clarendon Press, 1993.

**Slang: Topic by Topic Dictionary of Contemporary American Lingoes,** by Dickson, Paul. Pocket Books, Simon & Schuster, New York, 1990.

**Slang and Euphemisms,** by Spears, Richard A. NAL-Dutton, Penguin, New York, 1991.

**Slang and Its Analogies,** by Farmer, J.S. and W.E. Heneley. Amo Press of the New York Times, New York.

**Smaller Slang Dictionary,** by Partridge, Eric. Philosophical Library, New York, 1961.

**South Africa, Lesotho and Swaziland,** by Murray, John; Williams, Jeff and Everist, Richard. Lonely Planet Publications, Oakland, CA, 1998.

**South African Pocket Oxford Dictionary, The,** edited by Branford, William. Oxford University Press, Capetown, S.A., 1987.

**Story of English, The,** by McCrum, Robert, William Cran, and Robert MacNeil. Penguin Books, New York, 1992.

**Superior Persons Book of Words, The,** by Bowler, Peter and David R. Godine. Dell, New York, 1990.

**Translator's Handbook, The,** by Sofer, Morry. Schreiber Publishing, Rockville, MD, 1996.

**Understanding British English,** by Moore, Margaret E. Citadel Press, Carol Publishing Group, New York, 1989.

**Webster's Third International Dictionary.** Springfield, MA, 1969.

**What's the Difference? An American/British — British/American Dictionary,** by Moss, Norman. Hutchinson, London, 1974.

**When is a pig a hog? A Guide to Confoundingly Related English Words,** by Randall, Bernice. Prentice Hall, New York, 1991.

**Wicked Words,** by Rawson, Hugh. Crown Publishers, New York, 1989.

**Wired Style — Principles of English Usage in the Digital Age,** ed. by Hale, Constance. Hard Wired, San Francisco, 1996.

*Articles:*

"Business Acronyms," by Greenfield, Marian. *ATA Chronicle,* May 1996 (pp. 14-17); June 1996 (pp. 15-17); July 1996 (pp. 16-17).

"Proverbs," by Duval, John. *Translation Review* (No. 50), 1995.

"A Visit to the New York Public Library: Part 2" by Rainof, Alexander. *Proteus* (Vol., No. 2), pp. 8-9. Spring 1997.

## CHINESE

**English-Chinese Dictionary, The (Unabridged).** Shanghai Yiwen Publishing House, Joint Publishing (HK) Co., Ltd., Hong Kong, 1996.

**New English-Chinese Dictionary, A.** University of Washington Press, Seattle, Washington, 1988.

**Newton Dictionary of Current English, The.** Newton Publishing Co., Ltd., Taipei, Taiwan, 1992.

**Pinyin Chinese-English Dictionary, The.** Commercial Press, Hong Kong, 1979.

# FRENCH

**Bouquet d'expressions imagées, Le:** Encyclopédie thématique des locutions figurées de la langue française, by Dunton, Claude and Sylvie Claval. Seuil, Paris, 1990.

**Dictionary of Colorful French Language and Colloquialisms, A,** by Deak, Etienne and Simone. Dutton, New York, 1961.

**Dictionary of Modern Colloquial French,** by Hérail, René James and Edwin A. Lovatt. Routledge & K. Paul, Boston, 1984.

**Dictionnaire des abbréviations courantes de la langue française,** by Faudouas, Jean-Claude. Maison de Dictionnaire, Paris, 1990.

**Dictionnaire des expressions et locutions,** by Rey, Alain and Sophie Chantreau. Robert, Paris, 1987.

**Dictionnaire des proverbes, sentences, et maximes,** by Maloux, Maurice. Larousse, Paris, 1960.

**Harrap's Slang French Dictionary,** by Knox, H. Prentice Hall, New York, 1993.

**Majuscules, abbréviations, symboles, et sigles,** by Duppagne, Albert. Duculot, Paris, 1979.

**New French-English Dictionary of Slang and Colloquialisms, The,** Dutton, New York, 1971.

**Proverbes français, suivis des equivalents en allemand, anglais, espagnol, italien, néerlandais,** by Lig, Gérard. Elsevier Publishing Co., New York, 1960.


# GERMAN

**Abkürzungsbuch: Abkürzungen, Kurzwörter, Zeichen, Symbole** by Koblischke, Heinz. Bibliographisches Institut, Leipzig, Germany, 1969.

**Cassell's Colloquial German: A Handbook of Idiomatic Usage,** revised by Anderson, Beatrix and Maurice North. Macmillan Pub., New York, 1980.

**German Idioms,** by Stutz, Henry. Barron's Educational Series, Inc., New York, 1996.

**Lexikologie der Deutschen Gegenwartssprache,** by Schippan, Thea. Bibliographisches Institut, Leipzig, Germany, 1984.

**Lexikon der Sprichwörtlichen Redensarten,** by Rohrich, Lutz. 3rd ed. Verlag Herder, Freiberg, Germany, 1973.

**Mit Anderen Worten: Deutsche Idiomatik, Redensarten und Redewendungen,** by Griesbach, Heinz. Icedicum, Hamburg, 1993.

**Moderne Deutsche Idiomatik, Alphabetisches Wörterbuch mit Definitionen,** by Friederich, Wolf. Hueber, Munich, 1976.
**100 Deutsche Redensarten,** by Griesbach, Dr. Heinz and Dr. Dora Schulz. Langenscheidt, Berlin, Germany, 1985.
**1000 Deutsche Redensarten mit Erklärungen und Anwendungsbeispielen,** by Griesbach, Dr. Heinz. 5th ed. Langenscheidt, Berlin, 1981.
**Synonymwörterbuch der Deutschen Redensarten,** by Schemann, Hans. Ernst Klett Verlag für Wissen und Bildung, Stuttgart, Germany, 1991.


## ITALIAN

**Dizionario Fraseologico delle Parole Equivalenti, Analoghe e Contrarie,** 1988.
**Gran Dizionario Hazon Garzanti,** Garzanti Editore S.p.A., 1974.
**Il Nuovo Zingarelli Vocabolario della Lingua Italiana.** Nicola Zingarelli (publisher), Bologna, Italy, 1983.
**Sansoni-Harrap Italian-English/English-Italian,** by Macchi, V. 4 vols., London, 1981.


## JAPANESE

**Comprehensive Dictionary of Colloquial English.** Asahi Shuppan-sha, Tokyo, 1994 .
**Dictionary of Japanese and English Idiomatic Equivalents, A,** by Corwin, Charles. Kodansha International, New York, 1968.
**Dôgutoshiteno Eigo Hyogen Jiten,** ed. by Ishii, Shinji. JICC Pub., Tokyo, 1987.
**Dôgutoshiteno Eigo — Eigo de Zatsudan Hen** (Dictionary of Slang and Colloquialisms), by Kataoka, Miiko. JICC-Shuppan, 1990.
*Even Monkeys Fall from the Trees* **and Other Japanese Proverbs,** by Galef, David. Charles E. Tuttle, 1987.
**Japanese and English Idioms,** by Roger, Trey. Tokyo Hokuseido, Las Vegas, 1994.
**Kenkyusha's Lighthouse Japanese-English Dictionary,** ed. by Kojima, Yoshiro and Shigeru Takebayashi. Kenkyusha, Tokyo, 1986.
**Kotowaza no Izumi (Fountain of Japanese Proverbs),** by Takashima, Taiji. Hokuseidoshoten, Tokyo, 1993.
**Latest Dictionary of English Synonyms, The,** ed. by Kenkyukai, Gendai Eigo. Soutaku-Sha, 1991.

**Nichi-Ei Hikaku Kotowaza Jiten**, ed. by Yamamoto, Tadahisa. 2nd ed. Sogen-sha, Osaka, 1992.

**Saishin Nichibei Kôgo Jiten (Modern Colloquialisms Revised Japanese-English)**, by Seidensticker, Edward G. and Michiro Matsumoto. Asahi Shuppansha, Tokyo, 1984.

**Treasury of English Proverbs, A**, by Okutsu, Fumio. Sogen-sha, Osaka, 1983.

## KOREAN

**Basic Glossary of Korean Studies**, compiled by Song, Ki Joong. Korea Foundation, Seoul, 1993.

**Dictionary of New Electrical Terms**, by Park, Sang-hui. Kyomjisa, Seoul, 1995.

**English-Korean & Korean-English New Chemical Dictionary**, by Yi, U-yong. Tangwoodang, Seoul, 1985.

**Guide to Korean Characters, A**, by Grant, Bruce K. Hollym International Corp., Seoul, 1979.

**Hyondae Sisa Yongo Sajeon (English Dictionary)**, Tongo Ibosa. Seoul, 1987.

**Korean-English Glossary of Business Terms**, by Lee, Hyeon Kook. Nopun-orum, Seoul, 1995.

**Kukche Kyungyoung Sajeon (International Management Dictionary)**, by Hansoo, Kim and Park Se Woon. Kukche Kyungyound Yonguwon, 1995.

**Kyongje Sino Sajon, Maeil Kyongje Sinmunsa (Dictionary of Economic Terms)**. 4th ed. Seoul, 1996.

**Sin Kyongje Kyongyonghac Taesajon (New Economics and Management Greater Dictionary)**. Publishing Committee of Hankook Sajeon Yongusa, Seoul, 1995.

## NORWEGIAN

**Bokmålsordboka (Dictionary of bokmoål)**. Universitetsforlaget, Oslo.

**Engelske Idiomer (English Idioms)**, by Sverre, Follestad. 4th ed. Kunnskapforlaget, Oslo, 1994.

**500 Uttrykk og Vendinger (500 Proverbs and Phrases)**, Erichsen, G.M., 1993.

**Fremmedordbok (Dictionary of Foreign Words and Phrases)**, ed. by Berulfsen, et al. Kunnskapforlaget, Oslo, 1995.

**Moderne Norsk (Modern Norwegian Language)**, by Finn, Eric Vinje. 4th ed.. Universitetsforlaget, Oslo, 1987.

**Norsk-Engelsk Juridisk Ordbok,** Sivilrett og Strafferett (Norwegian-English Law Dictionary). Bedriftsøkonomensforlag, Oslo, 1992.

**Norsk-Engelsk Okonomisk Ordbok (Norwegian-English Dictionary of Economics),** by Janet, Aagenes. Kunnskapforlaget, Oslo, 1993.

**Norsk Idiomordbok (Norwegian Idioms),** by Kirkeby, Willy A. Scandinavian University Press, Cambridge, MA, 1990.

**Norsk Synonymordbok (Dictionary of Norwegian Synonyms).** Kunnskapsforlaget, Oslo, 1976.

**Nynorsk Ordboka (Dictionary of Norwegian).** Det Norske Samlaget, Oslo.

**Visual Dictionary.** Kunnskapsforlaget, Oslo.

## SPANISH

**El Chingole Primer Diccionario del Lenguaje Popular Mexicano,** by Pedro Maria de Usandizaga y Mendoza. 8th ed. Costa-Amic Pub., S.A., Mexico, DF.

**NTC Dictionary of Spanish False Cognates,** by Prado, Marcial. NTC Pub. Group, Lincolnwood, IL, 1996.

**101 Spanish Idioms,** by Cassagne, J.M. Passport Books/NTC Pub., 1995.

**Old Spanish Expressions,** compiled and translated by Nuñez, Mario A. Quixote Publications, Berea, OH, 1974.

**Old Spanish Sayings,** compiled and translated by Nuñez, Mario A. Quixote Publications, Berea, OH, 1959.

**2001 Spanish and English Idioms,** by Savaiano, Eugene.   Barron's Educational Series, Inc., Hauppauge, NY, 1977.

# INDEX

This index contains references to key words in Chapters Two through Five (covering proverbs, expressions, similes, and slang). While every chapter in this book is arranged alphabetically, this index provides additional help if one is not sure of the phrasing of a particular expression. The other chapters are actually an index unto themselves.

paddle 75
pain 72 142 149
paint 125 126
pair 105
pale 108
palm 93 95 133 135
pan 50 94 138
pancake 107 135
panhandle 135
panther 120
pants 92 115
papa 96
paper 98 120 128
parachute 128
parchment 108
parlay 140
part 44 50 56
parting 75
pass 82 99 140
path 61 75 96
patience 75 98
patriotism 75
Paul 98
pave 77
paw 121
pea 97 108 110 135
peace 82
peach 135
peachy 133 135
peacock 108 111
peanut 135
pearl 93
peck 85 121
peel 135
peeve 121
peg 73
pelican 121
pen 73 75
penguin 121
penicillin 156
penis 151
penny 45 62 75 81 98

105 129
people 44 63 75 88
Peoria 125
pepper 135
percent 81
percolate 135
perfect 72 76
perilous 66
perish 59
perk 129
perspiration 81
pet 121
Pete 94
Peter 98
Philadelphia 155
phony 129
pick 76 143 144
pick-up 110
pickle 135
picture 76 108 124
   125
pie 94 98 106 121 130
   132 133 135
pigeon 121 123 138
   155
pill 156
pilot 159
pin 108
pinch 100
pincher 129
pine 109
pineapple 135
ping 140
pink 129
pint 100
pipe 76
piper 68 125
piss 94 120 133 151
   152
pistol 158
pitch 108 140
pitcher 66 76

placid 108
plain 98 108
plan 46 139
plank 110
plate 139 141
player 44 140
plead 155
please 89
pleasure 48 64 78
plenty 82
plug 129
plum 135
plump 108
pocket 69 78 140
pod 97 108 110
point 76 78
poison 53 74
poke 71 121
poker 140 145
pole 110
police 155
policy 60
pond 92 108
pony 117 121
pooh-bah 126
pool 138 140
poor 77 82 108 121
   138
pop 128
popular 106
porcupine 121
pork 135
port 92
posh 162
possession 76
post 106
pot 54 76 85 135
potato 131 133 135
   136
pound 62 75
pour 86 98
poverty 86

# *Quick* Order Form

**Fax orders: (301) 424-2336. Send this form.**

**Telephone orders: Call 1 (800) 822-3213
(in Maryland: (301) 424-7737)**

**E-mail orders: spbooks@aol.com. www.schreibernet.com**

**Mail orders to: Schreiber Publishing, 51 Monroe St.,
Suite 101, Rockville MD 20850 USA**

Please send the following books, programs, and/or a free catalog. I understand that I may return any of them for a full refund, for any reason, no
questions asked:

❑ **The Translator's Handbook**, 3rd Revised Edition - All you need to know
about operating successfully as a translator (U.S. $24.95 Abroad $36.00)

❑ **The Translator's Self-Training Program** (circle the language/s of your
choice): Spanish French German Japanese Chinese Italian
Portuguese Russian Arabic Hebrew (U.S. - $69.00 Abroad - $89)

❑ **Multicultural Spanish Dictionary** - How Spanish Differs from Country
to Country (U.S. $24.95 Abroad - $36.00)

❑ **21st Century American English Compendium**, 2nd revised edition - The
"Odds and Ends" of American English Usage (U.S. $24.95 Abroad $36.00)

❑ **Translation Update** - A bimonthly newsletter for translators (One year -
U.S. $18.00 Abroad $24.00; Two years - U.S. $32 Abroad $42.00)

Name: _____

Address: _____

City: _____ State: _____ Zip: _____

Telephone: _____ e-mail: _____

Sales tax: Please add 5% sales tax in Maryland
Shipping (est.): $4 for the first book and $2.00 for each additional product
International: $ 9 for the first book, and $5 for each additional book
Payment: ❑ Cheque    ❑ Credit card:  ❑ Visa  ❑ MasterCard

Card number: _____

Name on card: _____ Exp. Date: ___ / ___